The Common Sense Diet

Robert Wayne Atkins, P.E.

How to loose weight
while eating most of the foods
you currently enjoy.

For more information please visit: https://www.grandpappy.org

The Common Sense Diet
Robert Wayne Atkins, P.E.

The image on the front cover of this book is the author of this book with his granddaughter, Olivia Ryan Atkins, at Nagshead Beach, North Carolina on October 18, 2004 after the author had lost 60 pounds in 8 months. The author was 55 years old and Olivia was 2 years old.

First Edition published by Grandpappy, Inc.

Bible scripture verses are from the following Bible translations:
1. Holy Bible, New King James Version (NKJV), Copyright © 1995 by Thomas Nelson, Inc., Pages 74, 130, 133, 166.
2. Holy Bible, King James Version, KJV, 1611. Public Domain. Pages 181, 237

This book does not contain any medical advice.
This book does not contain any medical recommendations.
Please consult a licensed medical professional to have your medical questions answered.

Disclaimer: The author, publisher, and distributors of this book do not make any claims about the accuracy of the information in this book or the suitability of the application of the information to specific individuals. Scientific research studies are being conducted continuously and some of those studies may not be in agreement with some of the information presented in this book. The information in this book should be used in conjunction with the advice of a licensed medical professional as to the suitability of the information to a specific person based on a physical exam and on the person's medical history.

How to Lose Weight
While Eating Most of the Foods
You Currently Enjoy.

ISBN: 978-1-7327883-7-4

Printed in the United States of America.
10 9 8 7 6 5 4 3 2

The Motivation for Writing This Book

On September 27, 2019 Dr. Graham Matthews gave me a thorough physical examination. He also authorized an extensive array of blood tests. I weighed 310.6 pounds on his scale and he told me that people weighing more than 300 pounds were seriously obese and they should lose weight if they wanted to extend their life expectancy and avoid a variety of health problems. Dr. Matthews told me to eat fewer calories than I burned each day to lose weight, and find a sugar substitute, and not eat seconds on potatoes or white rice, and to start exercising.

Two days later Dr. Matthews phoned me with my blood test results. My sugar level and my cholesterol level were both high and if I could not reduce those levels within six months then he was going to prescribe a sugar pill and a cholesterol pill for me. Then he repeated his advice on how I could lose weight.

I was not happy that I weighed more than 300 pounds. And I did not want to start taking two more prescription medications. Therefore I decided to follow Dr. Matthews advice and try to lose some weight.

I have always been able to lose weight by following almost any diet I tried. But my body always gradually adjusted to those different diets and my weight loss would stop. Then I would gain one or two pounds per month until I regained all the weight I lost plus a few more pounds.

This time I wanted to lose weight and keep that weight off my body for the rest of my life. I knew I could lose weight following almost any diet. But I also knew that no diet would help me keep the weight off my body indefinitely. As I was thinking about how to lose weight my "Common Sense Diet" slowly began to take shape in my mind.

On October 2, 2019 I implemented the first phase of my new dieting strategy and I kept detailed written records of the results. I gradually revised my diet based on what worked and what didn't. On a regular basis I ate bread, dietary fats, carbohydrates, dairy products, meat, pasta, and a few potatoes. I also drank beer. And two or three times each month, when I was in the mood, I ate at a nice restaurant and I ate their fresh bread with butter on it. After three months on December 31, 2019 I had lost 36 pounds without being hungry all the time.

Based on my successful weight loss I decided to formalize and publish my diet to help other people lose weight without being hungry all the time. This book explains how to create a diet that will help you lose weight by selecting a variety of low-calorie foods that you already enjoy eating, and by eating high-calorie foods only in moderation. There is lot more to the "Common Sense Diet" than this, but this is the basic foundation of my diet. If you will give the "Common Sense Diet" a try then you may be very pleased with the results.

Respectfully,

Robert Wayne Atkins, P.E. -- January 3, 2020

Preface to
The Common Sense Diet

Although I have read numerous scientific research studies about dieting and the health benefits of specific foods, this book only briefly summarizes a few of those research studies. I am 71 years old and most of this book is based on my successes and my failures when I actually tested a wide variety of "scientific" dieting advice on myself.

During my life there have been times when I was reasonably trim and healthy. But there have also been times in my life when I was overweight -- by 5 pounds at age 20, by 20 pounds at age 38, by 30 pounds at age 43, by 65 pounds at age 55, and by 110 pounds at age 70. My overweight problems increased as I aged. However at the ages of 20, 38, 43, and 55 I was able to bring my weight back down to what I considered to be very reasonable for a man with the amount of muscle I have on my body. Most of that muscle was acquired between the ages of 12 to 26 when I was extremely active and I participated in a lot of outdoor activities, such as canoeing, long-distance hiking, camping, riding bicycles, and playing tennis.

But after the age of 26 my family life dominated my daily activities and I became less active. This resulted in a very gradual weight gain each year until I would reach a point where I was very unhappy with my reflection in the mirror. Then I would read diet books and diet magazines, and I would listen to family and friends who had recently lost weight following some new diet. And I was always able to lose weight by eating more nutritious food and by exercising more regularly.

Because of my reoccurring weight problems I have always paid very close attention to anyone who talked about their actual experience following some type of diet. I also listened to true stories from people I knew who told me about one of their family members or friends who had lost a significant amount of weight following a "fad" diet and then the person died a few weeks after reaching their desired weight goal.

I have also had family members and friends who underwent surgical procedures to help them lose weight. But I made a personal decision that a surgical procedure was not an option for me.

After 50 years of reading diet books, and reading monthly diet magazines, and talking to people who had lost weight on a specific type of diet, I had gradually formed my own opinions about how to safely lose weight without sacrificing my health, and maybe even my life, by trying to lose weight in a reckless manner. In the year 2019, at the age of 70, I decided I would either lose weight in a common sense healthy manner or I would remain 110 pounds overweight.

At the age of 70 I also knew that my remaining years here on this earth were limited. And I did not want to spend those years being hungry most of the time, and not being able to think about anything except food most of the day. That helped me to decide that I was going to try to lose weight by eating low-calorie foods that I really enjoyed eating without worrying about whether or not the food contained dietary fat, or carbohydrates, or any other "forbidden" ingredient. I was also going to continue eating the Italian foods and the Mexican foods I really enjoyed but I was going to eat those foods in moderation. And I was going to continue eating bacon, beef, chicken, ham, turkey, beans, bread, cheese, corn, dairy, fruit, vegetables, nuts, and a limited amount of pasta, pizza, and potatoes. Finally I was going to continue drinking beer in moderation. Based on these parameters I put my new diet into action.

The good news is that my common sense approach to weight loss has been very successful for me and I am once again not ashamed to look at my reflection in the mirror. However, today a much slimmer, healthier, gray-haired old man is smiling back at me from the surface of the mirror. And I have the strength, energy, and stamina that I had 20 years ago. The reason is because I lost 50 pounds (22.7 kg) in 5 months without being hungry all the time. However, it was not unusual for me to get a little hungry just before my next regular meal.

My prayer is that the information in this book will help you lose weight without being hungry all the time, and that you will also be able to significantly improve your long-term health and your life expectancy.

Respectfully,
Robert Wayne Atkins, P.E.
March 2, 2020

The Common Sense Diet

Table of Contents

Chapter One

Introduction to Weight Loss

*This book does not contain any medical advice and
it does not contain any medical recommendations.*
*Please consult a licensed medical professional
to have your medical questions answered.*

Please stand in front of a full-length mirror and then completely relax. Now carefully look at yourself and consider your overall weight. Then turn sideways and carefully look at your profile in the mirror. If you are not pleased with what you see then the information in this book may help you to gradually and systematically trim down your body so that the image you see in the mirror several months from now will be significantly thinner than what you see today.

The First Critical Step

Before anyone begins any type of diet the first step should always be the same. Have your family doctor or your preferred medical practitioner give you a complete physical exam that includes a comprehensive blood analysis. The reason is simple -- **your objectives should be to lose weight and also become a healthier person**. Based on the results of your exam and blood tests, your doctor can give you some good advice about dieting and some specific foods to eat, and not eat, in order to help you avoid making some really bad choices that could negatively impact your health and your life expectancy. (Note: Your doctor will ask you to not eat anything for 12 or more hours before your blood test to improve the accuracy of the results.)

Most of us have had friends or family members who have lost weight following a specific type of diet but they died within six months or less after starting their diet. They didn't die accidentally, or due to some natural cause, or due to old age. They died because the food they were eating was lacking in something their body desperately needed, or the food included something that was harmful to their body's chemistry.

A simple example would be sodium or table salt. Some people have a sodium deficiency and their doctor will advise them to add salt to the food they eat to increase the amount of sodium in their body. Other people have an excessive amount of sodium in their body and their doctor will tell them to never add salt to their food and to avoid eating foods that have a lot of sodium. This is an example of the type of information that each one of us needs to know before we begin any diet. Based on our doctor's advice we can select foods that will help us lose weight and that will also help us become healthier people.

This is one of the reasons why a "one diet for everybody" is usually not a good idea. Just because a specific diet helped one of your friends or one of your family members lose a lot of weight does not mean that it would be a good diet for you. After you receive feedback from your physical exam and your blood tests then you can strategically evaluate any proposed diet with your doctor to see if the diet will help you to remain healthy while you lose weight.

Pregnant Women and Nursing Mothers

If you are pregnant, or if you are nursing a baby, then your body requires special nutrients because you are eating and drinking for two people. You should follow the advice of your doctor and eat the foods and drink the beverages specifically recommended for you. You should not attempt to follow any type of diet that is not in the best interests of your health and the health of your baby.

Some Practical Advice that can Help Almost Anyone Lose Weight on Almost Any Type of Diet

The remainder of this chapter will be devoted to strategies that can be successfully used with almost any type of diet, including "The Common Sense Diet."

The information in this chapter is based on the knowledge I have acquired during the past 50 years about dieting, exercising, how to lose weight, and how to have a healthier stronger body. This chapter will rarely quote specific scientific research to support my suggestions because I no longer have access to the books, magazines, and newspaper articles that I read during the past 50 years that helped me form my opinions. The suggestions is this chapter are based on applying the information I read and then seeing what impact it had on my own body. You can determine for yourself whether or not the suggestions in this chapter can help you lose weight without being hungry all the time.

Daily Multivitamin

Unless your physician has advised against it, a daily multivitamin tablet may help your body maintain a reasonable balance of vitamins, minerals, and other nutrients while you are on your diet. If possible, select a multivitamin that is designed for your age group and your gender in order to maximize its benefits. Gummy vitamins are not recommended because they will stick to your teeth and promote tooth decay. If your physician has also advised you to take specific vitamin supplements then you should follow your doctor's advise. This will help you maintain a healthy body as you lose weight.

Beginner's Headache

When we begin a new diet it takes our body between one to five days to adjust to burning some of our body fat each day instead of adding just a tiny bit more fat to our body each day. This chemical change inside our body may or may not cause us to have a headache. If the headache is more than you can tolerate then you can relieve the discomfort using your normal headache medicine. After our body adjusts to burning fat instead of adding fat then the headaches will stop.

Slow Down. Take Small Bites.
Chew Each Bite Completely Before Swallowing.

These are the eight reasons why you should: Slow Down, Take Small Bites, and Chew Each Bite Completely Before Swallowing.

1. **More Bites:** If each bite is small then you will have more total bites of food to enjoy from the same amount of food that is on your plate. This also means the food on your plate will last longer.

2. **Brain and Stomach Communication:** After you put some food into your mouth, immediately put your tableware down (knife, fork, or spoon). If you are eating a sandwich or finger food then put your partially eaten sandwich down on your plate. Put your empty hands on your lap or on the table beside your plate. Now focus on chewing and on thoroughly enjoying the food that you just put into your mouth. You are not in a hurry. The other food on your plate is not going anywhere. Do **not** prepare your next bite until after you have completely finished chewing and swallowing the food you just put into your mouth. This will give your stomach and your brain more time to communicate and it will require less food to make you feel full and satisfied. A side benefit is that it will also give other people the impression that you have good table manners and that you are not a glutton and that you don't just shovel food into your mouth.

3. **More Eating Pleasure:** The longer you chew each small bite of food, the more time the food stays inside your mouth, and the longer you will be able to enjoy its flavor and the eating pleasure it brings to you. Being able to chew food is one of the least appreciated pleasures of eating.

4. **Easier Swallowing:** If every small mouthful of food is completely chewed into miniscule pieces then you will be able to swallow your food more easily. And you may be able to live your entire life without choking on a piece of food that wasn't chewed well, and you may never need to have your back hit really hard or your chest squeezed really hard to help loosen a big piece of food that is caught inside your throat.

5. **Easier Digestion:** If you chew your food really well then you will be sending extremely tiny, tiny pieces of food down into your stomach and your stomach will be able to more easily digest that food. This means you should have fewer problems with indigestion or an upset stomach.

6. **Weight Control:** As you eat your stomach sends messages to your brain to let it know that you have eaten. Your blood automatically carries these messages to your brain and if you are eating slowly then your brain will receive these messages while you are still eating, and your brain will inform you that you are no longer hungry and you can stop eating. In other words, you will feel full by eating less food and this will help you control your weight and have a healthier body. Eating more slowly also increases the level of weight-reducing hormones in our body. One study discovered that people who thoroughly and completely chew their food usually eat about 12% less food per day than people who only chew their food long enough to be able to swallow it.

7. **Sensory Perception:** Our five senses (taste, touch, sight, smell, and hearing) are constantly sending messages to our brains and our brains are constantly responding to these messages on a subconscious level that we are normally not aware of. This is how the brain works to keep us alive and healthy. When we take smaller bites our eyes see us putting food into our mouths over a longer period of time. If the food has a pleasant aroma then our nose sends messages to the brain about what we are eating over a longer period of time. When we chew each bite completely our mouths are sending messages to our brain that we are still eating, and our taste buds are enjoying the flavor of the food longer, and our taste buds are constantly sending messages to our brain over a longer period of time. Even if our mouths are closed as they should be while we eat, our ears can still hear the sound of the chewing as it takes place inside our mouth and our ears are sending messages to the brain that we are still eating for a longer period of time. If we eat slowly then all of these sensory messages are being received by the brain over a longer period of time and our brain will gradually inform us that we can stop eating because we are full. This is an example of using the subconscious power of the brain to help us eat less, and still feel completely satisfied, and lose weight at the same time.

8. **Easier Bowel Movements:** If your teeth do a good job chewing your food, then your stomach can do a better job digesting that food. And when your stomach sends that food to the next part of your body then your body will have an easier job of processing that food and removing the nutrients from the food. When it is time to

expel the stuff your body doesn't need then you will have easier bowel movements for two reasons: the food will be more completely digested, and there will be less food to expel because you ate less and your body removed more of the nutrition from the food you did eat.

If you eat an entire meal in less than 20 minutes then you are eating too fast. It takes at least 20 minutes, or longer, for your stomach and your brain to effectively communicate with one another and inform you that you are full and that you should stop eating. If you are not eating alone then one way to help extend your meal is to engage in a pleasant topic of conversation during the meal with the people you are eating with. Please practice good manners and do not talk with food in your mouth. Please chew that food completely, swallow it, and then speak or answer a question. Avoid discussing unpleasant topics at mealtime because they can upset your digestion. Talk about unpleasant topics at some other time during the day.

Eat Until Your Hunger is Satisfied and then Stop Eating

A time honored weight loss strategy is to eat until you are full and then stop eating. Being full means you are no longer hungry. Being full does not mean you are so stuffed that you could not possible swallow another bite. This is overeating and it is not the same thing as feeling full. Feeling full is called being satisfied or satiated.

Use Smaller Plates

An easy and convenient way to begin eating smaller servings is to use smaller plates. Use an 8.5 inch diameter "bread or salad" plate instead of a standard 10.5 inch diameter "dinner" plate. A smaller plate will hold less food and this will automatically reduce the size of your meal. However, the smaller plate will appear full even though it contains less food than a 10.5 inch diameter plate. This is important because our eyes are constantly sending messages to our brain and the subconscious message will be that we will be eating a full plate of food instead of a skimpy portion of food. This may help make the meal more satisfying even though the meal contains less food than we used to eat.

Water

A generous amount of plain pure cold water should be consumed every day for the following reasons:
1. Water contains no calories but it helps the stomach feel full. This reduces the amount of food eaten and increases weight loss.
2. Water is absolutely necessary for the stomach and the intestines to properly digest food. If our bodies are not properly hydrated then digestive problems and several other health problems may result.

3. Water lubricates the digestive system so food flows more easily through the body.
4. Water facilitates normal bowel movements and helps prevent constipation. Water helps dissolve and flush toxins out of the body.
5. Water enhances kidney functions and may prevent kidney stones.
6. Water lubricates our joints and spine and makes movements easier.
7. Normal brain functions gradually slow down as the body becomes more dehydrated. The result is more frequent and severe headaches.
8. Our body's cells are continuously replacing themselves. A properly hydrated body makes it easier for new cells to replace old cells.
9. Water lubricates the skin and helps prevent premature wrinkles.
10. Drink a glass of cold water shortly after waking up in the morning and after you have weighed yourself for the day. The water will rehydrate your body and reactivate all your body's metabolic processes so you begin burning more calories all day long.
11. If cold water is consumed just **before** a meal then less food will be eaten during the meal and this will facilitate weight loss. Drinking water has the same weight loss benefit as eating a small bowl of broth based soup before a meal, or eating half a grapefruit before a meal because a grapefruit is mostly water and it has few calories.
12. Drinking 6 cups of cold water per day (1.5 liters) may help your body burn an additional 50 calories per day, or 18,250 calories per year, which is approximately 5.2 pounds of body fat per year.

Relieve Yourself Frequently

When you feel the urge to relieve yourself then you should do so as soon as it becomes possible. It is not healthy to postpone our normal bodily functions. Our body is an amazing organism and after it has removed all the nutrients from the foods and fluids that we eat and drink then our body tells us it is time to relieve ourselves of the food and fluids that our body has finished processing. If we will expel these items from our body at the earliest possible opportunity then our body can focus on processing other food and fluids that still require further processing. However, if we delay expelling foods and fluids from our body then our body may continue to extract stuff from that waste material that may not be healthy for our body. Therefore to maximize our weight loss and to minimize absorbing potentially harmful stuff into our bodies, we should relieve ourselves as soon as possible after we feel the urge to do so.

Weight Loss When We First Begin Dieting

The most significant and dramatic weight losses will occur the first week that we begin dieting. These exceptional weight losses will usually continue sporadically through the entire first month that we are on a new diet. This is because the human body will begin by eliminating the weight that is easy to shed. The human body is an amazing organism and it will gradually adjust itself to whatever food that it receives. Therefore weight loss will usually slow down during the second month of our diet. This is normal and it is something that we should expect. However, if we are aware of this issue when we first begin our diet then we can maximize our weight loss during our first month of dieting by staying on our diet as faithfully as possible, and we should attempt to avoid straying from our diet except on rare occasions. As we continue on our diet we will be very pleased with our weight loss that first month and this may motivate us to stay on our diet.

Weight Loss Does Not Happen Every Day

Be emotionally prepared for your weight to not decrease every day. Be prepared for your weight to actually increase on some days. There are factors other than your diet that can impact your daily weight, such as the amount of water your body retains from day to day, and the type of activities you participate in each day. In addition, some foods take longer to digest and those foods will remain inside you longer before your body expels the residue it does not need. The important issue is the long term trend in your weight from week to week until you approach your weight loss goal. As you approach your goal your weight loss will gradually slow down and then the important issue will be your weight from month to month as you maintain your desired weight.

Keep Track of Your Weight Every Day

Before you begin a diet weigh yourself and record your weight along with the date. At approximately the same time each day weigh yourself again and record your weight for that day. For most people the best time to weigh themselves is about 20 minutes after they get out of bed after a good night's sleep, and after they have relieved themselves in the bathroom, and before they get fully dressed, and before they have anything to eat or drink. After you have weighed yourself then drink some water to rehydrate your body and to activate your body's normal metabolic functions.

Daily feedback is a powerful incentive to stay on your diet. It can help you resist temptations to eat when you are only a little bit hungry. Being able to visually see the progress you are making on your diet will help you stick to your diet and not give up.

If your waistline is important to you then also use a cloth tape measure, such as the ones available in the sewing goods department of a store, to measure your waistline at your navel. If you always measure at your navel then you will be able to accurately determine the impact your diet is having on your waistline as you continue to lose weight.

I suggest measuring your waistline two ways as follows:

1. **Relaxed:** With your body totally relaxed measure the distance around your waist. Record the date and the measurement. This is what other people see when they look at you.

2. **Suck Your Tummy In:** Suck your tummy is as much as you can and then measure your waist again. Record the measurement beside your first measurement above. This is the smallest your waist can be for a very short period of time.

By measuring your waist both ways you will have a more accurate record of the impact of your new diet on the number of inches you lose around your waist. The reason is because the above method eliminates the temptation to suck your tummy in just a little bit when you measure your waist in a relaxed position. Your waistline will change slower than your body weight so you only need to measure your waistline once every two weeks, or once per month.

I have been reading dieting advice, off and on, for 50 years. I am fully aware that a few dieting professionals, but not all, recommend that you not weigh yourself every day. And some dieting professionals actually recommend that you get rid of your home weight scale completely. I disagree with that advice. I am an industrial engineer, a manager, and a teacher, and I intimately understand the importance and the benefits of feedback on a timely basis. Therefore I recommend that a person record their weight each day to receive an immediate benefit when the scale shows that they have lost some weight because this helps to reinforce their behavior and it helps them stay on their diet.

Therefore please do not become discouraged is someone criticizes you for weighing yourself every day. You are weighing yourself to help you stay on your diet and lose weight, and not to please anyone else.

Immediately after you weigh yourself in the morning, and after you have done your morning exercises, drink some water. Water will help to rehydrate your body and water will reactivate many of your body's metabolic processes. This will result in a long-term improvement in your health and in your weight loss.

How Much Weight Can Be Safely Lost in One Week?

If a person is overweight, then that person can safely lose up to one percent of their total weight in one week. For example, a person who weighs 300 pounds could safely lose 3 pounds a week. A person who weighs 200 pounds could safely lose 2 pounds a week. And a person who weighs 150 pounds could safely lose 1.5 pounds a week.

Get a Good Night's Sleep Every Night

Sleep deprivation negatively impacts your body in many different ways. When you are asleep your body is inactive and your body can perform its normal necessary nighttime functions. Lack of sleep can cause you to eat more food to compensate for the loss of sleep. Sleep deprivation may adversely impact your health and your judgment and it may result in poor choices on what to eat and not eat.

Sleeping in a cool room instead of a warm room may increase the number of calories you burn while you are asleep. In a cool room your body will burn more fat cells to keep your body temperature at a proper level. However, do not lower the room temperature below the point at which you can get a good night's sleep.

Eating Just Before Bedtime

If possible, schedule your last meal of the day at least two hours before bedtime. This gives your body a chance to partially digest the food you have eaten, and this provides some energy to your body so you can get a good night of sleep.

Eating just before retiring will usually result in a spike in blood sugar and insulin levels, and it can interfere with your normal digestive processes. Therefore eating just before bedtime is not compatible with getting a good night of sleep. And eating just before retiring can also result in weight gains instead of weight losses.

However, if you develop a strong craving for a specific food just before bedtime then it is usually a good idea to eat a small quantity of that food before retiring. A small quantity of the food, about 200 calories or less, will not require a significant digestive effort while you are sleeping. And a small quantity of the food may help minimize or eliminate the food craving you have for that specific food so you can go to sleep.

As an example, cherries contain the hormone melatonin which helps to regulate sleep. Cherries also contain a lot of antioxidants that are beneficial to weight loss. Fresh tart cherries are best. Frozen tart cherries or red tart cherries canned in water are fine when fresh cherries are out of season. Eating six or fewer cherries will not add too many calories to your diet and they may help you sleep better.

If you try to ignore a strong food craving just before bedtime then that food craving will normally interfere with your sleep and you will not get a good night of rest. Getting a good night of sleep is much more important than adding a few more calories to your diet.

Keep a Reasonable Supply of
Healthy Low-Calorie Foods in Your Home

If you have a variety of healthy low-calorie foods to pick from then when you get hungry it will be easy to select something that will satisfy your hunger without consuming too many calories.

Keep Food Out-of-Sight

Always store your food in a food cabinet or in the refrigerator or freezer. Do not put food on a counter or table where it can be easily seen. Food that is always visible encourages snacking and snacking will increase your daily consumption of calories. Food that is not visible will not encourage hunger or thoughts of eating.

Brush Your Teeth After Eating

Brushing your teeth after eating is obviously good dental advice. However, after we have brushed our teeth most of us automatically resist the temptation to eat something before the next normal meal. One reason is because our brain subconsciously interprets teeth brushing as an indication that more food will not be eaten for a reasonable period of time. Another reason is because food does not taste the same immediately after we have brushed our teeth because the toothpaste has temporarily desensitized the taste buds on our tongue. Not eating between meals can help some people lose a significant amount of weight. However, if possible, wait about 30 minutes after eating to brush your teeth because our tongue will continue to taste the food flavor that remains inside our mouth, and our mouth and our saliva will continue to remove small food particles out of our mouth for a short period of time after eating. This continues to send taste messages to the brain that we have eaten and this is a desirable consequence of waiting 30 minutes before we brush our teeth. If you can't brush your teeth then consider rinsing your mouth with a good mouthwash because this can have almost the same effect on your appetite as brushing your teeth.

Food Cravings

If you develop a strong desire to eat a candy bar, or some cake, or some ice cream, then it is usually best to resist the temptation and stick to your diet. However, sometimes the desire to eat a specific food is a message from our body to our brain telling us that our body is lacking something that can be provided by a specific type of food based on how that specific food has satisfied our body's needs in the past. In this situation it is advisable to eat the food item that you strongly crave for two reasons:

1. It you eat the specific food item you crave then it will satisfy your craving for that food, and your body will be able to extract

whatever nutrients it needs from that food, and you can think about something else instead of that specific food item.

2. If you don't eat that specific food item but you eat something else then your mind will keep reminding you that you are still hungry and that you need to eat that specific food. When you ignore this type of food craving then you will usually end up eating several different things that don't satisfy your real hunger and you will consume more calories than if you had just eaten the food item that you desire.

If your food craving is for something sweet then consider eating a sugar-free sweet that you enjoy. Detailed information about sweets that are compatible with weight loss are in chapter 24.

Hunger

It is normal for people to get a little hungry just before their next regularly scheduled meal *even if they are not dieting*. However, after we begin a diet and we start to lose weight then it is not unusual for us to get hungry more often than in the past. The reason is because hunger is the message our body sends to our brain in the hope that we will eat something to supply it with fuel to burn so our body doesn't have to consume the fat that has been stored on our body. Therefore a minor degree of hunger is a good thing because it lets us know our diet is working. If we can learn to say "no" to these minor hunger feelings between meals then we can be more successful in losing weight. However, when it is time for our next meal, or when our hunger reaches the point where all we can think about is how weak we feel and how hungry we are, then we need to eat something healthy. If it is almost time for our next meal then it is okay to eat our next meal a little early.

Will Power

When it comes to losing weight, "will power" is your ability to stay on your diet simply because you force yourself to do it through the strength of your will. There are very, very few people who can force their minds to think about something besides food when their bodies are telling them that they are really, really hungry and they should eat something. This would be similar to trying to force our brain to ignore a significant pain that we have somewhere on our body. Our brains help us stay alive by responding to the messages our brains receive from our bodies. Attempting to use "will power" to change the natural function of our brains is extremely difficult and most people cannot do it. Perhaps 1% of the people in the world can actually do this and these people will sometimes criticize the rest of us who can't do this as being "weak willed." In my opinion, we are not "weak willed." Instead we are normal people with normal body functions. Therefore please do **not** become discouraged if you cannot "force" your mind to think about something other than food when you become really hungry.

An easier way to use our brains to help us lose weight to do simple things that send subconscious messages to our brain that will help us to eat less. Previously in this chapter I have mentioned three activities that can send subconscious messages to our brains to help us lose weight:

1. Slow down. Take small bites. Chew each bite completely before swallowing.
2. Use a smaller 8.5 inch plate instead of a 10.5 inch plate.
3. Brush your teeth after eating.

Some of the chapters later in this book also contain some additional simply things you can do that send subconscious messages to your brain to help you more easily lose weight.

Calorie Counting

An entire chapter will be devoted to calories later in this book. However, in this introductory chapter a few basic comments about calories are absolutely necessary.

A lot of scientific research has been conducted over the years to determine the number of calories burned by the human body when it does different types of activities, such as running, playing tennis, playing golf, riding a bicycle, walking, swimming, standing, sitting, and sleeping. In addition, research has been done to estimate the number of calories that need to be burned by the body in order to remove one pound of fat from the body.

The result of all this research has shown that:

1. If we burn more calories than we eat per day we will lose weight.
2. If we eat more calories than we burn per day we will gain weight.
3. If we eat approximately the same number of calories that we burn per day then our weight will remain approximately the same.

On the average this is absolutely true. However, this simple calorie model does not take into consideration the nutrition per calorie.

Nutrition per Calorie

Some foods contain more nutrition per calorie than other foods. Nutrition is important for satisfying hunger and for maintaining a healthy body. Foods that are nutrient rich include beef, fish, pork, poultry, beans, dairy products, nuts, grains, fruits, and vegetables. These foods will satisfy your hunger and help you maintain a healthy body. Foods that are low in nutrition include cookies, candy, ice cream, white bread, white pasta, and potato chips. Foods that are low in nutrition will not help you maintain a healthy body nor will they provide you with a feeling of fullness after you eat them. Therefore although eating fewer calories per day than you burn per day will help you lose weight, you may be compromising your health if you are not careful in strategically selecting the types of foods you eat. That is why a diet should help you lose weight and improve your health. This can be accomplished by eating foods that have good nutritional values.

Nutrition Labels

Reading the nutrition labels and the list of ingredients on food packages will add a few minutes to the time you spend shopping. However, if you take positive action based on what you discover on those food labels then you may be able to add several years to your life. And your life may be a much healthier and more enjoyable one.

In the USA all commercially processed foods must contain a nutrition label. The information on that label must conform to the standards of the National Labeling and Education Act (NLEA).

However, nutrition labels are not required on fresh fruits, fresh vegetables, and fresh unprocessed meat, fish, and poultry.

Anyone on a diet should carefully read and understand the information of the nutrition label on every food item that they are considering to purchase and eat. Each of the nutrition items on a nutrition label is discussed in detail, and in simple language, in a chapter by itself later in this book. However, following is a very brief explanation of the basic information on a nutrition label:

1. **Servings per Container:** Either the exact number of servings or the approximate number of servings in the container.

2. **Serving Size:** The amount of food on which all the nutritional data on the label is based. If there is one serving per container then the data also represents the nutrition for the entire container. If there is more than one serving per container then multiply the number of servings per container by the nutrition per serving to determine the total nutrition in the entire container.

3. **Calories per Serving:** The number of calories based on the serving size specified on the label.

4. **Total Dietary Fat:** Dietary fat is one of the body's three primary sources of fuel. Fat helps keep the skin and hair healthy. Fat helps the body properly absorb some vitamins. Saturated fats raise your body's bad LDL cholesterol level. Saturated fats come from butter, cheese, milk, and meat fat. Unsaturated fats can lower your body's bad LDL cholesterol level. Unsaturated fats come from oils, such as olive oil, most nuts, peanut butter, vegetables, grain, meat, fish, and shellfish.

5. **Cholesterol:** Cholesterol is used to make body cell membranes, hormones, vitamin D, and it helps the body digest food. The liver can make all the cholesterol the body requires. Plant foods contain no cholesterol. Cholesterol is in animal products such as butter, cheese, egg yolks, and meat. Too much bad LDL cholesterol can result in plaque that sticks to the walls of the blood arteries and this can cause serious health problems including death (blocked artery). HDL cholesterol contains more protein and less cholesterol and it can benefit the body. The liver stores and releases cholesterol to the body as it is needed.

6. **Sodium:** Sodium is a mineral and it is regulated by the kidneys. Sodium is necessary for the body's nerves and muscles to function properly. However, extra sodium in the blood will attract more water into the blood (blood volume) and this increases blood pressure. Sodium is naturally present in most foods but it can also be added to foods. A lower sodium level can help control the fluid in your legs, heart, and lungs. Table salt is approximately 40% sodium and 60% chloride. Most commercially processed foods contain more sodium than the human body needs.

7. **Total Carbohydrates (Carbs):** Carbohydrates are one of the body's three primary sources of fuel. Carbohydrates contain carbon, hydrogen, and oxygen. They provide nutrients for the brain, for the nervous system, and for muscle functions. There are no carbohydrates in butter, fish, meat, or poultry. Simple carbs provide a quick energy burst. Simple carbs are in candy, cookies, sodas, sucrose sugar, and syrups. Complex carbs provide longer lasting energy. Complex carbs are in beans, corn, grain, nuts, peas, and potatoes. Total Carbs includes starches, fiber, and sugar. Fiber and sugar are usually shown below the Total Carb amount on the nutrition label. However the grams of fiber and sugar are already included in the Total Carb amount.

   a. **Starches:** Starches are not listed as a separate category on a food nutrition label but they are part of the Total Carb value.

   b. **Dietary Fiber:** Fiber is in plant foods (beans, fruit, grains, nuts, vegetables) but **not** in animal products (fish, meat, poultry, eggs, milk). Fiber is a nutrient that the body cannot absorb. However, fiber helps to clean the digestive system so the body can expel what it doesn't need. Fiber needs a reasonable amount of water to facilitate its effectiveness.

   c. **Total Sugars:** Includes all types of sugar including lactose and fructose.

* **Added Sugars, or Other Sugars, or Free Sugars:** Sugars that are added to the natural sugars that are in the food. Added sugars are for flavor and they are included in the Total Sugars amount. Added sugars may appear under a variety of different names.

8. **Protein:** Protein is one of the body's three primary sources of fuel. Protein is the basic nutrition the body uses to create muscles and tendons, and to rejuvenate and provide nourishment to the skin and to the internal organs. Protein can increase the number of calories you burn while simultaneously reducing your appetite.

9. **Vitamins:** Most nutrition labels will show the amount of vitamin D, Calcium, Iron, and Potassium per serving as a percent of the recommended daily dietary adult allowance (RDA) of that specific vitamin. The label may also include other vitamins if the food contains a reasonable percent of other vitamins.

Natural Foods, Processed Foods, and Fast Foods

Most commercially processed foods and fast foods contain too much sodium, added sugars, added fats and calories, and preservatives. Preservatives disrupt our stomach's normal process of sending messages to the brain to let it know that we have eaten and that we are full. The extra salt causes our body to absorb more water which can make us feel dehydrated and bloated. These foods are designed to temporarily satisfy our hunger but they also increase our hunger more rapidly after eating. They cause us to eat more at one meal, and to become addicted to that particular food. This helps to increase the sales and profits of the food processing company or the restaurant. However, it is bad for us because we gain weight.

Natural foods, such as fresh meat, fruit, and vegetables, are more nutritious and they do not contain added ingredients that can adversely impact our health and our weight.

Fad Diets

Anyone who has just a little age on them can probably remember some of the "fad" diets that were extremely popular for short periods of time. Most of these diets helped a lot of people lose an impressive amount of weight in one or two weeks. The weight loss was possible because these fad diets starved the person's body of some essential nutrient that their body was accustomed to obtaining on a regular basis. When that nutrient was eliminated from the person's diet then their body began burning stored fat in an effort to compensate for the loss of that nutrient. The problem is that the human body cannot remain healthy for very long when it is deprived of something it really needs.

When these people began feeling bad and they lacked the energy to do their normal daily activities then they began to eat some of the foods they had been denying themselves. The result was that they not only gained back all the weight they lost but they also put on additional weight because of their body's natural defense mechanism to protect itself from this type of nutrient starvation in the future. Therefore I strongly recommend that you carefully evaluate any diet that you are considering and verify that it is not totally lacking in some nutrient that your body needs. It is okay to eat less of a specified nutrient and to eat more of another nutrient. Depending on the nutrient that is minimized and the nutrient that is increased, there will be some health benefits associated with that particular type of diet. But there may also be some corresponding health problems depending on how extreme the diet is. This is where your doctor's advice can help you to not sacrifice your long-term health for a short-term temporary weight loss.

Exercise

Chapter 26 later in this book will be devoted to exercise. However, in this introductory chapter a few basic comments about exercise are absolutely necessary.

When we exercise we burn more calories. That is good. But any exercise you do should be approved by your doctor. For example, people with high blood pressure will usually be told by their doctor to **not** lift weights because it can aggravate their medical condition. Therefore listen to your doctor and select one or more types of exercise that your doctor recommends specifically for you.

Properly selected exercises can help tone specific parts of your body and help you become healthier and more attractive. When we first begin a regular exercise program our body's metabolism increases and we burn more calories. But eventually our body adjusts to our exercise routine and we are able to exercise regularly without burning as many calories as when we first began exercising because our body is now healthier and it is easier for our body to do the exercise.

In addition, exercise increases our feeling of hunger and it may take a little more food than before to help us feel satisfied. If this happens then our additional calorie intake may be equal to the number of calories we burn as a result of exercising and the net result will be that we don't lose any weight as a result of exercise. However, the exercise is still good because it helps to tone our bodies and improve our health. The reason I am including this paragraph is because some people frequently expect to see the same weight loss that they experienced when they first began exercising to continue for an extended period of time.

In my opinion a new exercise program should be delayed until after we have been on our new diet for four weeks. During our first month on a new diet most of us will have enough emotional stress to deal with that is related to the new diet. Therefore it will usually be easier to remain on a new diet if we do not immediately add a new exercise program to our schedule. In addition, weight is easier to lose the first four weeks on a new diet, and weight gradually becomes more challenging to lose the longer we remain on our diet. If we delay our new exercise program for four weeks then our body will be a little healthier, and our body will have adjusted to the foods we are now eating, and we will be emotionally, mentally, and physically ready to add a new exercise program into our schedule. And the new exercise program will help increase our total weight loss during our second month on a new diet which is when weight loss normally slows down for most people. This will add positive reinforcement to the benefit of our new exercise program and it may motivate us to continue our new exercises and not give up.

Fitness Tracking Watch or Wristband

Affordable attractive comfortable watches, or fitness wristbands, are now available on the internet. These devices will continuously monitor your daily activities, including sitting, walking, exercising, and sleeping, and those watches will keep track of and report the approximate number of calories you burn each day. This is a significant advantage for someone who is trying to lose weight.

Most watches require that you link to a smart phone to do almost everything, including updating the watch to the correct time. The most common functions on these watches when linked to your smart phone include: heart rate, blood pressure, total steps walked (pedometer), distance traveled, and the number of calories burned for a variety of different activities, exercises, and sports. Usually only a few of these functions are imbedded in the memory chip of the watch. Most of these functions will only work after you have linked to a smart phone. Most watches require you to download their recommended software into your smart phone. The software determines what the watch can do and how the information is monitored and reported. Therefore read the customer reviews on the exact software that is recommended for your watch. Some of the software is free but some of the software has a monthly fee that can range from $0.99 per month up to $39 per month. Almost all of the software apps require that you agree to their privacy policy which states something like: "We sincerely respect your privacy. However, to use our software you must now agree to allow us to access all the information on your mobile device without any restrictions, including your most private and personal information. We assure you we will use your information discretely but we will also sell your information to third parties. If you agree to our privacy police then you also agree that you forfeit all your rights to sue us or any third party for any damages of any type that may result from the release of your confidential personal private information from now on and forevermore." Although something may be legal that does not mean it is also ethical or moral.

When your smart phone is nearby and it is turned "on" then most watches will alert you of phone calls and text messages. Some watches have a "find phone" feature to help you locate a misplaced phone. Most watches only work with specific types of smart phones. Therefore verify that the watch you are interested in will actually link to the type of smart phone you have.

Waterproof and water resistant are interpreted differently by each watch manufacturer. Read the customer reviews to see what actually happens to a specific watch if you take a shower or swim in a pool.

Some watches have an adjustable wristband. This is an important feature for someone who is loosing weight because your wrist diameter will gradually be shrinking.

Some watches have to be charged every day and some last several days. Some optional features are a GPS function, a stopwatch, an alarm, and a display brightness adjustment. Some watches (software) monitor sleep duration and type of sleep (light and deep). And a few watches (software) have a sedentary alert reminder that will inform if you have been sitting for too long so you can get up and move around to reactivate your metabolism. Some watches (software) include calorie tracking data on a greater variety of activities, exercises, and sports.

All watches have setup instructions. Some watches have very easy to follow instructions that can be done in a very short period of time. However, some watches have very complicated instructions that can take a very long time to properly execute. Read the customer reviews to determine the difficulty of the watch initialization instructions.

A huge selection of affordable watches and fitness bands are available for less than $50 on the internet and many are less than $40. There are also some that cost a lot more than $100. However, the price is not always related to the quality of the watch. Read the customer reviews very carefully if you are interested in purchasing one of these watches or fitness bands. Some of the advertised functions on some watches and fitness bands, including some of the extremely expensive ones, do not work properly and they should be avoided.

Chapter Two

Scientific Research Studies

Some people will believe almost anything if it is supported by some type of "scientific research." And some people will not believe anything unless it is supported by "scientific research." Scientific research is usually very good but, in my opinion, it should not be used as the sole basis for what a person believes or does not believe.

I am now in my seventies and I have been exposed to scientific research since the age of five when I first watched television commercials and I listened to a variety of different advertising claims where some type of study had proved something about a specific product. In addition, since 1984 I have worked for a major state university and I have some personal "insider" knowledge about scientific research. Based on my life experiences I now have the following perspective about scientific research:

1. Scientific research does not always produce consistent results. Some scientific research is refuted by subsequent scientific research. I have seen this happen with the following common products: eggs, bacon, saccharin, aspartame, and milk.

2. Most scientific research draws valid conclusions based on the data that was collected. However, sometimes the data is very limited, or the data is not collected in a statistically valid manner, or the conclusion contains qualifying comments that restrict a broader application of the results to situations not addressed in the study.

3. Most research is done by prestigious independent universities or research facilities. However the money to fund the research is usually "donated" from outside sources. The source that provides the money may specify the issue to be researched along with certain stipulations or constraints. If the organization and the scientist wish to receive the money then they must agree to the guidelines provided by the source supplying the money. These guidelines do **not** restrict the scientist's interpretation of the final data but the guidelines sometimes specify how or where the data is to be collected. Obviously these restrictions can influence the final results of the study. It is always possible for the organization or the scientist to refuse to accept the money if they do not agree with the stipulations. If this happens then the sponsoring organization will offer their money and their research project to a different university or organization. This allows the source of the funding to remain in the background and it creates the illusion that the university or research facility was acting independently and impartially in the

execution of the research study. The scientist does not falsify or misinterpret the final results but the scientist sometimes knows that the final results are biased because of project guidelines that were provided by the sponsor of the research.

4. The journals in which research studies are published are controlled by a small group of people at each journal. These individuals make the decisions on which research studies they will publish and which studies they will not publish. Since space may be limited in some journals, or there may be a limit on the number of studies that will be published in some journals, then it is easy to select studies that are consistent with the policies of the journal, and to not publish studies that are not in the best long-term interests of the journal.

5. Food, beverage, and drug companies have significantly influenced medical research and health recommendations and this has been carefully documented from the 1960s to 2016. This is one of the primary reasons why it is possible to find research results that are in complete contradiction to one other based on how the research study was conducted and based on who funded the research.

In the year 2020 it is possible to find published scientific research that suggests that weight can be lost on a low-fat diet, on a high-fat diet, on a low-carb diet, on a high-carb diet, and on a high-fiber diet. Since these studies are usually focused on weight loss and not on the overall health of the people who lost the weight, it is possible that each of these diets did result in weight loss at the expense of some nutrient that the human body needs to maintain long-term good health.

It should also be mentioned that scientific studies only report the observed relationship between variables. Most studies cannot prove that one variable is the cause for a change in another variable. The reason is because there are many different variables that could have an impact on the results and it is not possible to monitor and control every possible variable in a scientific study. For example, a study may report that as the number of gas stations increased in a geographical area then the number of restaurants in that area also increased. But both variables increased as a direct result of an increase in the population in the geographical area, and the increase in the number of restaurants was not caused by an increase in the number of gas stations.

Many of the scientific research studies I read are very interesting. However, I currently do not put too much confidence in the results of "some" scientific research studies if the results are in complete opposition to my personal life experiences, or to the knowledge I have personally gained during my life that I know is reliable based on my profession as an engineer and as a scientist.

The Satiety Index Scientific Research Study

The reason the "Satiety Index" is included in this chapter is because in the early part of the year 2020 the Satiety Index is frequently mentioned in a variety of articles about food and dieting, and it is usually quoted as being a reliable source of very useful information.

The Satiety Index is a measure of how well a specific food satisfies hunger and reduces the eating of other foods during the day. The Satiety Index theoretically measures the following variables:

1. The ratio of the number of calories in a specific food to the food's ability to satisfy hunger.
2. How full a person feels after eating a specific food.
3. How much a person's hunger is reduced by eating a specific food.
4. The total number of calories eaten during the day including the specific food being evaluated.

The following factors influence the Satiety Index score:

1. **Volume:** Foods that contain more water or air are less dense so there is more of the food to eat.
2. **Protein:** Foods that contain more protein are more filling than foods that contain more carbohydrates and/or fat.
3. **Fiber:** Foods that contain more fiber slow the movement of the food through the digestive system with the result that hunger is delayed for a longer period of time.
4. **Energy Density:** Foods with fewer calories in comparison to its weight will fill you up on fewer calories.

The major shortcoming of the Satiety Index is that only 38 foods were tested. The original test only included one meat, one type of fish, two types of vegetables, four types of fruit, one type of nut, three types of bread, a few other healthy foods, and a lot of junk food.

The five foods with the highest Satiety Index scores were boiled potatoes (323%), ling fish which is a member of the cod family (225%), oatmeal and porridge (209%), oranges (202%), and apples (197%).

The only two ways that potatoes were evaluated were as boiled potatoes and as French fries. All the other ways to prepare potatoes, including baked potatoes, were ignored. This creates a significant bias in the final results because it suggests that boiling potatoes is the best way to prepare potatoes. The study fails to mention that the reason boiled potatoes may have received the highest satiety score is because all the other healthy ways to prepare potatoes were excluded from the study. French fries were the only other potatoes in the study. Most people already know from experience that French fries do not satisfy a person's hunger for an extended period of time. However, it is interesting to note that in the Satiety Index research study French fries scored *below* cookies and jelly beans. Most people would probably not agree that cookies and jelly beans satisfy their hunger for a longer period of time than French fries. This is another reason why the Satiety Index scores are questionable.

In summary, the Satiety Index Research Study only evaluated a total of 38 foods and many of those foods were junk foods. Therefore the Satiety Index scores should not be used to recommend the limited number of foods that were tested by the researchers in preference over the hundreds of other excellent foods that were not tested. This is an example of using *common sense* to avoid making food choices in favor of foods that are receiving a lot of favorable publicity and that publicity is based on a questionable scientific research study. Instead you should make your food choices based on other more reliable criteria.

Scientific Research Conclusion

This chapter began with the following two sentences:

1. Some people will believe almost anything if it is supported by some type of "scientific research."
2. And some people will not believe anything unless it is supported by "scientific research."

Believing the conclusions reached by scientific research without carefully examining how the research was conducted and how the data was evaluated is similar to believing a single sentence from the Holy Bible without reading the entire chapter from which it was extracted.

I am not implying that scientific research is not useful. What I am saying is that you should not simply believe something because it sounds good, or it is something you would like to believe, or it is something "new" that excites your imagination and you feel as if some new truth has been revealed to you.

Instead it might be more prudent to use good *common sense* and to compare any new information or any new concepts that are made available to you against information that you know is absolutely true based on your actual life experiences. If the new information is in complete agreement with what you already know to be true, then the new information may also be true. On the other hand, if the new information completely contradicts what you know to be true, or if the new information is something with which you have no previous experience, then perhaps it would be wise to postpone your acceptance of the new information until you can somehow verify its accuracy and its reliability.

Chapter Three

A Review of Popular Diets

Most weight loss diets can help people lose weight even though the people are in different age groups, and they have different occupations, and they participate in different leisure activities. However, some diets are better or worse than other diets in the following areas:

1. **Health Problems:** Some diets increase the risk of a variety of different health problems while the person is dieting.

2. **Total Weight Loss:** The actual amount of weight lost over a specified time period can vary significantly for different diets.

3. **Speed of Weight Loss:** The speed at which the weight is lost varies significantly for different diets.

4. **Hunger:** Some diets do not satisfy a person's hunger and all the person can think about is food even after the person has just eaten.

5. **Focus:** Most diets focus on achieving weight loss by eliminating one or more foods from the diet. They treat everyone the same and they do not allow for each person to be different with unique food likes and dislikes.

6. **Short-Term Health:** Most diets result in some weight loss by eliminating specific foods from the diet. If the diet is carefully followed then the diet will help a person lose weight in the short-term but usually at the expense of the person's short-term health.

7. **Sustainability:** Most diets are not sustainable for a long period of time because people are different. Most people can tolerate the elimination of specific foods from their diet for a short period of time but not for the long-term. Therefore people eventually abandon the diet because the person has cravings for foods that are not allowed on the diet.

8. **Weight Gain:** When the diet stops working for a person then the person gradually begins to gain back all the weight that was lost even though the person does not change their diet or their daily routine.

This chapter will briefly review some of the more popular diets based on the main features of each diet.

Some of the diets that are reviewed in this chapter are based on losing weight without compromising a person's health. However, some of the diets focus on losing weight without any regard to the short-term or long-term impact on a person's health.

It should also be mentioned that rapid weight loss diets are not sustainable, not healthy, and the weight that is lost will usually be regained along with some additional weight in a short period of time. Rapid weight loss diets may also result in the development of gallstones. Finally, diets that do not include any exercise are not focused on your long-term health.

Low Calorie Diets

1. **Cookie Diet:** Special low-fat cookies are eaten instead of a regular meal. (Note: This is similar to eating a health food bar that is a complete meal but which has minimal calories.)

2. **Noom Diet:** The Noom Diet was created in 2008. It is a mobile app that has a fee of about $129 per four months or $387 per year (estimated cost January 2020). The actual cost is not revealed to potential customers until after they register and agree to a fee of $1 for the first 14 days. After registering you can download the app onto your mobile device. The diet is based on a daily calorie deficit. The app also provides a variety of educational materials to help educate its customers in the advantages and disadvantages of specific foods. It also allows customers to answer a questionnaire and the app will calculate the number of calories a customer is allowed to eat each day to lose the number of pounds the customer desires to lose in the timeframe the customer specifies. The app will not recommend fewer than 1,200 calories per day for a woman or 1,400 calories per day for a man. The reason this diet may work is because it advocates a daily calorie deficit which means you eat fewer calories per day than you burn per day.

3. **Weight Watchers Diet:** Weight Watchers is a large organization with branches all over the world. Weight loss is based on diet, exercise, and a network of like-minded weight-conscious people. Dieters can attend regular meetings in person or online. Each food is assigned a specific number of points, and dieters can eat the foods they desire as long as they do not exceed their daily maximum point limit. The diet recommends a balanced diet and eating the foods you enjoy in moderation.

(Note: In 1987 I lost 20 pounds in about three months eating low-calorie frozen meals but I was always hungry. In 1992 I lost 30 pounds in about five months eating low-calorie frozen meals but I was always hungry. Each time I stopped eating the low-calorie frozen meals I very slowly and very gradually gained back all the weight I had lost, plus a little more weight, over a period of several years. The low-calorie frozen meals were purchased at local grocery stores.)

Low Carbohydrate Diets

Low carbohydrate diets reduce the consumption of carbohydrates and increase the consumption of protein and fats. Low carbohydrate diets have a good track record for reducing excess tummy fat.

1. **Atkins Diet:** This diet was created by Robert C. Atkins, MD during the 1960s by doing research on his patients who asked him how they could lose weight and who voluntarily followed his advice. (Note: To the best of my knowledge I am not related to Dr. Atkins although we may share one or more common ancestors somewhere in the distant past.) Dr. Atkins published his book "Dr. Atkins' Diet Revolution" in 1972. He founded "Atkins Nutritionals" in 1989 and the company began producing and selling diet products. In 2002 Dr. Atkins updated his diet. The basic premise of the Atkins diet is as follows: If we eat more carbohydrates than we need per day, then the extra food is converted into fat and stored on our body. If we eat fewer carbohydrates than we need each day, then our body automatically begins to burn our fat to provide the fuel it requires. Counting carbohydrates and **not** calories is the answer to successful weight loss. Eat any combination of beef, chicken, fish, pork, butter, cheese, eggs, mayonnaise, and olive oil until you feel full but not stuffed. Eat 2 or 3 cups each day of any combination of celery, cucumber, green peppers, lettuce, mushrooms, and radishes. Eat one cup per day of any combination of asparagus, avocado, broccoli, cabbage, cauliflower, eggplant, onion, spinach, and tomato. Do not eat bread, flour products, pasta, potatoes, rice, or sugar. Drink decaffeinated coffee, tea, diet soft drinks, and water. Exercise regularly. The main criticism of this diet is that it may increase the risk of some health issues. (Note: In 2004 I followed the Atkins diet and I lost 60 pounds in about eight months. But I was hungry most of the time and food occupied my thoughts almost continuously. My goal was to lose a total of 65 pounds. However I could not lose the final 5 pounds even though I stayed on the diet for another six months. Instead I gradually began gaining weight even though I did not change my diet or my daily routine. Therefore about three more months later I abandoned the Atkins diet. Then I slowly continued to regain all the weight I had lost, plus a little more weight, over a period of several years.)

2. **F-Factor Diet:** This diet was crated in 2006 by Tanya Zuckerbrot who is a registered dietician. The "F" stands for fiber. The diet is a low-carb diet that recommends lean protein and complex carbs that are rich in fiber. The diet permits eating at restaurants, drinking alcohol in moderation, and it minimizes the importance of exercise. These are probably the reasons this diet is liked by some people.

3. **Keto or Ketogenic Diet:** This diet has been used for several decades to help treat epilepsy. It is one of the most restrictive types of diets. It may be useful for people who have metabolic disorders or brain injuries. It is based on reducing carbohydrates and increasing fats in the diet. This forces the body to burn fats for fuel instead of carbohydrates. The body breaks down fat and creates ketones through a process called ketosis. The diet recommends healthy fats such as avocados, Brazil Nuts, coconuts, oily fish, and olive oil. This diet is not recommended for individuals with type 1 diabetes because it could result in a diabetic coma and death.

4. **South Beach Diet:** This diet was created by Miami Beach cardiologist Arthur Agatston, MD and by nutritionist Marie Almon in 2003. This diet is based on the premise that the key to quick weight loss and improved health does not depend on the number of carbohydrates or fats in your diet. Instead the critical issue is to strategically select the right type of carbohydrates and fats. The focus of the diet is on controlling insulin levels by recommending unrefined slowly digested carbohydrates instead of rapidly digested carbohydrates and by eating lean protein, low-fat dairy, healthy fats, fruit, vegetables, and whole grains.

High Starch and Low Fat Diets

1. **McDougall's High Starch Diet:** This high calorie, high fiber, low fat diet *excludes* all animal foods and all vegetable oils. This diet consists of foods that are high in starches such as beans, potatoes, and rice. Excluding all animal foods can result in a variety of health problems that are common among vegetarians who do not eat meat, eggs, or dairy products.

Pre-packaged Food Diets

The major shortcoming of these diets is the cost of the pre-packaged meals. Another shortcoming is that you have no control over the quality of the food that is put in the pre-packaged meals, and you have no control over the additives or preservatives in those meals.

1. **Jenny Craig Diet:** Created by Jenny Craig, Inc. The company provides weight counseling. Dieters must eat the pre-packaged food that is produced and sold by the company. (Note: In 1991 my stepfather-in-law was reasonably healthy except he was overweight. To lose weight he began to faithfully follow the Jenny Craig diet and he only ate the meals he was allowed to eat. He lost a lot of weight over a period of several months. However, while he was still faithfully following this diet, he died suddenly. It is possible that this may simply have been his time to die.)

2. **Nutrisystem Diet:** Created by Nutrisystem, Inc. Low-calorie meals are specially designed for each customer and those meals contain fixed ratios of carbohydrates, fats, and protein, which are the three sources of fuel in food. Dieters must eat the pre-packaged food that is produced and sold by the company.

Crash Diets and Fad Diets

These diets focus on fast weight loss by forbidding specific foods. These diets can be dangerous and some of them can result in sudden death if the person is not under the close supervision of a physician.

1. **Beverly Hills Diet** and the **New Beverly Hills Diet:** This diet was created by Judy Mazel. She published her first book "The Beverly Hills Diet" in 1981 and it was considered to be one of the first fad diets. She published her second book "The New Beverly Hills Diet" in 1996 and it is considered to be less extreme than her first diet. She believes that what a person eats is not important, and how much a person eats is also not important. What is important is that foods must be eaten in the correct combinations and in the correct order. Eating the wrong combinations of foods or eating foods in the wrong order will result in an increase in body fat. For example, fruit must be eaten alone and it must be eaten at least an hour before anything else is eaten. Two hours later carbohydrates may be eaten. Two hours later protein may be eaten. Protein and carbohydrates may not be eaten at the same time. However, fats may be eaten with either carbohydrates or protein. On some days only fruit may be eaten. Protein is excluded on a regular basis in the long-term execution of this diet. Water may be consumed with anything. Milk may be consumed with protein. Beer and liquor may be consumed with carbohydrates. Wine may be consumed with fruits. Exercise is **not** required. The entire diet is based on the opinions of Judy Mazel and there is absolutely no scientific reason why foods must be eaten in a specific order, or why foods cannot be eaten together. On the contrary, it is a scientific fact that some foods should be eaten with other foods because the nutrients in the foods combine together while being digested, and this enhances the overall nutritional value of the foods and the health impact of the foods. Weight loss in this diet occurs solely because the total number of calories that are consumed is reduced, and weight loss is not due to eating foods in the correct order. In addition, the diet results in weight loss at the expense of long-term health. The diet is not appropriate for pregnant women or for women who are breastfeeding their babies. This diet can result in serious deficiencies in nutrition, severe drops in blood pressure, and severe diarrhea which can result in dehydration. Any of these medical problems could result in death.

2. **Cabbage Soup Diet:** This is a seven-day, low-fat, high-fiber diet that became popular in the 1980s. Homemade cabbage soup is consumed in large quantities at each meal. The soup is made by the dieter and the soup must include cabbage. The soup should also include carrots, celery, green beans, green peppers, mushrooms, onions, spinach, tomatoes, and herbs and spices depending on what the dieter likes to eat. But beans, corn, and peas are forbidden. Dieters are allowed to eat as much cabbage soup as they want but most people do not like the soup and they only eat small quantities. Before the seven-days are over they become weak, dizzy, light headed, and they lose the ability to concentrate effectively. Some people experience cramping. The diet may also significantly change a person's normal blood sugar levels. The diet requires drinking a minimum of four glasses of water per day, and taking a multivitamin tablet every day. Unsweetened coffee or tea is permitted. Because the soup is low in calories, protein, carbs, and fats this diet does result in weight loss. But only about one-third of the weight loss is from burning fat cells and the other two thirds is from lost water weight and *decreased lean muscle mass*. This diet is not sustainable and when people stop this diet they frequently gain back all the weight they lost during their seven-day diet.

3. **Cottage Cheese Diet:** Only cottage cheese is eaten at each meal for at least three days. However, some people also eat fruits and vegetables in moderation. Carbonated sodas, fruit juice, sweetened beverages, and alcohol are excluded. Cottage cheese contains some vitamins but not all the vitamins needed by the body. One cup of cottage cheese contains 760 or more grams of sodium which is 30% or more of the RDA for sodium. Cottage cheese is high in protein that digests more slowly and this helps you feel full longer. However, cottage cheese contains no fiber and this may result in constipation, higher blood pressure, and higher blood sugar levels. This short-term diet will usually result in "water weight" loss but not the loss of fat. A better way to enjoy cottage cheese is to eat it as one of many different foods in a well-balanced diet.

4. **Grapefruit Diet:** This is a 10 to 12 day diet that first became popular in the 1930s. The advocates of this diet believe that grapefruit contains some special enzyme or chemical that helps the body to remove fat. However, this is just a myth and it is not true. This diet requires that grapefruit, or grapefruit juice, be consumed either before or during every meal. The diet also recommends a reduction to 1,000 calories per day, and a significant reduction in sugar and carbohydrates, and an increase in protein, fat, and cholesterol rich foods. Eight or more glasses of water should be

consumed each day. One cup of unsweetened coffee or tea is permitted. The diet does not include any type of exercise. This 12 day diet works for two reasons. First, if you only eat 1,000 calories per day then you will lose weight even if you don't eat grapefruit. Second, if you eat grapefruit, or if you drink water before or during a meal, then both grapefruit and water have the same exact effect of helping a person feel full and the person may eat a little less during the meal. It should also be mentioned that grapefruit and grapefruit juice can interfere with some prescription drugs for cholesterol, high blood pressure, antihistamines drugs, and anti-anxiety drugs. Grapefruit can reduce the amount of the drug that is absorbed by the body, or it can result in unhealthy side effects when combined with these drugs. However, it should also be mentioned that adding grapefruit, or any other citrus fruit, to a well-balanced diet may be a healthy choice for many people. (Note: In 1972 I ate half a grapefruit every morning for about six-months but I did not lose any weight. However, I was only 2 or 3 pounds overweight in 1972. Several other times during my life I occasionally consumed grapefruit juice at mealtime but I never lost any weight. On each occasion I stopped drinking grapefruit juice after about 4 to 6 weeks because it did not help me lose any weight.)

5. **Mediterranean Diet**: It is based on the foods that were normally eaten by people in the 1960s in the southern European countries of Crete, Greece, and southern Italy. In recent years it was expanded to include foods eaten by people in southern France, Portugal, and Spain. About one-third of the diet is fats but saturated fats should not exceed 8% of the calories. Monounsaturated fats, such as olive oil, nuts, and seeds, are recommended. Also recommended are polyunsaturated fats that are rich in omega-3 fatty acids such as herring, mackerel, salmon, sardines, shellfish, trout, and tuna. Olive oil should be used instead of butter, salad dressings, or marinades. Recommend foods include beans, fresh fruit, herbs, nuts, seeds, vegetables, and whole grains. The diet permits a limited amount of cheese, eggs, and yogurt. Fish is recommended over chicken, and a very small amount of red meat is allowed. Water is recommended but unsweetened coffee or tea are allowed. It allows four eggs per week, and low to moderate amounts of wine.

6. **Starvation Diet:** This is not fasting. Fasting is skipping one, two, or three meals, and fasting should not last for more than 24 hours. If a fast goes beyond 24 hours then it is not a fast and it is something else even if a person refers to it as a "fast." After 24 hours the body gradually begins to enter "starvation mode." Therefore most people call a long-term fast by its proper name

which is a "starvation diet." A starvation diet is an extreme diet. There are two basic types of starvation diets:

a. **No Food:** Only fluids are allowed and no food may be eaten. Some diets only allow water but other diets allow for fruit juice in addition to water.

b. **Limited Food:** An extremely limited amount of food is allowed but the number of calories is less than half of what the body needs to maintain its normal metabolic processes.

When the body realizes it is receiving no food, or very little food, then it automatically responds by gradually reducing its metabolic rate and the body burns fewer calories per day. This response is preprogrammed into the body's genes so it has a better chance of surviving a long-term famine. People who occasionally practice a starvation diet will lose a little weight in the short-term but they will gradually add that weight back, plus some more, in the long-term. In addition, if a starvation diet is practiced repeatedly then it can have long-term negative health consequences, and it may eventually result in the loss of muscle. Losing muscle is really bad because the basic purpose of dieting is to lose fat and to increase the amount of muscle in order to produce a slim healthy strong body.

7. **Subway Diet:** There is no "official Subway diet." This low-calorie, very low-fat diet was created in 1998 by a college student named Jared Fogle who lost 245 pounds by eating Subway Restaurant sandwiches at lunch and supper. Jared began his diet weighing about 425 pounds. Breakfast was a cup of coffee or a small bowl of cereal with skim milk. Lunch was a 6-inch turkey Subway sandwich with no mayonnaise and no cheese (about 290 calories), and a diet soda. Supper was a 12-inch Subway veggie sandwich with no mayonnaise and no cheese (about 460 calories), and water. Snacks were an apple, orange, or water. In three months Jared lost 94 pounds. At the end of 11 months he lost 245 pounds without doing any exercise except walking to his classes. (Note: Jared's weight loss was due to reducing his daily calorie intake and it had nothing to do with Subway sandwiches.) Jared received national publicity in 1999. Jared was hired by Subway and he appeared in their advertisements from 2000 to 2015. Subway included the following disclaimer in their advertisements: "The Subway diet, combined with a lot of walking, worked for Jared. We're not saying this is for everyone. You should check with your doctor before starting any diet program. But it worked for Jared." The FBI began investigating Jared in 2007. In 2015 Jared pleaded guilty in federal court to the charge of paying to have sex with minors and he received a 15 year prison sentence.

Vegetarian Related Diets

1. **Semi-Vegetarianism Diet:** Vegetables are the primary foods eaten but occasionally meat may be consumed. Some vegetarian diets allow for the consumption of butter, cheese, eggs, milk, and honey.

2. **Vegan Diet:** Only vegetables are consumed. Dieters refrain from butter, cheese, milk, eggs, honey, and all types of meat. This reduces the consumption of cholesterol and saturated fats. Dieters must figure out how to include an adequate amount of protein and vitamin B12 in their diet in order to maintain their health.

Other Diets

1. **Eat Stop Eat Diet:** Created by Brad Pilon in 2017. He emphasizes that you may eat each day just before you begin a 24 hour fast and you may eat again immediately after the 24 hour fast. The only way this would be an actual "day" would be if you started at midnight on one day and stopped at midnight the next day. As long as you don't start the diet at midnight then you will be eating something every day. The diet allows you to choose whether you will fast once a week (24 hours/week) or twice a week (48 hours/week) but not on consecutive days. The net impact is that you will skip two meals per week if you fast "one day or 24 hours" and you will miss four meals per week if you fast "two days or 48 hours." Breakfast is still allowed on the days you eat. On your eating days you may eat anything you want as often as you want but you are encouraged to eat responsibly. If you wish may also follow a specific diet, such as Paleo, or any other diet you desire on the days you do eat. The Eat Stop Eat Diet recommends between 100 to 300 grams of protein on the days you eat. Resistance training is required. But if you don't want to do strength exercises then you may do some other vigorous exercise. The reason this diet may result in weight loss is because it eliminates all intake of calories for two or four meals per week, and it recommends vigorous exercise. During your fasting days your metabolism shifts to burning body fat after about 10 to 12 hours of not eating. However, if you eat too much on the days you do eat then you will not lose weight and you may even gain weight.

2. **Gluten-Free Diet:** This diet is for people with celiac disease and for people who may be sensitive or intolerant to gluten. Wheat, barley, rye, and triticale all contain the type of gluten that can cause serious health problems in some people. Corn, rice, and quinoa contain a different type of gluten that can be eaten by some of these same people. The type of foods that are permitted in a gluten-free diet include fruit, vegetables, beef, fish, chicken, pork, eggs, and low-fat dairy products. Foods that are prohibited include bread,

pasta, cookies, pastries, cereals, crackers, pretzels, pizza, muffins, and any food that may be contaminated with gluten. The cost of gluten-free foods is usually higher than the same foods with gluten. Gluten-free foods are usually not fortified with B vitamins. The major risk of this diet is a deficiency in one or more essential nutrients. The major health problem with this diet is constipation.

3. **High-Protein Diet:** Foods that contain a lot of protein are eaten for the primary purpose of building muscles. In most other diets extra protein is eaten to compensate for the reduction in the amount of carbohydrates or fats that are eaten.

4. **Paleo Diet, or Paleolithic Diet, or Caveman Diet:** It emphasizes food eaten by our "distant ancestors" and it encourages exercise. Absolutely no sugar may be consumed except the natural sugar in fruit. No processed foods, no processed grains, no dairy, no alcohol, no beans or legumes, and almost no starches. The following foods are permitted: eggs, fish, some fruits, poultry, nuts, oils, seeds, sweet potatoes, vegetables, and grass-fed meat but no grain-fed meat. It recommends food in this order: vegetables, protein, fat, and a limited number of carbohydrates.

5. **Raw Food Diet:** The focus is on uncooked and unprocessed foods. No food that has been processed, pasteurized, or contains any type of additive or preservative may be eaten. The primary emphasis is on reducing the number of carcinogens in the diet. The diet may lack some important nutrients and it is difficult to follow for an extended period of time.

6. **Zone Diet:** The focus is on reducing the glycemic index. The glycemic index is the change in the glucose level after eating. Each meal must contain a nutritional balance of 40% carbohydrates, 30% fats, and 30% protein. The diet recommends high quality carbs, unrefined carbs, and fats. Some dieters have complained that the diet is too restrictive for long-term sustainability because it does not provide enough of some important nutrients.

Summary and Conclusion

Some of the diets reviewed in this chapter are based on losing weight without compromising a person's health. However, some of the diets focus on losing weight without any regard to a person's health.

If you are interested in knowing more about one of the diets mentioned in this chapter then you should do some additional research about the diet. And you should impartially consider the benefits and the shortcomings of the diet. You may discover that the shortcomings of the diet completely offset the benefit of the quick weight loss that is promised by the diet.

Chapter Four

The Common Sense Diet

Chapter one should be read before reading this chapter because the weight loss advice in chapter one should also be followed in addition to the new strategies presented in this chapter.

In my opinion the majority of the people in the USA who are overweight are truthfully not responsible for the extra pounds that we are carrying on our bodies. Instead I believe we are the innocent victims of a variety of different food processing companies, restaurants, and food advertisements.

In addition, we *too easily believe wrong information* about some foods, and about some diets, because that wrong information has been copied and repeated for so many years, in so many different sources, and by so many respectable intelligent people, that we simply accept it as being the truth. However, if something is not true then simply repeating that information in hundreds of different sources by hundreds of different people does not make the information true.

For example, some diets suggest that if you will just reduce your consumption of carbohydrates (or whatever) then the number of calories you eat each day will automatically be reduced and therefore calories can be ignored. However, these same diets stress that you cannot eat too much of some foods, such as cheese, because they contain too many calories. This clearly indicates that calories are important and you cannot lose weight if you eat too many calories.

The purpose of this chapter is to help separate truth from fiction. However, this will require an open mind and the ability to **not** pass judgment until after you have read all the facts. I do not expect everyone to agree with all the information presented in this chapter. However, a person with an open mind who sincerely desires to know the truth, may revise some of their opinions about some things that they had previously believed to be the truth. This may be very difficult for individuals who have previously expressed a firm opinion about some weight loss concept because it would require them to acknowledge that they may have been mistaken. (Note: One way to justify why you have changed you mind is to say that you have recently discovered some new information that you were not previously aware of.)

The primary objective of this chapter is to help you understand some simple *common sense* things you can do to improve your health and lose weight without starving yourself, and without having to join a gym or a weight loss club. This chapter will also explain how you can keep that weight off your body for the rest of your life.

No Claims and No Promises

Diets frequently make some type of claim or promise about what the diet can do for you if you will follow the diet faithfully, and if you will eat the foods that the diet recommends, and if you do not eat foods that the diet tells you to avoid.

The Common Sense Diet does not make any claims or promises. The reason is because you will design a diet that is just right for you, based on the foods you really enjoy eating, and which are also healthy for you, and therefore you will decide what to eat and what not to eat. Therefore the diet you design for yourself will be unique and it will help you lose weight while enhancing your long-term health. But your diet will probably not work for anyone else. The reason is because other people may not like the same foods you like.

Is There a Perfect Diet for Almost Everyone?

There is no "perfect diet" that will work for everyone. The reasons are as follows:

1. We have different jobs that consume a different amount of calories while we are working at our normal jobs.
2. We have different lifestyles and different leisure activities that consume a different amount of calories during our leisure time.
3. We have different food preferences and we may not enjoy eating some of the foods that are recommended by a specific diet.
4. We may have specific food allergies and we have to avoid specific foods in order to avoid health problems.
5. We may be part of a larger family unit and we may all eat at the same dining table at mealtime. It is more challenging to plan meals for more than one person when you are responsible for the health and happiness of all the people who eat at your dining table.

Three Reasons Why Most Diets Don't Work

There are three common problems with most diets. One or all of the following problems will result in the failure of the diet, either in the short-term or in the long-term.

1. **People are Different:** Although we are all members of the human race, each of us is a unique special person. We all have different likes and dislikes about specific foods. We all have different metabolic reactions to the same exact foods. And we all experience a different level of hunger satisfaction from the same exact type of food. For example, a specific food may do a good job of satisfying one person's hunger, but it may have only a minor impact on another person's hunger, and it may actually increase or aggravate

the hunger of another person. Therefore some of the foods that are recommended on some diets may help some people lose weight. But those same foods may not be effective at helping other people lose weight. In other words, one diet will not work for everyone.

2. **Significant Hunger:** Some diets may help you lose a lot of weight very quickly but these diets usually result in long periods of sustained hunger where all you can think about is food. Therefore most people abandon these diets after only a short period of time and they return to their normal eating habits. Then they gain back all the weight they lost plus some additional pounds.

3. **Forbidden Foods:** Some diets prohibit the eating of specific foods. If the food is one that you have enjoyed your entire life, such as bread, or milk, or meat, or Mexican food, or Italian food, then it is very difficult to follow the diet for an extended period of time because all you can think about is the food that you are no longer allowed to eat. These types of diets are doomed to fail in the long run because they are in opposition to your natural cravings for food that is basically healthy except it is forbidden by your diet.

Advantages of the Common Sense Diet

The common sense diet, as explained in this chapter, will allow you to customize a weight loss program that you design specifically for yourself, and it will include most of the foods you currently enjoy eating. *And the really good news is that you will lose weight without feeling hungry all the time.* However, you will probably get a little hungry just before your next regularly scheduled meal but this is normal for everyone regardless of whether or not they are losing weight.

Although the weight loss program you design specifically for yourself will help you lose weight, it will probably not be successful for someone else. The reason is because you will design a unique weight loss program that is customized for your individual needs, your abilities, and your food preferences. You will select foods that you enjoy eating, and that satisfy your hunger, and that reduce your cravings for more food. But these same food choices will probably not help someone else lose weight. Each person will need to gradually experiment with a variety of different foods until they find the best combination of foods that will help them to lose weight, increase the amount of lean muscles on their body, and improve their health.

As you read this book you will acquire a wealth of knowledge about why some foods are healthy, and why some foods should be avoided, and which foods can actually help you lose weight. When you combine this knowledge with your individual preferences for specific foods then you will be able to create an eating plan that will be perfect for you and it will enhance your long-term health and result in weight loss. And there is a good chance you will follow your new eating plan for the rest of your life because you will have created it specifically for yourself and you will be proud of what you have created and what it has accomplished for you. Pride of creation and ownership of your own customized diet are significant motivators for your continued long-term health, and for a slim healthy body that will enhance your enjoyment of everything you do. Unlike other diets you may have tried, this time your diet will be sustainable and you will be able to keep the weight you lose off your body for the rest of your life.

The Two Basic Principles on Which
the Common Sense Diet is Based

The two basic principles that form the foundation of the Common Sense Diet are: (1) the food should benefit the body and not be harmful to the body, and (2) the food must be satisfying and enjoyable to eat.

1. **Healthy:** Food is healthy if it meets all the following requirements:
   a. **Calories:** The food should not have too many calories based on the quantity and type of food that it is. *Calories are the most important criteria for selecting or rejecting any food.*
   b. **Cholesterol:** Foods with low or no cholesterol are preferred.
   c. **Sodium:** Sodium is naturally present in most foods and this is okay. Foods that contain high amounts of added sodium should be avoided, or the consumption of these foods should be minimized in our weekly diet.
   d. **Fat and Carbohydrates:** The food should contain a reasonable amount of the nutrients we desire and it should have very little or none of the nutrients we wish to avoid. Careful attention will be given to the type of fat and to the type of carbohydrates.
   e. **Protein:** Protein is desirable because it helps firm up our existing muscles and it helps us add new muscles.
   f. **Sugar:** Sugar that is a natural part of the food is okay as long as the total sugar content is not excessive. The food should contain very little or no added sugar or refined sugar.
   g. **Sugar Substitutes:** The food may contain a limited amount of sugar substitutes but preference should be given to foods that are naturally tasty and that do not need sugar substitutes.
   h. **Vitamins, Minerals, Amino Acids, and Antioxidants:** The food should contain some of the nutrition our body requires.
   i. **Preservatives:** If possible, the food should not contain any preservatives. Preservatives are extremely harmful to the body over an extended period of time.

j. **Allergies:** The food should not contain anything we have had an allergic reaction to in the past.

k. **Health:** The food should help us to not only help us retain our current health but it should also help us improve our long-term health and increase our life-expectancy.

2. **Satisfying:** Satisfying food meets all the following requirements:

a. **Appeal:** The food is something we really enjoy eating. Or at least we are not repulsed at the thought of eating it.

b. **Quantity (Amount, Volume):** There is enough food to satisfy us. A skimpy meal will rarely satisfy our hunger. There needs to be enough food in the meal to fill our stomachs.

c. **Sight (Appearance):** The food looks delicious.

d. **Smell (Aroma):** The food smells yummy if it has an aroma.

e. **Taste (Flavor):** The food has a delightful flavor. Or at least it has a neutral flavor and it does not have a disagreeable flavor.

f. **Chewability:** The food allows us to use our teeth to chew. Chewing food brings happiness and contentment. Swallowing a liquid meal does not result in happiness and contentment.

g. **Digestibility:** The food is something that is easy for our body to digest and it does not cause us problems after we eat it.

h. **Satisfying:** The food satisfies our immediate hunger and we do not get hungry again for several hours.

Weight Loss Goal

Before you begin your new diet may I suggest that you set a weight loss goal that you would like to achieve.

Please do not set your goal at your weight when you were 18 years old, or 21 years old, or any specific age. Instead it would be more reasonable to set a weight objective based on your current age, your current health, and your daily mandatory activities (such as a job).

Your weight loss goal should be the weight you would be satisfied with if you can achieve it. It should not be too ambitious because goals that are too ambitious are quickly abandoned. It should also not be too easy because goals that are too easy are only pursued in a half-hearted manner. Instead the ideal weight that you set as your goal should be something you believe you have a reasonable chance to achieve if you are persistent.

Please do not set a time limit on how long you will give yourself to achieve your goal. Time frames are important for organizational goals because progress will usually not be made towards a goal that has no due date or review date. However, a time frame is not relevant for a weight loss goal because there are too many variables that you have no control over that could slow down or delay reaching your goal within your allotted time period.

If you set a weight loss goal and a time limit goal then you will be setting two goals. The chance of being able to achieve two goals simultaneously is very slim.

Instead consider yourself to be on track towards your weight loss objective as long as you are making some type of gradual progress towards your goal and you are still losing some weight with the passage of time.

Finally, keep your weight loss objective a secret. Do not tell anyone what your goal is. This will prevent negative criticism from other people if you are not able to make continuous steady progress towards your goal. And it will eliminate the need to explain to anyone why your weight loss is taking longer than you originally estimated. As long as you are making some progress towards your goal then that should be enough to satisfy you. You do not need the praise or the condemnation of other people. The reason you are losing weight is to make yourself happy and you are not doing it to please anyone else.

One or Multiple Weight Loss Goals

Most weight loss professionals recommend setting a single weight loss goal as your desired final weight. In other words, set an "all or nothing" goal. You either achieve your goal or you don't. If you don't win then you have lost. If you don't succeed then you have failed.

A different option, or a *common sense* option, would be to set five goals or milestones instead of a single goal. As you achieve each of your five goals or milestones then you will have succeeded in that phase of your weight loss effort. This eliminates the "all or nothing," succeed or fail, win or lose, aspect of a weight loss effort.

Setting five goals also allows you to congratulate yourself each time you achieve one of your goals. This provides significant positive reinforcement that your weight loss plan is working and it helps to encourage you to stay on track towards your next weight loss goal or milestone.

If you decide to set five weight loss goals then you may set them any way you wish. One reasonable method is to consider how much total weight you wish to lose and then set your first goal at 10% of that weight, your second goal at 30% of that weight, your third goal at 60% of that weight, your fourth goal at 90% of that weight, and your fifth and final goal at 100% of that weight.

The following example is based on losing a total of 40 pounds in a total of five stages or phases:

Goal	Total Weight Lost	Additional Weight Lost
1	4 pounds (40 x 0.10)	4 pounds (4 - 0)
2	12 pounds (40 x 0.30)	8 pounds (12 - 4)
3	24 pounds (40 x 0.60)	12 pounds (24 - 12)
4	36 pounds (40 x 0.90)	12 pounds (36 - 24)
5	40 pounds (40 x 1.00)	4 pounds (40 - 36)

The above goals provide an easy weight loss goal for the first goal in order to provide quick positive reinforcement that your weight loss effort is working. But weight loss gradually becomes more difficult as you gradually approach your desired weight. Therefore the goals gradually become a little more difficult to achieve even though each goal does not require the same amount of weight loss. The last ten percent weight loss is usually the most challenging part of any weight loss effort. Therefore even though the fifth and final goal is only four pounds, it may take more time to lose those final four pounds than any of the previous weight loss goals.

Another method of setting five goals would be to simply divide the total desired weight loss by five and then use that weight loss as the amount of weight to lose for each of your five goals. For example:

40 pounds / 5 goals = 8 pounds per goal

Each time you lose another 8 pounds then you will have reached that goal.

You may set your weight loss goals any way you wish. The reason is because your goals need to make sense to you and that is the fundamental objective of the Common Sense Diet.

Now let's take a look at how the Common Sense Diet can be used to help you reach your total weight loss goal.

The Common Sense Diet

1. **Our long-term health is much more important than our weight loss.**
    a. **Long-Term Health:** The decisions we make about the foods we eat should always be based on their impact on our long-term health. Our long-term health should be the most important issue in the diet we design based on our food likes and dislikes. Damaging our body in order to lose weight is not a good idea. Our primary goal should be to improve our health so we can live a long life and enjoy every moment of it.
    b. **Weight Loss:** The foods we select should be low in calories and they should enhance our long-term health. The foods we

eat should satisfy our appetite so we are not always hungry and we are not constantly thinking about food. This will allow us to be more productive at whatever jobs we do because we will be able to focus on the task at hand.

2. **Calories are extremely important and calories should not be ignored.** Calories should not be put in second or third place after some other nutritional value such as fat, carbohydrates, or protein.

   a. **Number of Calories:** To lose weight we need to eat fewer calories per day than we burn that day.

   b. **Calorie Counting:** It is not necessary to count calories precisely and we don't need to record the number of calories we eat. We just need to roughly estimate the number of calories we eat each time we eat so we can keep the total number of calories we consume in one day to a reasonable level.

   c. **Calories per Serving:** We can eat almost any food we desire as long as we consider the number of calories in that food and how much of the food we eat. The actual number of calories is determined by the serving size. The "average" serving size is shown on the nutrition label for each food and that can help us determine how many calories are in the "actual" serving size we consume. If we consume a smaller serving than "average" then we will consume fewer calories. If we consume a larger serving than "average" then we will consume more calories. In dieting terminology this is called "portion control." By simply controlling the amount of each food we eat then we can control our total calorie consumption per day.

   d. **Calories in Foods Without Nutrition Labels:** The number of calories in most of the commonly available foods is in the Appendix at the end of this book

   e. **Calories per Day:** One pound of fat is equal to approximately 3,500 calories. Therefore, if we eat 500 to 750 fewer calories per day than we burn, then we will lose approximately 1 to 1.5 pounds of fat (0.45 to 0.68 kilograms) per week on the average. However, a person who is only a few pounds overweight may discover that their body's metabolism has already adjusted to their healthy lifestyle and they will not be able to lose weight as easily as someone who has a lot more weight to lose.

3. **Focus 100% of your attention on eating when you do eat.**

   a. **Distractions:** If possible, do not eat while working, talking on the phone, reading, playing a game, watching a movie, or doing almost anything else.

The Common Sense Diet

b. **Hunger:** If you get hungry while you are doing some type of activity, then stop doing that activity when you eat a meal or a snack. This will allow your brain to focus on the food you are eating, and it will help satisfy your hunger and reduce your appetite, and this will reduce the amount of food you eat later. This can significantly enhance your efforts to lose weight.

4. **Eat 2 or 3 normal meals per day.**
   a. **Breakfast:** You may eat breakfast if you want to. However, it is perfectly okay to skip breakfast. It is also okay to ignore the media propaganda that "breakfast is the most important meal of the day." It is okay to ignore the overwhelming number of dieting professionals that guarantee you that you will lose more weight if you will just eat a healthy breakfast. This may be true for the average person but it is not true for everyone. There are a lot of extremely healthy adults who never eat breakfast.
   b. **Fourth Meal:** If three normal meals do not satisfy your hunger then eat four smaller meals per day. However, eating four smaller meals per day may increase tummy fat, or prevent the loss of tummy fat.
   c. **Regular Meal Schedule:** Regardless of whether you eat two, three, or four meals per day, it is important to eat those meals at approximately the same time every day, seven days a week. If you eat at approximately the same time each day then your body will gradually become accustomed to this schedule and this will help you avoid eating snacks between meals because you will not start to get hungry until just before the next regularly scheduled meal. People who have a full-time job normally have a regular meal schedule on work days. If possible those same regular meal times should be observed on the days you do not work at your regular job. This will help your body regulate itself and it will be easier for you to remain on your diet and lose weight. On the other hand, if you eat your meals at different times on different days then your digestive system will not know when you intend to eat again and you will get hungry more often and at unpredictable times.

5. **Slow down. Take small bites. Chew each bite completely before swallowing.**
   a. **Chapter One Advice:** The above advice was first offered in Chapter One along with a very detailed explanation of the benefits of following this advice.
   b. **Additional Comments:** One of the most challenging eating habits to break is preparing our next bite of food while we are

still chewing the food in our mouth. This habit can be broken if you will follow the advice in Chapter One and put your knife, fork, or spoon down on your plate or napkin immediately after you have put some food into your mouth. But putting your eating utensils down can be a very difficult habit to acquire. It requires conscious thought and effort to acquire this highly desirable eating habit. The next suggestion may help you acquire this habit.

   c. **If Eating Alone, Close Your Eyes While Chewing:** After you have put some food in your mouth, and you have placed your eating utensils on your plate, then close your eyes while you chew. This will eliminate visual distractions from interfering with the pleasure of eating and it will automatically prevent you from preparing your next bite of food while you are still chewing. Your mind will focus on the delightful experience of chewing the food in your mouth, and on tasting the food completely, and this will significantly enhance the pleasure you receive from that meal.

   d. **Chewing Exercise:** The more bites of food you have to enjoy, and the longer you chew each bite will provide more exercise for your jaw muscles at each meal. All exercise, including the very modest exercise of chewing food, will help to increase the number of calories you burn each day. Some people may say there is no benefit in exercising your jaw muscles but those same people would probably not deny the benefits of squeezing a rubber ball in your hands many, many times in order to enhance the strength of your hands.

6. **Do not eat unless you are hungry.**

   a. **Hunger:** When you begin to feel hungry your body is telling you one or more of the following things:

      I. **Sugar Craving:** The food you recently ate contained a lot of sugar and your body is now loosing energy and it would like some more sugar. This type of hunger can be prevented if you will stop eating foods that contain added sugar.

      II. **Nutrition Deficiency:** The food you recently ate has been partially processed and it did not contain the nutrients or vitamins your body needs. Therefore even though there is still some food in your stomach you need to try again and eat something else. This type of hunger can be prevented if you will eat a reasonable variety and a reasonable quantity of healthy foods that contain a good mixture of healthy vitamins and nutrients at each meal.

III. **Energy Needed:** Your body has consumed the energy in the food you recently ate and your body is about to start burning some of your fat cells. This is good news and the longer you can delay eating then the more fat cells your body will burn.

IV. **Normal Hunger Just Before your Next Regular Meal:** Your stomach is empty or almost empty and your body would like some more food because it is almost time for your next regular meal. This type of hunger should be ignored so you can train your body to eat at the same time each day and to not eat a few minutes before the next meal.

b. **Breakfast:** If you are not very hungry when you wake up in the morning then do not eat breakfast. This will automatically eliminate approximately one-fourth of the calories that most people eat each day. Skipping breakfast will also allow your body to burn fat instead of food after you wake up, and your body will continue to burn fat until you eat your first meal of the day. However, if you wake up and you are really hungry then it is okay to eat a reasonable breakfast as long as you eat something healthy. A high-protein breakfast, such as eggs, may help reduce your food cravings and your calorie intake later in the day. A high-fiber breakfast, such as oatmeal, may improve your health and help you lose weight. Please remember that you are designing your diet to help you lose weight without becoming really hungry. Do not make your decision based on what is best for the "average" person based on some scientific studies. Your decision to eat or not eat breakfast should be based on what is right for you. If you skip breakfast then it is okay to eat lunch a little earlier in the day. If you eat breakfast then it is okay to eat lunch a little later in the afternoon. It is also okay to not eat breakfast shortly after you wake up. It is okay to delay breakfast until a little later in the morning.

c. **Satiation Occurs while Eating:** If you become full, or satisfied, with what you have already eaten, and there is still a reasonable amount of food on your plate, then it is okay to not eat that food. This violates our parents instructions that we received when we were young which was "Eat everything on your plate." However, when we are trying to lose weight it is okay to not "clean our plates." It is okay to allow the extra food to remain on your plate for about 30 minutes just in case you get hungry and you decide to eat the rest of it. After about 30 minutes if you are still not hungry then refrigerate the extra food that is on your plate for another time, or discard the extra food into the trashcan. In the future start each meal with a little less food on your plate and this will help you lose weight.

d. **Politely Refuse Food that is Offered to You Between Meals:** If someone offers you something to eat between meals, or something to eat during a meal that is not on your diet, then very politely say "No thank you. I am not currently in the mood to eat that." Some people may be very persistent about trying to get you to eat something and after you have politely refused the offer, then the only thing you need to say as they continue to try to force the food on you is, "No thank you." If the person will simply not leave you alone then you may accept a very small quantity of the food and say, "Thank you. However, I am not in the mood to eat this right now and I will set it aside until later." Later you can make a decision on whether or not the food item is consistent with your weight loss objectives, and you can decide to try a very small bite of it, or you can put all of it in the trashcan.

7. **Reduce the amount of refined sugar you consume each day.**

   a. **Sugar Substitute:** Find a sugar substitute that appeals to you and use that sugar substitute when you add sugar to something you wish to eat or drink, such as coffee, tea, or oatmeal. Also use it in place of sugar in recipes that you prepare yourself. Some sugar substitutes that you may wish to consider are: stevia, saccharine (Sweet'N Low, Sweet Twin, Necta Sweet), sucralose (Splenda), or aspartame (NutraSweet, Equal). These substitutes are discussed in detail in chapter 13. You may discover that the flavor of one of these sugar substitutes is acceptable to you. I recommend *Necta Sweet (saccharine).*

   b. **Nutrition Labels:** Read the nutrition labels on every food item and do not buy any food item that contains a significant percentage of sugar. Some foods may not have any added sugar. And some foods may be using one of the sugar substitutes mentioned above.

   c. **No Added Sugar**: Some foods packages mention that they contain "no added sugar." Read the nutrition label to verify that the amount of "natural sugar" is agreeable to your diet and that the food does not contain other stuff you are trying to avoid.

   d. **Sugar Free Foods:** Some foods packages indicate that they are "sugar free." Sugar free does not mean calorie free. If you are interested in one of these foods then carefully read the nutrition label on the package and verify that it does not contain other stuff you are trying to avoid and that the total number of calories is within acceptable limits.

e. **Sugary Sodas and Fruit Juices:** Avoid sodas and fruit juices that contain added sugar. These sugary beverages are one of the primary causes of obesity in the USA.

8. **Minimize or eliminate some starches from your meals.**
    a. **Minimize or Avoid Potatoes:** Stop eating French fries and potato chips because they are not healthy options. However, it is okay to eat potatoes when they are included in *small quantities* in a soup or low-calorie meal. It is also okay to eat a *modest quantity* of boiled potatoes, creamed mashed potatoes, or baked potatoes once or twice per week.
    b. **Minimize or Avoid All Rice:** All rice contains arsenic which is a poison. White rice contains the least arsenic. Read chapter 21 for more details. Do not eat rice as a side item with a meal. Avoid rice when it is used as the bottom layer of a meal that is spread across the top of the rice. However, it is okay to eat rice when it is included in *very small quantities* as part of a soup or a low-calorie meal.

9. **Reduce the total amount of carbohydrates in your meals.**
    a. **Carbohydrates:** They are one of the three primary sources of fuel and many foods contain carbohydrates. Foods that have a high percentage of *unhealthy* carbohydrates should be avoided.
    b. **Sugar and Starches:** They are carbohydrates and they have already been mentioned above and they should be avoided.
    c. **Dietary Fiber:** Fiber is a very healthy carbohydrate and if fiber is the primary component of the total carbohydrates in a food then that food is desirable.
    d. **Percentage:** Foods that contain a minimal percentage of unhealthy carbohydrates are okay it they meet the other requirements mentioned in this section.

10. **Include protein, fat, and fiber in every meal, if possible.**
    a. **Protein:** Your body requires protein to build new muscles and to maintain its existing muscles. Muscles require more calories to maintain when compared to fat and this extra consumption of calories happens automatically.
    b. **Dietary Fat:** Eating dietary fat will not automatically add fat cells to your body. Dietary fat helps your body absorb vitamins A, D, E, and K, which are the fat soluble vitamins. Dietary fat provides the essential amino acid called linoleic acid and this is an amino acid your body cannot make.
    c. **Dietary Fiber:** Fiber optimizes the body's digestive processes. This results in a healthier body. *Fiber may enhance weight loss regardless of the different types of foods that are eaten.*

11. **Whenever possible, purchase and eat organically grown fruit and vegetables, eggs from organically raised chickens, and the cheese and milk from organically raised and grass-fed cows.**
    a. **Organic Farming:** Organic farming does not use commercial fertilizers or pesticides that can be absorbed into the food and then ingested by the people who eat that food. Instead organic farming relies on crop rotation, crop residues, animal manures, and natural methods to control pests.
    b. **Benefits of Organic Food:** Rats, rabbits, and other animals that were fed organic foods were healthier, more fertile, and produced healthier offspring when compared to animals that were fed non-organic foods. When given the opportunity to eat either organic or non-organic foods, animals consistently ate the organic food even though there was no visible difference between the two foods they had to choose from.
    c. **Organic Labels:** Some foods have the word "organic" on the package label but they are not organically grown food. Look for the "USDA Organic" seal on the food package to verify that the food is truly organic.
    d. **More Information:** Additional detailed information about specific organic foods are in the chapters dedicated to those foods later in this book.

12. **If desired, eat a maximum of two sugar-free desserts or sweet treats per day.**
    a. **Food Cravings:** Desserts and sweet treats are one of the foods that many of us have strong desires to eat. If we completely eliminate them from our diet then we begin craving them and they can quickly become all we can think about. The simple solution is to eat desserts that satisfy your craving for something sweet but which do not add too many calories to your daily diet.
    b. **Calories:** Include the calories in each dessert in the total number of calories you consume during the day. Eating too many sugar free desserts can quickly add more calories than you can burn per day and they will cause you to gain weight instead of losing weight.
    c. **Information:** Detailed information about snacks and sugar free treats is in chapter 24.

13. **Eat your favorite meal once per week.**
    a. **Part of Your Weekly Diet:** Eating your favorite meal once per week is just another basic part of the Common Sense Diet. When you eat your favorite meal you can relax and really enjoy

your meal. You do not need to feel guilty or ashamed. You are still on your diet because you are doing what is best for your short-term and long-tem health.

b. **Food Cravings:** When we begin a new diet that contains a limited number of some foods then it is not unusual for us to gradually begin craving some of the foods we once ate on a regular basis. This is normal. Remember that the purpose of the diet you create is to help you lose weight without feeling hungry. Therefore it is okay to eat some of your favorite foods during one meal each week. However, be prepared for your body to gain a little weight that day. Depending on what you eat, a reasonable part of this extra weight may be water weight and your body can lose water weight easier than fat.

c. **Which Day?** Your favorite meal can be on any day of the week that pleases you and it does not have to be the same day every week. Your favorite meal day can vary based on your schedule and your food cravings.

d. **Which Meal?** You may eat your favorite breakfast, lunch, or supper meal based on what you desire each week.

e. **Long-Term Health and Weight Loss:** When your body craves a specific food then your body may need some of the nutrients in that specific food to reestablish some type of nutrient equilibrium in your body. Listening to the signals your body is sending you can help you remain healthier and lose more weight in the long run because your body is able to maintain a healthier balance of nutrients in your body. It will also help you remain on your diet because you know you can eat the foods you really crave once per week.

f. **Benefits of a Favorite Meal if it Includes Carbs:** A high-carb meal satisfies your body's craving for carbs so you can think about something else. And eating extra carbs can increase your levels of leptin and other fat-burning hormones that are depleted with a low-carb diet. These fat-burning hormones can help your body lose the extra weight you gained eating your one high-carb meal in just one or two days.

g. **Eat In or Eat Out:** Each week you can decide whether you will eat your favorite meal at home, such as a delicious delivery pizza with everything you like on it, or if you will leave home and eat at one of your favorite restaurants.

h. **Your Favorite Restaurants:** Eating one meal at a restaurant once per week will not significantly impact your diet as long as you do not overindulge in food at the restaurant and you eat so much food you gain back all the weight that you lost that week.

i. **Advantages of Eating at a Restaurant:** When we begin a new diet it is not unusual for us to crave food we used to eat at a specific restaurant. Eventually this food craving can become all we can think about. This usually results in our briefly ignoring our diet and eating at the restaurant. When we are finished eating we feel guilty about going off our diet. The good news is that it is okay to eat at your favorite restaurant because you are designing a diet that is just right for you. The purpose of your diet is to help you lose weight without feeling hungry. Ignoring a food craving to eat at your favorite restaurant can offset the joy you receive from losing weight. Therefore it is okay to eat a meal at your favorite restaurant once per week.

j. **Disadvantages of Eating at a Restaurant:** Restaurant food usually contains ingredients that are not compatible with weight loss or with your long-term health. Therefore if you can resist eating at a restaurant without feeling that you have been deprived on one of the important pleasures of your life, then you will discover it is easier to remain on your diet, and you will lose weight faster, and you will improve your health faster.

14. **Fasting is a time-honored way to enhance long-term health, lose weight, and extend a person's life expectancy.**

a. **Fasting Defined:** Skipping between one to three meals is called fasting. For many people breakfast is the first meal of the day and its name means "break fast" which means resume eating after fasting all night.

b. **History of Fasting:** Fasting is mentioned in the Holy Bible in the Old Testament (Jonah 3:5, Daniel 9:3), and in the New Testament (Matthew 6:16-18). John the Baptist and his disciples fasted regularly (Luke 5:33). Jesus fasted before being tempted by the devil (Matthew 4:1-11). Jesus approved of fasting (Matthew 6:17, Luke 5:35).

c. **Duration of a Fast:** In the Bible fasting began at sunset (6 PM) on one day and it ended at sunset (6 PM) the following day. A fast included 24 hours without eating any type of food. However water was consumed to prevent dehydration and to assist the body flush out any unhealthy things it had absorbed. Fasting is the time honored method of cleansing the body of unhealthy substances and it does not involve the use of any cleansing or purging chemicals. Therefore fasting does not provide any revenue to anyone or to any company. Since food is not eaten during a fast it actually reduces the revenue of some companies and some restaurants. Therefore fasting does not receive any favorable publicity.

d. **Fasting Research:** The December 26, 2019 issue of the "New England Journal of Medicine" contained some interesting research information on the benefits of intermittent fasting. It takes the body between 10 to 12 hours to consume all the energy stored in the liver and then the body switches modes and it begins to burn body fat for energy. Therefore people who eat three smaller meals per day do not burn as much body fat as someone who eats two larger meals per day that contain the same total number of daily calories, or someone who skips three meals and fasts for an entire day. According to the researchers, intermittent fasting may help stabilize blood sugar levels, minimize stress, reduce inflammation, decrease cholesterol and blood pressure, improve the resting heart rate, enhance memory, and facilitate weight loss. The benefits of intermittent fasting can be achieved by eating during a 6 to 8 hour time period each day and then do not eat for 16 to 18 hours per day. For example, eat *normal meals* during the 8 hours from 11 AM until 7 PM (or during the 6 hours from 12 noon to 6 PM) and then stop eating. The researchers also noted that it takes some people between two to eight weeks to adjust to intermittent fasting without being continually hungry or uncomfortable. The researchers do not recommend fasting for children, the elderly, or people who are underweight. (Note: I would also not recommend fasting for pregnant women or nursing mothers.)

e. **Fasting for 24 Hours (The Bible Method and the "Eat Stop Eat" Method):** If you wish to fast then it is okay to eat a normal meal just before 6 PM in the evening. Then do not eat anything until 6 PM the following day. But during your fast drink lots of water. If you wish you may also drink a limited number of calorie free beverages such as coffee or tea. When 6 PM arrives then eat a normal meal and break your fast.

f. **Fasting for One Meal (The Preferred Method):** Another way to fast is to skip breakfast each day. This will result in 7 skipped meals in one week and you will be giving your body some extra time each morning to flush out some of the unhealthy things it does not need. This could also help you lose weight and it could help you keep that weight off after you reach your desired weight goal.

g. **Fasting is Not for Everyone:** Fasting should not be attempted by individuals with diabetes because it may adversely impact their blood sugar levels. Fasting is also inappropriate for pregnant women, nursing mothers, or women who are trying to conceive. If you decide to try fasting and your body is not able to accept it then you should not fast. Instead you should try the other weight loss strategies discussed in this chapter.

15. **Drink a reasonable amount of plain pure cold water every day.** (This was mentioned in chapter one but it is also a very important part of the Common Sense Diet.)

   a. **Good Health:** Approximately 60% of our body is water, and approximately 75% of our brain is water, and approximately 83% of our blood is water and our blood transports nutrients and oxygen to the cells of our body. Water is absolutely necessary to maintain a healthy body.

   b. **Cold Water:** The body burns a few more calories increasing cold water to normal body temperature. And most people do not enjoy lukewarm beverages. Instead they prefer either a hot or a cold beverage. Cold water may increase your desire to drink water and this may help you drink more water each day.

   c. **Spring Water or Well Water:** If you have a choice then drink spring water, or well water that has been certified safe to drink. This type of water contains the natural minerals that are in our bodies and that are also included in most multivitamin tablets.

   d. **No Calories:** Water contains no calories but water helps the stomach feel full.

   e. **Digestion:** Water is absolutely necessary for the stomach and the intestines to properly digest food. If our bodies are not properly hydrated then digestive problems and an assortment of other health problems can result.

   f. **Lubrication:** Water helps lubricate our digestive system so food flows more easily through our body.

   g. **Bowel Movements:** Water helps facilitate normal bowel movements and water helps prevent constipation.

   h. **Cell Repair and Replenishment:** The cells in our body are continuously replenishing themselves. A properly hydrated body makes it easier for new cells to replace old cells.

   i. **Rehydration:** Drink a glass of water shortly after waking up in the morning and after you have weighed yourself for the day. The water will not only help to rehydrate your body but it will also help to reactivate all your body's metabolic processes so that you begin burning more calories all day long.

   j. **Appetite Reduction**: If some water is consumed just **before** a meal then less food will be eaten during the meal and this will facilitate weight loss. Drinking water before a meal may have the same weight lose benefit as eating a small bowl of broth based soup before a meal, or eating half a grapefruit before a meal because a grapefruit is mostly water.

k. **Weight Loss:** Drinking 6 cups of cold water per day (1.5 liters) may help your body burn an additional 18,250 calories per year, which is approximately 5.2 pounds of body fat per year.

l. **To Ignore or Not Ignore:** Drinking a lot of plain pure cold water is the most widely known and believed good dieting advice, but it is also the least followed dieting advice. A lot of people have made the decision they are not going to follow this advice for one reason or another. And their body suffers for their refusal to drink lots and lots of plain pure cold water. If you are truly serious about wanting to lose weight then do not ignore this advice. Just do it if you really want to lose weight.

16. **Put all food items where they cannot be easily seen.**

a. **Food Storage:** Always store your food in a cabinet, a pantry, or in the refrigerator or freezer. Do not put food on a counter or table where it can be easily seen.

b. **Out of Sight, Out of Mind:** Food that is always visible encourages snacking. And snacking will increase your daily consumption of calories. Food that is not visible will not encourage hunger or thoughts of eating.

17. **When beginning a new diet, phase in exercise and supplements.**

a. **New Diet:** During the first four weeks on your new diet it is advisable to focus your attention on staying on your diet and not begin any new exercises or take any new supplements.

b. **Exercise:** If your doctor has approved specific types of exercises for you, then begin those exercises the second month of your diet. This will allow you to properly evaluate the impact of the exercises on your weight loss, and on your energy level, and on the firmness of your muscles. Read chapter 26 on exercising. However, if your doctor has advised you to begin exercising immediately then follow your doctor's advice.

c. **Supplements:** Unless your doctor advises you differently, do not introduce any type of weight-loss supplement into your weight loss program until the third month of your diet. By the end of the second month you should have a reasonably good idea of the weight impact of your new diet and your new exercise program. This will allow you to properly evaluate the impact of any supplements beginning with the third month of your new diet. In order to properly evaluate the impact of a specific supplement on your body, it is best to only begin taking one new supplement every month beginning in the third month. This will allow you to determine if the new supplement is helping you, or causing you discomfort, or if it is having no noticeable impact on your health.

d. **Other Diets:** All the diets I have examined during the past 50 years offer the same basic advise: eat the foods they recommend, take the supplements they recommend, and also begin exercising the same day you start your new diet. Doing everything at the very beginning of a new diet has two benefits:

1. **More Weight Lost Sooner:** Weight is much easier to lose during the early days and weeks when we first start a new diet. This weight loss may be increased with supplements and exercise.

2. **Better Publicity for the Effectiveness of the Diet:** People who lose a lot of weight in a short period of time will usually praise the diet they are on and attribute all of their weight loss to the diet. However, some of their weight loss may be due to the exercises they are doing, or to the supplements they are taking, and this weight loss would have happened even if they were not eating the foods recommended on their new diet. But because they began doing everything at the same time they cannot determine the actual impact of their food choices on their weight loss.

The Common Sense Diet is **not** motivated by the above two short-term benefits. Instead the Common Sense Diet is motivated by two long-term benefits: (1) optimizing your health for the rest of your life, and (2) keeping the weight you lose off your body for the rest of your life. Although other diets claim that you will become a healthier person and you will not regain the weight you lost, the reality is that these two benefits do not materialize for the majority of the people who try a new diet. If these two long-term benefits occurred in addition to the two-short term benefits then the people who began these new diets would have stayed on those diets for the rest of their lives and they would not have abandoned their diet and gradually regained all the weight they lost. This is one of the differences between truth and fiction. The Common Sense Diet is not interested in favorable publicity or in quick weight losses. Instead it is focused on helping you maintain a sustainable gradual weight loss over a longer period of time and allowing your body to gradually adjust to the changes you are introducing it to. This is why I recommend delaying exercises until the second month of your diet, and delaying supplements until the third month of your diet. This gives you the ability to clearly identify the impact your food choices have on your weight loss during the first month, the impact of your new exercises during the second month, and the impact of any supplements beginning in the third month. By phasing exercise and supplements in gradually, this will result in a potential increase in weight loss in the second month, and a potential increase in weight loss beginning in the third month. These weight loss increases can have a positive impact on your morale and help encourage you to stay on your diet and not abandon it. In my opinion, this is just using good *common sense* to help sustain your weight loss over a longer time period, and not putting too much stress on your body in too short a time period which may not be conducive to your long-term health.

18. **How to create a diet that is perfect for you.**
    a. **Physical Exam and a Comprehensive Blood Test:** It is critical that you have your doctor give you a complete physical exam and a comprehensive blood test before you consider any type of diet, exercise, or supplements.
    b. **Foods to Avoid:** Your doctor will be able to properly advise you on which foods, nutrients, and vitamins you should avoid based on your physical exam, your blood test, and your medical history. Your doctor may also be able to suggest some foods, nutrients, and vitamins that would be very beneficial to your long-term health.
    c. **Foods to Consider:** Only you know which foods you really enjoy and which foods you do not like. Use your knowledge of yourself to select a wide variety of foods from the lists of recommended foods in future chapters of this book. Remember that it is important to include variety in your diet in order to receive the health benefits from all the different food groups.

19. **Recommended foods to avoid.** Detailed information about many of the following foods is included in future chapters in this book that are dedicated to the specific foods.
    a. **Foods that cause an Allergic Reaction:** Avoid any food that you have previously had an allergic reaction to, regardless of how healthy that food may be.
    b. **Refined Sugar:** Refined sugar is one of the primary causes of obesity. Candy, cookies, cakes, donuts, ice cream, pastries, and pies contain empty calories with very little nutrition. Avoid commercially available sweets. However, you may be able to

make delicious sugar-free treats at home by using saccharin instead of sugar in some recipes.

c. **Sugary Beverages:** Sugary drinks increase hunger because they only provide minimal nutritional benefits. Sugary drinks result in gradual but consistent weight gains and they should be avoided. Sugary drinks include fruit juices, flavored highly sweetened coffees, sport drinks, sodas, and sweetened tea. Use saccharin to sweeten your coffee or tea. Look for a brand of carbonated water that appeals to you. Some of these waters are available in a variety of flavors. Or you can add a little lemon juice or lime juice to carbonated water to make your own sugar-free carbonated beverage.

d. **Starches:** All rice contains arsenic, including brown rice, wild rice, and white rice. White rice contains the least arsenic. Avoid French fries, fried potatoes, and potato chips. Boiled potatoes, creamed mashed potatoes, and baked potatoes are okay in moderation.

e. **Low-Fat and Fat Free Foods:** Dietary fat is healthy. When the fat is removed from food to make a low-fat or fat free alternative, sugar is usually added to the food to compensate for the loss of flavor, and the total number of calories is not reduced. Therefore the words "low-fat" or "fat free" do not mean that the food is healthy. Instead those words mean that the food has been highly processed and the healthy fat has been removed and replaced with sugar. Whole-fat or full-fat foods are recommended for long-term health reasons.

f. **Foods with Artificial Preservatives:** Artificial preservatives extend the shelf life of food and this is good for the company that packages the food. However, artificial preservatives may contribute to a variety of long-term serious health problems, depending on the type of preservative. Therefore to maximize your long-term health try to eliminate or minimize the number of foods that you consume that have artificial preservatives. Fresh foods do not need artificial preservatives because they are sold to consumers for short-term consumption. Many foods that are refrigerated or frozen depend on the cold temperature to preserve the food and they do not need artificial preservatives. However, always read the ingredient label to verify that the food you are considering is preservative free.

g. **Foods with High Levels of Sodium:** Sodium is a natural preservative and a natural flavor enhancer. Sodium is present in many packaged foods. Sodium in small amounts is acceptable. However, excessive amounts of sodium in a food can contribute to a wide variety of long-term serious health problems. Therefore when evaluating the sodium content of a specific food, look at the percent sodium on the food nutrition label and consider if that amount of sodium, when consumed with other foods in your daily diet, will keep your total daily sodium consumption to 100% or less.

h. **Foods with Unnecessary or Artificial Ingredients:** Many packaged foods today contain ingredients that are not necessary. Some of these ingredients are habit forming, and they increase hunger, and therefore they increase the profits of the food company. However, this is bad for you because it results in an unhealthy diet, reduced long-term health, and weight gains. Carefully read the ingredient label and be cautious about buying foods with a long list of ingredients that you are not familiar with.

i. **GMO Foods:** Genetically modified organisms (GMO) are not healthy and they should be avoided. Look for the "NON GMO Project Verified" seal on the food package to verify that it does not contain any GMO ingredients.

j. **Vegetable Oils:** This includes canola oil (rapeseed oil), corn oil, soybean oil, sunflower oil, and vegetable oil. These oils may lower blood cholesterol levels and this is good. But there is a downside. These oils have consistently been shown to increase the risk of death from cancer and heart disease. Therefore use extra virgin olive oil instead.

k. **Breakfast Cereals:** Regardless of whether the cereals are made from corn, oats, rice, or wheat, most breakfast cereals contain added sugar, artificial preservatives, and unhealthy additives. Some breakfast cereals contain a few healthy ingredients in addition to the unhealthy cereal and they are a reasonable choice if you simply cannot live without breakfast cereal. Or you could eat oatmeal. Or you could sprout your own wheat berries to make your own healthy breakfast cereal.

l. **White Bread and Imitation Brown Bread:** All breads that are made from refined flour that does not contain the bran and the germ are long-term health disasters. Look for the "Whole Grain Council's" black and yellow stamp on a loaf of bread before you buy it. Also avoid bread that contains added sugar or artificial preservatives.

m. **Commercially Processed Meats:** Many processed beef, fish, pork, and poultry products contain a variety of unhealthy additives and artificial preservatives. This includes canned meats, deli meats sliced on demand, frozen meats, and most frozen dinners that contain meat. Processed meats increase the risk of colon cancer, heart disease, diabetes. However, most of the fresh meat or fish that is available at the butcher shop or at the fresh meat counter of a grocery store has only been cut and it does not contain additives and artificial preservatives.

n. **Processed Cheese**: Most processed cheeses contain additives and preservatives and they should be avoided. Instead buy fresh block cheese and cube or shred it yourself. However, it is okay to purchase ultra thin sliced cheese because it provides real cheese flavor but a lot fewer calories per slice.

o. **Pizza:** Pizza is one of the most popular junk foods in the world. Restaurant pizza is made from highly refined dough and with highly processed meats. A healthy alternative is to make your own pizza at home from scratch using healthy ingredients.

p. **Raisins:** They are delicious and they contain healthy nutrients. One small box of raisins contains about 90 calories. However, raisins are a sticky sweet food and small particles of raisins can get between your teeth where normal brushing cannot dislodge them. A very small raisin particle may stick to one tooth in a spot where even flossing won't remove it. When that happens it may start a cavity. After a cavity has been started then other foods can more easily get trapped in the cavity and the size of the cavity will increase. Raisins are not recommended.

q. **Fast Foods:** The food that is sold at most fast food restaurants contains unhealthy ingredients, and ingredients that increase hunger and that are habit forming. This is bad for you but it increases the profits of the fast food restaurants.

r. **Liquid Meals:** Unless you have digestive issues, avoid liquid meals such as a complete meal diet milkshake and a "smoothie" you make yourself. Liquid meals pass through your mouth without chewing and they quickly pass through your stomach. The brain does not respond to liquid food in the same way as food that has to be chewed and digested. Liquid foods will not satisfy your hunger.

s. **Irresistible Food:** If you cannot control yourself and you are not able to stop eating a specific food then you should omit that specific food from your diet. You should also remove that food from your home to eliminate the temptation to eat it.

t. **High Heat Cooking:** Foods that are fried, deep-fried, broiled, or grilled can form unhealthy compounds that can increase the risk of cancer and heart disease. The unhealthy compounds include acrolein, acrylamide, advanced glycation end products (AGEs), heterocyclic amines, oxysterol, and polycyclic aromatic hydrocarbons (PAHs). Cooking at low heat is preferred and this includes low temperature baking, low temperature frying, blanching, boiling, steaming, and stewing.

20. **Recommended foods to eat.**

   a. **Organic Foods:** Buy certified organic if it is available. Organic foods do not contain industrial pesticides and artificial fertilizers. The skins on organic fruits and vegetables are usually safe to eat after rinsing the food.

   b. **Raw Fruit and Vegetables:** Some vitamins and nutrients are lost during the cooking process. Therefore consider eating raw fruit or vegetables such as apples, broccoli, and carrots.

   c. **Natural Foods:** For example, buy butter and not margarine.

   d. **Dietary Fats:** Look for foods with more monounsaturated fats and polyunsaturated fats and with less saturated fats and with no artificial trans fats.

   e. **Dietary Fiber:** Fiber facilitates the digestive processes and enhances normal bowel movements. Fiber may contribute to weight loss.

   f. **Protein:** As you lose body fat, protein is necessary to build the lean muscles you add to your body.

   g. **Vitamins, Minerals, Amino Acids, and Antioxidants:** Foods that contain a reasonable variety of healthy nutrients will enhance your long-term health.

   h. **Specific Food Recommendations:** The next chapter contains information on the health benefits of specific foods. Many of the chapters later in this book contain additional detailed information about specific foods.

21. **Respect your body and be considerate of what you subject it to.**

   a. **Stress:** Do not subject your body to too many changes in too short a time. Gradually introduce your body to new things in order to reduce the stress you put on yourself. This will minimize the negative impact stress can have on your body.

   b. **Long-Term Perspective:** We only have the body we were born with and it is just good *common sense* to treat our body in a way that maximizes our long-term health and life expectancy.

   c. **Cleansing and Purging:** The body will gradually cleanse and purge itself of the bad stuff that has accumulated inside it. If we try to cleanse or purge our body too quickly then the cleansing may cause some undesirable side effects that we will not become aware of until some future date. However, if your doctor has recommended some type of cleansing then you should listen to your doctor's advice.

d. **Healing:** The human body is excellent at healing itself. Therefore we should be patient with our body and allow it to "naturally" heal itself at the speed it believes is best. However, if your doctor has informed you that something needs to be done immediately then follow your doctor's advice.

22. **Do the important things first. Delay things of lesser importance until a little later.**

a. **Prioritize your Plan:** When you first begin your new diet do not try to do everything the first day. Instead consider what you wish to accomplish during the first four weeks of your new diet and then implement those changes gradually during the first four weeks. Then gradually implement more changes beginning in month two and continue to try new things for the rest of your life at the speed you believe is appropriate.

b. **Week One:** Focus primarily on eating foods that are low in calories. Read the nutrition labels on the foods you are considering to eat. During week one try to keep your total daily consumption of calories to a level that will result in a little weight loss every day or two. During the first week avoid foods that contain added sugar. Stop drinking sugary beverages with added sugar such as sugary soft drinks, sport drinks, and most fruit juices. Try to find a sugar substitute that is acceptable to you. Sugar and sugar substitutes are discussed in detail in chapter 13. Reduce your intake of white rice and potatoes. Chapter 24 contains recommendations on tasty things you can eat to satisfy your hunger between meals. If it is possible during the first week, continue to eat the foods you have eaten in the past but avoid the high calorie foods and focus on the low calorie foods. Your body will gradually begin to burn a little body fat each day instead of adding fat to your body. This will help your body gradually adjust to your new diet without causing your body too much stress and you will still be able to lose some weight during the first week. And your body will appreciate the consideration you are showing it and your body may be more receptive to additional changes in the future as long as you continue to respect your body and you do not subject your body to the shock of too many changes too quickly.

c. **Week Two:** Read the nutrition labels on foods and try to avoid foods with artificial preservatives whenever possible. Sodium is not an artificial preservative but it can help to extend the shelf life of food. It is okay to eat food that contains sodium as long as the food does not contain an excessive amount of sodium. Too much sodium is not good for your body unless your doctor has told you to increase your sodium intake.

d. **Week Three:** If you enjoy eating bread then look for 100% whole wheat bread with no added sugar and no artificial preservatives. This type of bread usually has about 50 calories per slice instead of between 60 to 70 calories per slice. Read chapter 22. If you enjoy eating frozen meals then look for frozen meals that contain less than 300 calories per meal and which also contain no artificial preservatives and not too much sodium. Frozen meals do not need artificial preservatives or lots of sodium because their shelf life is automatically extended by freezing. See page 61 for specific recommendations. If you enjoy cooking then select fresh vegetables or frozen vegetables. Begin adding "organic" or "natural" foods to your diet even though they may be a little more expensive.

e. **Week Four:** Carefully consider all your meat choices. Some grocery stores sell "USDA Prime Beef" and some stores sell "USDA Choice Beef." These are the two best types of beef and the store will openly advertise that this is the type of beef they sell. "USDA Choice Beef" usually comes from grass-fed cows and it is more tender and healthier than the less expensive types of beef. Fresh meat rarely contains preservatives and it is significantly healthier than commercially processed meats. Some meats are soaked in water to improve their tenderness and to increase their total weight but water is not harmful to the human body. Read chapter 17 for more detailed information about the different types of meat.

f. **Month Two:** When month two arrives, gradually begin to implement an exercise program that is suitable for your age, gender, and physical abilities. Start slow and as time passes you can do more as your body gradually adjusts to doing exercises. Chapter 26 on exercises has some recommendations you may wish to consider. In addition, during the second month you should continue to refine your diet and gradually decrease the number and types of foods you know are not healthy for you, and gradually eat more of the nutritious and healthy foods you have come to enjoy.

g. **Month Three:** Gradually add any supplements you believe would be beneficial in the third month. However, only add one new supplement every two weeks so you can identify if that supplement is helping you, or causing you problems, or having no noticeable impact on your body. In addition, during the third month you should continue to enhance your exercise program, and also refine your diet and gradually decrease the number and types of foods that you know are not healthy for you, and gradually eat more of the nutritious and healthy foods that you have begun to really enjoy.

h. **Fourth Month and Beyond:** Continue to fine tune your exercise program, and experiment with any supplements you believe would be beneficial to you, and continue to modify your diet based on the slow gradual changes that are taking place in your appetite and in your taste for certain foods as you continue to try new healthy foods you have not eaten before.

23. **Never feel guilty about any of the foods you eat.**

a. **Calories are Important and Not Specific Foods:** As long as you eat fewer total calories than you burn each day then you will lose weight. Therefore you can eat almost any healthy food as long as it does not cause you to exceed your daily calorie allotment.

b. **Healthy Slim Muscular Body:** You are creating a diet that will help you lose weight, and add lean muscles to your body, and enhance both your short-term and long-term health. There is absolutely no reason to feel guilty about eating any food that helps you achieve these goals.

c. **Completely Ignore Bad Publicity About Any Food You Eat:** Every diet will say bad things about the foods that are excluded from the diet they recommend. Different diets recommended different foods, and they prohibit different foods. Anyone who attempted to avoid all the foods forbidden by all the different diets would starve to death. Anyone who uses *common sense* will realize that all foods cannot be bad even though each diet will condemn a different category of foods. It may help if you will remember that you are not trying to lose weight at the expense of your health and that it is okay to eat any food that is a healthy food.

d. **All Healthy Foods are Okay to Eat:** It doesn't matter if the food contains fat, or carbohydrates, or starch. It doesn't matter if the food is meat, dairy, vegetables, or fruit. Any healthy food is okay to eat regardless of what it is, and regardless of whether or not it is approved or forbidden by some type of diet. Never feel guilty about eating a healthy food, or eating any food in moderation if it helps you lose weight and not be hungry.

Chapter Five

Recommended Foods that may Help You Lose Weight and Improve Your Health

This chapter will focus on a few foods that may help you lose weight and improve your health.

Nutrient-dense foods contain more vitamins, minerals, and other beneficial ingredients per gram compared to less nutrient-dense foods.

High nutrient-dense foods include dairy products, fish, fruit, legumes, meat, poultry, nuts, vegetables, and whole grains. These foods may reduce the risk of diabetes and heart disease, and they have shown a correlation to a longer life expectancy.

Fruits, vegetables, nuts, and whole grains contain a variety of very healthy vitamins, minerals, and antioxidants.

Low nutrient-dense foods include candy, cookies, ice cream, potato chips, and soft drinks. These food should be avoided.

The chapter will begin with healthy meals options and then specific foods will be reviewed.

Frozen Meals

Frozen meals can be a convenient, quick, easy way to include some healthy meals in your weekly diet. However, home cooked meals are also a very healthy option and if you have the time and the skill then home cooked meals should also be included in your weekly diet.

There are a lot of different brands of frozen meals that have been targeted to people who wish to lose weight, or who wish to eat healthy foods. Some brands of frozen meals are a much better choice than other brands.

Before you purchase any type of frozen meal you should read the nutrition label on the package and evaluate the number of calories, the amount of sodium, the preservatives that are included in the meal, the variety of foods in the meal, and the quantity of food in the meal.

1. **Calories:** Some meals contain a lot more calories per meal than other meals. Preference should be given to meals with fewer calories. However, *common sense* should guide your choices. If you really enjoy the flavor of the food in a specific frozen meal then you should not eliminate if from consideration just because it contains more calories than other frozen meals. If the meal has

minimal sodium, no artificial preservatives, and there is enough food in the meal to satisfy your hunger, then it is the type of meal you should include in your weekly diet.

2. **Sodium:** Almost all raw foods contain sodium. Therefore all processed foods contain sodium. However, some frozen meals contain a significant amount of added sodium and some meals only contain a reasonable amount of added sodium. Preference should be given to frozen meals that contain less sodium.

3. **Artificial Preservatives:** Some meals include a lot of artificial preservatives and some meals do not contain any artificial preservatives. Preservatives are **not** necessary for a frozen meal. Freezing is all that is required to keep a frozen meal safe for human consumption. Therefore preference should be given to frozen meals that do not contain preservatives.

4. **Variety:** A meal that contains more different foods will usually contain a better blend of healthy nutrients than a meal that only has a few different foods. Preference should be given to frozen meals that contain a variety of the different types of foods you enjoy eating.

5. **Quantity of Food:** A meal that contains more food is usually more satisfying and more filling than a meal that contains less food. Preference should be given to frozen meals that contain enough food to satisfy your hunger.

In the early part of the year 2020 there is one brand of frozen meals that meets all the above requirements. However, as time progresses other brands of frozen meals may adjust the content of their meals and reduce the number of calories, reduce the amount of sodium, and eliminate artificial preservatives in their meals. If that happens then those brands of frozen meals should also be considered when you are purchasing frozen meals.

"Healthy Choice" is the frozen meal brand that has fewer calories, minimum sodium, no artificial ingredients, a reasonable variety of foods in each meal including an optional sauce, and there is enough food in each meal to satisfy the appetite of the average person. The meals have the optional sauce in the bottom of the primary food tray that is just below a smaller upper food tray. Therefore the sauce heats at the same time as the food in the upper food tray. If you do not want the sauce then you can simply eat the meal in the top food tray. If you want the sauce then you can easily lift up the top food tray and allow the food to slide down into the special sauce in the lower food tray. Then you can stir the sauce and food together.

Many of the "Healthy Choice" meals do not contain any white rice. However, about half of the meals do include white rice. Since rice is one of the few foods that are not recommended in the Common Sense Diet, you may wish to either avoid or minimize the number of white rice meals that you include in your weekly diet.

The "Healthy Choice" meals are inside a carton with three straight sides and one rounded side. This makes them easy to find among all the different brands of frozen meals. Some of the cartons are mostly white and some of the cartons are a light brown or tan color.

A few of the "Healthy Choice" meals that you may wish to examine more closely are the following frozen meals. The percents are based on the recommended nutrition in a 2,000 calorie daily diet as shown on the back of the meal carton.

"Healthy Choice" Meal	Cal.	Fat	Chol.	Sod.	Carb.	Fib.	Sug.	Prot.
Beef Merlot, Wine Sauce	180	4%	10%	25%	9%	14%	4%	20%
Chicken & Broc. Alfredo	190	6%	28%	26%	3%	14%	1%	42%
Chicken Linguini Alfredo	250	8%	13%	23%	10%	18%	2%	28%
Chicken & Veg. Stir Fry	190	5%	25%	22%	5%	14%	12%	40%
Meatball Marinara	280	8%	8%	21%	13%	21%	8%	20%
Mexican-Style Chicken	240	6%	13%	22%	11%	29%	2%	28%

Each of the above meals also contains a reasonable assortment of healthy vitamins. Therefore any of the above "Healthy Choice" meals could be included in the daily diet of an individual who desired to enhance their health and lose weight at the same time.

Different people have different taste preferences and some people may enjoy the "Health Choice" frozen meals and other people may not.

Sandwiches

The Common Sense Diet includes sandwiches in a person's weekly diet even though most popular diets forbid the consumption of bread. The reasons for including bread are explained in detail in chapter 22.

Two slices of a healthy 100% whole grain bread with the Whole Grain Council's stamp on the package will contain at total of approximately 120 calories for two slices. One ultra thin slice of cheese will contain between 40 to 45 calories per slice or about 85 calories for two slices of cheese. One ultra thin slice of meat will contain about 20 calories per slice or about 80 calories for four slices of meat. If you add lettuce at about 2 calories and sliced tomatoes at about 13 calories then the above sandwich will contain approximately 300 calories. And it will be a healthy meal because it will contain wheat, cheese, meat, a vegetable (lettuce), and a fruit (tomatoes). Most people consider tomatoes to be a vegetable but technically a tomato is a fruit. Most grocery stores display and sell tomatoes in the same area as their other fruits. However, in this book tomatoes are included in the vegetable chapter and the fruit chapter to make it easy to find them.

If you add two teaspoons of mustard then you will be adding zero calories. Mustard has a very tangy flavor and it doesn't take much mustard to do its job. One teaspoon of mustard may increase your metabolism by up to 25% for several hours after eating.

If you add four teaspoons of mayonnaise then you will be adding about 135 calories. It takes more mayonnaise because mayonnaise does not have a powerful flavor. Omitting the mayonnaise would be a good choice if this does not significantly impact the pleasure you receive from eating a delicious sandwich.

Healthy Food Recommendations

The following food recommendations are presented in alphabetical order. The foods are not listed in the order of their importance. Only a few healthy foods are very briefly mentioned in this chapter. Future chapters that are devoted to specific foods contain more information about the foods that are only briefly mentioned in this chapter.

Condiments

Extra Virgin Olive Oil: It is the oil that is pressed out of freshly harvested olives. Other types of olive oil may be extracted using chemicals and they may have other cheaper oils added to them. Some brands of extra virgin olive oil may also have been diluted. Always read the ingredient label. Olive oil contains vitamins E and K, healthy fatty acids, and healthy phenolic antioxidants. It contains oleic acid and oleocanthal, both of which have anti-inflammatory properties. It also contains oleuropein. It also contains adiponectin which is a hormone that helps break down fat cells.

Mayonnaise-Based Salad Dressings: When one or two tablespoons of these dressings are added to salads they help the body absorb the lycopene and the beta-carotene in the salads, and these nutrients reduce the risk of cancer and improve the overall health of the body. The healthiest salad dressings are refrigerated because they use refrigeration instead of artificial preservatives to extend the shelf life of the dressing. Avoid fat-free or low fat dressings because they usually contain more sugar and other stuff your body doesn't need, and they also have almost the same number of calories as regular salad dressings.

Mustard: In the year 2020 mustard contains no calories. One teaspoon of mustard included in a meal may increase your metabolism by up to 25% for several hours after eating.

Natural or Organic Peanut Butter: Read the nutrition label and look for a peanut butter that only contains nuts, a little sugar, and a little salt. Reduced fat peanut butter has less fat but more sugar and more salt and approximately the same number of calories. This means you are exchanging the healthy fat in regular peanut butter for more sugar and more salt that your body does not need.

Dairy

Organic Eggs from Cage Free Chickens: Eggs are high in protein and fat. Eating between one to three eggs per day may help reduce cholesterol and contribute to weight loss. However, eating a lot of eggs in one day can raise the bad "LDL" cholesterol in some people.

Organic Butter from Grass-Fed Cows: It is a good source of vitamins, minerals, and fatty acids, and it slows down the absorption of carbohydrates so you feel full for a longer period of time.

Cottage Cheese: Low in calories and fat but high in vitamins B2 and B12, calcium, phosphorus, selenium, and other important nutrients.

Cheese: Cheddar, Colby, Mexican, Monterey, muenster, provolone, mozzarella, and Swiss. See page 294.

Heavy Whipping Cream: Use it to reduce the bitterness of coffee and the negative impact that caffeine can have on some people's nerves. It helps stabilize blood sugar levels and it provides more energy over a longer period of time. Other types of creamers can increase insulin levels, increase inflammatory issues, and increase hunger cravings.

Whole Milk: Contains protein, calcium, phosphorus, vitamin B12, and almost every other nutrient the human body needs. It is more filling than reduced fat milk. Some of the acids in milk fat will increase your body's calorie burning hormones. If you only drink a small amount of milk then whole milk is a good choice.

2% Milk: It contains about 80% of the calories in whole milk and if you drink a lot of milk then 2% milk may help you achieve your weight loss goal.

Yogurt: Full-fat yogurt can reduce the risk of obesity and the risk of diabetes. Some yogurts contain healthy probiotic bacteria that can enhance your digestive processes. However, some yogurts contain no live bacteria. Avoid low-fat yogurt because it has a lot of sugar.

Desserts and Sweets

Atkins Snack Bars: They include sugar free candy, cookies, and protein bars. One or two of these treats per day can help you make the transition from a diet that contained candy and cookies to a healthy diet that does not include commercially processed candy and cookies.

Voortman Sugar Free Wafers: These wafers are available in chocolate, lemon, orange, peanut butter, and strawberry at 47 calories per wafer. Also key lime and vanilla at 43 calories per wafer.

Atkins, Voortman, and other sweets are discussed in chapter 24.

Fish and Shellfish

All fish and shellfish have a lot of protein and protein enhances bone health, energy, metabolism, lean muscle mass, skin health, and weight loss. They may help reduce blood pressure and cholesterol. They may enhance blood health, brain health, heart health, the immune system, metabolism, and nerve health. They may reduce the risk of cardiovascular diseases, dementia, depression, heart attack, and heart disease. They may help slow down the normal aging process and extend life expectancy.

Catfish: It contains a lot of vitamin D. It may facilitate a normal pregnancy and it may help reduce the risk of birth defects.

Halibut: It is low in calories and it is a good source of potassium, selenium, and vitamins B3, B6, B9, B12, and D.

Mackerel: Although it does have a lot of calories it has more vitamins A, B1, B3, and D than other fish, and it includes all nine essential amino acids. It is also a good source of iron, magnesium, selenium, and vitamins B2, B5, B6, B12, and E.

Salmon, Wild Caught: It contains omega-3 fatty acids which may help reduce blood pressure and triglyceride levels.

Tuna, Fresh or Canned in Water: It is low in calories. Tuna is a lean fish and it has no fat. Tuna packed in water is recommended because it has fewer calories than tuna packed in oil.

Other seafood options are discussed in chapter 17.

Fruit

Fruits are extremely healthy and they can make it easier to lose weight. They have a high water content and they contain a lot of nutrients, fiber, and antioxidants. Most studies on fruit have revealed that people who eat fruit regularly are usually healthier than people who only eat fruit occasionally or who rarely eat fruit. It should also be mentioned that on the average, people who eat more fruit weigh less than people who eat less fruit.

Most fruit is very filling, they contain a lot of healthy nutrients, they contain a modest number of calories, and they contain natural sugar that can satisfy your body's desire for sugar. Fruit is one of the best foods you should include with a meal or eat as a snack.

Apples (85 calories each): There is a significant amount of truth in the old saying "An apple a day keeps the doctor away." Apples are a low-calorie nutrient-dense source of healthy fiber.

Bananas (100 calories each): They contain a reasonable amount of vitamins and minerals and they may enhance digestion.

Blueberries (0.8 calories each): They contain fiber and a reasonable amount of vitamins and minerals.

Cantaloupe (52 calories per cup): It has a lot of vitamin A.

Cherries (4 calories each): They contain the hormone melatonin which helps regulate sleep. Cherries also contain a lot of antioxidants that are beneficial to weight loss. Fresh tart cherries are best. When fresh cherries are out of season, frozen tart cherries or red tart cherries canned in water are fine. Eating six or fewer cherries will not add too many calories to your diet and they may help you sleep better. Please remember that a good night's sleep can help you lose weight. (Note: Avoid maraschino cherries because they contain added ingredients that may be harmful to your health.)

Olives (4.6 calories each): They may help reduce the effects of seasonal allergies.

Oranges (65 calories each): They have a lot of vitamin C.

Peaches (40 calories each): They contain vitamins B3 (niacin), E, and antioxidants. Fresh peaches contain more healthy nutrients than canned peaches.

Pears (85 calories each): They contain copper, antioxidants, and several beneficial plant compounds. Pear skins contain a lot of fiber.

Other fruits are discussed in detail in chapter 19.

Grain

Wheat: Unless you are allergic to wheat or gluten, then whole wheat bread with the Whole Grain Council's stamp on the package is a very healthy food with significant health benefits. However do not eat so much bread that you cannot eat other healthy foods without gaining weight. More detailed information is in chapter 22.

Oats: Oats are an extremely healthy grain. Oats contain protein, fiber, magnesium, manganese, vitamin B1, and several other important nutrients. Steel cut, old fashioned, and instant oatmeal are all acceptable choices. Chapter 21 contains more information about oats.

Rice: No kind of rice is recommended, and that includes brown rice, wild rice, and white rice. Read chapter 21 for specific details.

Meat

Beef: Look for grass-fed beef that ate organically grown grass. This type of beef contains higher levels of omega-3 fatty acids which may help prevent heart disease. Grass-fed beef is leaner and it has fewer calories. Grass-fed beef only contains 60% of the calories and 30% of the fat as conventional beef.

Chicken: In the USA the most important thing to look for when buying chicken meat is a label that says it is *organic*. The reason is because organic means the chicken meat came from a naturally raised, free range chicken and the meat does not contain any GMOs, chemical fertilizers, or commercial pesticides. The second most important thing to look for is *no antibiotics*. If you can find a label that says *organic* and *no antibiotics* then you have found the healthiest chicken meat available in the USA.

Pork: All pork products should be completely cooked to neutralize any bacteria or parasites that may be present in the pork. When selecting pork products look for a thin layer of fat on the outside of the meat. The meat should be firm and grayish pink in color. Tenderness is enhanced if there is a small amount of internal fat marbling. Tenderloins are the most tender and the most flavorful cut of pork. The meat department butcher will usually slice a whole or a half tenderloin into pieces of any thickness you desire for free.

Turkey: It has about half the calories of beef, chicken, and pork.

More information about beef, chicken, pork, and turkey is in chapter 17.

Nuts

Nuts contain a reasonable balance of healthy fats, fiber, and protein. Nuts may enhance the body's metabolic processes and help enhance weight loss. A variety of different studies have shown that people who eat nuts in moderation are healthier than people who do not eat nuts.

Almonds (6.3 calories each): They contain a significant amount of protein, fat, fiber, vitamins B2 and E, calcium, copper, iron, magnesium, manganese, potassium, and antioxidants. Many studies have shown that almonds satisfy hunger, and they may reduce blood sugar, and they may enhance metabolism and weight loss. Almonds may enhance the creation of beneficial bacteria in the intestines. Almonds contain the anti-nutrient phytic acid which may reduce the absorption of some minerals but it may also have some positive health benefits. Almonds also have the highest ratio of omega-6 to omega-3 fatty acids which is not good. Therefore almonds should be consumed in moderation.

Cashews (8.5 calories each): They contain a lot of phosphorus, beta-carotene, and the antioxidants lutein and zeaxanthin. They may help lower blood pressure, cholesterol, and triglycerides.

Macadamia Nuts (7.2 calories each): They contain more monounsaturated fat and less omega-6 fatty acids than other nuts. They also have a relatively low amount of carbohydrates and almost no phytic acid. They may help lower blood pressure, cholesterol, and triglycerides.

Peanuts (5 calories each): Technically peanuts are a legume or vegetable. They are high in fiber, protein, and antioxidants. They may help lower blood pressure, cholesterol, and triglycerides. Peanuts may reduce the risk of heart disease and extend life expectancy. Mothers who ate peanuts during pregnancy gave birth to children with lower rates of asthma and allergies. Flavored peanuts do not have the same health benefits as unflavored peanuts. "Natural" peanut butter without added sugars or added oils is a practical way to add peanuts into your diet.

Other nuts and seeds are discussed in detail in chapter 23.

Vegetables

Asparagus: It is low in calories and carbohydrates but it contains a lot of vitamins E and K. It may help stimulate estrogen in women and testosterone in men. Try not to undercook or overcook asparagus.

Beans: Beans contain a lot of calories so they should be consumed in moderation. Beans are good sources of complex carbohydrates, fiber, protein, folate, iron, manganese, phosphorous, potassium, and several other nutrients. They may help decrease cholesterol, reduce blood pressure, stabilize blood sugar levels, and reduce tummy fat. The fiber in beans is both soluble and insoluble. Both types of fiber reduce the amount of fat the body stores. Digesting the fiber and protein in beans consumes extra calories during the digesting process.

Broccoli: Broccoli may be eaten raw or cooked. It is high in fiber, vitamin C, vitamin K, and antioxidants. It also contains more protein than many other vegetables. It contains the type of fiber that increases the thermic effect of food (TEF). It also contains a compound that may help neutralize some types of cancer, and it may slow down the progression of some diseases. It may facilitate a healthy pregnancy and the birth of a healthy baby,

Carrots: They may be eaten raw or cooked. They contain fiber plus a lot of vitamin A and vitamin B3 (niacin).

Green Peas: Green peas contain protein and fiber that digests slowly and this helps you feel full longer. They also contain folate, copper, iron, magnesium, manganese, phosphorus, potassium, thiamine, zinc, and vitamins A, C, and K.

Lentils: Lentils contain a lot of calories so they should be consumed in moderation. Lentils are a good source of fiber, protein, folate, copper, iron, magnesium, manganese, potassium, antioxidants, and a variety of other nutrients. They contain a type of carbs that are slowly digested. The fiber in lentils helps feed the healthy bacteria in the digestive system. Lentils may help reduce the risk of diabetes, heart disease, and some types of cancer. They may also enhance weight loss.

Okra: It has few calories and it contains about 25% of the RDA of vitamin C and 26% of the RDA of vitamin K. It may facilitate a normal pregnancy and reduce the risk of birth defects. It may be more filling and enhance weight loss.

Peppers: If you eat peppers occasionally then peppers may enhance your short-term metabolic rate. Simply add a few peppers to your salad, either mixed in with the salad or on a separate plate beside the salad. All the following types of peppers have approximately the same impact on increasing a person's metabolic rate: hot peppers, pimentos, rellenos, sweet banana peppers, and sweet bell peppers (green, red, and yellow). However, people who regularly eat spicy foods that contain hot peppers usually discover that their long-term metabolic rate adjusts to their spicy diet.

Potatoes: Potatoes may help reduce your appetite and minimize the amount of food you eat later in the day. If boiled potatoes are allowed to cool for a little while, then they develop a type of "resistant starch" that has a variety of health benefits including weight loss.

Other vegetables are discussed in detail in chapter 18.

Chapter Six

Beverages:
Caffeine, Fruit Juices, Sodas, Water, and Alcohol

Liquid Food Calories

Liquid food, such as a complete meal milkshake or a "smoothie," is not processed by the stomach or the brain in the same way as solid food. Therefore liquid food will not help you feel full, or relieve your hunger. Liquid food will add to the total number of calories you consume each day but it will not help you eat less or lose weight.

Caffeine

Caffeine is extremely popular worldwide. It occurs naturally in coffee, tea, and chocolate. It is also added to a variety of processed foods and beverages. It helps increase metabolism and energy levels and it is in a variety of weight-loss supplements. However, caffeine is addictive. It may cause insomnia, anxiety, nausea, and diarrhea in some people. It may delay the onset of sleep and reduce the quality of sleep.

Caffeine is a diuretic which helps eliminate excess bodily fluids. If high-fiber foods are added to your diet then the combination of caffeine and the additional fiber may result in constipation.

Coffee contains a significant amount of antioxidants and other beneficial compounds in addition to caffeine. Coffee can increase your energy level and reduce your risk of type 2 diabetes by 20% to 50%.

Caffeinated beverages, such as coffee or green tea, can increase the body's metabolic rate by 3% or more in the short-term. However, in the long-term the body gradually adjusts to these beverages and the body's metabolic rate returns to normal.

Green tea contains some caffeine and it contains a significant amount of antioxidants. It may increase the burning of overall body fat by 4% and it may increase the burning of tummy fat by up to 17%. Matcha green tea is a powdered green tea and it has more health benefits than other types of green tea. People who regularly drink hot coffee or hot tea may find the flavor of green tea acceptable to their palate. However, people who do not regularly drink hot beverages may not enjoy the flavor of green tea. Everyone should use *common sense* and if you don't like green tea then please don't force yourself to drink it just because it might be a healthy beverage.

Sweetened tea contains a significant amount of refined sugar. Avoid sweetened tea if you wish to lose weight and improve your health. However, if you really enjoy sweetened tea then you can make your own tea and then add a sugar substitute, such as saccharin, to create homemade sweetened tea that contains no refined sugar. If you carry a few saccharin tablets with you then you can make sweetened tea at a restaurant by adding your own saccharin to their unsweetened tea.

Heavy whipping cream is a healthy fat. When added to a cup of coffee it enhances the flavor of the coffee, and it helps stabilize blood sugar levels between meals, and it helps provide a steady source of energy. It can also minimize or eliminate the "jitters" which is a negative effect of drinking caffeine that is experienced by some people.

Fruit Juices

1. **Commercially Available Fruit Juice:** Most of the fruit juices that are sold in stores contain a significant amount of added refined sugar and these juices should be avoided. However, there are a few fruit juices available that only contain the natural sugar in the fruit and they do not have any added refined sugar. These juices are okay. However fresh whole fruit is a better choice.

2. **Fresh Squeezed Fruit Juice:** Some stores have a juice maker that will make juice from the fruit put into the machine. These juices are preferred over canned or bottled fruit juices.

3. **Homemade Fruit Juice:** A thick fruit juice can be made with a home juice maker. This is the best type of fruit juice because it contains the fruit in addition to its juice. It also allows you to make a juice that contains the exact combination of fruits you prefer. It is also a good option for people who like juice but not fresh fruit. If you prefer a thinner juice then add some pure water to the juice.

Sodas

1. **Carbonated Sodas:** If you enjoy carbonated beverages then you may wish to switch to the "mini cans" that only contain 7.5 ounces. If you do not increase the number of canned beverages you drink and you continue to consume the same number of canned beverages each day, then this could reduce your intake of these beverages by 1/3 while still satisfying your cravings for these beverages.

2. **Carbonated Water:** There are a variety of flavored carbonated waters available at many grocery stores. Read the nutrition label to verify that they don't contain any added refined sugar.

3. **Homemade Healthy Carbonated Sodas:** It is possible to make a healthy homemade carbonated soda by buying some pure carbonated water, and then adding an artificial sweetener such as saccharin if you desire a sweet beverage. If you wish you may add any flavor you enjoy, such as a little pure lemon juice and/or a little pure lime juice, or any other natural flavor you prefer.

Plain Pure Cold Water

Water contains zero calories. Drinking 1.5 liters (6 cups) of plain pure cold water per day may help your body burn about 50 additional calories per day, or approximately 5.2 pounds of body fat per year.

Water is discussed in detail in chapter one on page 5.

Alcohol

Alcohol should not be consumed by pregnant women, nursing mothers, or women who are trying to conceive.

One alcoholic beverage per day can increase your good HDL cholesterol, but too much alcohol can increase your triglyceride level which can damage your liver. The American Heart Association recommends no more than 2 drinks per day for a man and no more than 1 drink per day for a woman. This is based on the average weight of a person based on their gender. The human body cannot store alcohol like it does other liquids. Instead the body consumes glycogen to remove alcohol from the body. Glycogen is derived mostly from carbs. The depletion of glycogen therefore triggers a strong desire to eat carbs to replace the lost glycogen. Therefore alcohol should be consumed in moderation. If you develop a strong craving for carbs then select some type of healthy carb and not some type of junk carb.

1. **Beer:** When consumed in moderation beer may have the following impressive health benefits. It may enhance brain function and the immune system. It may increase bone density. It may reduce the risk of anemia, cataracts, heart attack, heart disease, kidney stones, strokes, and type 2 diabetes. It may help reduce blood pressure and decrease the bad LDL cholesterol. It may increase life expectancy. It also has a variety of healthy nutrients including healthy antioxidants and those antioxidants are different than the antioxidants found in wine. However, when too much beer is consumed the preceding health benefits are all neutralized.

2. **Wine:** When consumed in moderation wine may have the following impressive health benefits. It may enhance brain function and the immune system. It may increase bone density and lower cholesterol. It may reduce inflammation and the risk of heart disease, liver disease, stroke, and type 2 diabetes. It may reduce the risk of breast, colon, and prostate cancer. It may increase the amount of healthy digestive bacteria. It may increase life expectancy. It may help combat depression. Wine also contains healthy antioxidants and one of them may help control and reduce acne. However, when too much wine is consumed the preceding health benefits are all neutralized.

Is Drinking Alcohol Morally Wrong?

The following three scriptures from the Old Testament of the Holy Bible illustrate that God approves of the consumption of alcohol:

1. Deuteronomy 14:26 - And you shall spend that money for whatever your heart desires: for oxen or sheep, for *wine or similar drink*, for whatever your heart desires; you shall eat there before the LORD your God, and you shall rejoice, you and your household. (NKJV)

2. Isaiah 25:6 - And in this mountain The LORD of hosts will make for all people A feast of choice pieces, A *feast of wines* on the lees, Of fat things full of marrow, of *well-refined wines* on the lees. (NKJV)

3. Ecclesiastes 9:7 - Go, eat your bread with joy, And *drink your wine with a merry heart*, For God has already accepted your works. (NKJV)

In the New Testament Jesus Christ turned water into wine at a wedding feast and the master of that banquet praised the quality and the taste of the wine that Jesus made (John 2:1-11).

However, the Holy Bible also contains warnings about drinking too much alcohol. One example would be the following scripture verse.

1. Ephesians 5:18 - And *do not be drunk with wine*, (NKJV)

The Holy Bible therefore permits the consumption of alcohol in moderation. But it also contains numerous warnings about drinking too much alcohol. The Bible does not specify how much alcohol is too much. This is a decision each of us must make based on our body's ability to process alcohol without losing self-control.

Beverage Summary

1. **Water:** Pure plain cold water is the best beverage for the human body.

2. **Caffeine:** Caffeine can benefit the body if it is not consumed late in the day or too close to bedtime.

3. **Sugary Beverages:** Avoid sugary sodas, chocolate milk, fruit juices that contain added sugar, and energy drinks. However, energy drinks are okay in moderation if you need to replace lost electrolytes.

4. **Alcohol:** If alcohol is consumed in moderation it has some impressive health benefits. However if too much alcohol is consumed then all the health benefits are neutralized.

Chapter Seven

Calories

Definition of the Word "Calorie"

There are a variety of scientific definitions for the term "calorie." Nutritionists define the concept in terms of a food's energy producing potential that is released by oxidation inside the body. More specifically, a "food Calorie" it is the amount of heat required to raise the temperature of one kilogram of water 1°C (Celsius) at one atmospheric pressure. A "food Calorie" is also known as a nutritionist's calorie, a large calorie, a kilocalorie, and a kilogram calorie. A "food Calorie" is sometimes written with the capital letter "C" in order to distinguish it from other types of calories. Most countries require that food nutritional data be reported in terms of the "food Calorie" per serving, or per some unit of measure. Therefore the word is normally written as "calorie" for two reasons:

1. When "calorie" is used in reference to food the context makes the intended meaning of the word obvious since it is referring to food.
2. The International System of Units (SI) requires that the first letter of a "unit name" be written in a lower case English letter.

Calories are Important

Calories provide the fuel that allows the human body to function properly. If the minimum required number of calories are not eaten each day then serious long-term health problems may begin to develop.

The Basic Calorie Consumption Model

The following simple rules apply to daily calorie consumption:

1. If more calories are eaten than burned then weight will be gained.
2. If approximately the same number of calories are both eaten and burned then weight will remain approximately the same.
3. If fewer calories are eaten than burned then weight will be lost.

One pound of body weight is approximately equal to 3,500 calories. To lose one pound per week means that approximately 500 fewer calories should be eaten per day than burned. Or 500 more calories per day could be burned by exercise than eaten. However, the optimal solution would be to eat 250 fewer calories per day and burn 250 more calories per day by exercising.

Although the above basic rules are true, there is a lot more to losing weight than just eating fewer calories per day than you burn per day. Remember that your objective is to not only lose weight but to also become a healthier person. The remainder of this chapter will discuss other important concepts that apply to calories and weight loss.

Counting Calories

Some people believe they need to keep track of all the calories they eat each day in order to lose weight. There are a variety of "apps" that can be downloaded onto your mobile phone that will allow you to enter the type and quantity of food you eat and the "app" will keep track of your total daily calorie intake. It is also possible to keep track of calories on a piece of paper if that appeals to you.

Some people enjoy counting calories and it does not adversely impact their health or their personality. However, some people become overly obsessed with calories, and they forfeit the pleasure of eating when they do eat, and they develop unhealthy eating habits that can lead to disordered eating. Some of the symptoms of disordered eating include: obsessive calorie counting, feeling guilty about eating, frequently skipping meals, allowing food concerns to negatively impact the quality of your life, anxiety about specific foods or food groups, and refusing to eat anywhere except in your own home. If you suspect you may have disordered eating then you should discuss your concerns with a licensed medical professional.

Instead of keeping track of your exact total daily calorie consumption, a different method is to simply estimate the total number of calories you consume at each meal by adding up the calories on the nutrition labels of the food you eat. Also set a calorie limit on the number of calories you will consume between meals. This will help you easily control the total number of calories eaten per meal, and between meals, to a reasonable level so you can lose weight. When you weigh yourself the following morning you will receive prompt feedback on your previous day's efforts and you will know if the average number of calories you currently eat per meal, and between meals, is helping you lose weight. If not, then you can reduce the total number of calories per meal, or per snack, as you believe appropriate.

Different Types of Food Calories

Although all food calories are based on the same scientific definition of calorie, all food calories are not equal. Calories from healthy foods help you maintain a proper nutritional balance inside your body, and they help you feel full for a longer period of time, and they provide energy for a longer period of time. Calories from sugar, sweets, and most junk foods (frequently called "empty calories") do not provide the balanced nutrition your body needs, and they only provide a burst of quick energy. This will result in your becoming fatigued more easily. And you will quickly get hungry again and this will cause you to eat more and you will gain weight. You will also become more susceptible to a variety of health problems and diseases.

Calories Per Type of Nutrient

The following table shows the approximate number of calories per one gram of dietary fat, carbohydrates, protein, and alcohol:

Item	Grams	Calories
Dietary Fat	1	9
Carbohydrate	1	4
Protein	1	4
Alcohol	1	7

1. **Dietary Fat:** The gram weight of food is correlated to the amount of food. A food with more dietary fat has more calories than the same approximate weight of a different food that has more protein or carbohydrates. This means you can eat approximately twice as much food (weight) for the same total number of calories if the food has more carbohydrates and protein instead of dietary fat.

2. **Carbohydrates:** A low-carb diet and a low-calorie diet are both about equally effective for weight loss. However, carbohydrates include starch, fiber, and sugar, and reducing your fiber intake may cause health problems. An alternative to a low-carb diet is to eat fiber rich carbohydrates as explained next.

3. **Fiber in Carbohydrates:** Fiber is not digestible. Fiber calories are "free" calories and they do not add to your total daily calorie intake. Fiber sends messages to your brain that you are full and you stop eating so you eat less, and you are not hungry when you stop eating.

4. **Protein:** The protein in animal based food sends messages to your brain that you are full. And since protein has fewer calories than fat, you will feel full by eating fewer calories. And protein increases the metabolic rate at which you burn calories by approximately 80 to 100 calories per day. Protein also helps reduce food cravings and it helps reduce the desire to eat a snack before bedtime.

Liquid Calories versus Solid Calories

Liquid calories do not send the same messages to the brain as solid calories because liquid calories pass through the mouth and through the stomach faster than solid calories. Food that has to be chewed stays in the mouth longer and our taste, touch, smell, hearing, and seeing have more time to send messages to our brain that we are eating. And when the food is swallowed it takes longer to pass through the stomach. The result is that we feel full by consuming fewer calories.

Liquid calories include sugary sodas, fruit juices, chocolate milk, and sport drinks. In the USA these beverages are one of the primary reasons that adults and children are overweight.

In addition to causing weight gains, these sugary beverages adversely impact the body's metabolic rate, and they increase the risk of a variety of different health problems and diseases.

The long-term health benefits from avoiding these beverages can be significant. However, anyone who sweats heavily while working may benefit from an electrolyte beverage to replace the electrolyte deficiency in their body and to relieve their thirst. In addition, fruit juices that contains zero added sugar are okay if they are not consumed too often and if they contain the vitamins the human body needs.

However, complete meal diet milkshakes are a poor choice for avoiding hunger and for satisfying the human body's need for real food.

Average Daily Calorie Needs

The "average" man needs about 2,500 calories per day to maintain his body weight. The "average" woman needs about 2,000 calories per day to maintain her body weight. These are just averages and each one of us may need more or fewer calories per day to maintain our body weight based on our age, our metabolic rate, our normal job, and the types of recreational activities we participate in.

Food Choices and Calories

Eating healthy foods instead of junk foods helps us lose weight without starving ourselves. Although the type of food we eat (protein, carbohydrates, or dietary fat) may have a significant impact on how easily we lose weight, it is still the total number of calories we eat each day that determines whether or not we lose weight.

Long Term Effect of Calorie Reduction

The human body is excellent at adjusting to whatever it is fed. Although the impact of calorie reduction can result in significant weight losses in the short term, the human body very gradually reduces its metabolic rate to compensate for the reduction in calories. This means that after a reasonable period of time we will stop losing weight even though we eat the same number of calories per day.

Summary

Reducing your calorie intake does not mean that you have to feel hungry all the time. Foods with less fat, fewer carbohydrates, and more protein can help you feel full on less food and help you lose weight.

Being able to lose weight while improving your health involves more than just eating fewer calories than you burn each day. This does not mean that calories are unimportant. It means there are also other important issues. The remaining chapters in this book will help you understand how to strategically select foods that will help you lose weight and improve your health without feeling hungry all the time.

Chapter Eight

Dietary Fat

The human body must have fuel from food in order to survive. Dietary fat is one of the three primary sources of fuel that our body needs. The other two sources are carbohydrates and protein.

The body needs healthy fats to provide the energy it needs so it can function properly. Fats helps build cell membranes, and it helps keep your skin and hair healthy. Fat helps your body absorb vitamins A, D, E, and K, which are the fat soluble vitamins. Fats provide the essential linoleic amino acid which your body cannot make but which it needs to control inflammation and facilitate normal brain functions, muscle movement, and blood clotting when you are injured and bleeding. Our bodies need a *minimum* of 10% our total daily calories to come from fats in order to remain healthy. The USDA *recommends* that fats be between 20% to 35% of an adult's daily calories. Eating less fats will not reduce the risk of cancer, but eating less fats may help us lose weight, and losing weight is usually associated with a lower risk of different types of cancer and a longer and healthier lifespan.

Your body uses carbohydrates to provide fuel for the first 20 minutes of an exercise session. However, after the first 20 minutes your body uses fat to fuel your body.

In order to improve our health it is important that we consume the right type of fats. Food fats consist of saturated fats, unsaturated fats, and trans fats.

1. **Saturated Fats:** These increase your body's bad LDL cholesterol which increases your risk of heart attack, stroke, and a variety of other health problems such as clogged blood vessels. Foods that are high in saturated fats are oils that are solid at room temperature, and also in some oils that are liquid at room temperature such as coconut and palm oils. They are also present in animal products such as butter, cheese, cream, ice cream, whole milk, eggs, and in meats and poultry skin. Saturated fats should be less than 10% of our total daily calories, and less than 7% if possible.

2. **Unsaturated Fats:** These are liquid at room temperature but they will solidify if refrigerated. They include:

   a. **Monounsaturated Fats:** Also called MUFA for mono-unsaturated fatty acids. These fats are a good source of the antioxidant vitamin E. The are present in food such as canola oil, olive oil, peanut oil, and olives. They are also in nuts such as almonds, Brazil nuts, cashews, hazelnuts, macadamia, peanuts, pecans and in pumpkin seeds, sesame seeds, sunflower seeds, and in peanut butter. Olive oil has been linked to low levels of heart disease in Mediterranean countries where olive oil is a regular part of their normal daily diet.

b. **Polyunsaturated Fats:** These fats may help lower cholesterol and triglyceride levels. In women polyunsaturated fats can increase their reproductive hormone levels and improve their chances of successful child bearing. Polyunsaturated fats are essential fats. Your body cannot make essential fats but they are required for normal body functions. Therefore you must get them from the food you eat. Polyunsaturated fats include the following:

1. **Omega-3 Fatty Acids:** These acids include alpha linolenic acid (ALA), eicosapentaenoic acid (EPA), docosahexaenoic acid (DHA), and docosapentaenoic acid (DPA). The liver can convert EPA and DPA into whichever acid is needed at the time. DHA may help reduce tummy fat because it may deactivate the genes that add fat to the tummy, and this prevents tummy fat cells from expanding and becoming larger. The four omega-3 fatty acids may help relieve the symptoms of asthma, depression, and rheumatoid arthritis. They may help minimize the risk of cardiovascular diseases and heart attacks. They may help reduce blood pressure and inflammation, increase good HDL cholesterol, and decrease triglycerides. High amounts of omega-3 fatty acids, including DHA, are in fish such as bass, catfish, herring, mackerel, salmon, sardines, trout, and tuna. Small amounts of omega-3 are in canola oil, flaxseed oil, and walnuts. Eating fatty fish (but not deep fried) has been linked to a reduced risk of cardiovascular diseases. However, omega-3 *supplements* do not reduce the risk of heart disease, with the exception of people who have already been diagnosed with some type of heart disease.

2. **Omega-6 Fatty Acids:** Helps prevent heart disease. They are present in corn oil, safflower oil, sunflower oil, soy oil, and walnut oil. However, omega-6 fatty acids may *increase* the amount of the bad *oxidized* LDL cholesterol.

3. **Trans Fats:** These include natural and artificial trans fats.

a. **Natural Trans Fats:** Very small amounts of trans fats are naturally present in meat and dairy products and they are not a health concern.

b. **Artificial Trans Fats:** These are byproducts of hydrogenation which turns healthy oils into solids in order to prevent them from becoming rancid. On nutrition labels they are frequently listed as "partially hydrogenated vegetable oil." In the USA the USDA has required that artificial trans fats be eliminated from all foods no later than January 1, 2021. The reason is because trans fats have no known health benefits and they contribute to a wide variety of health problems and diseases.

Nutrition Labels

All dietary fats contain approximately 9 calories per gram.

Most foods contain a combination of fats but they are classified based on which fat is present in the highest percentage in the food.

A food label that says "trans fat free" may still contain a maximum of 0.5 grams of trans fat per serving.

Foods with labels that say "low-fat" or "fat free" usually replace the fat with refined sugars. Therefore these foods are generally not healthy food choices because most of them contain substitute ingredients that are not healthy.

The brain is at least 65% fat. Low-fat diets prevent young children from developing properly. Young children need fats to optimize the development of their entire body.

Low-fat diets are usually calorie restricted diets that require a person to be hungry almost all the time. Therefore low-fat diets are not recommended.

Fat Summary

1. Body fat is made from the extra calories that the body eats but which the body does not burn. Calories are contained in dietary fat, carbohydrates, and protein. Therefore body fat can come from any source of fuel that provides calories.

2. Dietary fat contains more than twice the calories per gram when compared to carbohydrates and protein. Therefore a high-fat diet will contain less food (less gram weight) than a diet that contains the same total number of calories where most of the calories are provided by carbohydrates or protein.

3. The body needs dietary fat to remain healthy. The gallbladder needs fats to break down foods and without an adequate intake of fat the result can be gallstones. Therefore a diet should not try to eliminate all, or most, of the fats from your meals.

4. Eating dietary food fat will **not** automatically add fat cells to your body.

5. Increasing unsaturated fats while decreasing saturated fats can reduce the risk of heart disease.

6. A few good sources of monounsaturated fat include lard, olives, peanut oil, extra virgin olive oil, and some nuts such as almonds, Brazil nuts, cashews, hazelnuts, macadamia nuts, peanuts, pecans, and pistachios.

Chapter Nine

Cholesterol

Cholesterol is a chemical the body needs. Cholesterol is a part of all the cells in the body. Cholesterol is used to repair cells and tissues throughout the entire body. The body needs cholesterol to make vitamin D and to make things the body needs to digest food. The liver can make most of the cholesterol the body requires. Cholesterol is present in animal products such as meat, poultry, seafood, dairy products, and eggs. Plant foods do not contain any cholesterol.

Cholesterol is used to make the sex hormones estrogen (females) and testosterone (males). If your cholesterol level drops too low then it may result in decreased sexual motivation in men and women, and an increase in infertility, and an increase in the chance of a miscarriage.

Approximately 60% of the brain is cholesterol. Low cholesterol levels have been associated with an increased risk of Alzheimer's disease, dementia, depression, mental illness, suicide, and committing violent crimes.

Your body's cholesterol level should be determined before you begin dieting during a complete physical exam that includes a comprehensive blood analysis. Cholesterol levels are based on a blood test called a lipid profile and your doctor can interpret the results for you based on your age, gender, race, and weight.

Cholesterol is absorbed from food by your small intestine and transmitted by your blood to your liver. Your liver stores cholesterol and releases it back into your blood as it is needed by your body.

If your blood contains too much cholesterol then it can combine with other substances and form plaque that will adhere to the walls of your arteries. Too much plaque can result in coronary artery disease.

Cholesterol is classified based on lipoproteins. A lipoprotein consists of fat (lipid) and protein. The lipid must be attached to a protein so it can travel through your blood. Lipoproteins are classified based on the ratio of cholesterol to protein. There are three different types of lipoproteins and each one has it own purpose:

1. **HDL or High-Density Lipoprotein or "Good" Cholesterol:** HDL transports cholesterol from all parts of your body back to your liver and then your liver removes the cholesterol from your body.

2. **LDL or Low-Density Lipoprotein or "Bad" Cholesterol:** LDL is composed primarily of cholesterol. It is bad because too much LDL can form into plaque that can build up on the inside of your arteries and cause health problems.

3. **VLDL or Very Low-Density Lipoprotein or "Bad" Cholesterol:** VLDL contains less cholesterol than LDL. VLDL is composed primarily of triglycerides. A high triglyceride level can result in coronary artery disease.

Factors that can Increase Cholesterol

1. **Saturated Fat:** Eating too much saturated fat.
2. **Sitting:** Spending more time sitting than standing.
3. **Lack of Exercise**: The lack of any type of exercise. Exercise can increase your good HDL cholesterol level.
4. **Smoking:** Smoking decreases HDL and increases LDL. Smoking is extremely harmful to a woman's health.

Other Factors Related to High Cholesterol

1. **Heredity:** High cholesterol may be an inherited family trait.
2. **Race:** Some races have higher levels of cholesterol. For example, African-Americans have higher HDL and LDL levels than whites.
3. **Age:** As we age our cholesterol level gradually increases.
4. **Weight:** Overweight people have higher cholesterol levels. Losing weight can help a person lower their cholesterol level.

Foods that may help Lower Cholesterol

1. **Soluble Fiber:** It helps reduce the bad LDL cholesterol. Good sources of soluble fiber include: apples, bananas, bran, Brussels sprouts, kidney beans, oatmeal, and pears.
2. **Omega-3 Fatty Acids (a Polyunsaturated Fat):** Helps increase the good HDL cholesterol, and reduce the bad VLDL triglycerides (but not the bad LDL cholesterol). Reducing triglycerides helps reduce blood pressure, the chance of harmful blood clots, and the chance of sudden death. The highest levels of omega-3 are found in fatty fish such as: bass, catfish, herring, mackerel, salmon, sardines, trout, and tuna. Small amounts of omega-3 are in canola oil, flaxseed oil, and walnuts. Omega-3 *supplements* do not reduce the risk of heart disease (with the exception of people who have already been diagnosed with some type of heart disease). Always discuss a supplement with your doctor before adding it to your diet.
3. **Nuts:** The monounsaturated fats in nuts may help to reduce cholesterol. Nuts are high in calories so do not overindulge.
4. **Olives and Avocados:** They contain monounsaturated fats and they may help lower LDL cholesterol in people who are overweight.
5. **Other Foods:** The following foods may help lower cholesterol levels: beans, fruits, oats, okra, and whole grains.

Prescription Medicines

Cholesterol may also be lowered with specific mediations that may be prescribed by your doctor.

Chapter Ten

Carbohydrates (Carbs)
Starches, Fiber, and Sugar

The human body must have fuel from food in order to survive. Carbohydrates are one of the three primary sources of fuel that our body needs. The other two sources are fat and protein.

Carbohydrates provide energy to the body, they prevent protein from being consumed for energy, and they assist in the metabolism of fat. Carbohydrates are critical for proper brain function. However, a diet that is extremely high in carbohydrates may negatively impact human social behavior. In addition, a diet that is extremely low in carbohydrates may increase anger, anxiety, and depression due to a decrease in the level of serotonin in the body. When we discover that our anti-social behavior is due to our hunger cravings then we abandon our low-carb diet in order to become socially acceptable once again.

Carbohydrates received their name because they contain carbon, hydrogen, and oxygen. Carbohydrates occur naturally in foods such as beans, fruits, grains, legumes, nuts, seeds, and vegetables. Meat, fish, and shellfish do not contain any carbohydrates.

Carbohydrates include the starches, fiber, and sugar contained in fruit, vegetables, grains, and dairy products. On a food nutrition label the total carbohydrates are shown as a separate category. Directly below the total carbohydrates there may be two or more sub-categories of carbohydrates such as fiber and sugar. These values are unusually indented a little to the right. This indicates that they are included in the total carbohydrate number. To estimate the amount of starches subtract the total fiber and the total sugar from the total carbohydrate number. If the answer is zero then the food does not contain any starch. If you get a number higher than zero then some of this value may be the starches in the food. It is unfortunate that starch is not listed on the nutrition label as starch.

The term "Net Carbs" is not regulated by law. Therefore it can mean whatever the food manufacturer defines it to mean. The two most common definitions of net carbs are:

1. The number of carbs remaining after subtracting fiber.
2. The number of carbs remaining after subtracting fiber and sugar.

The "glycemic index" is based on the impact of a specific food on your blood sugar level. There are some research studies that suggest that foods with a low glycemic index are healthier. However, there are also other studies that simultaneously evaluated diets that contained foods with a high index and diets that contained foods with a low index and the final result was that the index had no correlation to a person's overall health.

Carbohydrates are one of the body's three sources of fuel called macronutrients. Fats and protein are the other two macronutrients. The body requires large amounts of macronutrients in order to function properly. Since our body cannot produce macronutrients, they must be supplied to our body as part of the food we eat.

Carbohydrates are further classified as simple or complex. Simple carbs are digested and absorbed by the human body more easily and more quickly than complex carbs.

1. **Simple Carbs:** They can provide a quick burst of energy. They are classified as follows:

   a, **Monosaccharides or Single Sugars:** Includes fructose from sugar, and galactose (lactose) from milk.

   b. **Disaccharides or Double Sugars:** Includes sucrose (table sugar) from either sugar cane or sugar beets, and maltose which is in beer and in a few vegetables.

   Some simple carbs, called "empty carbs" or "empty calories" can be found in candy, cookies, pastries, sweets, sugary beverages, and syrups. These foods contain processed refined sugars and they are called "empty carbs" because they do not contain any fiber, vitamins, or minerals. Therefore they contribute directly to weight gains. The simple carbs that are present in some processed foods may increase the risk of heart disease and type 2 diabetes.

2. **Complex Carbs or Polysaccharides:** They provide a sustained level of energy over a longer period of time. They contain three or more sugars. They are called starches and they are in beans, bread, cereals, corn, lentils, parsnips, peas, peanuts, rice, and potatoes.

The human body breaks carbs down into smaller units of sugar. The small intestine absorbs these small units of sugar and transmits them into the blood and the blood carries them to the liver. The liver converts the small units of sugar into glucose and returns them to the blood along with insulin. This is known as blood sugar level (glucose level). Then the body uses the nutrients in the blood for energy to do work and to maintain the normal involuntary functions of the body. If the body does not need the energy then the liver can store about 2,000 calories in the liver, in the skeletal muscles, and in other cells in the form of glycogen. After all the glycogen storage cells are full any additional carbs are converted into fat cells that are stored in the body.

However, when there are not enough carbs or fat cells to fuel the body then the body will consume protein as fuel. This results in two significant problems:

1. The body needs protein to form muscles.

2. Using protein for fuel puts additional stress on the kidneys and this can result in painful byproducts being passed in the urine.

Low-carb diets are very effective for helping people lose weight and reduce their susceptibility to a variety of diseases. Eating fewer carbs and eating more protein and more fat may help some people feel less hungry so they eat less and consume fewer calories. This may result in more weight loss when compared to a basic low-fat diet. Therefore weight loss may be significantly increased by eating more fat and fewer carbs. However, if the low-card diet also decreases the amount of fiber below the minimum level required by the body then this will result in digestive problems and constipation. Therefore it is important to carefully evaluate the foods you eat to verify that the carbs you eat are higher in fiber than starches or sugar.

Carbs that are high in fiber are "good" carbs. Good carbs also provide vitamins, minerals, and phytochemicals. Carbs that are high in sugar are "bad" carbs.

Commercially processed carbs, called refined carbs, have most of their beneficial carbs and fiber removed. Only the easily digestible carbs remain and this contributes to overeating and it increases our susceptibility to a variety of diseases.

Food processors add carbohydrates to food in the form of starches and sugars in order to increase the chance that people will become addicted to their foods.

Refined carbs include breakfast cereals, pasta, pastries, sugary beverages, sweets, white bread, and white rice. (Note: All bread is refined.)

When you consume fewer carbs your body will provide fuel for your activities by burning some of the fat that is stored on your body.

Minimizing the number of carbohydrates we consume may help lower our insulin levels. It may also help our kidneys rid our bodies of excess salt and water. This may help minimize bloating and excess water weight.

A low-carb diet will usually reduce blood sugar levels, blood pressure, triglycerides, the bad LDL cholesterol, and increase the good HDL cholesterol.

However, a low-carb diet may increase your cravings for specific foods that contain carbs. When you don't consume enough carbs it is not uncommon for food to dominate your thoughts during most of the day, and for you to feel hungry even after you have eaten. Therefore a low-carb diet will usually not be sustainable for a long period of time.

Chapter Eleven

Starches

Starch is a carbohydrate. The other two carbohydrates are fiber and sugar.

Starches provide a quick burst of energy to the body in the form of glucose.

Starches are a complex carbohydrate which means they contain three or more sugars. *Therefore they also provide for a sustained level of energy over a longer period of time.* Vegetables that contain lots of starch include barley, beans, buckwheat, chickpeas, corn, lintels, oats, parsnips, peas, peanuts, potatoes, rice, sweet potatoes, water chestnuts, wheat, and whole grains. Processed foods that contain starch include bread, cereals, crackers, oatmeal, pancakes, pasta, popcorn, and tortillas.

Non-starchy vegetables include broccoli, carrots, celery, green beans, kale, and lettuces.

When starch is cooked it becomes more digestible.

When foods that contain a lot of starch are cooked and then allowed to cool for a little while, they develop a type of "resistant starch" that has a variety of health benefits including weight loss.

Starchy foods are also high in fiber, calcium, iron, and B vitamins.

Highly processed starches have been stripped of most of their nutrients and fiber. Therefore they are referred to as "empty calories" because they contain minimal nutritional value and they may increase the risk of type 2 diabetes, heart disease, and weight gains. Therefore highly processed starches should be avoided.

Whole grain cornmeal is healthier than de-germed cornmeal that has been stripped of some of its fiber and nutrients. You can grind hard dent corn kernels into fresh cornmeal at home as you need it.

Oats contain starch, fiber, fat, and protein. Oats may help reduce blood sugar levels, lower the risk of heart disease, and contribute to weight loss.

Uncooked rice contains a lot of starch (about 63%) but cooking significantly reduces its starch content to about 28% by weight.

Cooked corn contains about 18% starch by weight.

Cooked potatoes (boiled or baked) also contain about 18% starch by weight. Cook and eat potatoes with the skin on because the skins contain a lot of fiber which may help with weight loss. However French fries and potato chips are not healthy foods. If you are going to boil potatoes then only add just enough water to cover the potatoes in order to prevent the loss of too many of the nutrients into the water. Do not eat green or damaged potatoes or potatoes that have begun to sprout. More information about potatoes is on pages 154 and 155.

Chapter Twelve
Dietary Fiber

Dietary fiber is a carbohydrate. The other two carbohydrates are starches and sugar.

Dietary fiber is a complex carbohydrate. Fiber is usually listed on a food nutrition label directly below total carbohydrates. The amount of fiber shown on the nutrition label is also included in the total carbohydrates value shown above it.

Dietary fiber is also known as roughage or bulk. Dietary fiber is the indigestible part of plant foods. Most people know that fiber may help prevent constipation. However, fiber may also help with weight loss. And fiber may help lower the risk of hemorrhoids, heart disease, type 2 diabetes, and some types of cancer. Wheat fiber may help neutralize stomach acid and it may be of benefit to individuals with stomach ulcers.

Indigestible fiber is present in good quantities in brown rice, potato skins, whole wheat pasta, and whole wheat bread.

Partially digestible fiber is present in apples, carrots, oats, and potatoes, and these foods may help reduce cholesterol.

Fiber requires water to do its job properly. Therefore it is important to drink an adequate amount of water each day if you wish to be healthy.

Fiber is necessary for proper digestion and fiber facilitates normal bowel movements. Fiber is the part of plant foods that your body cannot absorb. Fiber passes relatively intact through your stomach, and it is not absorbed by the small intestine and it is not converted into glucose. Instead fiber continues into the large intestine where it is converted into hydrogen, carbon dioxide, and fatty acids. As the fiber passes through your system it collects a lot of the harmful stuff in your body and that harmful stuff is expelled with the fiber in your stools.

Fiber is classified as follows:

1. **Soluble Fiber (pectin, gum, mucilage):** It dissolves in water into a gel-like substance. Soluble fiber slows down digestion. It may help lower cholesterol and glucose levels. Soluble fibers may help you lose tummy fat more easily. It is present in apples, ripe bananas, barley, beans, blueberries, carrots, citrus, lentils, peas, oats, oatmeal, onions, nuts, and strawberries.

2. **Insoluble Fiber (cellulose, hemicellulose, lignin):** It will not dissolve in water and it retains most of its original shape as it passes

through the digestive system. It helps to prevent and relieve constipation, and it facilitates normal bowel movements. Insoluble fiber is present in avocados, beans, unripe bananas, brown rice, carrots, cauliflower, celery, cucumbers, dark leafy vegetables, green beans, fruit, nuts, potatoes, seeds, tomatoes, wheat bran, and whole wheat flour.

Beans, carrots, and nuts are good sources of both types of fiber.

Other foods that contain fiber are artichokes, blackberries, broccoli, corn, popcorn, raspberries, and turnip greens.

The highest insoluble fiber content is found in the skin on fruits and vegetables. However, unless the food is USDA certified organic then the skin may also contain residual amounts of harmful insecticides. Foods that are certified as organic outside the USA may not meet the standards that are used inside the USA.

Fiber rich foods have all the following advantages:

1. **Fewer Calories:** High fiber foods are less energy dense and they contain fewer calories for the same amount of food.

2. **More Filling:** Foods that contain more fiber are more filling than foods that contain less fiber.

3. **Weight Loss:** Soluble fiber helps slow down the digestion of other foods eaten at the same time. This results in an expansion of the stomach and the release of satiety hormones. This helps us feel full for a longer period of time. This automatically results in our eating less food, and fewer calories, and therefore we lose weight.

4. **Blood Sugar:** Soluble fiber helps to maintain a more consistent blood sugar level. This helps prevent blood sugar spikes. Insoluble fiber also helps regulate blood sugar. Insoluble fiber may reduce the risk of type 2 diabetes.

5. **Blood Pressure:** Fiber may help to reduce blood pressure, inflammation, and artery stiffness.

6. **Cancer:** Fiber may attach itself to the chemicals that cause cancer and steer them away from the cells in the breasts and the colon and this may help prevent breast and colon cancer.

7. **Cholesterol:** Soluble fiber may help decrease cholesterol. As digestion improves the liver removes cholesterol from the blood in order to create the acid required for digestion. This lowers the bad LDL cholesterol level.

8. **Gallstones:** Fiber may help prevent the formation of gallstones.

9. **Normal Bowel Movements:** Insoluble fiber increases the bulk, weight, and softness of your stool, and this helps the stool to more easily pass out of your body. Stools are approximately 75% water. Fiber also absorbs water and this helps solidify the stool and thereby prevent loose watery stools.

10. **Healthy Colon:** A high-fiber diet may help reduce the risk of hemorrhoids and small pouches in the colon. It may also reduce the risk of colon cancer.

11. **Cardiovascular Disease:** Soluble fiber may help reduce the risk of cardiovascular disease, heart disease, and cancer.

12. **Respiratory Disease:** Fiber may help reduce the risk of respiratory diseases.

13. **Longer Life:** Because of all the above health benefits, a fiber rich diet may increase life expectancy.

Commercially processed foods or refined foods are usually lower in fiber when compared to the same foods before processing. Refined foods will usually add some artificial vitamins back into the food but fiber is not added back into the food.

The best source of fiber is in whole foods instead of fiber supplements. Fiber occurs naturally in fruits, grains, nuts, peas, and vegetables. Also barley, brown rice, bulgur wheat, wild rice, whole wheat pasta, and whole wheat tortilla chips. Beans, lentils, legumes, and peas contain a lot of fiber.

Although fiber supplements contain fiber, they do not contain the variety of fibers, vitamins, minerals, and other nutrients that are contained in whole foods. Some fiber supplements can also interfere with some medications.

Prebiotin, a prebiotic, contains all the fiber your body needs, and it may help grow healthy gut bacteria. It is plant based, contains very few calories, has a slightly sweet taste, and it can be added to water or sprinkled on foods.

Always talk to your doctor before you add any supplement to your diet because your doctor can advice you if the supplement will be beneficial for you based on the results of your physical exam and your medical history.

Total daily fiber intake should be increased slowly over a period of three or four weeks. This will allow the natural healthy bacteria in your digestive system to adjust to the change. This will help minimize or prevent stomach discomfort, bloating, and diarrhea. And please remember to drink a lot of water because water helps the body maximize all the benefits of fiber.

Numerous studies over a period of several decades have reported a significant link between eating more fiber and losing weight. Eating more fiber may also help prevent obesity.

One study found that eating more fiber resulted in weight loss regardless of the total number of calories eaten per day, or the types of foods eaten. This is significant because any diet that seriously limits carbohydrates without permitting those carbohydrates that contain a lot of fiber are in complete opposition to the findings of many research studies that report that fiber can contribute to weight loss.

Chapter Thirteen

Sugar and Sugar Substitutes

Sugar is a carbohydrate. The other two carbohydrates are starches and fiber.

Sugar is the common name for the sweet-tasting water-soluble carbohydrates normally present in many foods.

The natural sugars in milk, fruit, and vegetables are present in conjunction with enzymes, fiber, and vitamins which slow down and assist in the digestion of the sugar. Commercially processed sugars are different and they contain "empty calories" because they have no enzymes, fats, fiber, minerals, vitamins, or other nutrients.

Sugar can be subdivided into two basic categories:

1. **Simple Sugars:** Simple sugars consist of fructose, glucose, and galactose. Honey and fruit contain simple sugars.

   a. **Fructose:** Can increase blood sugar levels, triglycerides, and LDL (bad) cholesterol levels when compared to the same amount of glucose consumption. However the natural fructose in fruit does **not** have this same bad effect. Fructose increases the hunger hormone called ghrelin when compared to the same amount of glucose.

   b. **Glucose (sometimes referred to as dextrose):** It does a better job of stimulating the part of the brain that tells you that you are full when compared to fructose.

   c. **Galactose:** It is present in small quantities in milk, yogurt, and green peas. It is important for mothers who are breastfeeding. The human body can produce galactose from glucose so it is not essential to include galactose in the diet.

   d. **Honey:** It contains as many antioxidants as spinach. Honey is a natural sweetener that is produced by bees from the nectar in flowers. Honey contains both fructose and glucose but they are not joined together into a single compound. Honey is approximately 53% fructose and in its natural form it has many health benefits when consumed in *moderation.* Honey may be used as a sweetener in coffee and in recipes instead of commercially processed sugar. The Holy Bible mentions honey as being a desirable healthy food when consumed in moderation (Proverbs 24:13, Proverbs 25:15, Exodus 3:8, Leviticus 20:24, Numbers 14:8, Deuteronomy 6:3, Joshua 5:6, 2 Samuel 17:29, Isaiah 7:22, Jeremiah 11:5, Ezekiel 20:6).

e. **100% Pure Maple Syrup:** It is a natural sweetener.

f. **Molasses:** It is a natural sweetener and it is a byproduct of the process of removing sugar from sugarcane or sugar beets.

g. **Corn Syrup:** It is made by converting cornstarch into fructose and glucose sugars.

h. **High Fructose Corn Syrup (HFCS):** It is made by converting some of the glucose in corn syrup into fructose. It contains 55% fructose and 45% glucose.

2. **Compound Sugars:** Compound sugars consist of two simple sugars joined together by a chemical bond. Examples would be lactose (glucose plus galactose), maltose (glucose plus another glucose joined together), and sucrose (fructose plus glucose).

a. **Lactose:** It is present in milk, including human breast milk, and in some dairy products.

b. **Maltose:** It is produced by malting grains.

c. **Sucrose:** It is present in sugarcane and sugar beets. It is commonly known as granulated sugar, regular sugar, and table sugar. Powdered sugar, or confectioners' sugar, is granulated sugar that has been milled into a fine powder. Brown sugar is granulated sugar coated with molasses. Using more molasses results in a darker brown sugar.

Liquid sugar is one of the most significant causes of obesity in the USA. Liquid sugar is present in sugary sodas, sugary beverages, fruit juices with added sugar, and sport drinks.

Sugar in small amounts does not result in obesity. However, foods that contain a lot of sugar may become addictive. This is more likely when the sugar is added to high fat foods. Sugar addiction may lead to increases in weight instead of decreases in weight. Sugar may reduce alertness and increase fatigue within one hour of consumption. Eating foods with added sugar may contribute to acne, cancer, dementia, depression, gout, heart disease, kidney disease, liver fat, skin wrinkles due to age, tooth decay, and type 2 diabetes.

The good news is that it is not necessary to completely eliminate all sugar from the diet. However, reducing the total amount of sugar consumed is an excellent first step to improving your overall health.

The easiest way to reduce your total sugar intake is to read the nutrition labels on foods and to select foods with no added sugar or "free sugar." Many of the foods you enjoy probably contain added sugar. But if you read the nutrition labels on different competing brands of your favorite foods, then you may be able to find many of your favorite foods that contain no added sugar. These brands will usually contain fewer calories and they will allow you to continue eating the foods you enjoy while simultaneously helping you reduce your sugar intake, lose weight, and improve your health.

All sugars provide approximately the same number of calories per gram.

Sugar Substitutes

Before you experiment with a sugar substitute you should discuss it with your doctor because your doctor is knowledgeable about your health, your medical history, and any prescription medicines you may be taking. Your doctor can advise you of any potential problems that you may experience with a specific sugar substitute.

The impact of sugar substitutes on a person's health may be influenced by the quantity consumed and the time of day it is consumed. Sugar substitutes may adversely impact intestinal bacteria (flora), and increase the risk of glucose intolerance and metabolic disorders.

The consumption of some artificial sweeteners may increase your cravings for sweets and carbohydrates. Artificial sweeteners may increase your appetite and lead to the accumulation of fat on your body and an increase in your weight.

All the different sugar substitutes have their own unique sweet taste. Therefore you may wish to experiment with several different sugar substitutes until you find one that has a sweetness you enjoy. You may also discover that you prefer one type of sweetener in your coffee and a different type of sweetener in your baked goods. In addition, it takes different amounts of the different sweeteners to achieve the same final result. Therefore you will need to follow the specific instructions that accompany each type of sweetener and use the recommended amount of that sweetener to achieve the desired result.

1. **Sugar Alcohols:** They are sweet but they are not classified as sugars even though they are referred to as "sugar alcohols." Sugar alcohols do not contain any alcohol (ethanol). Sugar alcohols can cause gas, cramping, and diarrhea in some people. However, in some people these symptoms are temporary and they pass as the person's system gradually becomes accustomed to sugar alcohols. On a nutrition label sugar alcohols may be listed as: erythritol, glycerol, lactitol, maltitol, mannitol, sorbitol, xylitol, and a few other less common names. Some sugar-free foods may contain sugar

alcohol in addition to better known artificial sweeteners such as aspartame (NutriSweet) or sucralose (Splenda).

    a. **Erythritol** is a sugar alcohol that is naturally present in some plants. It contains approximately 6% of the calories and 70% of the sweetness of sucrose (table sugar). It may have a mild aftertaste and if consumed in quantity it may cause digestive problems. It does not cause spikes in blood sugar or insulin levels and it has no impact on cholesterol or triglyceride levels.

    b. **Xylitol** is a sugar alcohol. It has almost the same sweetness as sucrose but it only has about 65% (2.4 per gram) of the calories of sucrose. It doesn't cause spikes in blood sugar or insulin levels. If consumed in large amounts it may cause digestive problems. It is extremely toxic to dogs so you should not store it, or foods that contain it, where a dog can get to it because it could kill the dog.

2. **Aspartame:** It was discovered by accident in 1965 by James Schlatter while working as a chemist for G.D. Searle & Company. When submitted for FDA approval in 1975 the FDA found serious deficiencies in Searle's operations and practices. In 1980 the FDA concluded there was no relationship between aspartame and brain damage. However, the FDA did not approve aspartame in 1980. Later in 1981 aspartame was approved for use in a few foods. In 1983 it was approved for use in soft drinks. In 1996 is was approved as a general purpose sweetener. Aspartame is a combination of the two amino acids aspartic acid and phenylalanine. The human body can produce aspartic acid but phenylalanine must be obtained from food. When the body digests aspartame it breaks it down into methanol. Methanol is naturally present in very small quantities in some foods. However, in large quantities methanol may be harmful to the body. The human body converts methanol into formaldehyde which is then oxidized into formic acid. The amount of formaldehyde is trivial and theoretically it should not cause any harm to the body. Aspartame is approximately 200 times sweeter than table sugar so only a small amount is needed to achieve the desired degree of sweetness. In the year 2020 the internet contains approximately the same number of articles that praise aspartame as articles that condemn aspartame. This allows each person to make up his or her mind on whether or not aspartame is safe or not safe.

3. **Saccharin:** It was discovered by accident in 1879 at John Hopkins University by a researcher named Constantine Fahlberg. In 1884 he obtained a patent and he began to mass produce saccharin. In 1911

President Theodore (Teddy) Roosevelt made the following official statement: "Anybody who says saccharin is injurious to health is an idiot." Sales for saccharin increased significantly during World War II because sugar was rationed. Sales increased again in the 1960s and 1970s when people gradually became "weight and sugar conscious." Saccharin is an artificial sweetener that is about 300 to 400 times sweeter than table sugar so only a very small amount of saccharin is needed to achieve the desired level of sweetness. It is made by oxidizing o-toluene sulfonamide or phthalic anhydride which results in a white crystalline powder. In high concentrations saccharin may have a bitter aftertaste. Saccharin has **no calories**. It also has no nutrients. It is safe for diabetics to consume because saccharin does not impact blood sugar levels. It contains no carbohydrates and the human body cannot breakdown or absorb saccharin so it is expelled from the body unchanged. Therefore saccharin does not contribute to tooth decay or cavities. Saccharin is stable and it has a shelf life of many years. Studies on rats in the 1970s resulted in saccharin being banned in 1977. This was at approximately the same time that the artificial sweetener aspartame was first being introduced into the market. (Do you suppose this was just a convenient coincidence or could it have been intentionally orchestrated?) A careful and impartial review of the saccharin studies of the 1970s revealed that they were seriously flawed. Subsequent studies systematically reputed the original studies and those studies resulted in the removal of warning labels from products that contained saccharin in 2000 by the Department of Health and Human Services. In 2001 the Food and Drug Administration (FDA) declared that saccharin was safe for human consumption. In 2010 the Environmental Protection Agency (EPA) declared that saccharin was not a potential hazard to human health. Saccharine has been declared safe for human use by the World Health Organization (WHO) and by the European Food Safety Authority (EFSA). Saccharine may be used to sweeten beverages, or sprinkled on foods like table sugar, or used in baking recipes. However, only a very small amount is needed when compared to table sugar. Saccharin is sold under the brand names Necta Sweet, Sweet 'N Low, and Sweet Twin. Some of these brands may also contain dextrose (glucose) in addition to saccharin so you should read the ingredient label. (Necta Sweet does not contain any dextrose or lactose.) Saccharin is available in granular and liquid form in many grocery stores where table sugar is sold. According to the FDA, adults and children can consume saccharin in moderation without risk.

4. **Sucralose (Splenda):** Sucralose was discovered in 1976. Splenda was released in 1998. Sucralose is not a sugar even though it is advertised as being "made from sugar." It is a zero-calorie chlorinated artificial sweetener where 3 hydrogen-oxygen groups are replaced with chlorine. In simple terms, sucralose is chlorinated sugar. As chlorine gradually accumulates inside our bodies, chlorine may result in a variety of health problems. Although pure sucralose has no calories, Splenda contains the sugar glucose (dextrose) and the starch maltodextrin so it contains about 3.4 calories per gram. Maltodextrin may cause blood sugar spikes in some people. Sucralose is between 400 to 700 times sweeter than table sugar and this means that only a tiny amount of it is needed. In addition, it does not have a bitter aftertaste like some artificial sweeteners. Sucralose may *reduce the friendly bacteria* in your intestines without impacting the harmful bacteria. This can have a negative impact on your digestive system. At the beginning of the year 2020 it is not clear if sucralose increases, decreases, or has no impact on blood sugar and insulin levels. Studies on different groups of people have yielded conflicting results. Sucralose may be stable up to 350°F (120°C) and it might be safe to use in baking up to this temperature. However, it will decrease the baking time and the finished volume of the baked good. In addition, at temperatures higher than 350°F (120°C) sucralose breaks down and it may then interact with other ingredients with the result being that it may increase the risk of cancer.

5. **Stevia:** Stevia is a sweet herb that is called stevia rebaudiana and it can be grown in a home garden. It is considered safe to consume in its natural form. The leaves are harvested and then dried. The dried leaves can be steeped in hot tea to sweeten the tea. Or the dried leaves can be ground into a powder and then 1 teaspoon of the powder can be added to 2 cups of water and boiled for about 12 minutes and then strained through some cheesecloth to yield a sweet syrup. In the USA the FDA has not approved whole leaf stevia in processed foods primarily due to the lack of scientific research information about its short-term and long-term health impact. Whole leaf stevia and stevia extract may not be safe to consume during pregnancy primarily due to the lack of research on its effects. However, in Asia and in South America stevia leaves have been used for medicinal purposes and as a sweetener for centuries. Stevia leaves contain several sweet compounds. The two most important sweet compounds found in stevia leaves are stevioside and rebaudioside A (Reb-A). Both compounds are hundreds of times sweeter than sucrose (table sugar). In the USA

the FDA has approved one refined form of stevia as being safe to use. On an ingredient label it may be listed as stevia extract or as stevia rebaudiana. The commercially processed stevias available in grocery stores, such as Stevia in the Raw and Truvia, do not contain the entire stevia leaf. Instead they are made from a refined stevia extract called rebaudioside A (Reb-A). Rev-A is about 200 times sweeter than table sugar. Most of the commercially processed stevias are blends of Reb-A and other sweeteners, such as sugar alcohol (erythritol), or sugar glucose (dextrose), or the starch maltodextrin. Maltodextrin may cause blood sugar spikes in some people. Many of the stevias also contain "natural flavors" which may be highly processed chemicals and they are not healthy. Commercially processed stevias contain almost no calories. Some commercial brands of stevia may be used in place of sugar in baking but you should follow the baking instructions for the type of stevia you purchase. However, stevia may add a licorice aftertaste to your baked goods. Reb-A stevia may help to reduce bad LDL cholesterol, increase good HDL cholesterol, reduce triglycerides, and reduce the risk of some types of cancer, such as breast, leukemia, lung, and stomach cancers. Stevia is stable up to 392°F (200°C) and it can be used in baked goods that are baked below this temperature. Some people like the taste of stevia and some people do not.

Chapter Summary and Recommendation

Based on all the information presented in this chapter, saccharin is the one sweetener that has performed well in research studies since the 1980s. It does not appear to have any unhealthy long-term side effects. The human body cannot breakdown or absorb saccharin so it is expelled from the body unchanged. Saccharin does not contribute to tooth decay or cavities. Saccharin can be safely added to baked goods. The FDA has stated that adults and children can consume saccharin in moderation without risk. Therefore in the early part of the year 2020, saccharin might the best choice for a sweetener because it has no calories and it does not cause the health problems attributed to table sugar.

Saccharin is sold under the brand names Necta Sweet, Sweet 'N Low, and Sweet Twin. Some of these brands may also contain dextrose (glucose) in addition to saccharin so you should read the ingredient label.

Necta Sweet does not contain any dextrose or lactose. Necta Sweet is sold in the following two sizes. Both of the following sizes of Necta Sweet tablets quickly dissolve in water:

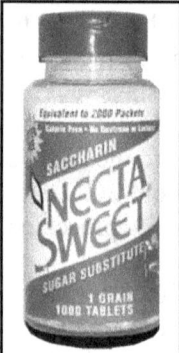

Saccharin
Tablets
1 Grain Each

a. 1/4 Grain per tablet which is equivalent in sweetening power to 1 teaspoon of sugar.
b. 1 Grain per tablet which is equivalent in sweetening power to 4 teaspoons of sugar.

In reasonable amounts saccharin does not have any aftertaste. However, if too much saccharin is used then it may result in an unpleasant aftertaste.

Chapter Fourteen

Protein

The human body must have fuel from food in order to survive. Protein is one of the three primary sources of fuel that the body needs. The other two sources are fat and carbohydrates.

About 20% of a person's body consists of protein. However, the human body does not store extra protein. The daily protein intake required by the human body depends on a person's age, gender, muscle mass, activity level, and health. Another important issue is a person's physical goals for their body, such as sport athletes, professional dancers, boxers, and weight lifters.

Protein is used by the body to make muscles, tendons, organs, and skin. It is also used to manufacture hormones, enzymes, and other molecules that are essential to the proper function and health of the human body.

Proteins are composed of amino acids. Some amino acids can be manufactured by the human body and some cannot. The amino acids that the body cannot make are called "essential" amino acids. These "essential" amino acids must be acquired from food sources. Since the bodies of animals perform the same basic functions as the bodies of people, animal products provide all the "essential" amino acids that are required by people. And animal amino acids are in the proper proportion required by people. Animal products include beef, fish, lamb, pork, poultry, dairy products, and whole eggs.

Protein From Animal Sources and Plant Sources

When protein is eaten it is broken down inside the body into amino acids. Protein and amino acids are necessary for almost every metabolic process within the human body. Protein from animal sources contain the proper balance of amino acids needed by the human body including all the essential amino acids. However, protein from plant sources are low in some necessary amino acids such as isoleucine, lysine, methionine, and tryptophan. Beans, lentils, and nuts are lacking one or more of the essential amino acids. Although soy contains all the necessary amino acids, two of the amino acids are present in trivial amounts and soy cannot supply enough of these amino acids to maintain a healthy body.

In addition the following nutrients that are present in animal protein are frequently lacking in plant protein:

1. **DHA:** This is an essential omega-3 fat called docosahexaenoic acid and it is found in fatty fish. It helps maintain a healthy brain.

2. **Heme Iron:** It is present in meat and the highest amount is in red meats. The heme iron in meat is more easily absorbed by the human body than heme iron from plant sources.

3. **Vitamin B12:** It is present in dairy products, fish, meat, and poultry.

4. **Vitamin D:** It is present in dairy, eggs, and oily fish. Although it is present in some plants, the vitamin D in animal products is more efficiently absorbed and used by the human body.

5. **Zinc:** It is present in beef, lamb, and pork. Although it is present in some plants, the zinc in animal products is more efficiently absorbed and used by the human body.

On the other hand, plants contain several nutrients that are not found in animal sources. In order to maintain optimal health we should eat plant foods in addition to animal products.

The Importance of Protein

Protein rich foods are important for the following reasons:

1. **Age:** As we age our bodies gradually need more protein in order to maintain optimal health. Protein helps to minimize muscle loss as we age.

2. **Injuries:** When people are recovering from injuries their bodies need more protein to repair the damaged tissues in their bodies.

3. **Muscles:** Protein rich foods help to build new muscles and they help to maintain existing muscles in firm condition.

4. **Strength:** To add more muscle to our body we need to synthesize more protein than we burn. This is called a positive nitrogen balance because protein has a high nitrogen content. Building new muscles and properly maintaining existing muscles results in a stronger body.

5. **Prevent Muscle Loss:** Dieting is frequently the cause of muscle loss. Insufficient protein intake will cause our body to automatically burn muscle tissue instead of fat tissue to compensate for the protein deficiency.

6. **Diabetes:** Protein may help reduce the risk of diabetes.

7. **Physical Activity:** People who are physically active require more protein that people who are less active.

8. **Metabolism:** Protein rich foods may increase the body's normal metabolism by as much as 100 calories per day.

9. **More Filling:** Protein rich foods are more filling than foods that contain less protein. Protein is more filling than fats or carbs.

10. **Calorie Intake:** Protein rich foods may reduce our appetite and this may reduce the total number of calories we eat each day.

11. **Food Cravings:** Protein rich foods may minimize our food cravings and the desire for a late-night snack with the result that we may voluntarily eat less food each day.

12. **Weight Loss:** When protein is approximately 30% of our total daily calories this results in the optimal weight loss following any diet. And protein makes it easier to stick to any weight loss diet regardless of whether it is high carb, low carb, high fat, or low fat.

Protein Myths

Protein does not cause kidney damage in healthy people. A high protein diet helps to reduce blood pressure and prevent diabetes which are two of the causes of kidney diseases. However, people who have already been diagnosed with kidney problems may need to restrict their protein intake if their physician recommends it.

Protein does not cause osteoporosis or bone or joint diseases. A protein rich diet can actually help prevent bone and joint problems and improve bone heath.

Good Sources of Protein

1. **Red Meat:** Some scientific studies have reported that commercially processed red meat is correlated to an increase in some health risks. However, studies on fresh red meat do not show any correlation between fresh red meat and increased health risks. Fresh red meat does not contain the additives and the preservatives that are added to commercially processed red meat. This indicates that the additives and the preservatives are the real health risks and not the red meat to which they have been added. This is an example of how some scientific research studies that failed to account for all the important variables reached a conclusion that was not valid.

2. **Animal Protein:** It helps lower cholesterol levels, reduce the risk of heart disease, facilitate weight loss, and increase the amount of lean muscles. It also helps reduce the loss of muscles that gradually occurs with increasing age. Good sources of animal protein include beef, chicken breast with the skin removed, cheese, cottage cheese, eggs, whole milk, fish, shrimp, and turkey breast.

3. **Plant Protein:** Plants that are rich in protein include almonds, artichokes, asparagus, beans, broccoli, Brussels sprouts, corn, green

peas, lentils, quinoa, oats, peanuts, potatoes, raw nuts, spinach, sweet potatoes, and wild rice. Some fruits contain low amounts of protein.

4. **A Balanced Healthy Diet:** A healthy diet should include plants that contain protein and a variety of sources of animal protein in order to reap the benefits of both types of protein. A balanced diet will result in optimal health.

Chapter Fifteen

Vitamins, Minerals, Amino Acids, Antioxidants, and Supplements

On pages 278 to 282 in the appendix there are tables that show the Recommended Daily Dietary Allowances (RDA) for the vitamins and minerals mentioned in this chapter.

Balanced nutrition is critical to the optimal functioning of the body because different types of nutrition compliment one another. If the body has a deficiency in any of the nutritional elements that it requires then some of the body's normal functions will not be able to do their work efficiently. This reduction in performance may negatively impact health in different ways, and the long-term cumulative impact of this deficiency could have serious long-term health consequences.

Natural versus Artificial Nutrients

The human body absorbs and uses nutrients from natural food sources in a more efficient manner than artificial nutrients such as supplements, or as "enriched" or "fortified" nutrients added to specific foods. These artificial nutrients may not contribute to long-term good health as effectively as natural nutrients. However, it is important to remember that artificial nutrients are better than no nutrients.

The Amount of Nutrients in Different Foods

Most foods contain a reasonable number of different vitamins, minerals, amino acids, and antioxidants. A specific food may contain an average amount of a nutrient, or a small amount of a nutrient, or a lot of a nutrient. The appendix contains tables on pages 284 to 298 that show how much of each nutrient is in a variety of the more popular foods. The foods that are specifically mentioned in this chapter will be foods that contain a lot of the nutrient being discussed. If a food is not mentioned then that does not mean the food is missing that nutrient. It simply means that the food contains a low amount or an average amount of the nutrient being reviewed. Or the food may be a food that is not as popular as other foods and therefore it is not mentioned.

Vitamins

Vitamins can help prevent and/or treat some diseases. Vitamins also facilitate some body functions, and they perform some functions that cannot be performed by other nutrients. Natural vitamins occur in food. Artificial vitamins are available as supplements. However, the human body processes and uses natural vitamins more efficiently than artificial vitamins. Although the human body can benefit from a reasonable amount of each type of vitamin, too much of some vitamins can have a negative impact on the body. Therefore it is important to avoid consuming an excessive amount of any one vitamin unless you have been advised to do so by your physician.

Most vitamins are sensitive to light, temperature, and moisture. Therefore the way that foods are stored and processed can significantly impact the viability of the vitamins that were originally in the food. Raw foods contain a superior quantity and quality of vitamins and they should be considered when unprocessed foods are a healthy option, such as raw carrots, broccoli, cabbage, cauliflower, and fruits.

Do not chop, cut, slice, or peel any fruit or vegetable until you are ready to eat it or use it in a recipe because the nutrients in food gradually begin to decline after it has been cut.

Classification of Vitamins

Vitamins are divided into two major groups based on how they dissolve. The way that vitamins dissolve also determines how they are absorbed, stored, and expelled from the body. Water soluble vitamins cannot be stored in the body but fat soluble vitamins can be stored in the body. The word soluble means how something dissolves.

It is extremely rare for an excessive quantity of any vitamin to be consumed when eating a variety of foods in a well-balanced diet. However, vitamin supplements that contain an excessive amount of any vitamin may not be a healthy choice.

1. **Water Soluble (Vitamins B, C, and Choline):** They dissolve in water and are quickly transported by the blood to all the tissues of the body. However, the body cannot store these vitamins and any vitamins that are not needed simply pass through the body and they are soon expelled in the urine. Therefore these vitamins need to be supplied to the body on a daily basis. The exception is vitamin B12 which can be stored in the liver. Also an excessive amount of vitamin C may result in diarrhea. Vitamin A in the form of beta-carotene is also water soluble until the body converts the beta-carotene into vitamin A and then vitamin A becomes fat soluble. Although unneeded quantities of these vitamins will be removed by the kidneys and expelled in the urine, it is not advisable to consume an excessive amount of these vitamins.

2. **Fat Soluble (Vitamins A, D, E, and K):** They dissolve in fats and they are absorbed into fat globules that travel in the blood to all parts of the body where they are absorbed into body tissues. After fat soluble vitamins are absorbed into the tissues of the body they usually remain there until they are needed, except for vitamin K. Fat soluble vitamins are more efficiently absorbed by the body if they are consumed with fats. Therefore a low-fat diet may not be a

healthy choice. If an excessive amount of these vitamins are absorbed then they may increase the body's susceptible to specific diseases. Therefore vitamin supplements that contain excessive amounts of fat soluble vitamins may not be healthy unless they have been specifically prescribed for you by your doctor.

List of Vitamins

1. **Vitamin A (Retinol and Retinal):** It may improve the vitality of the hair. It may help prevent eye problems, night blindness, cataracts, and macular degeneration. It may help treat acne and other skin problems. It may help optimize your body's immune system by enhancing the creation and function of the white blood cells that help wounds to heal, and remove bacteria from the blood, and prevent infection. It may be beneficial to bone growth and healthy bones. The small intestine converts beta-carotene into vitamin A and this form of vitamin A may help reduce the gradual deterioration of vision with age, and it may help reduce the risk of cancer (bladder, cervical, lung, prostate). Vitamin A supplements do not have these same benefits. Vitamin A is fat soluble and it can be stored in the body. Therefore an excessive consumption of vitamin A from supplements can negatively impact your health. The best way to obtain vitamin A is by eating foods that are rich in vitamin A or beta-carotene. Vitamin A is in apricots, avocados, butter, cantaloupes, carrots, cheese, eggs, fish, lettuce, milk, pistachio nuts, and shrimp. Beta-carotene is in apricots, beef liver, Brussels sprouts, butter, cantaloupes, carrots, green peas, lettuce, peppers (sweet and hot), pumpkins, spinach, squash, sweet potatoes, and tomatoes. Many people get an adequate amount of vitamin A from their normal diet and a vitamin A supplement is not necessary and a vitamin A supplement may lead to health problems.

2. **Vitamin B1 (Thiamine):** It may improve the health of hair, skin, and muscles. It may enhance blood circulation, brain function, heart function, nerve function, and the body's metabolism of food. It may help prevent heart disease and indigestion. It may help prevent or slow down the onset of Alzheimer's disease or dementia that is due to the normal aging process. Vitamin B1 is in beans, Brazil nuts, hazelnuts, ham/pork, lentils, macadamia nuts, peanuts, pecans, pistachio nuts, red potatoes, and squash.

3. **Vitamin B2 (Riboflavin):** It may improve blood health, brain functions, hair health, and skin health. It may help treat anemia, cataracts, and skin problems. It may enhance the body's immune system, nervous system, and the body's metabolism of food. Vitamin B2 is in almonds, cheese, corn, eggs, ham/pork, herring, mackerel, milk, mushrooms, salmon, sardines, trout, and turkey.

4. **Vitamin B3 (Niacin):** It may improve blood health, brain functions, and nerve functions. It may lower blood pressure and cholesterol levels. It may help prevent diabetes, diarrhea, heart problems, and indigestion. It may enhance eye, hair, and skin health. It may help treat skin problems and relieve migraine headaches. Vitamin B3 is in food and the body can make B3 with the assistance of vitamin B6 and the amino acid tryptophan. Vitamin B3 is in avocados, beans, beef, carrots, chicken, cocoa powder, fish, green peas, ham/pork, lentils, mushrooms, nuts, peanut butter, potatoes, shellfish, squash, turkey, and whole grains.

5. **Vitamin B5 (Pantothenic Acid):** It may help metabolize food and help the body make hemoglobin, lipids, and steroid hormones. It may help treat arthritis, infections, and skin problems. It may help reduce blood pressure and stress. It may help delay the natural graying of the hair. Vitamin B5 is in avocados, beans, cashews, chicken, eggs, hazelnuts, lentils, lobster, macadamia nuts, mackerel, peanuts, pecans, salmon, trout, turkey, walnuts, and wheat.

6. **Vitamin B6 (Pridoxine, Pyridoxine, and Pyridoxamine):** It is a water-soluble essential vitamin that your body cannot make. It may help control appetite, make red blood cells, reduce clogged arteries, and reduce the risk of heart disease. It may enhance brain functions, nerve functions, and the immune system. It may help treat anemia, convulsions, diabetes, insomnia, excessive menstrual bleeding, motion sickness, piles, and stress. It may help reduce the risk of retinal disorders and age-related macular degeneration (AMD). It may reduce the risk of cancer (breast, colon). It may help treat morning sickness, nausea, and vomiting during pregnancy. It may improve mood and reduce depression in older people. Vitamin B6 is in bananas, beans, corn, hazelnuts, lentils, pistachio nuts, salmon, sunflower seeds, tuna, turkey, and walnuts. However, a vitamin supplement that contains too much B6 may cause health problems.

7. **Vitamin B7 (Biotin):** May also be referred to as vitamin H. It may enhance healthy bones, hair, and nails. It may help regulate blood sugar levels. It may improve the body's metabolism of food, and it may help treat skin problems. Vitamin B7 is in almonds, cauliflower, eggs, green peas, lentils, mushrooms, oatmeal, pecans, spinach, sunflower seeds, sweet potatoes, and walnuts. Raw or lightly processed foods contain more B7 than cooked foods.

8. **Vitamin B9 (Folate, Folacin, Folic Acid):** It may enhance nerve functions. It may be very useful in the treatment of anemia, gout, indigestion, skin problems, and unusual brain growth. It may increase the growth of red blood cells and it may help prevent colon

cancer and heart diseases. It may help prevent breast cancer in women who consume alcohol. It is very important for the creation of new cells. It may help prevent brain and spinal birth defects if consumed at the beginning and during a pregnancy. It is in avocados, asparagus, beans, beets, broccoli, Brussels sprouts, cauliflower, green peas, hazelnuts, kale, lentils, peanuts, pistachio nuts, spinach, and walnuts. Many people do not get enough vitamin B9.

9. **Vitamin B12 (Cobalamin or Cyanocobalamin):** It may help in the production of the cells necessary for healthy hair, nails, and skin. It may help in the production of healthy red blood cells. It may help minimize the symptoms and the side effects of anemia, kidney problems, liver problems, mouth ulcers, pregnancy, and smoking tobacco. It may help improve bone health and decrease the risk of osteoporosis. It may help prevent macular degeneration in the eyes as a result of the normal aging process. It may help prevent memory loss or dementia due to aging. It may help prevent birth defects due to a vitamin B12 deficiency in the early stages of pregnancy, and it may also help prevent a premature birth or miscarriage. When used in conjunction with vitamins B6 and B9, it may help prevent heart problems and strokes. Vitamin B12 is only present naturally in animal and dairy products such as butter, cheese, eggs, milk, yogurt, beef, chicken, fish, ham/pork, shellfish, and turkey. However, artificial B12 may be added to some food products and it is also available as a vitamin supplement. As the human body ages it has more difficulty absorbing vitamin B12 from food and your doctor may recommend a vitamin B12 supplement, such as *sublingual vitamin B-12*, based on your blood test results.

10. **Vitamin C (Ascorbic Acid):** It is a powerful antioxidant that may help neutralize harmful molecules that can cause cell damage. It may enhance the healing of wounds. It may help prevent or treat some cancers (breast, mouth, throat, stomach), diabetes, eye problems (cataracts), heart disease, inflammation, internal bleeding, kidney problems, lead poisoning, piles, scurvy, and stress. It may help lower cholesterol levels, enhance skin health, and enhance the immune system. Scientific evidence that it has any beneficial impact on the common cold is questionable. It is in blackberries, broccoli, Brussels sprouts, cabbage, cantaloupes, cauliflower, chestnuts, green peas, kiwi, oranges, peppers (sweet and hot), pineapples, and strawberries.

11. **Vitamin D:** It is called the "sunshine vitamin" because your body can make vitamin D when your skin is exposed to sunlight (about 15 minutes per day). Vitamin D is a fat-soluble vitamin and it can be stored in the human body. It includes vitamins D1, D2, and D3. It may help the body absorb calcium and phosphorus. It may help in the normal growth and health of the bones and teeth. It may help reduce the risk of catching the flu. It may help treat arthritis, depression, diabetes, and rickets. It may help lower blood pressure, lower blood sugar levels, prevent tooth decay, enhance the body's immune system, and facilitate bone mending. It may help prevent cancer and heart disease. It may help prevent multiple sclerosis in people who have osteoarthritis. It may help reduce appetite and increase weight loss in people who are overweight. Foods that contain natural vitamin D include eggs, catfish, halifut, mackerel, salmon, and sardines. Foods that are usually "fortified" with artificial vitamin D include milk, orange juice, and yogurt. Vitamin D supplements are also a reasonable option if your physical exam indicates that you have a deficiency and your doctor recommends a vitamin D supplement.

12. **Vitamin E (Alpha-Tocopherol):** It acts as an antioxidant that may help neutralize harmful molecules that can cause cell damage. It may facilitate tissue healing. It may improve blood circulation and help prevent Alzheimer's disease, brain malfunction, heart disease, and sterility. It may help provide relief from eye problems, menopause, and menstrual discomfort. It may be used to enhance the condition of the skin but it does not prevent wrinkles or slow down the normal aging process. Vitamin E is in almonds, apricots, asparagus, avocados, blackberries, Brazil nuts, Brussels sprouts, corn, hazelnuts, herring, kiwi, lobster, mackerel, olives, peanuts, pine nuts, pistachio nuts, raspberries, salmon, sardines, snapper, spinach, squash, walnuts, and wheat.

13. **Vitamin K (Phylloquinone):** It is sometimes called the "forgotten vitamin." It may help prevent internal bleeding, kidney stones, excessive menstrual flow, menstrual pain, osteoporosis, and plaque buildup inside the arteries. It may enhance bone metabolism, nerve communications, and blood clotting. Individuals who are taking a blood-thinner medication should avoid consuming too much vitamin K. Vitamin K is in cashews, hazelnuts, most fruits (except citrus), pine nuts, and most vegetables (except mushrooms). It is extremely high in asparagus, broccoli, Brussels sprouts, cabbage, blackberries, blueberries, cashews, grapes, kiwi, lettuce, pears, plums, pine nuts, raspberries, spinach, and tomatoes.

Not Yet Formally Classified as a Vitamin or a Mineral

1. **Choline:** Because it has benefits similar to B vitamins it is usually discussed with vitamins. It is water soluble. It may enhance brain, liver, muscle, and nerve functions. It may help the body metabolize and transport fats, and make cells. It may reduce the risk of breast cancer, heart disease, strokes, and the loss of memory. If pregnant women consume an adequate amount of choline it may help to prevent a variety of birth defects in their babies. The consumption of alcohol can increase the body's need for more choline. The liver can make small quantities of choline but it may not be enough for optimal health, especially with advancing age. Choline is in asparagus, beef, broccoli, Brussels sprouts, butter, cauliflower, chicken, cheese, eggs, fish, green peas, milk, mushrooms, nuts, shellfish, spinach, turkey, whole grains, and yogurt.

Minerals

Minerals work in harmony with vitamins in the formation, growth, and function of healthy cells. The difference between a vitamin and a mineral is that a vitamin contains carbon and it is organic, but a mineral does not contain carbon and it is inorganic. Health problems due to a vitamin deficiency are usually easily treatable once the deficiency is identified. However, a deficiency in some minerals can result in serious health problems that could result in death if not properly treated.

Minerals assist in a variety of normal body functions such as helping to keep your bones, teeth, brain, eyes, heart, and muscles in good condition. Some minerals are components of enzymes which are protein based molecules that enhance the chemical reactions within the body.

Minerals are separated into two groups:

1. **Major Minerals or Macro-minerals:** Required in large quantities to keep the body functioning properly. They include calcium, chloride, magnesium, phosphorus, potassium, sodium, and sulfur. (Table salt contains 40% sodium and 60% chloride. Iodized table salt also includes the trace mineral iodine.)

2. **Trace Minerals or Micro-minerals:** Only necessary in small amounts and they help facilitate normal body functions. They include chromium, copper, iodine, fluoride, iron, manganese, molybdenum, selenium, and zinc.

List of Minerals

1. **Calcium (Ca):** It may help build and maintain healthy bones and teeth. It may help with blood clotting, muscle movements, nerve functions, and kidney functions. It may help lower cholesterol

levels and blood pressure. It may help regulate the rhythm of the heart. It may assist in hormone secretion and the activation of enzymes. It may help reduce the risk of colon cancer. It may help with insomnia. Calcium is present in large quantities in beans, black pepper, broccoli, cheese, crab, eggs, garlic, herring, kale, lobster, milk, oats, olives, oranges, nuts, seeds, sardines, shrimp, spinach, and yogurt. However, diets that include too much calcium may increase the risk of prostate cancer.

2. **Chloride (Cl):** It is essential to the efficient digestion of food inside the stomach. It may help the liver remove waste from the blood stream. It may function as an electrolyte and enhance the electrical communication between cells. It may help balance fluids inside the body. Chloride is in table salt (40% sodium and 60% chloride) and soy sauce.

3. **Chromium (Cr):** It may help to process glucose, and maintain normal blood sugar levels, and enhance the function of insulin. It may help reduce cholesterol and triglyceride levels which may reduce the risk of heart attacks and strokes. It may also help reduce the risk of cancer and diabetes. It may help reduce the appetite and control the amount of fat inside the body. It may help generate and maintain muscles. Chromium is in barley, broccoli, eggs, grapes, grass-fed beef, oatmeal, potatoes, red wine, and sweet potatoes.

4. **Copper (Cu):** It may help make red blood cells, metabolize iron, maintain healthy bones, improve skin health, and enhance the immune system. It may help produce hemoglobin and it may help protect cells from damage due to free radicals. Copper is in asparagus, avocadoes, beans, black pepper, cocoa powder, celery, corn, crab, garlic, green peas, haddock, herring, kiwi, lentils, lobster, mahi mahi, mushrooms, oats, nuts, olives, peppers (hot), pineapples, sardines, seeds, shrimp, tomatoes, trout, and wheat.

5. **Fluoride (F):** It may help in the formation of strong bones. It may help in the creation of tooth enamel and it may help prevent tooth cavities. It may help in the prevention of osteoporosis. Fluoride is in grapes, potatoes, raisins, red wine, and shellfish. However, too much fluoride can cause serious health problems in children.

6. **Iodine (I):** It may help the thyroid function properly, help regulate body temperature, enhance muscle and nerve functions, reduce fatigue, and aid in reproduction and growth. It may help prevent goiter and congenital thyroid disorder. It may help reduce the risk of mental retardation in babies inside pregnant women. Iodine is in eggs, seafood, seaweed, whey, and iodized salt.

7. **Iron (Fe):** It may benefit blood hemoglobin and muscle myoglobin.

It may improve the health of the skin. It can prevent anemia. It may be necessary for the production of some amino acids, collagen, hormones, and neurotransmitters. It may help the body resist disease and minimize fatigue and stress. Iron is in asparagus, beans, beef, chicken, cocoa powder, corn, eggs, ham/pork, herring, lentils, mackerel, nuts, oats, olives, sardines, seeds, spinach, trout, tuna, turkey, and wheat. However, it is easier for the human body to absorb iron from animal products compared to plant foods.

8. **Magnesium (Mg):** It may help build and maintain healthy bones and teeth. Approximately two-thirds of the magnesium in the body is stored in the bones. It may help metabolize calcium and vitamin C. It may work with calcium to enhance muscle and nerve functions and joint flexibility, and it may help control blood clotting, blood sugar, and blood pressure. It may help regulate the beating of the heart and minimize the risk of heart disease and heart failure. It may help reduce migraine headaches, muscle spasms, stress, and tension. Magnesium is in beans, cocoa powder, corn, mackerel, oats, nuts, seeds, spinach, and wheat.

9. **Manganese (Mn):** It may help form and maintain healthy bones. It may act as an antioxidant that may help neutralize harmful molecules, such as free radicals, that can cause cell damage. It may help repair damaged tissues and heal wounds. It may improve digestion and help metabolize amino acids, vitamins B1 and E, carbohydrates, cholesterol, fats, and protein. It may help provide nourishment to the brain and the nerves. It may help regulate blood sugar levels. It may help maintain the production of normal sex hormones and enhance fertility. Manganese is in beans, cocoa powder, grapes, lentils, nuts, seeds, spinach, trout, and wheat.

10. **Molybdenum (Mo):** It is a part of several different enzymes. It may help metabolize carbohydrates, copper, fats, and iron. It may help prevent tooth decay and cavities. It may help prevent anemia and it may enhance the mental perception of well-being. Molybdenum is in almonds, beans, cashews, cheese, chestnuts, cottage cheese, lentils, milk, peanuts, peas, soy beans, tomatoes, leafy vegetables, whole grains, and yogurt.

11. **Phosphorus (P):** It may help build and maintain healthy bones and teeth. It may help metabolize calcium and vitamin C. It may reduce the risk of heart disease. It may help make bile and prevent the accumulation of fatty acids in the liver. It may enhance bowel movements, digestion, and sexual health. Phosphorus is in beans, beef, chicken, cocoa powder, corn, eggs, fish, garlic, green peas, lentils, milk, oats, pork, nuts, seeds, shellfish, turkey, and wheat.

12. **Potassium (K):** It may help balance body fluids, lower blood pressure, maintain a steady heart beat, assist in muscle and nerve functions, and improve the condition and health of the skin. It may help in the metabolism of carbohydrates. It may function as an electrolyte and enhance the electrical communication between cells. It may work with sodium to regulate waste and it may stimulate the kidneys to remove poisonous wastes from the body. It may help reduce the discomfort of, or prevent, muscle cramps. Potassium is in avocados, bananas, beans, cod, cocoa powder, halibut, herring, lentils, oats, nuts, sardines, seeds, spinach, tuna, and wheat. The natural potassium in food does not cause health problems but too much potassium in supplements may result in health problems.

13. **Selenium (Se):** It may act as an antioxidant that may help neutralize harmful molecules, such as free radicals, that can cause cell damage. If may enhance the immune system. It may help regulate the hormone activity of the thyroid and it may assist in the proper function of the pancreas. It may enhance testosterone production and male fertility. It may help reduce the risk of some cancers and heart disease. It may help repair DNA. It may slow down the natural aging process that results from the hardening of tissues due to oxidation. Selenium is in beans, beef, Brazil nuts, cashews, cheese (cheddar, Swiss), chicken, cocoa powder, corn, eggs, fish, ham/pork, oats, peanuts, seeds, shellfish, turkey, walnuts, and wheat.

14. **Sodium (Na):** It may help balance body fluids, maintain proper levels of acidity and alkalinity, and assist in muscle and nerve functions. It may help metabolize carbohydrates, fat, and protein, and help prevent blood clots. It may function as an electrolyte and enhance the electrical communication between cells. Too much sodium may increase blood pressure but a decrease in the amount of sodium to a normal level may lower blood pressure. Sodium is in table salt (40% sodium and 60% chloride) and soy sauce.

15. **Sulfur (S):** It may contribute to healthy hair, nails, and skin. It may assist in enzyme reactions and the metabolism of protein. It may help remove toxins from the body. Sulfur is a component of thiamin and some amino acids. Sulfur is present in apricots, asparagus, broccoli, Brussels sprouts, cauliflower, chicken, collard greens, eggs, garlic, grass-fed beef, kale, milk from grass-fed cows, nuts, onions, peaches, pork, radishes, spinach, and wild caught seafood.

16. **Zinc (Zn):** It may act as an antioxidant that may help neutralize harmful molecules, such as free radicals, that can cause cell damage. It may help form new cells, enzymes, proteins, and it may help wounds to heal. It may help release vitamin A stored in the

liver. It may help in the metabolism of phosphorus. It may help the prostate to function correctly and aid in the creation of male hormones. It may help stabilize the blood and maintain a proper alkalinity balance. It may help the immune system defend against bacteria and viruses and it may help in the healing of wounds. It may enhance the senses of smell and taste. It may be essential during pregnancy and it may help in the healthy growth and development of young children. It may help in the development of the reproductive organs during the different stages of growth. A zinc deficiency may contribute to hair loss. Zinc is in beans, beef, cheese, chicken, cocoa powder, corn, eggs, green peas, ham/pork, herring, lentils, oats, nuts, sardines, seeds, shellfish, tuna, turkey, and wheat. It is easier for the human body to absorb zinc from animal products compared to plant foods.

Amino Acids

Amino acids are any organic compound that contains carboxyl and an amino group. Amino acids can help build muscles, enhance the immune system, and provide energy. Amino acids may help increase lean muscles and reduce body fat. Amino acids may help prevent the loss of lean muscles during a prolonged illness that requires bed rest. Amino acids may also help prevent the loss of lean muscles in athletes, and in elderly adults as a result of the normal aging process.

Amino acid deficiencies may impact the growth and repair of muscles, and also negatively impact the body's digestive, immune, nerve, and reproductive systems. Some of the symptoms of a possible amino acid deficiency are bone loss, brittle nails, dry skin, increased appetite, puffiness, swelling, and hair thinning, loss, and splitting.

Good sources of amino acids in animal foods include beef, cheese, chicken, duck, eggs, halibut, lamb, mackerel, meat, milk, salmon, sardines, tuna, turkey, venison, and yogurt. Good sources of amino acids in plant foods include almonds, amaranth, beans, buckwheat, chia seeds, chickpeas, flaxseeds, lintels, oats, peas, pistachios, pumpkin seeds, quinoa, soybeans, walnuts, and whole grains.

It is unlikely that an unhealthy amount of amino acids can be consumed from natural sources. However, amino acid or protein supplements may cause an excess of amino acids in the body and this may result in bad breath, constipation, kidney problems, and an increase in weight.

The body needs 20 different amino acids to function efficiently.

Amino acids may be separated into three groups:

1. **Essential Amino Acids:** They cannot be produced by the body and they must be acquired from food sources. The nine essential amino

acids are histidine, isoleucine, leucine, lysine, methionine, phenylalanine, threonine, tryptophan, and valine. Foods that contain all nine essential amino acids are called "complete proteins" and they are present in animal foods and some plant foods. Animal foods include dairy, eggs, fish, meat, and poultry. Plant foods include buckwheat, hemp seed, quinoa, and soy.

2. **Conditionally Essential Amino Acids:** These are nonessential amino acids that the body can produce in sufficient quantity when the body is healthy. However, during sickness or stress or when fighting cancer, the body cannot produce enough of them to supply the body with the quantity it needs. In these situations the body requires that additional quantities of these nonessential amino acids be obtained from food sources or supplements. Conditionally essential amino acids include arginine, cysteine, glutamine, glycine, proline, serine, and tyrosine. However, under normal circumstances these are classified as nonessential amino acids.

3. **Nonessential Amino Acids:** They can be produced by the body. They eleven nonessential amino acids include alanine, arginine, asparagine, aspartate, cysteine, glutamate, glutamine, glycine, proline, serine, and tyrosine.

List of Amino Acids

1. **Alanine:** It may help the body metabolize food and provide energy for the brain, muscles, and the central nervous system.

2. **Arginine:** It may help reduce the effect of fatigue, and enhance the immune system, and improve the health of the heart.

3. **Asparagine:** It may act as a diuretic (promotes urination) and it may enhance brain and nerve functions.

4. **Aspartate:** It may help in the production of several amino acids including arginine, asparagine, and lysine.

5. **Cysteine:** It is the primary protein in the hair, nails, and skin, and it may be necessary for the production of collagen.

6. **Glutamate:** It may function as a neurotransmitter in the central nervous system.

7. **Glutamine:** It may enhance a variety of metabolic processes and it may provide energy to the various cells of the body.

8. **Glycine:** It may function as a neurotransmitter to enhance brain functions.

9. **Histidine:** It may help protect nerve cells. It may help with digestion, sleeping, the function of the sexual organs, and enhance the immune system.

10. **Isoleucine:** It may help maintain healthy muscles, and produce hemoglobin, and enhance the immune system. It may help injured bones and wounds to heal. It may help stimulate the loss of body fat. It may help reduce muscle soreness, and build new muscles, and reduce the effect of fatigue after exercising.

11. **Leucine:** It may help in the metabolism of protein and the repair of muscles. It may help control blood sugar levels, stimulate wound healing, and produce growth hormones. It may help stimulate the loss of body fat. It may help reduce muscle soreness, and build new muscles, and reduce the effect of fatigue after exercising.

12. **Lysine:** It may help in the metabolism of protein and calcium, and in the production of enzymes and hormones. It may help provide energy, produce hemoglobin, and enhance the immune system.

13. **Methionine:** It may help in the maintenance of the hair, nails, and skin. It may help in the metabolism of selenium and zinc. It may help in the detoxification of the body by helping to remove heavy metals such as lead and mercury. It may be essential to the growth of tissues.

14. **Phenylalanine:** It may help proteins and enzymes perform their functions, and it may help produce other amino acids.

15. **Proline:** It is present in collagen, and it may help improve metabolism, joint health, and skin elasticity.

16. **Serine:** It may be required for the metabolism of fat, and it may enhance muscle growth and the immune system.

17. **Threonine:** It may help in the maintenance of the skin and connecting tissues. It may help in the metabolism of fat and it may enhance the immune system. It may help reduce anxiety, depression, and indigestion.

18. **Tryptophan:** It may contribute to drowsiness. It may help maintain a proper balance of nitrogen, and it may help control the appetite and your mood. It may help synthesize serotonin which may help reduce anxiety, depression, and epilepsy, and it may enhance sleep. It may help in the normal growth of infants.

19. **Tyrosine:** It may help synthesize melanin and epinephrine which are thyroid hormones.

20. **Valine:** It may help provide energy and minimize fatigue and enhance physical activity. It may help decrease muscle soreness and it may help stimulate the growth and regeneration of muscles after exercising. It may help stimulate the loss of body fat.

Antioxidants

Antioxidants received their name because they prevent or stop damage to cells from "oxidants." Oxidants are free radicals created by the body or absorbed from the environment (air pollution, cigarette smoke). The purpose of oxidants created by the body is to enhance the body's natural immune system and help defend the body against microbes and viruses. However, unhealthy amounts of oxidants may be created by the body due to high blood sugar levels, excessive and prolonged exercise, and excessive consumption of polyunsaturated fats, vitamin C, vitamin E, copper, iron, magnesium, or zinc. An excess amount of oxidants (usually from supplements) may reduce your autoimmune response system, damage DNA, and increase the risk of diabetes, cancer, heart disease, and a premature death. The body needs to establish a healthy balance between oxidants and antioxidants because they both contribute to good health. Therefore high-dose antioxidant supplements should be avoided. Most multivitamins are low-dose sources of antioxidants. It is extremely rare to get too many antioxidants by eating healthy foods. Antioxidants are naturally present in berries, fruits, vegetables, coffee, green tea, chocolate, and wine. Small quantities of antioxidants are also in beef, ham/pork, poultry, and seafood. The oleocanthal in extra virgin olive oil has both antioxidant and anti-inflammatory properties. Antioxidants include vitamins A, C, and E, beta-carotene, magnesium, selenium, catechins, flavanols (chocolate), lutein, lycopene, phytoestrogens, and resveratrol (wine),

Supplements

Supplements are not supervised by the government and therefore the producers and sellers of supplements can make claims about their supplements that may or may not be true. The government does not monitor supplements for dosage, purity, quality, or safety.

Since the government does not inspect supplements, the companies that make supplements do not have to prove to the FDA that their products are safe, or that their products are what they are supposed to be, or that their products are effective. Therefore many weight-loss supplements are simply not effective despite the advertising claims made by those supplements. However, a few supplements may help you lose a small amount of weight.

If you decide to purchase some type of supplement you should research the company that makes the supplement very carefully before purchasing any type of supplement.

Also, before taking any type of supplement, including vitamin supplements, you should discuss the supplement with your physician and follow your doctor's advice about the supplement because your doctor is aware of your physical condition, your medical history, and any potential adverse interactions the supplement may have with any prescription medications you may be taking.

Glucomannan

The fiber supplement glucomannan may reduce tummy fat. It is a natural fiber obtained from the konjac plant which is also called elephant yam. It has few calories and it helps keep food in the stomach longer which delays the feeling of hunger for a longer period of time. It also reduces the absorption of protein and fat which may enhance weight loss. It feeds the beneficial bacteria in the intestines. It may reduce blood sugar, cholesterol, and triglycerides. It may help relieve constipation. However, it may cause bloating, soft stools, and it may interfere with some medications if they are taken at approximately the same time. It should be taken with water 30 minutes before a meal.

Prebiotics

Prebiotin, which is a prebiotic, contains all the fiber your body needs. It may also increase the amount of healthy bacteria you already have in your digestive system. It is plant based, contains very few calories, has a slightly sweet taste, and it can be added to water or sprinkled on foods. A healthy balance of good bacteria in your digestive system may enhance weight loss and the immune system, minimize or eliminate digestive problems, and improve mental health.

Probiotics

Probiotics are bacteria that may have a healthy impact on the body. Probiotics may add healthy bacteria to your digestive system. They may increase the healthy bacteria in the intestines and they may reduce the absorption of dietary fat. They may improve digestion, improve the function of the heart, and assist in weight loss. However, there are two potential problems with probiotics:
1. The heat and acid in the stomach may destroy some or most of the probiotic bacteria before it passes into the intestines.
2. There is no way to know if the bacteria in the probiotic is the type of bacteria that your body actually needs.

Sublingual Vitamin B-12

Sublingual B-12 with B-6, B9 (folic acid), and B12 (biotin) may enhance the nervous system, cardiovascular functions, and metabolism, and it may reduce stress and enhance energy.

Wheat Germ Oil Capsules

Although wheat germ has many impressive health benefits, it is not for everyone.
1. People who have an allergy or intolerance to wheat or gluten should avoid wheat germ supplements.

2. Wheat germ contains triglycerides and therefore it should not be used by people with heart disease.
3. When ingested, wheat germ may cause mild side effects in some people such as nausea or diarrhea.
4. When applied externally to the skin some people may experience an allergic skin reaction.

Consult your doctor before using wheat germ. If your doctor approves the use of wheat germ then you should begin using very small amounts to determine if you are allergic to it before using it regularly in normal amounts.

Wheat germ oil has a feel or consistency similar to olive oil, and a dark golden yellow color. It has a mild wheat smell and an oily nutty wheat taste. When you first purchase a new brand of wheat germ oil capsules you should crush or cut one capsule and verify that the oil has the correct feel, color, smell, and taste. If it doesn't then what you purchased is not pure wheat germ oil and it may not produce the many health benefits of real wheat germ oil.

Wheat germ oil that is derived using a "cold pressing" process is clean, and it does not require any added chemicals, and it preserves all the nutrients and fatty acids in the oil because many nutrients are degraded or destroyed by heat. Oil from organically grown wheat will not contain any residue from artificial fertilizers or from commercial pesticides. However, I could not find any "cold pressed" oil that was made from organically grown wheat.

Wheat germ oil is perishable. Wheat germ oil capsules should be stored in a cool dry place and they should not be exposed to intense light. The vitamins and nutrients in wheat germ oil are heat sensitive and they will degrade or be destroyed by heat, or when exposed to the air, or when exposed to an intense light. This is why most wheat germ oil capsules are sold in a container that is not transparent in order to protect the oil from light. A capsule helps to protect the oil from air. Store the capsules in a cool dry place but not in the refrigerator.

Many of the healthy nutrients in wheat germ are degraded or destroyed when exposed to heat. Therefore if you desire the maximum health benefit from wheat germ oil then it should not be used as a cooking oil or added to baked goods.

Wheat germ oil can be used both internally and externally. Wheat germ oil may have all of the following health benefits:
1. **Weight Loss:** It may enhance your metabolism and help reduce the extra fat on your body. It may also help by supplying one or more essential ingredients your body may not be receiving and thereby reduce your appetite.

2. **Antioxidant and Anti-Inflammatory:** It contains omega-3, omega-6, and omega-9 fatty acids which have antioxidant and anti-inflammatory properties.

3. **Brain and Nerve Functions:** It may enhance the function of the brain and the nervous system. It may help minimize the effects of stress. It may reduce the risk of dementia.

4. **Cardiovascular System:** It may help create healthy red blood cells. It may help improve the circulation of blood in the body. It may help regulate blood sugar levels. It may help normalize blood pressure. It may help decrease bad LDL cholesterol and increase good HDL cholesterol. This may help reduce the buildup of plaque inside the arteries which may help prevent hardening of the arteries and improve heart health.

5. **Cellular Metabolism:** It may help repair damaged cells. It contains the vitamins B1, B3, and B9 which are essential to cellular metabolism and which may improve alertness and energy levels, and facilitate weight loss.

6. **Digestion:** It contains fiber which is essential to the proper function of the digestive system, and fiber also helps prevent constipation.

7. **Disease Prevention:** It may help reduce the risk of cancer, diabetes, heart disease, and neurological disorders.

8. **Energy, Stamina, and Strength:** It may help enhance athletic performance.

9. **Hair:** It may help improve the health of hair, and it may help repair damaged hair. It may enhance the growth of hair and minimize hair loss.

10. **Immune System:** It may be an immunity booster. It may help destroy free radicals and prevent other germs from multiplying.

11. **Muscles:** It contains protein which may help build new muscles and repair existing muscles.

12. **Fertility, Pregnancy, and Birth Defects:** It may enhance fertility. It contains folates which may facilitate a healthy pregnancy and reduce the risk of neural defects in the baby. It may help prevent miscarriage and impotence. When applied externally to the skin it may help prevent stretch marks during pregnancy.

13. **Skin:** When consumed it may help improve skin health. When applied externally to the skin it may help reduce wrinkles and it may improve the appearance of blemishes and scars. It may help relieve dry skin, eczema, psoriasis, and sunburn.

14. **Vitamin E:** It is a good source of vitamin E. Vitamin E has a lot of health benefits including slowing down the normal aging process.

Wheat germ oil is an oil and it is not a solid. Any company that advertises dry wheat germ is selling something that has been refined and that product may or may not have all the health benefits you desire.

Wheat germ oil capsules are extremely difficult to find at local pharmacies and at health food stores, including GNC. You will probably have to shop online.

The following five brands of "cold pressed" wheat germ oil in soft gelatin capsules were available on Amazon at the beginning of the year 2020 and they were the only brands of "cold pressed" wheat germ oil I could find on Amazon at that time.

| Best Naturals | Puritan's Pride | Solgar | Swanson EFAs | Wholistic Botanicals |

The table on the next page shows a comparison of the five different brands of wheat germ oil capsules.

Explanation of the Information in the Table

Wheat germ oil should have an oily feel, a dark golden yellow color, a mild nutty smell, and a nutty wheat taste. Wheat germ oil should be rich in vitamin E.

All five brands felt oily.

The Swanson EFAs (Essential Fatty Acids) was the only brand that had the correct color, smell, and taste of wheat germ oil.

The other four brands had no noticeable color, smell, or taste.

The Swanson EFAs brand contains 10% of the RDA of vitamin E. The Wholistic Botanicals brand contains 7% of the RDA of vitamin E. The Best Naturals brand states that it contains vitamin E but it does not indicate how much. The other two brands do not mention vitamin E.

The Puritan's Pride brand does not indicate that it was "cold pressed" on the bottle label. "Cold pressing" is only mentioned in the "Product Description" on the Amazon page that advertises this product.

Natural caramel color is not the same thing as caramel color that is made from ammonia. Caramel color made from ammonia may

Item Description	Best Naturals	Puritan's Pride	Solgar	Swanson EFAs	Wholistic Botanicals
Number of Softgels	120	100	100	60	60
Cost per Bottle	$13.49	$10.16	$16.37	$9.26	$15.99
Cost per Softgel	$0.1124	$0.1016	$0.1637	$0.1543	$0.2665
Calories	10	10	10	10	10
Total Fat	1 g	1 g	1 g	1 g	1 g
Vitamin E	Yes	?	?	**10%**	7%
Listed Ingredients:					
Wheat Germ Oil	1130 mg	1130 mg	1130 mg	1130 mg	1130 mg
Gelatin	Yes	Yes	Yes	Yes	Yes
Vegetable Glycerin	Yes	Yes	Yes	No	No
Glycerin	No	No	No	Yes	No
Glycero	No	No	No	No	Yes
Purified Water	Yes	No	No	Yes	Yes
Natural Caramel Color	Yes	Yes	Yes	Yes	No
Capsule Color:	CLY	VDB	VDB	VDB	CLY
Oil Characteristics:					
Feel	Oily	Oily	Oily	Oily	Oily
Color	AC	VMYT	AC	**DGY**	VMYT
Smell	NS	NS	NS	**MS**	NS
Taste	NT	NT	NT	**NWT**	NT

Comparison of Five "Cold Pressed" Wheat Germ Oil Capsules

All Capsules were oval, 15/16 inch long, and 3/8 inch round.

Capsule Colors:
     CLY = Clear Light Yellow.
     VDB = Very Dark Brown.

Oil Characteristics:

Color: AC = Almost Clear.
     VMYT = Very Minor Yellow Tint.
     DGY = Dark Golden Yellow.

Smell: NS = Negligible or No Smell,   MS = Mild Smell.

Taste: NT = Negligible or No Taste,   NWT = Nutty Wheat Taste.

increase the risk of cancer.

    Based on the above very simple analysis, the Swanson EFAs brand has all of the easily identifiable characteristics of wheat germ oil and it has the most vitamin E. Swanson EFAs brand also has a reasonable average price per capsule, and it is not too cheap or too expensive.

I strongly recommend that the first time you purchase wheat germ oil capsules that you cut one capsule open and carefully examine the oil inside the capsule so you can recognize the color, smell, and taste of real wheat germ oil. You should continue to do this each time you purchase a new supply of wheat germ oil capsules to verify that the quality of the wheat germ oil has not changed.

My personal experience with the Swanson EFAs brand of wheat germ oil capsules at the end of the year 2019 was very good. In the second month of my diet I began exercising. In the third month of my diet I began taking one Swanson EFAs wheat germ oil capsule each day. This was the only change I made during the third month of my diet. During the entire third month (30 days) of my diet I lost 30% more weight than during the entire second month (30 days) of my diet. My opinion is that wheat germ oil does **not** contain some special ingredient that enhances weight loss. Instead my opinion is that wheat germ oil contains the healthy nutrients that are now missing from all commercially baked bread because of the time lag between when the wheat is ground into flour, and the flour is baked into bread, and the bread is delivered to the store, and the bread is gradually consumed by us. Some of the nutrients and vitamins in bread simply degrade with the passage of time and we no longer receive the true benefits of wheat that used to be ground into flour and then immediately baked into bread within one or two days, and then eaten within one or two days. When I began taking wheat germ oil capsules the nutrients in the wheat germ oil were positively received by my body. Very gradually I began to realize that I did not get hungry as quickly as I used to, and I did not need to eat as often or as much as I used to eat before I began taking the wheat germ oil capsules. In my opinion this is the reason I lost 30% more weight during the 30 days after I began taking the Swanson EFAs wheat germ oil capsules. If you decide to experiment with wheat germ oil capsules you may or may not receive the same benefits I received.

It might be helpful if you will remember that Jesus told us to ask God for our daily bread (Matthew 6:11). Until the 1880s wheat grains were ground into flour and then baked into bread within two days, and the bread was then eaten within two days. The allowed the human body to receive all the benefits of wheat as God originally intended. But if there is a significant time delay from milling to eating then some of the vitamins and the nutrients in the wheat and in the wheat germ may degrade and be lost. Cold pressed wheat germ oil capsules can provide the natural essential nutrients that are currently missing in all the breads that are now available at a local store.

Chapter Sixteen

Salt, Black Pepper, Seasonings, Condiments, and Oils

On page 296 in the appendix there is a table that shows the nutrition, vitamin, and mineral data for most of the food items mentioned in this chapter.

Sodium

Sodium is a mineral the human body needs. Sodium is regulated by the kidneys. Sodium helps maintain the normal balance of fluids in the body. Sodium helps regulate blood pressure and blood volume. Sodium is also needed for proper muscle and nerve functions.

When there is **too much** sodium in your blood the sodium will attract more water into your blood. This increases the amount or volume of blood inside your blood vessels and this causes your blood pressure to increase which puts extra stress on your heart. High blood pressure can stretch the walls of your blood vessels.

Consuming less sodium can help offset the body's increase in blood pressure due to age. Consuming less sodium can also reduce the risk of heart attack, heart failure, kidney disease, stroke, and stomach cancer. It may also reduce the frequency and severity of headaches.

The daily recommended amount of sodium for an adult is 2,300 mg.

Commercially processed foods and restaurant foods contain a significant amount of sodium. Read the nutrition label on processed foods to discover the amount of sodium in each serving.

Salt

1. **Table Salt:** It contains 40% sodium and 60% chloride. One teaspoon of table salt contains 2,300 mg of sodium which is the entire daily requirement of sodium for an adult.

2. **Sea Salt:** It contains some trace minerals in addition to sodium and chloride.

3. **Iodized Salt:** A small amount of iodine is added to table salt. Iodine is an important nutrient the human body needs.
   a. 1/2 teaspoon of regular iodized salt contains 48% of the **maximum** RDA of sodium and 90% of the **minimum** RDA of iodine.
   b. 1/2 teaspoon of Morton's Lite Iodized Salt contains 24% of the **maximum** RDA of sodium and 80% of the **minimum** RDA of iodine.

Iodine

Iodine deficiency can result in *weight gain*, goiter (enlarged thyroid gland), reduced metabolism, fatigue, cold intolerance, an impaired immune system, an increase in bodily toxins, and neurological, gastrointestinal, and skin abnormalities. Iodine deficiency in a pregnant woman is the most common preventable cause of mental retardation in her baby. Iodine deficiency can contribute to miscarriages and stillbirths. *The salt in processed food and fast foods is not iodized.* Regular table salt and sea salt are widely available as iodized or non-iodized. Unless your doctor has advised otherwise, iodized salt should be purchased instead of non-iodized salt.

Salt and a Healthy Diet

A healthy diet will normally include fresh vegetables, fresh fruit, and fresh meats. Although fresh vegetables, fruit, and meat contain natural sodium, the amount is trivial except for sweet potatoes and canned olives. And most vegetables, and some fruit (watermelons), and most meats will taste significantly better if a little iodized salt is added to these foods. Remember your body needs sodium and if you reduce or eliminate processed foods, fast foods, unhealthy snack foods, and unhealthy beverages from your diet then your sodium intake will be significantly reduced. Therefore adding a little iodized salt to the fresh foods you eat will probably not increase your daily sodium intake above a safe level and it will also allow you to add iodine to your diet.

Low-Sodium Diet

If your doctor has advised you to decrease or eliminate extra sodium from your diet then do not add table salt to the food you eat. Read the nutrition label on all food items before you purchase and eat them. Verify that the food has no sodium or a trivial amount of sodium. Avoid barbeque sauce, broth mixes, canned soup, celery salt, Chinese food, gravy mixes, garlic salt, instant cereals, ketchup, meat tenderizers, MSG (monosodium glutamate), mustard, onion salt, soy sauce, steak sauce, teriyaki sauce, and Worcestershire sauce. Avoid salty snack foods such as popcorn, potato chips, pretzels, salted crackers, and salted nuts. Select fresh foods or frozen foods that contain little or no salt. Select low-sodium or heart healthy foods.

Salt Substitute

Ask your doctor before you begin using a salt substitute. Your doctor can advice you if the salt substitute will be beneficial or harmful to you based on the results of your physical exam and your medical history.

Black Pepper

Dried ground black pepper is one of the most common and most popular spices added to foods worldwide. It is normally used as a companion to salt. Black pepper is a good source of vitamin K, iron, manganese, and potassium. It enhances the digestion of fats and meat proteins, and it enhances the absorption of the nutrients and vitamins in food. Black pepper is grown in tropical regions and when the pepper fruit is dried it is called a black peppercorn. Black peppercorns can be course ground, normal ground, or fine ground. Fine grind is normally used when cooking because there are more particles per teaspoon and therefore it distributes itself more evenly with the rest of the ingredients in the recipe. Coarse grind is good when a burst of pepper flavor is desired while eating. Black pepper stimulates the taste buds on the tongue and this sends a message to the brain and stomach to start producing digestive compounds. This enhances digestion because food is processed quicker through the stomach and this reduces the chance of heartburn or indigestion. It also enhances digestion in the intestines and this results in easier, more gentle bowel movements because the food is more fully digested. Black pepper helps prevent both constipation and diarrhea. Black pepper is a carminative (prevents gas) and a diaphoretic (promotes sweating) and a diuretic (promotes urination). In addition, black pepper has antioxidant and antibacterial properties. It stimulates the breakdown of fat cells to help a person stay slimmer while giving the person extra energy and vitality. Therefore adding a little black pepper to a food will: (1) enhance the flavor of the food, (2) make the food easier to digest, (3) make the food more enjoyable to eat, (4) decrease the chance of heartburn or indigestion, (5) enhance health, and (6) enhance weight loss. Black pepper loses some of its flavor the longer it is cooked so it should normally be added near the last step in a recipe if the food will be cooked a long time.

Seasonings

The following seasonings may be used to flavor the foods you eat or they can add a unique flavor to your own homemade beef jerky.

Cajun or Creole Seasoning: It contains a mixture of herbs that adds a Cajun (or Creole) flavor to foods.

Italian Seasoning: It contains a mixture of herbs that adds the Italian-American flavor preferred by people in the USA.

Lawry's® Seasoned Salt: Created in 1938 for use in the world-famous Lawry's® Prime Rib Restaurant in Beverly Hills, California to season prime rib beef. It is currently used to season prime rib, beef, chicken, potatoes, and casseroles.

Old Bay Seasoning: Created in 1939 by a German immigrant named Gustav Brunn in the Chesapeake Bay area for the purpose of seasoning crabs with a salt mixture that would encourage restaurant customers to purchase more beverages. It gradually became a standard seasoning on Navy ships. It was named after the passenger ship called "The Old Bay Line" that sailed the Chesapeake Bay in the early 1900s between Baltimore, Maryland and Norfolk, Virginia. The seasoning is used to season crabs and shrimp, and sometime clams and oysters.

TexMex Seasoning: It contains a mixture of herbs that adds a unique Mexican or Hispanic flavor to foods.

Condiments

Ketchup (or Catsup): One tablespoon of regular ketchup with added sugar contains 20 calories. One tablespoon of ketchup with no added sugar contains 10 calories. It may enhance bone health, eye health, skin health, teeth health, and male fertility. It may reduce cholesterol, and the risk of cancer (breast, prostate) and heart disease.

Mayonnaise: One tablespoon contains about 100 calories. It contains a significant amount of vitamin K and omega-3 fatty acids. It may enhance blood circulation, digestion and lung function. It may help stabilize blood sugar levels. It may reduce inflammation. It may reduce the risk of arthritis, heart attack, and stroke.

Mustard: One tablespoon contains about 0 calories and 9% of the RDA of sodium. (Mustard has no calories in the year 2020.) It contains a lot of fiber, calcium, iron, magnesium, selenium, and omega-3 fatty acids. It may reduce the bad LDL cholesterol and increase good HDL cholesterol. It may enhance bone health, hair health, and teeth health.

Peanut Butter: One tablespoon contains about 94 calories and it has a significant combination of healthy nutrients. Its high fiber and protein content may help you feel full longer so you eat less. It may reduce the bad LDL cholesterol and increase the good HDL cholesterol. It may help stabilize blood sugar levels. It may enhance brain function, digestion, energy levels, heart health, muscle health, and skin health. It may reduce the risk of cancer (breast, colon, prostate), diabetes, gallstones, and migraine headaches.

Honey

Warning: Never give honey to an infant. Honey contains some types of bacteria that may kill a young baby who does not yet have a fully developed immune system.

The Holy Bible says, "My son, eat honey because *it is* good, And the honeycomb *which is* sweet to your taste." (Proverbs 24:13, NKJV)

Honey should be used instead of sugar in some recipes. However, if honey is pasteurized or cooked then a few of its benefits will be lost. For example, the friendly probiotic bacteria will be destroyed by heat.

None of the following potential health benefits have been scientifically proven by medical research. Most medical research is done in areas that could increase the profits of the company funding the research and doing research on honey would not financially benefit any organization.

1. **Weight Loss:** Honey may help reduce the fat stored in your body.
2. **Digestion:** Honey is a probiotic and it contains large quantities of friendly bacteria.
3. **Blood Sugar Levels:** Honey may help the human body better regulate its blood sugar levels.
4. **Antibacterial:** When bees make honey they add an enzyme that makes hydrogen peroxide. This gives honey its antibacterial properties, and a very long shelf life.
5. **Antifungal and Antioxidant:** Honey also has antifungal and antioxidant properties.
6. **Cancer, Ulcers, and Heart Disease**: Since honey contains antioxidants it may help reduce the risk of some types of cancer, and some types of ulcers, and heart disease.
7. **Mouth Cold Sores, Sore Throat, and Coughing:** The World Health Organization classifies honey as a demulcent because it forms a protective coating inside the mouth that may relieve minor mouth irritations. Honey may help relieve the pain of a sore throat and it may help reduce coughing in children who have an upper respiratory tract infection. A study that included 139 children reported that honey was more effective in reducing nighttime cough and helping children sleep when compared to a commercially available children's cough syrup that contained a cough suppressant (dextromethophan) and an antihistamine (diphenhydramine).
8. **Allergies:** Locally made honey contains pollen from local plants. If a small quantity of this honey is consumed each day then it may introduce a small quantity of the allergen into your body to help your body build its natural immunity to it. Honey made in other parts of the country may not provide this health benefit because that honey may not contain the local pollens you may be allergic to.

Oils, Shortening, Lard

Oils: Canola (rapeseed), coconut, corn, peanut, and vegetable oils do not contain any carbohydrates, cholesterol, or protein. The only vitamins they contain are E and K. They contain trivial amounts of a few minerals. They all contain 120 calories per tablespoon. They will add to your weight without providing any significant amount of nutrition. These oils have consistently been shown to increase the risk of death from cancer and heart disease. If you use oil then extra virgin olive oil is the best choice and it is discussed on page 64.

Shortening: Shortening is made by hydrogenating vegetable oil. It does not contain cholesterol. However, it may contain saturated fat depending on how it is made (read the nutrition label). Some brands of shortening may also contain harmful artificial trans-fats until January 1, 2021.

Lard: Lard is rendered (melted) pork fat. Lard is used in traditional Mexican restaurants more often than butter, shortening, or oil. Lard has all the following advantages:

1. Lard has a neutral flavor and it does **not** add a pork flavor to food.
2. Lard is heat stable. It contains about 48% monounsaturated fat (heart healthy fat) and 40% saturated fat. Saturated fat helps keep other fats from oxidizing when exposed to heat. If the fats oxidize then they create free radicals which are harmful to the human body.
3. Until 1900 lard was the primary cooking fat used in most restaurants and in most homes. Our ancestors used lard and prior to the 1900s heart disease was **not** as common as it is today.
4. Modern scientific research has **not** been able to show any correlation between saturated fat and an increased risk of heart disease or cancer. Instead research has found just the opposite -- saturated fat decreases the risk of heart disease. On the other hand, a **low-fat** diet has been shown to increase triglycerides which can increase the risk of heart disease.
5. Lard is the 18th richest food in good HDL cholesterol, which helps control inflammation and improve hormone production which control many of the body's important functions. Research has shown a correlation between **low** blood cholesterol and an increased risk of depression, dementia, Alzheimer's disease, suicide, and committing violent crimes.
6. Lard has a smoking point of about 370°F (188°C) and it is excellent for frying and deep frying at temperatures of 370°F or below.
7. Lard is excellent for baking and it produces the best tasting fried chicken, biscuits, rolls, cookies, and piecrusts.
8. If eaten regularly lard may help prevent wrinkles as you age.
9. Do not purchase lard from a grocery store because it may have added ingredients. Instead purchase lard from a local Farmers' Market because it may contain between 500 to 1000 I.U. of vitamin D if the lard is from farm raised pigs that were allowed to spend part of the day in the sun because the sun's vitamin D collects in the fat under the skin of the pig. Ask the person selling the lard if they raised and butchered the pigs, and if so, then ask how much time the pigs spent in the sun on an average day.
10. You can make your own "lard substitute" by straining and saving the grease from bacon after you bake (or fry) the bacon.

Chapter Seventeen

Beef, Pork, Poultry, and Seafood

On page 284 in the appendix there is a table that shows the nutrition, vitamin, and mineral data for most of the meats mentioned in this chapter.

Beef in the Holy Bible

The Old Testament tells us that the following men had herds of cattle: Abraham (Genesis 12:16), Jacob (later called Israel) (Genesis 32.5), and Joseph (Genesis 47:17). All of these men lived for more than 100 years and eating beef did not shorten their life spans.

God required that the firstborn of the cattle be offered to him as a sacrifice (Exodus 22:30, Leviticus 22:19). A small part of the sacrifice was burned in a fire, and some of the meat was eaten by the priests, but most of the meat was eaten by the people who offered the sacrifice. Deuteronomy 14:26-27 (NKJV) says, "And you shall spend that money for whatever your heart desires: for oxen or sheep, for wine or similar drink, for whatever your heart desires; you shall eat there before the LORD your God, and you shall rejoice, you and your household. You shall not forsake the Levite who is within your gates, for he has no part nor inheritance with you." The Levites were the priests who sacrificed the animals to God, and the priests ate some of the meat along with the people who provided it.

God loves His children and God gave His children permission to eat beef because beef is a healthy meat to eat. God also told His children not eat bats, owls, camels, and a variety of other creatures because their meat would cause His children to get sick (Leviticus 11:3-23).

Most of the cattle owned by the Israelites were not offered as a sacrifice. They were simply eaten by the people whenever they desired to eat beef. Deuteronomy 11:15 (NKJV) says, "And I will send grass in your fields for your livestock, that you may eat and be filled." The cattle ate grass and they roamed freely about the pasture lands in Israel.

Modern ranching techniques have changed and most cattle are not raised in pastures where they can eat grass. Most cattle are fed a special diet in order to increase the amount of fat on the cattle because this results in a higher USDA beef grade, and higher grades of beef sell for more money. However, it is still possible to buy grass-fed beef in some stores if you look carefully for it. The beef from grass-fed cattle is still healthy beef just like it has been ever since God first gave mankind permission to eat meat (Genesis 9:3-4).

However, if your doctor has specifically advised you to not eat beef then you should follow your doctor's instructions.

Some False Claims about Beef

Several research studies have reported that beef is not a healthy meat to eat. These studies were conducted on commercially processed meats that contained a variety of additives and artificial preservatives. Subsequent research studies on fresh beef reported that beef without any additives or artificial preservatives did not have unhealthy side effects. This is an example of how some "scientific research" can be true based on the data that was collected, but subsequent scientific research studies that are more carefully executed arrive at a completely different conclusion. The final answer is that the additives and artificial preservatives in commercially processed beef are unhealthy but fresh beef is not unhealthy.

Beef does not increase the risk of diabetes or heart disease. Two recent studies on a huge number of different people found that there was no correlation between beef and cancer in women, and only a very minor possible correlation between beef and cancer in men.

Health Benefits of Beef

Beef contains at least 8 times more L-carintine than chicken, milk, or plant foods. L-carintine may reduce inflammation, enhance weight loss, and reduce the risk of heart failure. Beef contains the amino acid glutathione and it may slow down the normal aging process, extend life expectancy, enhance the immune system, minimize inflammation, and it protects every cell in the human body from cellular damage. Beef has a lot of protein and protein enhances bone health, energy, metabolism, lean muscle mass, skin health, and weight loss. Beef reduces food cravings. Beef contains a lot of iron, phosphorus, selenium, and zinc. Beef contains heme iron which is the easiest type of iron for the body to metabolize and this helps prevent iron deficiency anemia especially in females. Vitamin B12 is only present in animal products and beef contains significantly more B12 than chicken, pork, or turkey. A four ounce serving of beef contains approximately 100% of the RDA for B12. Vitamin B12 enhances blood health, brain health, nerve health, skin health, and sleep, and B12 minimizes depression and fatigue. Beef reduces the risk of heart disease and hair loss. However, eating extremely well done beef may increase the risk of cancer (breast, colon).

Beef Grading

Grading of beef is voluntary in the USA. If a meat processor wishes to have its beef graded, then they must pay a trained United States Department of Agriculture (USDA) inspector to evaluate and grade its beef as the cattle are being slaughtered. If the beef has been graded then the USDA's shield or label will be on the beef package. If the beef does not display a USDA label then it has not been graded, or the beef received a low grade and the meat processor decided not to report the low grade that the beef received.

The two factors that impact the tenderness of meat are the meat's maturity (age) and its marbling. Marbling is intramuscular fat and it does not include the fat on the outside edge of the beef. Younger cattle (age 2 years or less) have beef with a lighter red color and the beef contains more marbling and it is more tender than older cattle with less marbling. Fat marbling contributes to the flavor, juiciness, and tenderness of beef. The age of the beef contributes to its color, flavor, firmness, and texture, and younger cattle have the highest ratings.

There are eight different grades of meat but only the top five grades are sold to consumers.

1. **U.S. Prime:** Less than 2% of all graded beef is prime. It has the most fat marbling (11% or more), and it is the juiciest, the most tender, and it has the most desirable texture. It is usually only sold to very expensive restaurants and to very wealthy consumers. Prime beef may be baked, broiled, fried, grilled, or roasted.

2. **U.S. Choice:** About 50% of all graded beef is choice. Grocery stores that sell USDA Choice beef will usually proudly display the USDA Choice shield in their fresh beef area. It has a reasonable amount of fat marbling (between 9.5% to 11%). Choice beef may be baked, braised, fried, grilled, or roasted.

3. **U.S. Select:** It has less fat marbling, it is less tender, it is less juicy, and it has a coarser texture. It is the most common type of beef available in most grocery stores and fresh cuts of beef will display the "USDA Select" label. Select beef may be braised, poached, steamed, stewed, or cooked in a slow cooker. These moist cooking methods help break down the tougher fibers in select beef.

4. **Standard and Commercial Grades:** It has very little fat marbling and it is not very tender. Stores that sell these grades of beef will usually advertise their beef using their "Store Brand," or words such as Black Angus, or Blue Ribbon, or Premium. If they use the words Prime, Choice, or Select but they do not display the USDA shield then the beef is not true USDA Graded Prime, Choice, or Select beef. Frying or grilling these lower grades of beef will usually result in the beef tasting dry and chewy. These grades of beef should be stewed or cooked in a slow cooker to help reduce the toughness of the beef.

5. **Utility, Cutter, and Canner Grades:** Usually cut from older cattle with no fat marbling. These grades of raw beef are usually not sold

directly to consumers. However, these grades of beef are used in processed meats, and in canned meats, and in some frozen dinners such as some frozen beef pot pies.

Different Cuts of Beef

The cut of the meat is usually much more important than the grade of the meat. Some cuts of meat (such as filet mignon, rib eye, or porterhouse steak) are always more flavorful, juicy, and tender than other cuts of meat (such as strip steak or rump roast) from the same exact steer.

When buying fresh meat at a grocery store or butcher shop look for the presence of more finely dispersed fat marbling running through the lean red meat. Also look for a lighter red color instead of a darker red color. Unfortunately the type of lighting used in the fresh meat display area of most stores is carefully selected to enhance the appearance of the red beef. Therefore color is not as good an indicator of the quality of the beef as the amount of dispersed fat marbling in the lean red meat.

Pasture Raised Grass-Fed Beef

The United States Department of Agriculture (USDA) and the Food Safety and Inspection Services (FSIS) inspects 100% of all beef for diseases and for safety. The FSIS is the public health agency of the USDA. On the other hand, grading the beef is optional and it is at the discretion of the slaughterhouse.

Beef grades are not relevant for grass-fed cattle. USDA beef grades are only based on the amount of fat marbling and the age of the steer. USDA beef grades do not consider how the steer was raised, or what it was fed while it was alive, or how much healthy nutrition is in the beef.

Grass-fed beef contains higher levels of omega-3 fatty acids which help prevent heart disease. Grass-fed beef is leaner and it only contains 60% of the calories and 30% of the fat compared to conventional beef. Many people prefer the flavor of grass-fed beef.

Lamb

Lambs are typically grass-fed which results in high levels of omega-3 fatty acids. Lamb contains a lot of the beneficial conjugated linoleic acid (CLA). CLA is also present in beef and dairy products. CLA may help decrease body fat and enhance weight loss. CLA may enhance the immune system, and it may help reduce the risk of cancer (breast, colon, liver, prostate, stomach). Lamb has a lot of protein and protein enhances bone health, energy, metabolism, lean muscle mass, skin health, and weight loss.

Pork

Pork contains all 9 essential amino acids. Pork is high in protein and protein enhances bone health, energy, metabolism, lean muscle mass, skin health, and weight loss. Pork may enhance brain health, heart health, and thyroid function. It may help reduce fatigue. However, over-cooked pork may increase the risk of cancer.

All pork is inspected but grading is voluntary. There are only two grades of pork:

1. **Acceptable:** This is the only grade of pork sold to consumers. It has a high proportion of lean mean in relation to fat and bone.

2. **Utility:** This grade is only sold to food processors.

Although pork has been marketed as "the other white meat," pork is actually classified as a red meat just like beef, lamb, and veal. All pork products should be completely cooked, but not over-cooked, to neutralize any bacteria or parasites that may be present in the pork.

When selecting pork products look for a thin layer of fat on the outside of the meat. The meat should be firm and grayish pink in color. Tenderness is enhanced if there is a small amount of internal fat marbling. Tenderloins are the most tender and the most flavorful cut of pork. The meat department butcher will usually slice a whole or a half tenderloin into pieces of any thickness that you desire for free.

Poultry

Poultry includes chicken, duck, goose, and turkey.

Chicken contains a lot of protein and protein enhances bone health, energy, metabolism, lean muscle mass, skin health, and weight loss. Chicken may enhance brain function, cardiovascular health, digestion, eye health, heart health, the immune system, nail health, and oral health. It may help treat anemia and the common cold. It may help reduce blood pressure, cholesterol, and stress. It may reduce the risk of Alzheimer's disease, colon cancer, heart disease, and stroke.

Turkey has approximately half the calories of beef, chicken, and pork. Turkey has a lot of protein and protein enhances bone health, energy, metabolism, lean muscle mass, skin health, and weight loss. Turkey may enhance blood health, cardiovascular health, hair health, the immune system, nail health, oral health, sleep, testosterone production, and thyroid function. It may help treat anemia. It may help reduce cholesterol, depression, and stress. It may help reduce the risk of cancer. However, turkey may trigger gout attacks.

There are three grades of poultry. However, gizzards, necks, tails, and wing tips are not graded. Ground chicken is also not graded.

1. **Grade A:** This is the only type of poultry that is sold to consumers. The meat does not have any bruises, defects, or feathers. If the meat is on the bone then none of the bones are broken. If it is a whole bird then there should be no tears in its skin.

2. **Grade B and Grade C:** These are not sold to consumers. They are sold to food processors to make processed poultry products.

Since all poultry products sold to consumers are Grade A, sellers of poultry meat use the following terms to describe their birds:

1. **Cage-Free:** Cage-free simply means the chickens were free to roam the building or the area where they are raised. Since chickens are slaughtered at the age of 13 weeks, cages have no benefit. Therefore "cage-free" means nothing when purchasing chicken meat. However, cages may help simplify the egg gathering process for hens that are allowed to live long enough to lay eggs.

2. **Free Range:** The animals must have continuous and unrestricted access to outdoor pasture during their entire lives. For poultry this simply means there should be a small door from the indoor area that leads to an outdoor area of an unspecified size, and the outdoor area does not have to be large enough to accommodate all the birds at the same time. The outdoor pasture may or may not have anything edible growing in it. Chickens are slaughtered when they reach the age of 13 weeks so there is a good chance that many chickens never venture outdoors during their short life expectancy.

3. **No Antibiotics or Raised without Antibiotics:** The chickens cannot receive any type of antibiotic in any form or in any way during their entire life. This means the breeder has to immediately identify any sick birds and remove and separate them from the rest of the flock. The breeder must then either dispose of the birds or label those birds differently if they are given antibiotics.

4. **No Hormones:** In the USA giving hormones to chickens has been illegal since 1959. Therefore in the USA all chickens are "hormone free" and this advertising claim on a label means nothing.

5. **Natural:** The chicken received minimal processing after it was slaughtered and no artificial colors, flavors, or preservatives were added after slaughtering. Since all chicken meat is "natural" this advertising claim on a label does not mean anything.

6. **Naturally Raised:** "Naturally raised" is not the same thing as "natural." Naturally raised chickens were fed grains and plant matter and they were not fed slaughter byproducts which are cleverly called "animal protein."

7. **Organic:** The chicken had to be naturally raised and free ranging beginning the second day of its life. The feed has to be certified organic and it cannot contain any GMOs, chemical fertilizers, or commercial pesticides. *This is the one marketing claim that has real merit when trying to select the healthiest chicken meat to eat..*

Based on the above information, the following claims are either important or not important when making a choice on which packages of fresh chicken meat to purchase at the supermarket:

1. **Not important:** In the USA all chickens that are sold for meat are Grade A, hormone free, cage free, and natural. These four advertising claims can be completely ignored.

2. **Important:** In the USA the most important thing to look for when buying chicken meat is a label that says it is *organic*. The reason is because organic means the chicken meat came from a naturally raised, free range chicken and the meat does not contain any GMOs, chemical fertilizers, or commercial pesticides. The second most important thing to look for is *no antibiotics*. If you can find a label that says *organic* and *no antibiotics* then you have found the healthiest chicken meat available in the USA.

Seafood

People who eat a lot of fish have longer life expectancies and they become sick less often. They also have a lower risk of dementia, depression, and heart disease.

Fish contains high-quality protein. Many studies have reported that fish is more filling than beef or chicken. When fish is consumed as part of a meal it may decrease the number of calories you eat at your next meal.

All fish and shellfish contain docosahexaenoic acid (DHA) which is an omega-3 fatty acid. DHA may help reduce tummy fat because it may deactivate the genes that add fat to the tummy, and this prevents tummy fat cells from expanding and becoming larger. Bass, herring, mackerel, salmon, sardines, and trout contain the most DHA.

Wild caught fish generally have more omega-3 fatty acids than farmed fish of the same species. In the USA most fish farms meet higher health standards than fish farms in other parts of the world. Therefore if you have a choice then select a USA farmed-raised fish instead of a farmed-raised fish from some other country. The package label should indicate the country of origin of the seafood. The most common farmed fish are bass, catfish, cod, salmon, and tilapia.

Omega-3 Fatty Acids, Selenium, and Mercury in Seafood

Omega-3 fatty acids are a type of polyunsaturated fat. Seafood contains a lot of healthy omega-3 fatty acids and a reasonable amount of iodine which is necessary for proper thyroid function. The thyroid regulates the body's metabolic processes and it assists in weight loss.

Seafood contains heavy metals, mercury, and polychlorinated biphenyl (PCB), and they are all harmful to the body if consumed in high quantities. The reason is because humans have polluted the land, the rivers, and the oceans with harmful chemicals, and the seafood that live in these polluted waters absorb these harmful substances into their bodies. These unhealthy substances are present in higher concentrations in fish with longer life spans and larger fish. For example, whales contain a significant amount of mercury. Small fish with a shorter life span, such as sardines, contain very little mercury.

Seafood choices should include seafood that contains low quantities of the harmful stuff and high quantities of the healthy stuff.

Pregnant women, nursing mothers, and young children should avoid mercury if possible, or at least they should avoid seafood with high mercury levels.

Seafood contains high quantities of selenium. Selenium may help neutralize harmful free radicals, enhance the immune system, enhance the functions of the pancreas and thyroid, reduce the risk of some cancers and heart disease, help repair DNA, and help slow down the normal aging process.

Selenium also helps to minimize the amount of mercury absorbed by the body. If a fish contains more selenium than mercury then the selenium helps to neutralize the mercury so the mercury passes through the body and it is expelled. This relationship of selenium to mercury has been known since the 1960s and it has been documented in birds, fish, and mammals. In the USA the amount of selenium in the soil is relatively consistent and this impacts the selenium in freshwater and in freshwater fish. A lot of selenium is present in ocean water and this impacts saltwater fish. However, selenium only minimizes the health risks of mercury and it has no impact on other pollutants.

The table on the next page shows the amount of omega-3 fatty acids, selenium, and mercury in a variety of fish and shellfish. The last column in the table shows the ratio of selenium to mercury for each specie of seafood. A ratio less than one indicates that the mercury level exceeds the selenium level and this should discourage you from eating that specific type of seafood. Ratios between one to two may also be a

Fish and Shellfish - Nutrients and Contaminants
Per 100 Grams of Fish (or a 3.53 ounce serving)

Fish Species	Omega-3 Fatty Acids g	Selenium (S) μg	Mercury (M) μg	Ratio (S/M)
Bass, Striped, Ocean	0.754	36.5	16.7	2.2
Carp	0.434	12.6	11.0	1.1
Catfish	0.464	12.6	2.4	5.3
Cod	0.194	33.1	11.1	3.0
Grouper	0.257	36.5	44.8	0.8
Haddock, Atlantic	0.138	25.9	5.5	4.7
Halibut	0.221	45.6	24.1	1.9
Herring, Atlantic	1.626	36.5	7.8	4.7
Kippers (smoked herring)	2.224	52.6	7.8	6.7
Mackerel, Atlantic	2.511	44.1	5.0	8.8
Mackerel, Pacific	1.574	36.5	8.8	4.1
Mackerel, King	0.330	36.5	73.0	0.5
Mackerel, Spanish	1.442	36.5	45.4	0.8
Mahi Mahi	0.117	36.5	17.8	2.1
Perch, Freshwater	0.661	12.6	15.0	0.8
Perch, Ocean	0.240	28.6	12.1	2.4
Salmon, Sockeye	0.848	29.8	2.2	13.5
Salmon, Canned	1.417	30.1	1.4	21.5
Sardines, Canned	0.982	52.7	1.3	40.5
Snapper	0.376	38.2	16.6	2.3
Tilapia, Farmed	0.167	41.8	1.3	32.2
Trout, Rainbow	0.693	12.6	7.1	1.8
Tuna, Canned Light	0.279	80.4	12.6	6.4
Tuna, Skipjack	0.269	36.5	14.4	2.5
Shellfish				
Clam	0.036	30.6	0.9	34.0
Crab	0.320	37.4	6.5	5.8
Lobster, North Atlantic	0.176	63.6	10.7	5.9
Scallops	0.109	12.8	0.3	42.7
Shrimp	0.150	29.6	0.9	32.9

Sources of Data:
Omega-3 and Selenium values are from the
United States Department of Agriculture (USDA).
Mercury values are from the Food and Drug Administration (FDA).

concern to someone who wishes to avoid any seafood that may not be healthy. The higher the ratio the better the chance that the selenium can help neutralize the mercury in the seafood. However, the total amount of mercury in a specific type of seafood should also be considered because a seafood with a lot of mercury may contain more mercury than your body can safely process in a short period of time.

This is an example of how *common sense* can be used to evaluate the above information. Many different research studies have reported that people who eat a lot of fish are healthier, they have fewer diseases, and they live longer than people who eat less fish. Therefore eating fish is a very healthy choice, and the negative publicity about the amount of mercury in fish is not a valid reason to abstain from fish. The choice of the best seafood to include in your diet can be based on the total mercury content in the seafood, and its selenium-mercury ratio, and whether or not you enjoy eating that type of seafood.

Fish Species and Fish Grading

Fish Health Benefits: All fish has a lot of protein and protein enhances bone health, energy, metabolism, lean muscle mass, skin health, and weight loss. All fish may help reduce blood pressure and cholesterol. All fish may enhance blood health, brain health, heart health, the immune system, metabolism, and nerve health. All fish may reduce the risk of cardiovascular diseases, dementia, depression, heart attack, and heart disease. All fish may help slow down the normal aging process and extend life expectancy.

Fish Grading: Fish is only graded in terms of breed, color, fat, size, and weight.

1. **Bass:** It has all the health benefits listed above for fish. In addition, it may enhance eye health, and it may reduce the risk of asthma, cataracts, diabetes, and macular degeneration.

2. **Catfish:** It contains a lot of vitamin D. It has all the health benefits listed above for fish. In addition, it may enhance oral health, and it may facilitate a normal pregnancy, and it may help reduce the risk of birth defects.

3. **Cod:** It has all the health benefits listed above for fish. In addition, it may enhance bowel movements, digestion and hair health. It may minimize asthma, arthritis, gout, inflammation, and migraine headaches. It may reduce the risk of Alzheimer's disease, diabetes, and macular degeneration.

4. **Halibut:** It is a good source of potassium, selenium, and vitamins B3, B6, B9, B12, and D. It has all the health benefits listed above for fish. In addition, it may enhance digestion, hair health, liver

health, nail health, and sexual health. It may lower trigylcerides. It may minimize fatigue and stress. It may help reduce the risk of Alzheimer's disease, anemia, cancer (colon, kidney), leukemia, osteoporosis, and stroke.

5. **Herring:** It has more vitamin B12 than other fish. It has all the health benefits listed for fish on page 142. In addition, it may enhance eye health and lung function. It may lower triglycerides. It may help minimize arthritis, asthma, and inflammation.

6. **Mackerel:** It has more vitamins A, B1, B3, and D than other fish, and it includes all nine essential amino acids. It has all the health benefits listed for fish on page 142. In addition, it may enhance hair health, oral health, and thyroid health. It may reduce inflammation and triglycerides. It may help reduce the symptoms of rheumatoid arthritis. It may help reduce the risk of anemia, asthma, cancer (breast, colon, prostrate, renal), diabetes, and macular degeneration. It may help stabilize blood sugar levels. In January 2020 some brands of canned mackerel only contain mackerel, water, and salt, and they do not contain any additives or artificial ingredients. Always read the ingredient list before buying canned mackerel.

7. **Perch:** It has all the health benefits listed for fish on page 142. In addition, it may enhance digestion and sexual health. It may help minimize fatigue. It may help stabilize blood sugar levels.

8. **Pink Salmon:** It has all the health benefits listed for fish on page 142. In addition, it may enhance digestion, energy, eye health, joint flexibility, and thyroid health. It may help lower triglycerides. It may help minimize inflammation and rheumatoid arthritis. It may reduce the risk of Alzheimer's disease, asthma, cancer, diabetes, and stroke. Wild salmon have a pink color due to the shrimp and krill they eat. Wild salmon have 11 times more omega-3 fatty acids than omega-6 fatty acids and this is good. Farmed salmon have naturally beige flesh because they are fed food pellets that contain ground fish, soy, chicken poop, and hydrolyzed chicken feathers. The result is that farmed salmon have 10% less omega-3 fatty acids than omega-6 fatty acids and this is bad. And pink dye is added to the food pellets to change the farmed salmons' flesh from its natural beige to pink. Farmed salmon only contains one-fourth of the vitamin D as wild salmon. Farmed salmon also contain cancer causing chemicals and herbicides and they also have internal parasites. Therefore when you are buying fresh salmon look for "wild caught salmon" and avoid "farmed salmon." In January 2020 the "Double Q" brand of canned salmon contains "wild caught Alaskan" salmon and salt, and it does not contain any additives or

artificial preservatives. Always read the ingredient list if you are buying canned salmon.

9. **Sardines:** They have all the health benefits listed for fish on page 142. In addition, they may enhance eye health, joint flexibility, and oral health. They may help lower triglycerides. They may help minimize anemia, asthma, arthritis, blood clotting, fatigue, and inflammation. They may reduce the risk of cancer (colon, prostate), macular degeneration, osteoporosis, and pneumonia. They may help stabilize blood sugar levels. Sardines are small oily fish that contain a wide variety of healthy nutrients including healthy omega-3 fatty acids.

10. **Snapper**: It has all the health benefits listed for fish on page 142. In addition, it may enhance digestion, eye health, and oral health. It may help minimize arthritis discomfort. It may reduce the risk of cancer, diabetes, kidney stones, osteoporosis, and stroke.

11. **Tilapia:** It contains more omega-6 fatty acids than omega-3 fatty acids and this is bad because it may contribute to inflammation. It has all the health benefits listed for fish on page 142. In addition, it may enhance hair health, oral health, and thyroid health. It may reduce the risk of cancer. It is the fourth most popular fish eaten in the USA. About 73% of it comes from China because China has a climate that is suited to tilapia. It is more challenging to farm tilapia in the USA. Chinese farmed raised tilapia may contain antibiotics, harmful pesticides, and cancer causing pollutants due to the unsanitary conditions of the fish farm. Farm raised tilapia and mahi mahi have the lowest omega-3 fatty acids of all fish and both fish are imported from China. Tilapia raised in Canada, Ecuador, or the USA are a better choice.

12. **Trout:** It has all the health benefits listed for fish on page 142. In addition, it may enhance fertility, hair health, kidney health, liver health, nail health, and oral health. It may reduce triglycerides. It may reduce the risk of asthma and cancer (breast, colon, prostrate).

13. **Tuna:** It has all the health benefits listed for fish on page 142. In addition, it may enhance eye health and kidney health. It may help minimize inflammation, arthritis, and gout. It may help reduce triglycerides. It may reduce the risk of cancer (breast, colon, kidney), kidney disease, macular degeneration, and stroke. Tuna is a lean fish that has almost no fat. Toxic mercury levels are highest in the larger tuna species such as bluefin and albacore tuna. Smaller tuna have a lower mercury level and the smaller tuna are processed into canned chunk light tuna. Tuna packed in water has fewer calories than tuna packed in oil.

Shellfish

Shellfish Health Benefits: All shellfish has a lot of protein and protein enhances bone health, energy, metabolism, lean muscle mass, skin health, and weight loss. All shellfish may help reduce blood pressure and cholesterol. All shellfish may enhance blood health, brain health, heart health, the immune system, metabolism, and nerve health. All shellfish may reduce the risk of cardiovascular diseases, dementia, depression, heart attack, and heart disease. All shellfish may help to slow down the normal aging process and extend life expectancy.

1. **Crab:** It has all the health benefits listed above for shellfish. In addition, it may enhance eye health and thyroid health. It may help minimize inflammation, arthritis, and gout. It may help reduce the risk of Alzheimer's disease, cataracts, macular degeneration, osteoporosis, and stroke. It may facilitate a normal pregnancy and help prevent birth defects.

2. **Lobster:** It has all the health benefits listed above for shellfish. In addition, it may enhance eye health and thyroid health. It may help minimize arthritis and inflammation. It may reduce the risk of Alzheimer's disease, cancer (breast, colon, esophageal, lung, ovarian, prostrate), diabetes, hearing loss, macular degeneration, and osteoporosis.

3. **Scallops:** They have all the health benefits listed above for shellfish. In addition, they may enhance hair health and kidney health. They may minimize inflammation and fatigue. They may reduce the risk of colon cancer, diabetes, and stroke.

4. **Shrimp:** They have all the health benefits listed above for shellfish. In addition, they may enhance eye health, hair health, nail health, oral health, prostrate health, and thyroid health. They may help minimize inflammation and menstrual discomfort. They may reduce the risk of cancer (prostrate), diabetes, hair loss, macular degeneration, and stroke.

Deli Meats Sliced On Demand

Deli meats that are sliced on demand to the thickness you desire are **not** healthy. They contain a variety of artificial colors, flavors, nitrates, and unhealthy preservatives. At the beginning of the year 2020 this includes all the following brands that are available in most delis: Boar's Head, Prima Della, and Sara Lee.

Prepackaged Sliced Meats

1. **Hillshire Farm** provides a nice selection of different meats that are sliced ultra thin. Their meats contain no artificial preservatives, no

artificial flavors, and no nitrates. Sodium is added to their meats in the form of sea salt. Other nutrients vary based on the type of meat and the seasonings used in the meat. Each slice of meat contains approximately 20 to 30 calories because it is sliced ultra thin. This is nice because a person can eat one or two slices to satisfy their craving for a "meat snack" without consuming too many calories.

2. **Hormel "Natural Choice"** contains no hormones and no nitrates. Hormel meats are sliced thicker than Hillshire Farm meats and they contain approximately 70 calories per slice.

3. **Oscar Mayer** prepackaged meats contain no artificial preservatives, no added hormones, and no nitrates. Oscar Mayer meats are sliced thicker than Hillshire Farm meats and they contain approximately 50 calories per slice. Some of their meats also contain caramel coloring and caramel coloring may increase the risk of cancer.

Depending on the thickness of the slices, one, two, three, or four slices of prepackaged sliced meat may be added to a sandwich, or a salad, or eaten alone (or with a thin slice a cheese) as a healthy snack. When the meat is thinly sliced, different types of meat may be eaten at the same time instead of a single type of meat. This can provide some interesting variations in flavor.

Chapter Eighteen

Vegetables, Salads, and Salad Dressings

On page 286 in the appendix there is a table that shows the nutrition, vitamin, and mineral data for most of the vegetables mentioned in this chapter. Salad dressings are on page 296.

Vegetables are extremely healthy and they can make it easier for a person to lose weight. They have a high water content and they contain a lot of fiber, vitamins, minerals, and amino acids. They also have a low energy density.

Vegetables contain few calories so a large quantity of vegetables can be eaten without adding a significant number of calories to the diet. On the average, people who eat more vegetables and a wider variety of vegetables, weigh less than people who eat fewer vegetables and a limited variety of vegetables.

Vegetables may enhance the normal function of the digestive system and they may help prevent constipation, diarrhea, irregularity, hemorrhoids, and colon cancer.

Vegetables may help maintain healthy bones, hair, skin, and teeth.

Vegetables contain antioxidants that may help control blood sugar levels, decrease blood pressure, and prevent cardiovascular problems. They may enhance immunity, prevent infections, and reduce the risk of cancer and disease.

Vegetables may help reduce hypertension and stress.

A diet that consists primarily of meats and vegetables will contain all the protein, fiber, vitamins, and minerals a person needs to stay healthy and lose weight. Therefore some type of vegetable should be eaten at every meal, if possible.

The healthy nutrients in vegetables, including vitamin C, quickly degrade with the passage of time. Therefore, if possible, smaller quantities of fresh vegetables should be purchased more often.

Raw vegetables contain more of their original nutrients than the same vegetable after cooking. However, some vegetables must be cooked. And cooked vegetables are easier for some people to digest. And cooking activates some of the nutrients in some vegetables.

Raw or cooked vegetables are healthier than vegetable juices. However, if you have difficulty digesting vegetables then vegetable juices may be a reasonable option. However, the body processes liquid nutrients differently than solid nutrients and vegetable juices may not satisfy your hunger for the same length of time as solid vegetables.

Do not chop, cut, slice, or peel any vegetable until you are ready to eat it or use it in a recipe because the nutrients in vegetables gradually begin to decline after the vegetable has been cut or peeled.

Types of Vegetables

Low-carb vegetables include: broccoli, Brussels sprouts, cabbage, cauliflower, cucumber, kale, lettuce, spinach, Swiss chard, and tomatoes.

Non-starchy vegetables include artichokes, asparagus, beets, broccoli, carrots, cucumbers, eggplant, leafy greens, leeks, mushrooms, onions, peppers, spinach, squash, and tomatoes.

Cruciferous vegetables include broccoli, Brussels sprouts, cabbage, cauliflower, collard greens, and kale. They contain a lot of fiber and they are very filling. They also contain nutrients that may help the body defend itself against cancer and they may help reduce the free radicals that can cause inflammation.

Leafy green vegetables include collards, kale, lettuce, spinach, and Swiss chard. They are low in calories and carbohydrates, but they contain a lot of healthy dietary fiber. They also contain many vitamins, minerals, and antioxidants.

Root vegetables include beets, carrots, onions, potatoes, radishes, sweet potatoes, and turnips. Root vegetables have many health benefits.

Asparagus

Asparagus is low in calories and carbohydrates but it contains a lot of vitamins E and K. Avoid undercooking or overcooking asparagus. If asparagus is boiled in water then some of the vitamins will be lost in the water. Steaming asparagus or baking asparagus at a low temperature are better options. Asparagus may help prevent urinary tract infections. It may enhance digestion and the immune system. It may help minimize depression. It may help prevent gas and it may help the body flush out excess liquids that can cause bloating. It may help stimulate estrogen in women and testosterone in men. Asparagus may cause a temporary change in the odor of your urine.

Beans

Beans contain protein and fiber that digests slowly and this may help you feel full longer and reduce food cravings and the desire to overeat. Beans contain a lot of vitamins B1 (thiamine), B2 (riboflavin), B3 (niacin), B5 (pantothenic acid), B6, B9 (folate), calcium, iron, magnesium, manganese, phosphorous, potassium, selenium, and zinc. Beans also contain some "resistant starch." Beans need to be properly cooked in order to minimize digestive problems. However, some people have difficulty digesting properly cooked beans. The protein in beans helps build and maintain muscles. Beans may lower cholesterol, blood pressure, and stabilize blood sugar levels. They may reduce the risk of diabetes, colon cancer, intestinal cancer, heart attack, heart disease, and stroke. Beans may increase the amount of healthy bacteria in the intestines. Beans may enhance eye health, bone health, and joint function. They may help minimize depression. They may contribute to a healthy pregnancy and also help prevent birth defects. Beans contain a lot of calories and those calories need to be strategically included in the total number of daily calories that are eaten. Beans may contribute to the formation of intestinal gas.

Kidney beans contain toxic chemicals that can be leeched out of the beans by processing them correctly.

Beets

Beets may help lower blood pressure, and reduce the risk of artery damage, heart disease, hemorrhoids, and inflammation. Beets may enhance brain function, endurance, and stamina. Beets may enhance digestion and help prevent constipation.

Broccoli

Broccoli may be eaten raw or cooked. It is high in fiber, vitamin C, vitamin K, and antioxidants. It also contains more protein than many other vegetables. It may reduce cholesterol. It may reduce the risk of cancer (bladder, breast, colon, kidney, prostate, stomach), heart disease, and inflammation. Broccoli may enhance bone health, brain function, dental health, digestion, eye health, and the immune system. It may help prevent constipation. Broccoli may slow down the normal aging process and help protect the skin from sun damage. Broccoli may contribute to a healthy pregnancy and the birth of a healthy baby.

Brussels Sprouts

Brussels sprouts contain high levels of vitamin C, vitamin K, selenium, and antioxidants. They also contains more fiber and more protein than many other vegetables. They may enhance digestion and help relieve constipation. They may help reduce triglycerides and inflammation. They may help stabilize blood sugar levels and reduce the risk of diabetes.

Cabbage

Cabbage is low in calories and carbohydrates but it contains a lot of vitamins C and K. It may help minimize inflammation. It may help lower blood pressure and bad LDL cholesterol. It may enhance brain functions, digestion, eye health, and the immune system. It may reduce the risk of coronary artery disease, heart attack, and heart disease.

Carrots

Carrots may be eaten raw or cooked. They contain fiber plus a lot of vitamin A and vitamin B3 (niacin). They are an excellent source of carotenoids, including a significant amount of beta carotene which the body can convert into vitamin A. They may enhance eye health, reduce the risk of cataracts, and help prevent night blindness. They may enhance the oral health of the teeth and gums, minimize tooth decay, and they may help reduce the accumulation of plaque and prevent teeth stains after eating. They may enhance the health of the hair, nails, and skin. They may enhance brain functions and the immune system. They may help stabilize blood sugar levels and reduce cholesterol and blood pressure. They may enhance digestion and help the kidneys, liver, and intestines flush toxins from the body. They may help reduce the risk of diabetes, heart disease, and strokes. They may help reduce the risk of cancer (breast, cervical, colon, esophageal, gastric, lung, oral, prostrate). They may slow down some of the normal effects of aging. Carrots may not be appropriate for individuals with diabetes. Nursing mothers should probably avoid carrots because carrots can change the flavor of breast milk. Finally, eating an excessive quantity of carrots may cause a temporary discoloration of the skin which can be easily reversed by reducing the number of carrots consumed in the future.

Cauliflower

Cauliflower may be eaten raw or cooked. Cauliflower contains a lot of vitamins B5 (pantothenic acid), B9 (folate), C, K, choline, and antioxidants. It may lower blood pressure. It may improve bone health, brain functions, and eye health. It may help reduce inflammation, enhance the immune system, and help reduce the risk of cancer (breast, colon, lung, prostate, stomach), dementia, diabetes, heart disease, liver disease, and stroke. It may help protect the skin from sun damage.

Celery

Celery may be eaten raw, cooked, or steamed. Celery has fewer calories and carbohydrates than most other vegetables. It contains a reasonable amount of vitamin A, vitamin B9 (folate), vitamin K, and antioxidants. It may help reduce inflammation and relieve the symptoms of arthritis, rheumatism, and gout. It may help stabilize blood sugar levels. It may help minimize depression. It may enhance bone and joint health, digestion, eye health, heart health, the immune system, and mental functions. Celery leaves contain the most nutrients so they should be eaten in addition to the stalks. The leaves should be crisp looking and a pale to light green color. Celery with yellow or brown spots are unacceptable.

Cucumbers

Cucumbers are mostly water and they have fewer calories and fewer carbohydrates than most other vegetables. They have small amounts of most vitamins, minerals, and antioxidants but they do have a reasonable amount of vitamin K. They may help stabilize blood sugar levels. They may contribute to regular bowel movements. They may enhance bone and joint health. Cucumbers may be eaten with the peel or the peel may be discarded depending on what you prefer.

Garlic

Garlic nutritional information is shown in the seasonings table on page 296 in the appendix. Garlic contains reasonable amounts of vitamin B1 (thiamine), vitamin C, calcium, copper, manganese, phosphorus, potassium, and selenium. Garlic contains bioactive organosulfur compounds that have many health benefits that may enhance the immune system and extend life expectancy. Garlic may help reduce blood pressure, the bad LDL cholesterol, and fatigue, It may reduce the risk of Alzheimer's disease, dementia, and heart disease. It may enhance eye health. It may help expel toxins from the body. It may help relieve the symptoms of asthma and reduce the occurrence of yeast infections in women. The aroma of garlic will be noticeable on your breath and this may influence when you decide to eat some of it.

Green Peas

Green peas contain protein and fiber that digests slowly and this helps you feel full longer. They also contain reasonable amounts of vitamins A, B1 (thiamine), B9 (folate), C, K, choline, copper, iron, magnesium, manganese, phosphorus, potassium, and zinc. They may help stabilize blood sugar levels and reduce the bad LDL cholesterol. They may reduce the risk of bowel disease, cancer (colon, stomach), diabetes, and heart disease. They may help reduce inflammation. They may enhance bone health, digestion, eye health, the immune system, and skin health. However green peas may contribute to bloating and intestinal gas in some people.

Kale

Kale may be eaten raw, cooked, or steamed. Kale contains a reasonable amount of fiber. It contains high amounts of vitamins A, C, E, and K. It contains reasonable amounts of calcium, copper, iron, magnesium, manganese, potassium, selenium, zinc, and antioxidants. Kale has twice as much vitamin C as the average orange. Kale is low in oxalate which is good because oxalate may interfere with the proper absorption of some minerals. Kale may improve cholesterol levels by decreasing the bad LDL cholesterol and increasing the good HDL cholesterol. It may help reduce blood pressure. It may help stabilize blood sugar levels. It may help expel toxins from the body. It may reduce the risk of anemia, cancer, eye problems (cataracts, macular degeneration), heart disease, and stomach ulcers. In may enhance bone health and skin health.

Lentils

Lentils contain protein and fiber that digests slowly and this may help you feel full longer and reduce food cravings and the desire to overeat. Lentils contain a lot of vitamins B1 (thiamine), B2 (riboflavin), B3 (niacin), B5 (pantothenic acid), B6, B9 (folate), E, copper, iron, magnesium, manganese, phosphorous, potassium, and zinc. They also contain antioxidants. The protein in lentils helps build and maintain muscles. Lentils may help stabilize blood sugar levels. They may help reduce blood pressure and cholesterol and reduce the buildup of plaque inside the arteries. They may enhance digestion and bowel movements and minimize constipation. They may reduce the risk of heart disease. They may help slow down the normal aging process. They may contribute to a healthy pregnancy and also help prevent birth defects. Lentils should be avoided by individuals who have a history of kidney stones. Lentils may contribute to the formation of intestinal gas. Lentils contain a lot of calories and those calories need to be strategically included in the total number of daily calories that are eaten.

Lettuce

Lettuce has fewer calories and carbohydrates than most other vegetables. It has a significant amount of vitamins A and K. Lettuce contains lactucarium which may contribute to a feeling of relaxation, and help prevent insomnia, and enhance the quality of sleep. It may reduce cholesterol and inflammation. It may enhance brain functions. It may contribute to a healthy pregnancy and help prevent birth defects.

Mushrooms

Mushrooms may be eaten raw or cooked. Mushrooms contain a lot of vitamin B2 (riboflavin), choline, copper, selenium, and zinc. They may help reduce blood pressure and cholesterol and reduce the buildup of plaque inside the arteries. They may help reduce inflammation. They may help minimize depression. They may enhance brain functions, digestion, the immune system, and the quality of sleep.

Fresh mushrooms should be stored in the container in which they were purchased because that container was designed to help maintain the freshness of the mushrooms. Transferring fresh mushrooms to a plastic bag or plastic container will hasten their demise. To enhance the vitamin D in freshly purchased mushrooms place them upside down (with their stems pointing straight up) in the sun in front of a window for about one hour. This would make mushrooms the only plant source of vitamin D. Store fresh mushrooms in the refrigerator.

Okra

Okra has few calories and 3.5 ounces contains about 25% of the RDA of vitamin C and 26% of the RDA of vitamin K. It may enhance bone health, bowel movements, brain health, digestion, eye health, the immune system, joint flexibility, kidney and liver health, metabolism, and muscle, nerve, and skin health. It is a diuretic (promotes urination) and it may enhance detoxification. It may reduce blood pressure, LDL cholesterol, depression, fatigue, inflammation, migraine headaches, and triglycerides. It may reduce the risk of Alzheimer's disease, asthma, cancer (breast, colon), diabetes, heart disease, kidney disease, liver disease, osteoporosis, and stomach ulcers. It may help stabilize blood sugar levels. It may enhance a normal pregnancy and reduce the risk of birth defects. It may be more filling and enhance weight loss.

Peppers

Different types of peppers contain different amounts of calories, nutrients, vitamins, and minerals. The summary table on page 286 in the appendix shows this information for sweet green bell peppers and hot green chili peppers.

Sweet bell peppers may enhance brain functions, digestion, eye health, and the immune system. They may reduce inflammation. They may help protect the skin from sun damage.

Hot peppers contain capsaicin. Capsaicin may help minimize hunger, reduce the number of calories consumed, increase metabolism, and increase the burning of fat. Hot peppers may reduce arthritis pain, headache discomfort, and inflammation. They may help reduce the risk of cancer (pancreatic, prostrate, skin), sinus infections, sinus related allergies, and stomach ulcers. They may enhance digestion.

If you eat peppers occasionally they may enhance your short-term metabolic rate. Simply add a few peppers to your salad, either mixed in with the salad or on a separate plate beside the salad. All the following types of peppers have approximately the same impact on increasing a person's metabolic rate: hot peppers, pimentos, rellenos, sweet banana peppers, and sweet bell peppers (green, red, and yellow). However, people who regularly eat spicy foods that contain hot peppers usually discover that their long-term metabolic rate adjusts to their spicy diet.

1. **Banana Pepper:** Sweet mild flavor if allowed to ripen. Has a banana shape up to 6 inches long. Yellow when mature but red if allowed to fully ripen on the vine.

2. **Bell Pepper:** They have a mild sweet crunchy flavor and they contain vitamin C. They may be eaten raw or cooked. Varieties differ in size, shape, thickness, and color and they may be yellow, green, or red. They are usually green at maturity but they will turn red if allowed to fully ripen on the vine. They have their strongest flavor when mature and their flavor becomes milder and sweeter as they continue to ripen. Red bell peppers contain the antioxidants beta carotene, capsanthin, and quercetin.

3. **Chile (or Chili) Peppers:** There are more than 200 varieties of different sizes, shapes, and flavors that range from mild to extremely hot. Generally the smaller the pepper the hotter it is. They may be eaten raw or cooked. Fresh peppers are best stored wrapped in a clean dry cloth inside a paper bag in the refrigerator but sun-dried peppers are best stored in a cool dark dry area.

   a. **Cayenne Peppers:** Very common chili pepper with a very hot taste that is often used in Cajun and chili recipes.

   b. **Jalapeño Peppers:** One of the most popular chili peppers because of their spicy flavor and the ease with which their seeds can be removed. Green when harvested but will gradually turn red if allowed to ripen over a long period of time. Smoked and dried jalapeño peppers are called "Chipote Chiles" and they can be ground into a powder.

   c. **Pepperoncini (or Tuscan) Peppers:** Mild, sweet, slightly hot flavor commonly added to Greek and Italian salads to add crunch.

   How to Process Peppers: Wear disposable kitchen gloves when processing hot peppers and do not touch your eyes. Rinse the pepper. Remove and discard the stem. Cut pepper in half (or quarters) and use a thin sharp knife (or a spoon) to scrap out the ribs (or membrane) and the seeds and discard them. It may be left as a half pepper if it will be stuffed. Or it can be cut into thin slices, or diced into small pieces.

Potatoes

Potatoes may enhance digestion.

Potato Color: Red potatoes and white potatoes both contain similar amounts of starch, nutrients, vitamins, minerals, and antioxidants.

Potato Skin: A lot of nutrients are contained in the potato skin. The skin should not be removed when potatoes are baked or boiled because the skin helps to contain the nutrients inside the potato during baking or boiling. The potato skin should be eaten to maximize the nutritional value of the potato. However, if you do not like the flavor of the skin then don't eat it. But you will be missing a significant amount of the nutritional value in potatoes.

Boiling: If potatoes are boiled then bring a small amount of water to a boil and then add the potatoes. This will reduce the amount of time the potatoes are in the water and this will reduce the amount of nutrition that is lost during boiling. If boiled potatoes are allowed to cool for a little while then they will develop a type of "resistant starch" that has a variety of health benefits including stabilizing blood sugar levels, reducing the risk of colon cancer, and enhancing weight loss.

Frying: Frying adds calories and fat that results in weight gains.

Potato Chips: Fried potato chips are not filling, they contain an excessive amount of sodium, they are not healthy, they do not contribute to weight loss, and they are not recommended.

Green Potatoes: Potatoes that are green, or that contain green spots, are poisonous and they should be discarded and not eaten.

Sprouted Potatoes: Do not eat potatoes that have begun to sprout.

Squash

Squash contains significant amounts of vitamin A, vitamin E, and iron. Squash may enhance bone health, brain functions, digestion, and the immune system. It may reduce blood pressure and inflammation. It may reduce the risk of anemia, cardiovascular diseases, eye problems, heart attack, lung cancer, and stroke. It may reduce the accumulation of plaque on the inner walls of the arteries. It may reduce the symptoms of asthma. If you have low blood pressure then you should talk to your doctor before including squash in your diet.

Sweet Potatoes

Sweet potatoes contain about 50% more calories than regular potatoes. They also contain a significant amount of vitamin A, even more than carrots. They may enhance brain functions, digestion, eye health, and the immune system. They may reduce the risk of cancer (bladder, breast, colon, and stomach). They may reduce blood pressure and inflammation. They may help stabilize blood sugar levels.

Swiss Chard

Swiss chard may help stabilize blood sugar levels. It may enhance bone health, brain functions, digestion, eye health, and nerve and muscle functions. It may improve the condition of the hair, nails, and skin. It may reduce blood pressure. It may reduce the risk of cancer (breast, colon, lung, prostate), heart attack, and stroke.

Tomatoes (See Appendix Page 288)

Technically tomatoes are a fruit but most people think of them as a vegetable. They may enhance bone health, digestion, hair health, eye health, and skin health. They may reduce inflammation. They may reduce the risk of cancer (breast, colon, lung, ovarian, prostate, stomach), heart attack, heart disease, and stroke.

Turnips

Turnips have a lot of vitamin C. They may enhance bone health, digestion, heart health, the immune system, metabolism, and skin health. They may reduce inflammation. They may reduce the risk of cancer (breast, colon, lung, prostate).

Salads

The vegetables in a salad contain a variety of nutrients and plant compounds that may enhance long-term health. When a salad is eaten before a meal it has the same impact as consuming a bowl of soup before a meal. A salad may reduce the total number of calories eaten during a meal by 10% to 20%. A salad can be an appetizer before a meal, or a salad can be a complete meal.

In order for a salad to be a complete meal it should contain some dairy and some protein. A salad does not have to fit on one plate or in one bowl unless you prefer your salad on a single plate. It is okay to put the leafy salad greens on one plate, or in one bowl, along with some diced tomatoes, shredded carrots, chunks or thin slices of your favorite meats, croutons, and a small amount of your favorite dressing. On a different plate you can put a sliced hard-boiled egg, some cubes of cheese, and some sliced mushrooms. Or arrange things anyway you desire. By having the egg and cheese on a different plate, it is possible to eat a slice of egg by itself and experience the pleasure of eating the egg. Then eat a cube of cheese by itself and experience the pleasure of eating cheese. Then eat some mixed salad greens with your favorite dressing. You can switch back and forth between the two plates as you desire. This allows you to enjoy the unique flavors of each of the foods so when you finish eating you feel extremely satisfied with your meal.

Mayonnaise-Based Salad Dressings: When one or two tablespoons of these dressings are added to salads they help the body absorb the lycopene and the beta-carotene in the salads, and these nutrients reduce the risk of cancer and improve the overall health of the body. Avoid fat-free or low fat dressings because they usually contain more sugar and other stuff your body doesn't need, and they have almost the same number of calories as regular salad dressings. Carefully read the nutrition label and the ingredient list because many salad dressings contain added sugar, unhealthy additives, and artificial preservatives. Usually the healthiest salad dressings are refrigerated because they depend on refrigeration instead of artificial preservatives to extend the shelf life of the dressing. However, if your weight loss slows down significantly or stops, then salad dressing is one of the things you can omit from your diet to reactivate your weight loss.

Chapter Nineteen

Fruits

On page 288 in the appendix there is a table that shows the nutrition, vitamin, and mineral data for most of the fruits mentioned in this chapter.

Fruits are extremely healthy and they can make it easier for a person to lose weight. They have a high water content and they contain a lot of nutrients, fiber, and antioxidants. Most studies on fruit have revealed that people who eat fruit regularly are usually healthier than people who only eat fruit occasionally or who rarely eat fruit. It should also be mentioned that on the average, people who eat more fruit weigh less than people who eat less fruit.

Fresh whole fruit is healthier, more satisfying, and more filling, than pureed fruit such as applesauce or fruit juice.

Do not chop, cut, slice, or peel any fruit until you are ready to eat it or use it in a recipe because the nutrients in fruit gradually begin to decline after the fruit has been cut or peeled.

Apples

There is truth in the old saying: "An apple a day keeps the doctor away." Apples are a low-calorie nutrient dense source of healthy fiber and antioxidants. Apples contain pectin, a water-soluble fiber, that helps you feel full. It digests slowly to decrease your appetite for more food. Apples may enhance cardiovascular health, dental health, digestion, hair health, liver health, respiratory health, and skin health. They may reduce the risk of cancer (breast, colon, prostrate, skin), cataracts, dementia, hemorrhoids, and stroke. They may help relieve the symptoms of asthma. They may slow down the normal aging process.

Apricots

Apricots contain vitamins A, B3, phosphorus, and potassium. They may enhance bone health, brain functions, digestion, eye health, heart health, the immune system, muscle functions, and skin health. They may reduce inflammation and the risk of liver disease.

Avocados

Avocados contain fiber, protein, vitamins A, B9 (folate), C, E, K, magnesium, manganese, potassium, and monounsaturated fats that may help reduce the bad LDL cholesterol. They may help relieve the symptoms of arthritis, and they may help protect the skin from the sun. They contain oleic acid, which is also found in olive oil, and this nutrient may help reduce the feeling of hunger. They contain antioxidants that may destroy the harmful free radicals in your body.

The healthy fats in avocados may increase the absorption of carotenoid antioxidants from other vegetables eaten during the same meal. They contain a lot of water which makes them less dense than most fruits. At the beginning of the year 2020 avocados are highly recommended by a variety of very popular diets, including the keto diet and the paleo diet. However, if you use *common sense* and you examine the nutrition data on page 288 in the appendix then you will immediately notice that avocados contain significantly more calories than any other fruit. Avocados contain two or three times more calories than most fruits, and more than four times the calories as cantaloupes, honeydew melons, peaches, and strawberries. Although avocados have a pleasant taste, and they are rich in nutrients, avocados are not filling and they do not satisfy a person's hunger. This means more avocados need to be eaten to satisfy hunger compared to all other fruits. Therefore *common sense* suggests that avocados be consumed in moderation when compared to fruits that are more filling, and that have a variety of healthy nutrients, and fewer calories. However, professional athletes may significantly benefit from the calories and nutrition in avocados. Also ripe avocados that are finely smashed or pureed may be fed to a baby as an extremely nutritious high-calorie baby food that is packed with natural vitamins, minerals, and antioxidants, and that is also tasty (but not too sweet), and that is easy for a baby to chew and digest. However first ask your pediatrician if this type of baby food is appropriate for your baby.

Bananas

Bananas contain carbohydrates, vitamins B2 (riboflavin), B3 (niacin), B6, B9 (folate), plus magnesium, potassium, and antioxidants. They may enhance digestion, heart health, and kidney health. They may help lower blood pressure and stabilize blood sugar levels. They may reduce the risk of stroke.

Blackberries

Blackberries contain vitamins B3 (niacin), B9 (folate), C, E, K, iron, magnesium, manganese, zinc, and antioxidants. They may enhance bone health, brain functions, digestion, eye health, heart health, the immune system, oral health, and skin health. They may reduce cholesterol, stabilize blood sugar, and reduce the risk of heart disease.

Blueberries

Blueberries contain vitamin C, vitamin K, and manganese. They are one of the best sources of antioxidants in the world. They may enhance bone health, brain functions, heart health, the immune system, and skin health. They may lower blood pressure and stabilize blood sugar levels. They may reduce inflammation and the oxidized bad LDL cholesterol. They may minimize muscle soreness after exercising. They may slow down the normal aging process. They may reduce the risk of heart attack, heart disease, and urinary tract infections. They may enhance a healthy pregnancy and reduce the risk of birth defects in a baby.

Cantaloupes

Cantaloupes (also called muskmelons) contain vitamin A, vitamin B3 (niacin), vitamin C, and potassium. Cantaloupes have ten times or more beta-carotene than any other fruit. They may enhance bone health, brain functions, digestion, eye health, hair health, kidney health, lung health, the immune system, oral health, and skin health. They may reduce blood pressure and inflammation. They may reduce the risk of arthritis, asthma, cancer (breast, colon, lung, pancreatic, prostate, uterine), diabetes, and heart disease. They may enhance a healthy pregnancy and reduce the risk of birth defects in a baby.

Cherries

Cherries may enhance heart health. They may reduce the bad LDL cholesterol. They may reduce the risk of diabetes and heart disease. They may reduce inflammation and the discomfort of gout and osteoarthritis. They may reduce the frequency of gout attacks. They may minimize muscle soreness after exercising. They contain a lot of antioxidants that are beneficial to weight loss. They contain the hormone melatonin which helps regulate sleep. Fresh tart cherries are best. When fresh cherries are out of season, then frozen tart cherries, or red tart cherries canned in water, are fine. Eating six or fewer cherries will not add too many calories to your diet and they may help you sleep better. Please remember that a good night's sleep can help you lose weight. (Note: Avoid maraschino cherries because they contain added ingredients that may be harmful to your health.)

Grapefruits

Grapefruits contain more than 85% water and they will fill you up for very few calories. They contain the water-soluble fiber pectin that helps you feel full and it digests slowly to decrease your appetite. Grapefruits contain vitamin B5 (pantothenic acid), vitamin C, selenium, and antioxidants. They may enhance digestion, heart health, and the immune system. They may help reduce blood pressure and the bad LDL cholesterol. They may reduce the risk of cardiovascular disease, diabetes, and kidney stones. Unfortunately they may gradually erode tooth enamel. They may also adversely interact with some prescription medications. Grapefruit first became popular as a diet food in the 1930s. Since then eating grapefruit or drinking grapefruit juice has been recommended in a lot of different diets. However, drinking a glass of water before a meal will have the same weight loss effect. There is no special enzyme or chemical in grapefruit that burns fat cells.

Grapes

Grapes contain vitamin B1 (thiamine), vitamin K, manganese, and antioxidants. The highest concentration of antioxidants is in the grape skins, and red grapes (and red grape wine) have the highest levels. Grapes may reduce blood pressure, the bad LDL cholesterol, and inflammation. They may help stabilize and decrease blood sugar levels. They may enhance bone health, brain functions, eye health, and the immune system. They may reduce the risk of cancer, diabetes, eye diseases, heart disease, and stroke. They may slow down the aging process. They may reduce the occurrence of yeast infections in women.

Honeydew Melons

Honeydew melons (also called honeymelons) contain potassium and antioxidants. They may enhance bone health, digestion, eye health, the immune system, and skin health. They may reduce blood pressure. They may help stabilize blood sugar levels. They may reduce the risk of diabetes. They may enhance a healthy pregnancy.

Kiwi

Kiwi contains vitamin B9 (folate), vitamin C, vitamin K, calcium, manganese, zinc, and antioxidants. It may enhance digestion, eye health, heart health, the immune system, kidney health, lung function, and skin health. It may lower blood pressure and stabilize blood sugar levels. The entire kiwi with its peel may enhance the onset and duration of sleep. It may reduce blood clotting and inflammation. It may relieve constipation. It may reduce the risk of cancer (colon, intestinal, stomach). It may reduce the symptoms of asthma. It may enhance a normal pregnancy and reduce the risk of birth defects in a baby.

Lemons

Lemons contain vitamin C and iron. They may enhance digestion, gall bladder function, the immune system, liver function, metabolism, and blood, eye, hair, lung, oral, and skin health. They may reduce blood pressure and cholesterol. They may reduce the risk of cancer (colon, liver, pancreatic, skin, stomach), kidney stones, and throat infections. They may reduce the symptoms of asthma and skin acne.

Limes

Limes contain vitamin C, iron, and zinc. They may enhance blood circulation, digestion, the immune system, and eye, hair, heart, and skin health. They may help stabilize blood sugar levels and reduce cholesterol. They may reduce inflammation. They may reduce the risk of anemia, cancer (blood, breast, colon, kidney, lung, pancreatic, prostate, stomach), heart disease, kidney stones, stroke, and urinary tract problems. They may reduce the symptoms of asthma.

Olives

Olives contain vitamin E, calcium, copper, iron, and zinc. They contain healthy monounsaturated fats, a variety of antioxidants including oleuropein, and several beneficial plant compounds. They may enhance blood circulation, bone health, brain functions, digestion, eye health, heart health, and the immune system. They may reduce blood pressure, cholesterol, and inflammation, and the risk of anemia, cancer (breast, colon, stomach), diabetes, heart disease, and osteoporosis. They may help reduce the effects of seasonal allergies.

Oranges

Oranges contain more than 85% water and they will fill you up for very few calories. They contain pectin which is a water-soluble fiber that helps you feel full and it digests slowly to decrease your appetite. Oranges contain vitamin B5 (pantothenic acid), vitamin C, calcium, and antioxidants. They may enhance brain functions, digestion, the immune system, and eye, hair, heart, oral, and skin health. They may reduce blood pressure, cholesterol, and inflammation. They may help relieve constipation. They may increase the production of sex hormones. They may reduce the risk of cancer (breast, colon, lung, skin, stomach), diabetes, kidney stones, rheumatoid arthritis, and ulcers. They may reduce the symptoms of asthma and rheumatoid arthritis.

Peaches

Peaches contain vitamins B3 (niacin), E, and antioxidants. Fresh peaches contain more healthy nutrients than canned peaches. They may enhance bone, brain, eye, heart, and skin health. They may enhance the central nervous system, digestion, and the immune system. They may reduce the bad LDL cholesterol, triglycerides, blood pressure, and the risk of cancer (breast, colon, lung). They may help stabilize blood sugar levels. They may slow down the aging process. They may reduce the effects of seasonal allergies. They may enhance a healthy pregnancy and reduce the risk of birth defects in a baby.

Pears

Pears contain copper, antioxidants, and several beneficial plant compounds. Pear skins contain a lot of fiber. Pears may enhance digestion and minimize constipation. They may enhance blood circulation, bone health, eye health, hair health, heart health, the immune system, and skin health. They may reduce blood pressure, cholesterol, and inflammation. They may reduce the risk of diabetes, cancer (bladder, breast, lung, ovarian, stomach), heart disease, and stroke. They may help relieve the discomfort of arthritis and gout.

Pineapples

Pineapples contains vitamin B3 (niacin), vitamin B5 (pantothenic acid), vitamin C, manganese, copper, and antioxidants. They may enhance digestion, eye health, gum health, the immune system, and skin health. They may reduce inflammation. They may reduce the risk of cancer (breast, colon, skin). They may help relieve the discomfort of arthritis. They may minimize muscle soreness after exercising.

Plums

Plums contain vitamin K. They may enhance blood circulation, bone, brain, eye, hair, heart, and skin health. They may enhance the central nervous system, the immune system, and metabolism. They may reduce cholesterol and triglycerides. They may reduce intestinal gas and help relieve constipation. They may reduce the risk of cancer (breast, intestinal, liver, lung), heart attack, and stroke. They may enhance a healthy pregnancy and reduce the risk of birth defects.

Raspberries

They contain vitamins B3 (niacin), B9 (folate), C, E, K, iron, magnesium, manganese, zinc, and antioxidants. They may enhance brain functions, digestion, eye health, the immune system, skin health, and reduce blood pressure and the risk of diabetes and heart disease.

Strawberries

Only buy *organic* strawberries. If you can't afford organic then avoid strawberries because they are sprayed with powerful insecticides that can seriously damage your health. Strawberries contain vitamin B9 (folate), vitamin C, manganese, and antioxidants. They may enhance bone, brain, eye, hair, heart, and skin health. They may enhance digestion, the immune system, reduce blood pressure, and help relieve constipation. They may reduce the risk of diabetes, esophageal cancer, and stroke. They may slow down the normal aging process. They may reduce the pain of arthritis and gout. They may enhance a healthy pregnancy and reduce the risk of birth defects

Tomatoes

Technically tomatoes are a fruit but most people think of them as a vegetable. They may enhance bone health, digestion, hair health, eye health, and skin health. They may reduce inflammation. They may reduce the risk of cancer (breast, colon, lung, ovarian, prostate, stomach), heart attack, heart disease, and stroke.

Watermelons

Watermelons contain vitamins A, B5 (pantothenic acid), beta-carotene, and antioxidants. They may enhance digestion, eye health, gum health, hair health, heart health, kidney health, the immune system, and skin health. They may reduce blood pressure, cholesterol, and inflammation. They may minimize muscle soreness after exercising.

Chapter Twenty

Dairy Products
Milk, Butter, Cheese, Eggs, and Yogurt

On page 294 in the appendix there is a table that shows the nutrition, vitamin, and mineral data for most of the diary products mentioned in this chapter.

Organic Dairy Products

Organic dairy products are created from the milk of cows that are raised in a healthy environment and those cows eat healthy stuff. The cows must have access throughout the year to outdoor pastures, sunlight, shade, shelter, areas to roam about, and clean drinking water. Continuous confinement indoors, or in feeding pens, or in feedlots is prohibited. Organic milk cannot contain any antibiotics or any insecticide residuals, and it may only contain a trivial amount of growth hormones.

Ten different brands of organic dairy products that were actually on grocery shelves and that were being sold to people at different locations all across the USA were randomly tested. 100% of the products that were tested met all of the above requirements for organic dairy products and they contained no antibiotics, no insecticide residuals, and only a trivial amount of growth hormones. The same study also examined 18 different brands of regular dairy products and they all contained some antibiotics and insecticide residuals, and they contained 20 times more growth hormones than what was found in organic dairy products.

Organic milk contains more nutrition, 62% more healthy omega-3 fatty acids, and more healthy antioxidants when compared to conventional milk. The butter, cheese, and yogurt that is made from organic milk also have all of these very desirable characteristics.

Dairy Dietary Recommendations

In the USA the dietary recommendation for adults is 2 to 3 cups of milk, or its equivalent, per day. Equivalents include butter, cheese, ice cream, and yogurt.

Milk Allergies and Lactose Intolerance

Milk, butter, cheese, ice cream, and yogurt should be avoided by people who are allergic to milk or who are lactose intolerant.

No Fiber

Milk, butter, and cheese contain no fiber. Therefore consumption of too much milk, butter, and cheese and not enough other healthy foods that are rich in fiber, may result in constipation.

Milk

Milk is sometimes severely criticized in the media and in some scientific studies. However, the Holy Bible praises the benefits of milk, including cow's milk, goat's milk, and mother's milk (Exodus 3:8, Leviticus 20:24, Numbers 14:8, Deuteronomy 6:3, Joshua 5:6, 2 Samuel 17:29, Isaiah 7:22, Jeremiah 11:5, Ezekiel 20:6). The Holy Bible says that Abraham served curds and milk to the LORD and to the two angels who were with the LORD (Genesis 18:1-18). The fat in milk can be separated into curds and whey.

Whole milk contains *casein* which helps the body absorb calcium and phosphorus. Casein may also help lower blood pressure.

Whole milk contains *whey* which helps grow and repair muscles. Whey contains the amino acids isoleucine, leucine, and valine. Whey may help lower blood pressure and minimize the effect of stress.

Milk is one of the most nutritious foods we can enjoy. Milk contains almost every nutrient needed by a person. Milk has an abundant amount of the following nutrients:

1. **Vitamin B2 (riboflavin):** Milk is one the highest and best sources of vitamin B2.
2. **Vitamin B12:** Milk contains a high amount of vitamin B12.
3. **Calcium:** Milk is one of the best sources of calcium, and the calcium in milk is easily absorbed by the body.
4. **Phosphorus:** Milk is a good source of phosphorus.
5. **Vitamin D:** Cow's milk does not contain vitamin D. However, fortifying milk with vitamin D is mandatory in the USA and many other countries. One cup of fortified milk contains approximately 65% of the recommended daily amount of vitamin D.
6. **Fat:** Milk fat contains about 400 different fatty acids. The fat in whole milk is about 2/3 saturated fat, and 1/4 monounsaturated fat, and about 1/20 polyunsaturated fat. Healthy dairy (ruminant) trans fat is also in milk and this is not the same thing as commercially processed trans fats which are not healthy.

Health Benefits of Milk

1. **Healthy Bones:** One of the primary functions of cow's milk is to enhance healthy bone growth and development in newborn calves. Milk provides this same benefit to children and adults because of the calcium and protein in milk. Milk may even improve the bone density in older people and this may help prevent osteoporosis.
2. **Blood Pressure:** The calcium, casein, magnesium, and potassium in milk may help reduce blood pressure.
3. **Diabetes:** Milk may help reduce the risk of type 2 diabetes.

However, milk may have some unhealthy side effects in some people. For example, milk may contribute to acne.

Raw milk inside a cow is rarely contaminated unless the cow is sick. However, the milking process, the raw milk storage containers, and the transportation method may allow a variety of bacteria to contaminate the raw milk. Therefore drinking raw milk can be hazardous to your health. The pasteurization process neutralizes these bacteria so commercially available milk is usually safe to drink.

Milk is available in the following forms:

1. **Whole Milk:** Contains 3.25% to 3.5% of the original 4% fat that is present in fresh milk from a cow before it is processed. Most commercially available milk has been *pasteurized* to kill bacteria, and *homogenized* to prevent the milk fat (cream) from separating from the milk and rising to the top of the milk. Homogenization also helps improve the flavor of milk, extend the shelf life of milk, and enhance the white color of milk. Whole milk contains the most calories but it is also the most filling. Drinking whole milk, instead of low-fat or skim milk, may help with weight loss because whole milk helps burn calories. Whole milk does **not** increase the chance of diabetes or heart disease.

2. **Reduced 2% Fat Milk:** Contains 2 percent fat. If you drink a lot of milk then this is a very reasonable option because it only contains about 80% of the calories in whole milk.

3. **Low Fat Milk:** Contains 1 percent fat.

4. **Skim Milk:** Contains less than 1/2 percent fat. Children who drink skim milk have at least three times more occurrences of diarrhea than children who drink whole milk.

5. **Cream:** This is the fat that is removed from low fat milk and from skim milk and it is sold as cream. Cream will rise to the top of milk that has not been homogenized where it can be easily removed and used for other purposes.

   a. **Sour Cream:** Contains 18 percent fat. It is used on potatoes, tacos, and in soups.

   b. **Light Cream:** Contains between 16 to 29 percent fat. It is used in sauces and soups.

   c. **Whipping Cream:** Contains 30 percent fat. When whipped it will thicken but not as much as heavy cream. It is only available in the USA.

   d. **Heavy Whipping Cream:** Contains 36 to 40 percent fat. It will not curdle when heated and it does not form a skin on top. Heavy whipping cream is the best cream to use to flavor coffee.

Butter

In the Holy Bible, Proverb 30:33 says, "churning of milk produces butter," (NKJV). The book of Proverbs was consolidated into its final form sometime around 539 BC or before.

Butter is made by churning either milk or cream and this separates the solid fats from the liquid. Butter has a rich creamy flavor and texture. There are several types of butter including salted, unsalted, butter from grass-fed cows, and clarified butter (ghee).

Butter contains about 2/3 saturated fat, 1/4 monounsaturated fat, and 1/20 polyunsaturated fat.

The most recent research has found **no** relationship between saturated fat and an increased risk of heart disease. However, replacing some of the saturated fat with polyunsaturated fat may decrease the risk of cardiovascular problems.

Butter resists oxidation and it has a high smoking point so it is a good choice for high-temperature cooking because it can prevent the formation of harmful free radicals in the food.

Butter is the best source of natural vitamin A, and the vitamin A in butter is easily absorbed and processed by the body. Vitamin A is essential for thyroid and adrenal health.

Butter also contains iodine which is critical to the proper function of the thyroid gland.

The type of cholesterol in butter fat is essential to the normal development of the brain and the nervous system in children.

Butter may help prevent gastrointestinal infections in young children and in senior adults.

Butter contains a variety of antioxidant trace minerals including chromium, copper, manganese, iodine, selenium, and zinc. Antioxidants help protect the body from free radicals that can damage the arteries. They may also enhance the growth and maintenance of healthy bones, and reduce the risk of arthritis and the symptoms of premature aging.

Butter contains lecithin which helps metabolize cholesterol.

Butter contains conjugated linoleic acid (CLA) which is a type of dietary fat. CLA may help decrease body fat and enhance weight loss. CLA may enhance the immune system, and it may help reduce the risk of cancer (breast, colon, liver, prostate, stomach). Free range grass-fed cows produce higher levels of CLA than stall fed cows.

Butter contains oleic acid and myristic which are both fatty acids. These two acids have significant cancer fighting properties.

Butter contains butyrate which is a fatty acid. Butyrate may enhance metabolism, and help prevent the formation of fat cells, and assist in weight loss. Butyrate may enhance digestion, reduce intestinal inflammation, reduce irritable bowel syndrome, and enhance the balance of electrolytes in the body.

Butter contains beta-carotene which may enhance vision by stimulating cellular growth, and reduce the risk of cataracts, and minimize the gradual deterioration of vision due to age.

Butter contains a rare hormone-like substance called the "Wulzen Factor" (or the "anti-stiffness factor") and it is not present in pasteurized milk because the heat of pasteurization destroys it. This nutrient may help prevent the calcification of the joints which results in arthritis, and it may be especially beneficial in the treatment of rheumatoid arthritis. This same nutrient may help prevent hardening of the arteries and calcification of the pineal gland. It may also help prevent cataracts.

Butter may enhance fertility in women. When butter is eaten by a pregnant woman it may help facilitate the proper development of the brain and bones of her new baby while the baby is still in her womb.

Butter may help prevent tooth decay.

Butter consumed in moderation may help reduce the risk of type 2 diabetes, heart attack, and stroke. However, consuming too much butter may increase the bad LDL cholesterol.

Although butter contains a lot of calories per tablespoon, butter should not be completely eliminated from your diet. If butter is consumed in moderation then it may enhance weight loss and your overall long-term health.

The optimal amount of butter that will result in health benefits without causing health problems has not been determined. However, consuming 1 tablespoon or less of butter per day may be okay for some people. On the other hand, consuming 3 tablespoons or more of butter per day is probably very unhealthy for everyone.

1. **Butter:** Butter is a dairy product made by churning cream to separate the butterfat from the buttermilk. Butter contains cholesterol and saturated fat. Different brands of butter have different amounts of cholesterol and fat (read the label). Organic butter made from grass-fed cows is highly recommended because it contains more omega-3 fatty acids than regular butter.
2. **Unsalted Butter:** Unsalted butter does not contain any salt. It is recommended because it contains no sodium and this allows you to add table salt to your food or to your recipes if you desire.

3. **Salted Butter:** Salted butter contains salt. It is not recommended. However, if you use salted butter in a recipe then omit the salt in the recipe.

4. **Margarine:** It is a non-dairy product that is made from any one of a variety of different vegetable oils. The vegetable oil is heated to a very high temperature which makes it rancid. Then nickel (a toxic heavy-metal) is added as a catalyst to solidify the oil. Even after the nickel is removed, trace amounts of the nickel is still present in the finished margarine. Deodorants are then added to hide the disgusting smell of the rancid oils. Finally artificial colors are added to change the natural gray color of margarine to the color of real butter. Margarine increases bad LDL cholesterol, decreases good HDL cholesterol, and decreases the body's automatic immune response to invading harmful microorganisms. Therefore margarine is **not** recommended, and margarine in all of its many different forms should be avoided.

Cheese

In the Holy Bible Abraham served curds and milk to the LORD and to the two angels who were with the LORD (Genesis 18:1-18). This occurred sometime around 1700 BC or before.

Separating milk into curds and whey is the first step in making cheese. The fat in the milk separates during churning and the fat collects together into a solid. The whey is the liquid that remains after the curds have been extracted. The curds are then pressed into cheese. Different varieties of cheese can be made using either fresh cheese or aged cheese. There are at least 300 different varieties of cheese. Cheese is available in different forms, such as blocks, chunks, cubes, shredded, slices, spreads, sticks, and wheels.

One slice of cheese has approximately the same amount of nutrition as one cup of whole milk.

Cheese contains an average of about 100 calories per ounce, with a range of approximately 85 to 115 calories per ounce, more or less. Thinly sliced cheese that contains less than one ounce per slice will contain fewer calories but still contain all the flavor of that cheese. Cheese made from low-fat milk will also contain fewer calories but at the expense of some of the nutrients in the fat of whole milk.

Cheese should be eaten in moderation because the calories can quickly add up. Eating cheese in moderation may help reduce the risk of cardiovascular disease and type 2 diabetes, and it may help extend life expectancy.

Hard cheeses require more sodium to create them so they are higher in sodium.

Cheese made from cows that are 100% grass-fed contain more nutrients and omega-3 fatty acids.

For individuals who are lactose intolerant, some aged chesses, such as cheddar, Parmesan, and Swiss, contain little or no lactose and some individuals may be able to enjoy these cheeses if consumed in moderation.

Cottage Cheese: Cottage cheese is made from the solid curd that results from churning milk. The curd is drained and dried. The curd is then crumbled into smaller pieces. Cream, salt, and spices may then be added to create cottage cheese with the desired flavor and consistency. Cottage cheese has approximately 110 calories per 1/2 cup. Cottage cheese contains vitamins B2 (riboflavin), B12, calcium, phosphorus, and selenium. One-half cup of cottage cheese contains about 15% of the RDA for sodium.

Some brands of cottage cheese are 100% cottage cheese. And some brands contain a variety of other ingredients that may or may not be healthy. Read the nutrition label before buying cottage cheese.

The high protein content of cottage cheese may enhance the feeling of fullness, and this may result in a decrease in appetite, and the consumption of fewer calories, and the loss of weight. Because of its high protein content it may help form lean muscle mass as you lose weight. Casein is approximately 80% of the protein in cottage cheese and casein is as effective as whey protein for building muscles. Some bodybuilders eat cottage cheese before going to sleep at night, and this results in a slow release of amino acids into the blood during the night, and this may facilitate the creation of muscles while sleeping.

The flavor of cottage cheese can be enhanced in any one of the following ways:

1. **Fruits:** Stir diced pieces of your favorite fruit into the cottage cheese.

2. **Jello Flavor:** Sprinkle a *small amount* of your favorite flavor of Jello gelatin on top of one serving of cottage cheese, and then stir until the powdered gelatin is mixed evenly throughout the cottage cheese. Small curd cottage cheese evenly absorbs the flavor and color of the gelatin. By flavoring one serving of cottage cheese at a time, you can use different flavors of Jello gelatin to change the flavor of the cottage cheese each time you eat it into a different taste that you really enjoy.

Greek Yogurt

Greek yogurt contains approximately 20 grams of protein per cup and it is high in calcium, iodine, and probiotics. It may enhance blood health, bone health, digestion, the immune system, muscle formation, tooth health, and thyroid function. It may decrease the risk of diarrhea. It may reduce blood pressure. It may reduce the occurrence of yeast infections in women.

Eggs

Individuals with egg allergies should avoid eggs.

Most of the nutrients in an egg are in the yellow yolk. Eggs are high in protein and fat. Eggs are a complete protein which means they contain all nine essential amino acids.

One egg contains more than 30% of the RDA for choline and selenium. Eggs may increase the good HDL cholesterol. Eggs may enhance bone health, brain health, eye health, and muscle health. Eggs may reduce blood pressure, and reduce the risk of breast cancer, cardiovascular disease, cataracts, heart attack, heart disease, macular degeneration, and stroke. Eggs may minimize fatigue and enhance energy. Pasture-raised eggs may reduce triglycerides. Eggs may be more filling and enhance weight loss. However, eating a lot of eggs in one day can raise the bad LDL cholesterol in some people.

There is no nutritional difference between eggs based on the color of the eggshell. Some breeds of chicken lay brown eggs, and other breeds of chicken lay white eggs. The color of the shell has no impact on the nutrition that is inside the shell.

Organic eggs are more expensive that conventional eggs but they are worth it. The table on page 380 in Appendix A illustrates the nutritional differences between a normal egg and an organic egg. A normal egg contains an impressive amount of nutrition and 72 calories. On the other hand, an organic egg only contains about 60 calories, the same amount of protein, more omega-3 fatty acids, less saturated fat, less cholesterol, less sodium, and more vitamins and minerals.

Eggs should be stored in the refrigerator at 40°F (4.5°C) or a little less. Eggs should not be eaten raw. Eggs should always be cooked long enough to avoid potential health problems.

Hard Boiled Eggs: Let the eggs come to room temperature for 4 hours or overnight. Do not add salt or baking soda to the water. Bring water to a fast boil. Then add eggs using tongs, cover the pot, reduce heat to a slow boil, and cook 10 minutes. Use tongs to move each egg to an ice water bath. Chill 8 minutes. Crack the shell in many, many, many places. Peel by lifting the cracked shell pieces up using the thin inner membrane that is between the shell and the egg.

Chapter Twenty-One

Grain: Corn, Oats, Rice, and Wheat

On page 290 in the appendix there is a table that shows the nutrition, vitamin, and mineral data for most of the grains mentioned in this chapter.

When whole grains (such as corn, oats, rice, and wheat) are included in a diet that also contains fish, then this combination of foods can reduce the chance of asthma in children.

Corn

There are three basic types of corn as follows:

1. **Dent Corn or Field Corn** (used for cornmeal, hominy, and for corn chips, tortillas, and taco shells): A small depression or dent appears in each kernel of corn on an ear of corn. This is the best type of dried corn to grind into "fresh cornmeal" because home ground cornmeal does not contain any additives or artificial preservatives. Only grind the amount you need to make fresh cornbread, hush puppies, and similar foods.

2. **Popcorn or Flint Corn**: When it is heated the steam builds up inside the kernel until it explodes. If unpopped popcorn is ground into cornmeal then it will be grittier than cornmeal made from dent corn. Popcorn contains more fiber than other snack foods and it is a very healthy snack because popcorn is a whole grain. Most diets recommend air-popped popcorn instead of popping the corn in a little oil or using the microwave. However, since air-popped popcorn is 100% popcorn without any oil or flavors it has a relatively flat boring taste. Adding a little salt and drizzling a little melted butter or oil on the popcorn does not make a big improvement in its flavor. Most people have become accustomed to the flavor of popcorn that has been popped in oil, or in the microwave, and air-popped popcorn just isn't the same. It is not reasonable to give up the delightful flavor of traditional popcorn to save a few calories or to avoid a few additives. The Common Sense Diet recommends that you enjoy your popcorn the way you like it and that you should not force yourself to eat something you don't enjoy. However, consider the calories of anything that you add to your popcorn, such as butter or cheese, and be reasonable in the quantities you use. Some popcorn suggestions are on page 210.

3. **Sweet Corn or Table Corn** (yellow or white corn): It contains a high sugar level. It is usually eaten as corn on the cob. But it can be removed from the cob and either canned or frozen for future consumption. The best way to purchase sweet corn is at a grocery

store or a farmers' market. The green husks should still be on the fresh ears of corn on the cob. Another way to purchase healthy sweet corn is to buy frozen corn at a grocery store. The least desirable way to buy sweet corn is canned corn because most canned corn may contain sodium, artificial preservatives, and other unhealthy ingredients.

Corn, including popcorn, may enhance bone health, bowel movements, brain health, colon health, digestion, energy, eye health, heart health, the immune system, kidney health, nerve health, and skin health. It may reduce bad LDL cholesterol. It may reduce the risk of Alzheimer's disease, anemia, cancer (colon, lung), cardiovascular diseases, diabetes, and hemorrhoids. It may facilitate a normal pregnancy and it may help prevent birth defects. It may be more filling and enhance weight loss.

Oats

Oats contain a lot of water-soluble fiber and the fiber has two benefits: it soaks up water which makes it more filling, and the fiber digests very slowly which helps reduce the desire to eat more food.

Oats do not contain any gluten. Oats contain complex carbohydrates and they are a good source of B vitamins. Oats contain beta-glucan which is a water-soluble fiber that may help decrease bad LDL cholesterol, enhance metabolism, increase satiety, reduce the appetite, and enhance weight loss.

Oats may reduce blood pressure and inflammation. Oats may enhance bowel movements, digestion, heart health, and the immune system. Oats may reduce the risk of asthma, cancer (breast, colon, ovarian, prostate), cardiovascular diseases, diabetes, heart attack, and stroke. Oats may help stabilize blood sugar levels. Oats may have an anti-itching benefit.

Oats are available in the following forms:

1. **Whole Oats:** This is the oat as it is grown and harvested, and it still contains its inedible outer hull.
2. **Whole Oat Groats:** This is the oat kernel with its inedible outer hull removed. Groats may or may not be roasted at a very low temperature. This gives the groats their toasty flavor and it extends the shelf life of the groats because it neutralizes the enzymes that can cause groats to become rancid.
3. **Steel Cut Oats:** These are also sometimes referred to as Irish oats or as Scottish oats. The whole oat groat is chopped or cut into smaller pieces that look almost like rice. The cooking time for steel cut oats varies based on the amount of processing they receive. Follow the cooking directions on the package.

4. **Rolled Oats:** These are oat groats that have been steamed, dried, pressed down into flat flakes under heavy rollers, and then lightly toasted. This stabilizes the desirable oils in the oats and they have a longer shelf life. Rolled oats are sometimes used in cookie, candy, bread, and muffin recipes.

There are two basic types of rolled oats as follows:

    a. **Old Fashioned or Regular:** The cooking time is about 5 minutes.

    b. **Quick or Instant:** The cooking time is about 1 minute. These oats are cut into smaller pieces, and then they are pressed down thinner, and sometimes steamed longer, than regular oats. Therefore they absorb water faster and they cook faster.

5. **Oat Flakes:** The tough outer bran is removed before rolling, steaming, and toasting. Oat flakes are usually thicker than rolled oats.

6. **Oat Flour:** You can grind oat groats, steel-cut oats, rolled oats, or oat flakes into an oat flour.

All the different types of processed oats have the same basic nutritional values because they are all made from the same type of oats.

Rice

This section on rice will review white rice, brown rice, and wild rice. However, before you make a final decision about rice, may I humbly suggest that you read all the information about all the different types of rice, and especially the summary at the end of this section. You may discover that the type of rice that you believed was a healthy choice was not so healthy after all.

Introduction to Rice

Rice is a whole grain. Rice is gluten free. Before processing, all rice contains a hard inedible exterior hull (or husk), and inside the hull is the edible bran, germ, and endosperm. The hard inedible exterior hull of all rice products is removed and discarded.

Rice is mostly carbohydrates with a little protein and even less fat. Rice contains healthy "resistant starch" when it is cooked and allowed to cool for just a little while. Rice is a very popular grain all over the world. It goes well with beef, chicken, seafood, and most vegetables.

White Rice

White rice has been popular in the USA since the late 1800s. It was popular in the rest of the world long before that.

White rice is brown rice without its hull, bran, and germ. The bran and the germ are the healthiest parts of the grain but they are removed from white rice. White rice is a highly polished rice. Almost all of the fiber and essential fatty acids are destroyed during the milling process. Therefore white rice is "enriched" with artificial vitamins and nutrients but not in the same quantities in which they were removed. And artificial vitamins and nutrients are not processed by the human body as efficiently as their natural counterparts.

Eating white rice regularly doubles the risk of developing type 2 diabetes.

Brown Rice

The color of brown rice may be brown, purplish, or reddish. Brown rice is made by removing the hard exterior hull from rice. The embryo may or may not be removed depending on the milling process. If the embryo is not removed then the brown rice contains a lot more nutrition.

Brown rice may have the following health benefits:

1. **Antioxidants:** Brown rice is rich in antioxidants on the same level as fresh fruit and vegetables. The antioxidants in brown rice may be part of the reason for the low occurrence of some chronic diseases in some countries where brown rice is one of their staple foods.
2. **Cholesterol:** The bran of brown rice may help lower bad LDL cholesterol and increase good HDL cholesterol.
3. **Fiber:** Brown rice contains fiber. Fiber attaches itself to the chemicals that cause cancer and steers them away from the breasts and colon. Fiber may also enhance cardiovascular health.
4. **Vitamin B1**: Brown rice contains vitamin B1.
5. **Magnesium:** Brown rice contains magnesium.
6. **Manganese:** Brown rice contains a lot of manganese.
7. **Selenium:** Brown rice contains selenium.
8. **Type 2 Diabetes:** Brown rice releases its sugar slowly and this is important for someone with diabetes.

Unhealthy Ingredients in Brown Rice

Brown rice also contains the following unhealthy ingredients:

1. **Phytic Acid (Phylate):** Phylic acid is an anti-nutrient. Anti-nutrients reduce the body's ability to absorb some of the good nutrients from food. Phytic acid does offer a few health benefits but it interferes with the body's ability to absorb iron and zinc. In the long-term consuming a lot of phytic acid may cause mineral deficiencies in the body.
2. **Arsenic:** Arsenic is one of the world's most toxic heavy metals and it is naturally present in most parts of the world. The amount of arsenic has been steadily increasing due to the effect of pollution in

all of its different forms. Significantly higher amounts of arsenic is present in brown rice, and brown rice products, when compared to white rice. Long-term consumption of arsenic may result in several chronic diseases, such as cancer, heart disease, and type 2 diabetes.

Arsenic if present in almost all foods and beverages but in very negligible amounts. There are two forms of arsenic:

a. **Organic Arsenic:**   It is present in very small quantities in animals and plants. Fish, shrimp, and shellfish contain organic arsenic.

b. **Inorganic Arsenic:** Inorganic arsenic is the most toxic form of arsenic. Mussels and some types of seaweed contain inorganic arsenic. It is naturally present in the soil and rocks. When it is dissolved it is also present in water. Polluted waters that contain the highest levels of arsenic are common in Asia and in South America. The polluted water eventually finds its way into flooded rice paddies where rice is grown. Rice naturally absorbs more arsenic from soil and water than other food crops. Rice is the single highest food source of inorganic arsenic, which is the most toxic form of arsenic. This includes rice milk, rice bran, rice breakfast cereal, rice baby cereal, rice based infant formulas, rice crackers, rice pudding, brown rice syrup, rice pasta, and food bars that contain rice or brown rice syrup. The short-term impact of arsenic may result in a minor degree of confusion, drowsiness, diarrhea, vomiting (which may include blood in the vomit), blood in the urine, hair loss, stomach pain, severe muscle cramps, and eventually convulsions. Long-term consumption of inorganic arsenic may result in blockage of blood vessels, high blood pressure, heart disease, cancer (bladder, liver, lung, skin), type 2 diabetes, severe diarrhea, nerve cell damage, and brain damage. Eventually it may result in a coma or death. In children and teenagers arsenic may contribute to the inability to concentrate, to remember, and to learn new material, and it may result in reduced intelligence and impaired social behavior. In pregnant women it may hinder the normal development of the baby and result in birth defects.

Wild Rice

"Wild rice" is actually not a rice despite its name. It is not even directly related to rice. It is called "rice" because it looks like rice and it can be cooked like rice. However, it has a stronger taste than rice and it is more expensive. It also takes between 45 to 60 minutes to properly cook wild rice.

Wild rice is a grass that grows in shallow freshwater marshes and on the shores of some streams and rivers. The grass produces edible seeds that look like rice.

There are four varieties of wild rice. One variety is grown in Asia and it is harvested as a vegetable. Three varieties are grown in North America primarily near the Great Lakes and they are harvested as a grain. Wild rice was grown and harvested by Native American Indians for hundreds of years before the arrival of European settlers.

Wild rice is a complete protein because it contains all nine essential amino acids. Wild rice contains a lot of antioxidants. The glycemic index (GI) of wild rice is 57 which is similar to brown rice and oats and therefore it may help stabilize blood sugar levels.

Unhealthy Aspects of Wild Rice

Since wild rice is grown in the wild it may contain the following unhealthy stuff:

1. **Ergot:** This is a toxic fungus that can infect the seeds of wild rice. If consumed it may cause diarrhea, nausea, vomiting, dizziness, headaches, mental impairment, and seizures.

2. **Toxic Heavy Metals:** The waters in which wild rice grows is frequently saturated with harmful pesticides, industrial wastes, and pollution in all of its different forms. Arsenic, cadmium, and lead have been found in 26 different brands of wild rice in the USA. In the long-term heavy metals can accumulate in the human body and result in a variety of medical problems.

How to Remove Some of the Arsenic in Rice

White rice has been popular in the USA since the late 1800s. The artificial vitamins that are added to white rice are primarily on the exterior of the rice. If the rice is rinsed before cooking then most of the vitamins on the outside of the rice will be rinsed off and lost. Therefore in the USA rinsing the rice before cooking is not recommended by the companies that make and sell white rice. When white rice is cooked the vitamins on the rice are cooked off into the water. Therefore in the USA the cooking instructions for white rice indicate that twice as much water should be added to the cook pot as rice. This allows for most of the water to be absorbed back into rice as it cooks which keeps the artificial vitamins with the rice. Gradually the instructions for cooking white rice in the USA have been applied to all types of rice that is cooked in the USA.

White rice from California, India, and Pakistan, and sushi rice from the USA, all contain about half the amount of inorganic arsenic as all other types of rice from other regions. In the USA approximately 75%

of all types of rice are grown in Arkansas, Louisiana, Mississippi, Missouri, and Texas and they contain the highest levels of inorganic arsenic.

Brown rice has an average of about 80% more inorganic arsenic than white rice because white rice has its bran removed. Brown basmati rice from California, India, Nepal, and Pakistan all have about one-third less inorganic arsenic than brown rice grown in other areas. Jasmine rice may also contain lower levels of inorganic arsenic.

Organically grown rice absorbs arsenic in the same way as rice grown in conventional paddies so there is no difference in the amount of arsenic in organic rice. The important consideration for rice is where the rice is grown and not how it is grown.

In most of the countries in the world where rice is a significant part of the diet, the rice is thoroughly rinsed before it is added to the cooking pot. Then six times as much water is added to the cook pot as rice. When the rice is done the extra water is drained off the rice and then the rice is served. The water that is drained off the rice contains a reasonable amount of the arsenic that was originally in the rice.

Therefore the arsenic in all types of rice can be reduced by using the following preparation and cooking procedures:

1. **Rinsing:** Different studies have arrived at different conclusions about the value of rinsing rice before cooking. Some studies have reported that almost none of the arsenic is removed by rinsing in clean arsenic-free water. Other studies have reported that between 10% to 28% of the arsenic is removed by rinsing the rice in clean arsenic-free water before cooking.

2. **Cooking:** Add six times the amount of clean arsenic-free water to the cook pot as rice. After the rice is cooked drain off and discard the water that is now contaminated with arsenic, and serve the rice. Different studies have reported that this cooking method may remove between 30% to 60% of the arsenic in the rice. However, the studies do not indicate whether or not this includes any arsenic that may have been removed during the above rinsing procedure.

If white rice is prepared following the above instructions then almost all of the artificial vitamins that were added to the white rice will be lost. However, a significant amount of the arsenic in the rice will also be removed. This will result in a rice that may satisfy a person's desire to eat rice, but the rice will not contain any artificial vitamins. However, the cooked white rice will have the lowest amount of toxic arsenic when compared to brown rice and wild rice. If other healthy nutritious food is consumed at the same meal then the meal may still contain vitamins and nutrients and it will also contain less toxic arsenic.

Rice Summary

1. **Arsenic:** All rice contains arsenic which is a toxic heavy metal. It can very gradually accumulate in the human body over time, and eventually arsenic can cause a variety of health problems. However, about 70% of the arsenic that is consumed is expelled in the urine a few days after eating if the amount of arsenic is not significant and rice is not consumed frequently. However, before the arsenic is expelled from the body the arsenic may begin to cause health problems that the body will have to deal with after the arsenic is expelled from the body.

2. **White Rice:** White rice has the lowest amount of healthy nutrition but it also contains the lowest amount of arsenic.

3. **Brown Rice:** Brown rice contains phylic acid in addition to arsenic. Phylic acid is an anti-nutrient. Anti-nutrients reduce the body's ability to absorb some of the good nutrients from food.

4. **Wild Rice:** Wild rice may contain the toxic fungus ergot in addition to arsenic.

If your primary objective is to improve your long-term health while you are losing weight, then you may wish to consider removing, or minimizing, all forms of rice from your diet and replacing rice with other healthier whole grains. However, if you really like rice then you may wish to include some white rice in your diet because it does not contain as much arsenic as other types of rice, and then eat other healthy foods to make up for the missing nutrition in white rice. Rinse the white rice in clean arsenic-free water, and then add six times as much clean arsenic-free water as rice to the cook pot. After cooking drain the rice and discard the water that is now arsenic contaminated.

You should make a decision about rice based on what you believe would be best for you. The reason is because you are designing a diet that is just right for you.

Wheat

Wheat may enhance bone health, bowel movements, brain health, digestion, energy, eye health, hair health, the immune system, metabolism, muscle health, oral health, and skin health. It may minimize depression, inflammation, and skin acne. It may reduce blood pressure, cholesterol, and triglycerides. It may reduce the risk of asthma, cancer (breast, colon), cataracts, type 2 diabetes, gallstones, heart attack, heart disease, macular degeneration, and stroke. It may help stabilize blood sugar levels. It may facilitate a healthy pregnancy and reduce the risk of birth defects. It may be more filling and enhance weight loss, especially in women.

The major types of wheat are:

1. **Hard Red Wheat** (Spring and Winter Wheat):
   a. The berry has a reddish brown color and it has a long thin shape with one rounded end and one pointed end.
   b. It is the most common type of wheat.
   c. It is used to produce a heavier, darker colored bread with a strong wheat flavor.

2. **Hard White Wheat** (Spring and Winter Wheat):
   a. The berry has a yellowish brown color with more of a long oval shape with rounder ends.
   b. It creates the *best all-purpose wheat.*
   c. It can be used to make bread, tortillas, oriental noodles, or cookies.

3. **Soft White Wheat** (Spring and Winter Wheat):
   a. The berry has a light yellow color with more of an oval shape with rounder ends.
   b. It has a very mild flavor.
   c. It makes outstanding piecrusts, cakes, cookies, and pastries.
   d. It can also be used to make excellent pizza crusts.
   e. It is preferred for breads that contain herbs, cheese, or meat.
   f. It can be used to make rolls with a milder flavor.

4. **Soft Red Wheat** (Winter Wheat):
   a. This is the least popular of all the different types of wheat.
   b. It has a stronger wheat flavor than white wheat and its primary uses are for flatbreads and crackers.

If you can only afford to purchase one type of wheat berry then you should consider purchasing the hard white wheat berries because they can be ground into the best all-purpose flour. If you can afford to invest in more than one type of wheat berry then you should also consider the soft white wheat berries because they can be ground into an excellent pastry flour that can be used to make pizza crusts and rolls. If you are not limited in what you can afford then you should also consider purchasing a small quantity of hard red wheat berries and then mix them into your loaf bread recipes in a ratio of about 1/4 red wheat berries to 3/4 white wheat berries to add a little variety to the flavor of your homemade loaf breads.

Other Grains

1. **Amaranth:** 102 calories per 100 grams. It is gluten-free and it contains a significant amount of protein, fiber, micronutrients, and antioxidants. It is also a good source of manganese, magnesium, phosphorus, and iron.

2. **Barley:** 354 calories per 100 grams. It has a chewy texture and a nutty taste. It is the fourth highest produced grain in the world. Hulled barley is a whole grain but pearled barley has had it bran removed and it is not a whole grain. When it is cooked barley doubles in size. Barley contains vitamins, minerals, and antioxidants. It is a good source of fiber, thiamine, manganese, and selenium.

3. **Buckwheat:** 353 calories per 100 grams. Buckwheat is not a wheat. It has very few vitamins but more minerals than corn, rice, or wheat. It is a good source of fiber, resistant starch, copper, magnesium, manganese, phosphorus, and iron.

4. **Bulgur:** 83 calories per 100 grams of cooked bulgur. Bulgur is a whole grain. It is made by parboiling dried cracked durum wheat. It is a good source of fiber and manganese.

5. **Millet:** 378 calories per 100 grams. Millet is a small grained grass cereal. Millet is a good source of fiber.

6. **Quinoa:** 120 calories per 100 grams. Quinoa is gluten-free. It is an edible seed and it is one of the most popular health foods in the world. Although it is not a cereal grain it is still counted as a whole grain. It has a high fiber content but most of the fiber is insoluble and only about 10% of the fiber is the healthy soluble type.

7. **Rye:** 335 calories per 100 grams. Rye is a cereal grain. It has less gluten than wheat. It can be used to make flour, bread (pumpernickel), beer, whiskey, and vodka. The whole rye berries can be boiled or rolled (like rolled oats or oatmeal).

8. **Sorghum:** 329 calories per 100 grams. It is the fifth most important cereal crop in the world because it is drought tolerant and heat resistant. It contains a lot of protein, vitamins, and minerals. It is used to make sorghum molasses, sorghum syrup, alcohol, and biofuels. It may be eaten by some people who are allergic to wheat. It is also an important animal feed.

9. **Teff:** 367 calories per 100 grams. Teff is a gluten-free type of millet. It has a nutty flavor similar to hazelnuts. It is the most expensive type of grain because it is the smallest type of grain and it is difficult to harvest. Teff can be purchased as ground flour.

10. **Triticale:** 338 calories per 100 grams. It is a hybrid grain with wheat as its mother and rye as its father. It is typically available in health food stores.

Chapter Twenty-Two

Bread, Cereal, and Pasta

Introduction to Bread

A lot of people become angry, upset, furious, outraged, shocked, and traumatized when they discover that their favorite "wheat bread" that they have been eating for many, many years is nothing more than "white bread" that has been cleverly disguised, and that their bread's brown color is artificial, and that they have been deprived of the many health benefits that they believed they were getting by eating their favorite "brown bread."

The information in this chapter will help you evaluate the bread your family is now eating so you can determine exactly how healthy that bread is. You may discover that your family has been eating extremely nutritious bread for a very long time. Or you may discover that you have been feeding your family a bread that has very little nutritional value except for a lot of calories and some artificial vitamins.

Is Bread Good for You or Bad for You?

Some diets, such as low-carb diets, strongly recommend that you minimize or eliminate bread from your diet. Other sources recommend that you eat grain products, including bread, as a part of every meal during the day. However, eating too much bread, or too many grains, and not enough other healthy foods is probably not a good idea for most people. For most people the best answer is probably a compromise between none and a lot. Most of us should eat a reasonable amount of grain, which includes bread, but not so much that we are not able to include other healthy foods in our diet without gaining weight.

The Lord's Prayer in the Holy Bible includes this statement, "Give us this day our daily bread," (Matthew 6:11, KJV). Since Jesus encouraged us to pray for daily bread, then eating some bread each day is probably a healthy thing for most of us to do, unless we have an allergy or an intolerance to wheat or gluten.

Whole Grains

Whole grains include amaranth, barley, brown rice, buckwheat, bulgur, corn, millet, quinoa, oats, rye, sorghum, teff, triticale, wheat, and wild rice. Rolled oats are a whole grain if they contain all of their original bran, germ, and endosperm. "Quaker Oats" original, quick, steel cut oats, and packets of instant oatmeal are all 100% whole grain oats. Corn flour and cornmeal may be whole grains if they contain the pericarp, seed coat, germ, and endosperm. Whole grains contain a lot of healthy dietary fiber and a variety of other healthy nutrients. Whole grains can be cooked for human consumption without crushing. An example would be popcorn which is a cooked whole grain. When whole grains are processed by crushing the result is a flour that can be used in a variety of recipes that require some type of cooking, frying, or baking.

Definition of Whole Grain

The terms "whole grain" and "whole wheat" mean that the product contains some of the bran, germ, and endosperm that was present in the original grain or in the original wheat.

1. **Bran (or Brain):** The bran is the thin husk that surrounds the grain. The bran contains protein, vitamins, minerals, and nutrients such as calcium, magnesium, niacin, phosphorus, potassium, phytic acid, and dietary fiber. The bran contains a minimum of 50% of the nutrients in the grain.

2. **Germ:** The germ is the smallest part of the grain. It is the embryo inside the grain and it contains about 25% of the nutrition in the grain including protein, vitamins, minerals, fiber, heart-healthy fats, lipids, and sugar. The germ contains tocopherol which is a critical nutrient that is necessary to maintain a healthy reproductive system.

3. **Endosperm:** The endosperm is the starchy inside part of the grain. The endosperm is primarily carbohydrates and it contains essential amino acids and the components of gluten. The endosperm is relatively dry and it is the only part of the grain that is absolutely necessary to make flour as we know it today. Flour that is made using only the endosperm after the bran and the germ has been removed is sometimes called "refined flour." (Note: Gluten is formed when bread flour is mixed with water. Gluten is what causes bread dough to rise and gluten yields a light airy soft bread.)

Converting Whole Grains into Flour

Whole grains can be converted into flour in the following ways:

1. **Roller Milling:** A series of high-speed steel rollers are used to squeeze the grain into flour. This is a relatively hot process and the high temperatures can cause the vitamins to degrade and the heat can cause any oils in the grain to become rancid. Therefore the bran and the germ are usually sifted away from the endosperm and only the endosperm is milled.

2. **Hammer Milling:** Steel hammers rotating at high speeds impact the grain. The grain is gradually reduced into smaller pieces by repeated impacts with the hammers, and with the walls of the grinding chamber, and with other grain particles inside the chamber. Particles of the correct size can pass through the discharge screen but larger particles remain inside the grinding chamber until they are reduced to the correct size.

3. **Stone Grinding:** This is the method that was used to grind grain for thousands of years. It was first done by hand, and then it was done using animal power, and then waterpower, and eventually wind power. Two large stones are used to grind the grain into flour. One of the stones rotates against the other stone which is stationary. This is a relatively cool process and if done at a slow speed it may not cause any oils that are present to become rancid. However, if it is done at moderate or high speeds then it may cause the oils to become rancid. Therefore if stone grinding is done at moderate or high speeds then the bran and the germ are first removed, and then the endosperm is processed by stone grinding. After grinding, some of the bran and germ may be added back into the flour. In the year 2020 there is no federal standard that defines stone ground wheat so each miller can create stone ground wheat any way they desire. Some millers stone grind some of their wheat and then mix it with their roller milled flour and sell it as "stone ground flour." If you want real stone ground flour then look for a product that states that it is 100% stone ground whole wheat flour. If the 100% stone ground whole wheat flour contains some natural oils then it will spoil more quickly than flour that has had some or all of its bran and germ removed. Also please remember that there are no regulations that govern what stone ground flour should be and therefore different millers are at liberty to use the term "stone ground" as they see fit.

Types of Bread

White Breads: Most white breads, and some "wheat breads," are made from flour that does not contain any bran or germ. The flour is made from the endosperm and therefore most of the nutrients have been removed from the flour. To meet the legal requirements for bread these breads must be artificially "enriched" with some of the vitamins and nutrients that were in the bran and germ. However, fiber is rarely added back into these breads and this is a serious deficiency in most white breads.

Some "white breads" are made using some whole grains and this will be indicated on the bread package with the words "white whole wheat bread" or "white bread made from whole grain." This type of white bread is a healthier option than ordinary white bread and it is an option for people who have digestive issues with whole wheat bread. However, these white breads do not contain all the germ that was originally inside the wheat grain.

Whole Grain Breads: Foods labeled as "whole grain" should contain some grain that contains the bran, germ, and endosperm. The whole grains should be at least 51% of the ingredients by weight. The other 49% can be any type of flour, including white flour but the white flour will probably be listed using one of the many different technical names for white flour.

Most whole grain breads contain the same unhealthy additives and preservatives that are in white bread. Reading the ingredient label will reveal if the bread contains all natural ingredients or if it is saturated with unhealthy stuff.

Some millers begin by sifting out the bran and the germ, and then they process the endosperm by itself. After processing the endosperm they add some (or all) of the bran and germ back into the flour so that they can legally refer to it as "whole wheat." However, the amount of bran and germ that is added back into some flours may be a lot less than what was removed. The reason is because bran attracts moisture and it can increase the speed at which the flour and the bread becomes stale, and the speed at which the bread attracts mold. The amount of germ is usually significantly reduced because the germ is what causes the flour to become rancid. In simple terms, the bran and the germ reduce the shelf life of the flour, and the shelf life of the bread, so they are undesirable from a profit perspective.

The terms "100% wheat" and "cracked wheat" and "enriched" and "multigrain" and "stone ground wheat" and "wheat flour" do not automatically mean that the product contains whole grain flour.

1. **100% Wheat Bread:** The bread only contains wheat flour and it does not contain any other grains, such as corn, oats, or rye. However, the bread may or may not contain any bran or germ. If the bread contains little or no fiber then this is the clue that the bread was stripped of its bran and germ.

2. **Cracked Wheat Bread:** Raw whole wheat berries are broken, cracked, crushed, or cut into smaller pieces instead of being ground or milled. The cracked wheat may then be mixed with some milled flour which may or may not contain bran and germ, and then it is baked into a bread that has a courser texture than regular bread.

3. **Enriched Bread:** The bread contains no (or very little) bran or germ and it is supplemented (enriched) with artificial vitamins and nutrients.

4. **Multigrain Bread:** The bread contains more than one type of grain, such as wheat plus corn, oats, or rye. It may or may not contain any bran or germ. If the bread contains little or no fiber then this is the clue that the bread was stripped of its bran and germ.

5. **Stone Ground Wheat Bread:** The bread contains some grain that was made into flour using a stone grinding process. The higher the

percent of stone ground wheat the coarser the texture of the bread.

6. **Wheat Bread:** Some of these breads are made using approximately 25% whole wheat flour and 75% white flour. Some of these breads are made with 100% white flour. Since whole wheat flour and white flour are both made from wheat grain these breads can be labeled as a "wheat bread." If the bread contains little or no fiber then this is the clue that the bread was stripped of its bran and germ.

Food Nutrition Labels

Food nutrition labels are required to list the ingredients in descending order based on the weights of those items in the finished product. The ingredient that is present in the highest amount (weight) should be listed first. Then the other ingredients are listed in descending order based on the amount (weight) of that ingredient in the finished product.

Some nutrition labels are very ingenious in the way they legally list the ingredients in the food. White flour may be listed as "enriched wheat flour" or as "unbleached wheat flour" or as "unbromated wheat flour." These are all just different technical names for white flour. Even the term "unbromated unbleached enriched wheat flour" is actually just white flour with a long fancy name.

When reading a nutrition label look for the word "whole" before the first ingredient in the list of ingredients. If "whole" appears in front of the first ingredient then that indicates that the food contains more of that ingredient than any one of the other ingredients in the list. However, that doesn't mean that the food contains at least 50% of that ingredient. It just means that the food contains more of that one ingredient than any of the other ingredients in the list. For example, it may contain 35% of the first ingredient, and the food will contain less than 35% of each of the other ingredients whatever they may be.

In the 21st century food labels can be somewhat misleading. Some products that are labeled "whole grain" or "whole wheat" may actually contain more white flour than whole wheat flour and the product may contain some artificial brown coloring or caramel to produce a brown color and then a few seeds are sprinkled on top to create the illusion of a whole grain brown bread. The reason is because the FDA only "recommends" that products follow some specific guidelines when using the terms "whole grain" or "whole wheat" and there is no penalty if the FDA's recommendations are not followed. Therefore do not make your purchase decisions based on what appears in BIG BOLD LETTERS on the front of the food package. Instead make your purchase decisions based on what appears in the list of ingredients on the back or on the side of the food package.

The Whole Grain Council

In 2005 the Whole Grain Council created their "Whole Grain Stamp" to help consumers identify foods that contained "whole grains" instead of "refined grains." At the beginning of the year 2020 the stamp is on more than 13,000 products in 61 different countries.

The stamp has a rectangular black border around a golden-yellow interior that shows an artistic sheaf of grain and the number of grams of whole grain per serving. Examples of the different stamps are shown below in black and gray instead of black and golden-yellow.

100% Stamp	50% Stamp	Basic Stamp
100% WHOLE GRAIN 23g or more per serving 100% OF THE GRAIN IS WHOLE GRAIN	50%+ WHOLE GRAIN 32g or more per serving 50% OR MORE OF THE GRAIN IS WHOLE GRAIN	WHOLE GRAIN 20g or more per serving EAT 48g OR MORE OF WHOLE GRAIN DAILY

The above stamps are based on the 2005 Dietary Guidelines for Americans that recommend that everyone over the age of 9 should eat a total of 48 grams of whole grains per day, or 16 grams of whole grains during each of their three daily meals.

The requirements for each of the above three stamps are as follows:

1. **100% Stamp:** All of the grain is whole grain that includes the bran, germ, and endosperm and the product does not contain any refined grains. In addition, one serving must contain a minimum of 16g (16 grams) of whole grain.

2. **50% Stamp:** At least half of the grain is whole grain that includes the bran, germ, and endosperm. The rest of the grain will be refined grain that has been stripped of its bran and germ. In addition, one serving must contain a minimum of 8g (8 grams) of whole grain.

3. **Basic Stamp:** Less than half of the grain is whole grain that includes the bran, germ, and endosperm. More than half of the grain are refined grains that have been stripped of their bran and germ. In addition, one serving must contain a minimum of 8g (8 grams) of whole grain.

Each of the three stamps will also show the actual number of grams of whole grain per serving.

Very few food products have the 100% stamp. However, if a food has a minimum of 8 grams of whole grain per serving then it meets the **minimum** guidelines of the Whole Grain Council and that food package is allowed to display their black and yellow **basic** stamp on the package that states the number of grams of whole grain per serving. Any food that meets any of the Whole Grain Council's guidelines will proudly display the appropriate Whole Grain Council's black and yellow stamp on their package along with the number of grams of whole grain per serving. However, you should still read the ingredient list because the food may also contain a lot of sugar, or a lot of sodium, or hydrogenated fat, or unhealthy preservatives.

Now that you understand how to evaluate the nutritional value of bread, perhaps you should take a look at the nutrition label and the ingredient list on the favorite brown bread that your family now eats. Carefully examine the bread package and look for one of the Whole Grain Council's stamps. If you can't find one of those stamps on your favorite brown bread then that means the bread does not meet the **minimum** requirements for healthy bread. If the first ingredient is listed as "enriched wheat flour" or "unbleached wheat flour" or "unbromated wheat flour" then the bread is simply white bread with some brown coloring in it.

The next time you are in the bread aisle at your favorite store, please pause for a moment and examine one loaf of bread from each of the different "brown breads" that are for sale. Look specifically for one of the Whole Grain Council's stamp somewhere on the package. You may be surprised at what you discover.

100% Whole Grain Bread

100% whole grain bread has a stronger wheat taste than most people are accustomed to. Most of these breads do **not** contain a lot of added sugar and therefore they do not taste as sweet as people expect their bread to taste. These breads are also usually heavier and denser. People who are not accustomed to digesting 100% whole wheat bread may experience some digestive issues if they switch too quickly to this type of bread.

Healthy whole grain bread should contain a **minimum** of 8 grams of whole grain per slice (or serving), at least 2 grams of fiber, at least 3 grams of protein, less than 2 grams of sugar, and less than 150 milligrams of sodium. Also look for the absence of artificial coloring, artificial flavors, and preservatives. If the bread does not clearly specify the number of grams of whole grain per slice then this means it has less than 8 grams per slice and therefore it does not qualify for one of the Whole Grain Council's certification stamps.

Even if a package says "100% whole wheat" this does not mean that the food has been approved by the Whole Grain Council if the package does not display one of their stamps. The food may contain other stuff, such as added sugar, caramel, brown coloring, lots of sodium, and a variety of unhealthy preservatives.

If you are not able to find a whole wheat bread in your area that meets all your requirements for whole wheat bread, then one possible option is to purchase the healthiest whole wheat bread you can find and then consider taking one or more "wheat germ oil capsules" every day. You should discuss this option with your doctor and then follow your doctor's advice on the amount of wheat germ oil that would be healthy for you to consume. Wheat germ oil capsules are extremely difficult to find at local pharmacies and health food stores, including GNC. You will probably have to shop online. If you begin looking for a wheat germ oil capsule then you may wish to look for one that is "cold pressed" and that is derived from organically grown wheat (if possible). Wheat germ oil begins to degrade when exposed to air, heat, or intense light. Therefore a capsule helps protect the oil from air, and cold pressing avoids the use of heat to extract the oil. Wheat germ oil is an oil and it is not a solid. Any company that advertises dry wheat germ is selling something that has been refined and that product may or may not have all the health benefits you desire. Food companies have been experimenting with genetically modified wheat for several years but that wheat is not yet available for sale at the beginning of the year 2020. However, sometime in the near future it may also become important to look for non-GMO wheat germ oil. Wheat germ oil capsules are discussed in detail on pages 121 to 126.

Additives and Preservatives

In the USA and in Canada, a variety of additives and preservatives are legally allowed to be included in flour and in bread. However, in Europe the use of additives is almost completely prohibited due to the unhealthy long-term impact of those chemicals.

Local Bakery Bread and Bread Shelf Life

Freshly baked bread from a local bakery may be made from whole grains that contain the bran, germ, and endosperm. Some local bakeries may grind wheat berries into flour each day and then use that freshly ground flour to bake bread. These breads often do not contain any preservatives and therefore they may only remain fresh for a few days. You should read the nutrition label on a bakery bread to verify that it is made from whole grains and that it does not contain unhealthy stuff you do not desire.

Prepackaged breads delivered to a grocery store may contain some preservatives to extend the shelf life of the bread to one week or more beyond the printed "sell by date" on the bread package.

It should be mentioned that a rancidity study conducted by Larsen in 1988 revealed that rancidity could be detected in some flour as soon as 2 to 14 days after milling. Many studies have shown that after milling the vitamins, unsaturated fatty acids, lipoproteins, lipids, and amino acids in flour begin to gradually degrade.

Fresh bread will remain fresh longer at room temperature. Bread will stale twice as fast if refrigerated. On the other hand, mold is more likely to grow on bread at room temperature if the conditions for the growth of mold are present. Bread that has begun to mold is not safe to eat and it should be discarded.

However, fresh bread can be frozen inside a large heavy-duty plastic zipper freezer bag to extend its shelf life to about 3 months. However, some people do not enjoy the taste of frozen bread after it has been unthawed.

Bread Nutrition

The nutritional benefits of bread can be enhanced if bread is consumed in the same meal as butter, cheese, fish, meat, nuts, or legumes. Some of the heat sensitive vitamins in bread will be reduced if the bread is heated by toasting, grilling, or frying.

Cereal

Many companies make advertising claims about how healthy their breakfast cereals are. Examples are "low-fat" or "a good source of ..." or "whole grain." However, breakfast cereals are made from processed grains that have had their healthy bran and germ removed. Then artificial vitamins and other nutrients are added into the cereal along with a significant amount of sugar. Many breakfast cereals list sugar as the second or third ingredient which means sugar is a significant part of the cereal. Starting your day with a high sugar meal will spike your blood sugar and approximately one or two hours after you have eaten you will become really hungry again.

Most breakfast cereals have been targeted primarily at children for many decades. Most adults in the USA in the 21st century probably remember eating one or more of these cereals when we were young. For many of us this has resulted in a favorable attitude towards breakfast cereals and we may feed a variety of "new" breakfast cereals to our children or grandchildren because they ask for them by name, or because they beg for them when they see them on a grocery store shelf due to the colorful package and the cartoon characters on the box.

Breakfast cereals that are targeted towards adults are also made from refined grains. Although they may have less sugar and they may contain some things like nuts, or raisins, or dried fruit, these cereals are still not healthy foods.

If you are addicted to breakfast cereals then read the nutrition label on the box. Look for a cereal that has 5 grams or less of sugar per serving, and that has 2 grams or more of fiber per serving. Then limit yourself to one bowl of cereal per day if you truly wish to control your weight and improve your long-term health.

Another cereal option would be to eat oatmeal for breakfast instead of a bowl of cereal. "Quaker Oats" oatmeal displays the Whole Grain Council's 100% Whole Grain Stamp on all their packages. Their steel cut oats contain 45 grams of whole grain per serving (almost 100% of your daily needs). Their old fashioned oatmeal and their quick oatmeal both contain 40 grams of whole grain per serving. Their individual serving packets contain between 20 to 29 grams of whole grain per serving depending on the quantity of fruit and other flavors per serving.

Some senior adults eat a bowl of corn flakes or some other cereal for their evening meal because it does not cause them indigestion that wakes them up in the middle of the night. If you are one of these senior adults then you should not change your diet just because cereal is not a healthy food. You should continue to do what is best for your body.

Pasta

Pasta noodles are usually made from durum flour or from semolina flour. Durum wheat is a variety of hard spring wheat. Semolina is course ground durum wheat.

If you only eat pasta once per week then forcing yourself to switch from regular white pasta to brown whole grain pasta may not have any significant impact on your weight or on your long-term health. However, if you eat pasta several times per week then your body may benefit from pasta that includes some whole wheat.

Pasta made from 100% whole wheat has a nuttier flavor. It also has a gummier texture after cooking due to its high fiber content and the noodles may stick together. To minimize this problem carefully follow the cooking directions on the package. The choice of a good sauce or topping may help minimize the unique taste of whole wheat pasta and it may help make the pasta more pleasant to eat and enjoy.

It should be mentioned that some brands of whole wheat brown pasta contains some whole wheat flour and some refined flour without the bran and the germ.

If you desire 100% whole wheat pasta then read the ingredient information on the package and look for the word "whole" in front of the first ingredient and verify that no other type of wheat is included in the list. There are several national brands of pasta that are 100% whole wheat pasta and they contain nothing but whole durum wheat. This includes spaghetti noodles, lasagna noodles, and spiral shaped noodles.

Grinding Whole Grains at Home

The digestive system of many people in the USA has become accustomed to digesting bread that was made from flour that was ground using metal rollers and that flour has had all or a lot of its bran and germ removed. This is important if you decide to begin grinding wheat berries into flour at your home with a home flour mill, and then baking your own bread. Many people who attempt this discover that their bodies do not approve of "real" wheat bread because their bodies have not been digesting "real" wheat bread that contains 100% of the original bran and the germ.

One way to allow your body, and the bodies of your family members, to adjust to "real" bread is to mix a small amount of your freshly ground flour with some commercially ground whole wheat flour that you buy at the store. As your bodies gradually begin to adjust to digesting "real" food with real vitamins, minerals, and fiber, then you can slowly and gradually increase the amount of your own freshly ground flour in the bread you bake.

Some brands of whole wheat flour display the Whole Grain Council's 100% stamp and those flours contain nothing except whole wheat flour. They are significantly healthier than the other flours available at a grocery store. However, it is important to remember that the vitamins and nutrients in flour gradually begin to degrade as soon as the grain is ground into flour. Although these flours may be considered "fresh" from a safety perspective, they will not contain the quality or quantity of vitamins and other nutrients of whole grain flour that you grind at home.

Approximately 1 cup of wheat berries will yield 2 cups of wheat flour. As you gain some experience with your home grain mill you will be able to grind exactly the amount of grain you need each day.

Since the nutritional value of flour begins to very gradually decline immediately after grinding please do not grind more flour than you need for a recipe. If you do not use all of your freshly ground flour the same day that you grind it, then refrigerate the rest of it and use it as soon as possible. If you cannot use it in two or three days then you should consider tossing it in the trashcan.

If you don't have the time to bake bread then you can purchase an electric bread machine. Simply toss all of the necessary ingredients into the machine as explained in the instructions that come with the machine and the machine will mix, knead, pause to allow the dough to rise, and bake a delicious loaf of bread for you. By changing the ingredients that you put into the bread machine, the bread machine can produce a remarkable variety of different types of delicious bread.

A Research Study on Flour and Bread

The following is not the type of research study that would be funded in the USA. If it were financed by an independent source then it would not be accepted for publication in any scientific journal that had any credibility. If it were published in a second rate journal or on the internet, then it would never be quoted by other researchers, or by Ph.D. students, or by any professional who understood the harm it could do to their reputation and to their future career. Now that you understand the serious academic and professional shortcomings of the following study, let's take a look at what the study revealed.

In 1970 a research study in Germany conducted by Bernasek evaluated the long-term impact of feeding flour, and bread made from flour, to some rats. The flour or the bread consisted of one-half of the daily diet of the rats. The rats were divided in five groups as follows:

1. **Group 1:** The rats were fed fresh stone ground wheat flour.

2. **Group 2:** The rats were fed bread made from fresh stone ground wheat flour.

3. **Group 3:** The rats were fed stone ground wheat flour that had aged for 15 days.

4. **Group 4:** The rats were fed bread made with the type of flour fed to Group 3.

5. **Group 5:** The rats were fed white flour without the bran and germ.

After four generations the rats in Groups 1 and 2 were still fertile and they were capable of reproducing offspring. The rats in Groups 3, 4, and 5 were infertile and they could not reproduce offspring. For reference purposes four generations of rats is considered to be about 100 years for people.

There have been several other studies on rats that were fed white bread as a part of their diet and all of those studies reported that the health of the rats declined, the life expectancy of the rats decreased, and the number of rats born dead increased, when compared to rats in the same study that were fed whole grain bread.

It is not appropriate to extrapolate conclusions from a rat study to people. However, please allow me to make a few casual observations that may or may not have any relationship to the above study.

1. In the 21st century in the USA approximately 20% of the adult men in all age groups have a significantly reduced sex drive. In the 21st century in the USA approximately 15% to 20% of men over the age of 20 have requested medical assistance for erectile dysfunction which is the same thing as impotence. An additional 9% of adult men are naturally sterile and they cannot father children. Many men under the age of 30 have no desire to marry or to father children.

2. From the year 1998 to 2008 in the USA sales of the prescription drug viagra steadily increased until sales peaked in 2008 at $1,934,000,000. In the year 2019 generic viagra became available. Viagra is used to treat erectile dysfunction in men.

3. In the 21st century in the USA approximately 10% of the women under the age of 44 cannot conceive, or they have trouble conceiving, or they cannot maintain a healthy pregnancy.

4. In the 21st century in the USA approximately 10% of adult women cannot give birth to a live baby.

5. In the 21st century in the USA "secondary infertility" is becoming more common where a woman can successfully give birth to one or two children but then the woman can no longer conceive. The official medical explanation is that this is the result of the normal aging process. However, could this problem be due to the foods these women continue to eat?

Many people probably know someone on a personal basis who is in at least one of the above five groups of people.

In 1872 high-speed roller mills began producing bread for sale in Britain. The new bread was stripped of its bran and germ. In 1876 the birth rate in Britain was 36 per 1,000 people. Sixty-five years later in 1941 the birth rate had declined to 14 per 1,000 people which was a 61% decrease in births. During this same time period medical care in Britain was significantly improved, including improvements in prenatal care and improvements in the delivery process. Despite these improvements in medical care, and the improvements in the quality of life for many people, the birth rate declined by 61% in Britain.

Except for the above statistics, there is no data or scientific research to support the relationship between commercially processed bread and infertility in people. However, if this relationship were scientifically documented, and if a causal effect were discovered that was linked to infertility, then it would have a devastating impact on the food industry in the form of lawsuits and the loss of future sales. It would also interfere with the agenda of those people who wish to control the worldwide population explosion.

The milling of wheat grain into flour is done at a milling facility. The flour is then shipped to a baking facility. The baking facility then processes the flour into bread. The bread is then shipped to distributors who deliver the bread to grocery stores. I could not find any data on the internet for how much time elapses from when the grain was first ground into flour, and when the flour was baked into bread at a bakery. But I suspect that more than 14 days elapse from the time the grain is ground into flour and the flour is baked into bread. If this is true, then the above study on rats has some significant implications for the bread we purchase at a grocery store even if the bread is 100% whole wheat bread with 100% of its original bran and germ.

If you think that the above information might be important to the future of your family line, then one possible solution would be to grind your own non-GMO wheat berries into flour at home in very small quantities using an electric grain mill, and then immediately use that freshly ground flour to make your own homemade bread. This is what mankind did for thousand of years prior to the late 1800s. Your children, grandchildren, and future posterity may be eternally grateful to you if you decide to do this.

At the very minimum, this would allow you to create healthy nutritious bread without adding any extra sugar or preservatives and this could help you lose weight and improve your long-term health. In my opinion, this would be an example of using good *common sense*.

If you do not bake then you could use a bread machine and it will do all the work for you including baking the bread. However you will still need a grain grinder to grind wheat berries into fine flour.

Another option would be to sprout wheat berries using water and then eat the sprouted wheat as a cereal.

On the next two pages there is a comparison of three different breads that were all baked by the same bakery.

A Comparison of Different Breads Baked by One Company

All the following breads were baked by "Sara Lee ®."

Page 1 of 2

Serving Size: 1 Slice or 28 grams (Data collected January 2020)

Type of Bread ➝ Nutrients:	100% Whole Wheat Bread	Classic White Bread	White with Whole Grain
Calories	60	70	70
Total Fat	1 g	1 g	1 g
Saturated Fat	0 g	0 g	0 g
Trans Fat	0 g	0 g	0 g
Polyunsaturated Fat	0 g	0 g	0 g
Monounsaturated Fat	0 g	0 g	0 g
Cholesterol	0 mg	0 mg	0 mg
Sodium	120 mg	130 mg	125 mg
Total Carbohydrates	12 g	14 g	13 g
Dietary Fiber	2 g	0 g	1 g
Total Sugars	1 g	1 g	1 g
Added Sugars	1 g	1 g	1 g
Protein	3 g	2 g	3 g
Vitamin D	0 mcg (0%)	1.1 mcg (6%)	0.6 mcg (2%)
Calcium	35 mg (2%)	150 mg (10%)	140 mg (10%)
Iron	0.7 mg (4%)	1.5 mg (8%)	0.7 mg (4%)
Potassium	60 mg (0%)	20 mg (0%)	35 mg (0%)
Vitamin A	(0%)	50 mcg (6%)	
Vitamin E	?	1.1 mg (8%)	
Thiamin	(4%)	0.1 mg (10%)	0.1 mg (8%)
Riboflavin	(0%)	0.1 mg (6%)	0.1 mg (6%)
Niacin	(4%)	1.1 mg (8%)	1.0 mg (6%)
Folate (Folic Acid)	(2%)	45 mcg (10%)	30 mcg (8%)
Grams of Whole Grain	**13g**	**0g**	**9g**

(Ingredients are listed on the next page.)

A Comparison of Different Breads Baked by One Company

All the following breads were baked by "Sara Lee ®."

Serving Size: 1 Slice or 28 grams (Data collected January 2020)

Type of Bread ⟶ Ingredients:	100% Whole Wheat Bread	Classic White Bread	White with Whole Grain
Enriched Wheat Flour		Yes	Yes
Whole Wheat Flour	Yes		Yes
Soy Flour			Yes
Water	Yes	Yes	Yes
Wheat Gluten	Yes	Yes	Yes
Sugar	Yes	Yes	Yes
Molasses	Yes		
Yeast	Yes	Yes	Yes
Soybean Oil	Yes	Yes	Yes
Salt	Yes	Yes	Yes
Preservatives	Yes	Yes	Yes
Datem	Yes	Yes	Yes
Monoglycerides	Yes	Yes	Yes
Cellulose Gum	Yes		
Cellulose Fiber			Yes
Monocalcium Phosphate	Yes	Yes	Yes
Calcium Phosphate	Yes		
Calcium Sulfate	Yes	Yes	Yes
Ferrous Sulfate		Yes	
Soy Lecithin	Yes	Yes	Yes
Citric Acid	Yes	Yes	Yes
Grain Vinegar	Yes	Yes	Yes
Potassium Iodate	Yes	Yes	Yes
Enrichment		Yes	
Vitamin D3			Yes

(Nutrition is shown on the previous page.)

Chapter Twenty-Three

Nuts and Seeds

On page 292 in the appendix there is a table that shows the nutrition, vitamin, and mineral data for most of the nuts and seeds mentioned in this chapter.

Nuts contain a reasonable balance of healthy fats, fiber, protein, vitamins, minerals, and antioxidants. Nuts may enhance the body's natural metabolic processes and nuts may enhance weight loss.

A variety of different studies have shown that people who eat minimally processed nuts in *moderation* are:
1. Healthier than people who do not eat nuts.
2, Have fewer chronic diseases than people who do not eat nuts.
3. Have a longer life expectancy than people who do not eat nuts.

When you eat nuts you can obtain the maximum eating pleasure by putting one nut in your mouth, chewing it thoroughly, and then swallow it before you put the next nut into your mouth. This will give your taste buds the maximum amount of time to enjoy the flavor of the nuts and it will give your jaws the maximum amount of time chewing the nuts. Being able to chew crunchy food is one of the least appreciated pleasures of eating.

Mixed Nuts

Mixed nuts contain approximately 166 calories per ounce (28 grams) based on the current USDA data on page 370. Lightly salted mixed nuts are a good choice because they contain a mixture of nuts that enhances the health benefits of some nuts while minimizing the negative aspects of other nuts. Eating mixed nuts in moderation can enhance weight loss.

After you have read the information in this chapter, the Common Sense Diet recommends that you prepare your own selection of fresh mixed nuts in some small plastic zipper snack bags as follows:
1. Purchase a small quantity of each of the different types of fresh nuts that you enjoy. Some grocery stores sell fresh nuts in a variety of different large containers where you can scoop out the quantity of nuts you desire from each container and put them into a plastic bag by themselves. Then write the nut container code number on a small sticky label and put the label on the bag, and pay for the nuts at the checkout register on your way out of the store.
2. Consider the actual nutrients in each type of nut and create an extremely healthy well-balanced snack in each or your nut snack bags. A "healthy nut snack" example is at the end of this chapter.

3. Consider the disadvantages of some nuts (such as the huge quantity of the mineral selenium in Brazil nuts) and include those nuts in moderation in your nut snack bags.

4. Continue to add nuts until you reach the total number of calories that you desire in one snack bag of mixed nuts based on the number of calories in each type of nut as shown later in this chapter.

5. When you get hungry and you are in the mood for a healthy snack then you will have the option to consume one of your snack bags of mixed nuts if you are in the mood for nuts.

Nuts

Almonds: (Approximately 6.3 calories per nut, or 162 calories per 28 grams or 1 ounce.) They contain significant amounts of protein, fat, fiber, vitamin B2 (riboflavin), vitamin E, calcium, copper, iron, magnesium, manganese, potassium, and antioxidants. They may enhance bone health, bowel movements, brain health, digestion, energy, hair health, the immune system, lung health, metabolism, lean muscle mass, oral health, skin health, and weight loss. They may help minimize anemia and inflammation. They may lower blood pressure and cholesterol. They may reduce the risk of Alzheimer's disease, cardiovascular diseases, colon cancer, diabetes, and heart disease. They may help stabilize blood sugar levels. They may help slow down the normal aging process. Almonds may enhance the creation of beneficial bacteria in the intestines. Almonds contain the anti-nutrient phytic acid which may reduce the absorption of some minerals but it may also have some positive health benefits. Almonds also have the highest ratio of omega-6 to omega-3 fatty acids and this is not good. Therefore, almonds should be consumed in *moderation*. Almonds are frequently added to cereals, salads, and to some dessert recipes.

Brazil Nuts: (Approximately 18.9 calories per nut, or 184 calories per 28 grams or 1 ounce.) They are the best source of dietary selenium in the world (about 55 µg per nut or 100% of the RDA of selenium). To avoid an overdose of selenium only 1 or 2 of these nuts should be eaten per day. These nuts also contain a lot of vitamin E, calcium, magnesium, phosphorus, potassium, zinc, and antioxidants. They may enhance blood health, brain health, bowel movements, digestion, male fertility, hair health, heart health, the immune system, lean muscle mass, life expectancy, nerve health, skin health, sleep, testosterone production, thyroid health, and weight loss. They may help minimize inflammation and depression. They may help lower cholesterol and triglycerides. They may reduce the risk of cancer (esophageal, stomach) and heart disease. They may help treat acne and erectile dysfunction.

Cashews: (Approximately 8.5 calories per nut, or 155 calories per 28 grams or 1 ounce.) They contain a lot of phosphorus, beta-carotene, and the antioxidants lutein and zeaxanthin. They may enhance blood health, bone health, eye health, male fertility, heart health, the immune system, liver health, lean muscle mass, nerve health, oral health, skin health, testosterone production, and weight loss. They may help minimize anemia and migraine headaches. They may help lower blood pressure, cholesterol, and triglycerides. They may reduce the risk of cancer (colon, prostrate, testicular), cardiovascular disease, cataracts, diabetes, gallstones, heart disease, macular degeneration, osteoporosis, and stroke. On the downside cashews contain a lot of carbohydrates. Cashews are frequently added to oriental recipes such as stir-fries, cashew chicken, and chicken salad.

Chestnuts: (Approximately 14 calories per nut, or 63 calories per 28 grams or 1 ounce.) They contain a lot of carbohydrates and starch but only a modest amount of fat. They do not contain high amounts of any vitamin or mineral. However, some people enjoy the taste of chestnuts. If chestnuts are stored in the refrigerator for a few days then some of the starches will convert into sugar.

Coconut: (99 calories per 28 grams or 1 ounce.) It contains fiber and fatty acids. It may be shredded and added to desserts or it can be made into coconut oil. A small amount of "coconut milk" is on the hollow inside of a fresh whole coconut.

Hazelnuts (Filberts): (Approximately 7.1 calories per nut, or 176 calories per 28 grams or 1 ounce.) Hazelnuts contain the most vitamin E of all nuts, or 15 mg per 100 grams, or 100% of the RDA for vitamin E. They also contain a lot of polyphenols which have antioxidant benefits. They may enhance blood health, bowel movements, brain health, energy, hair health, heart health, the immune system, metabolism, nerve health, skin health, and weight loss. They may help minimize anemia, depression, and inflammation. They may help lower cholesterol and triglycerides. They may reduce the risk of cancer (breast, cervical, colon, liver), cardiovascular disease, diabetes, and heart disease. They may help stabilize blood sugar levels. They may help reduce the risk of birth defects. They may help slow down the normal aging process. Hazelnuts will remain fresh inside their shells for several months. However, after they have been removed from their shells they will only remain fresh for a few weeks. Hazelnuts should be eaten with their exterior paper-thin skins to maximize their health benefits.

Macadamia Nuts: (Approximately 7.2 calories per nut, or 201 calories per 28 grams or 1 ounce.) They contain more monounsaturated fat and less omega-6 fatty acids than other nuts. They also have a relatively low amount of carbohydrates and almost no phytic acid. They may enhance bone health, brain health, digestion, eye health, hair health, heart health, the immune system, metabolism, lean muscle mass, nerve health, oral health, skin health, and weight loss. They may help minimize inflammation and arthritis. They may help lower blood pressure, cholesterol, and triglycerides. They may reduce the risk of Alzheimer's disease, anemia, cancer (breast, cervical, lung, prostate, stomach), cardiovascular diseases, cataracts, diabetes, heart attack, heart disease, kidney disease, and stroke. They may help stabilize blood sugar levels. Macadamia nuts are expensive and they contain a lot of calories.

Peanuts: (Approximately 5 calories per nut, or 159 calories per 28 grams or 1 ounce.) Technically peanuts are a legume or vegetable. They are high in fiber, protein, and antioxidants. They may enhance brain health, hair health, heart health, the immune system, joint flexibility, lean muscle mass, nerve health, skin health, and weight loss. They may help minimize arthritis, depression, and inflammation. They may help lower blood pressure, cholesterol, and triglycerides. They may reduce the risk of Alzheimer's disease, cancer (breast, colon, prostate, skin, stomach), dementia, diabetes, gallstones, hair loss, heart disease, nerve disease, and stroke. They may help slow down the normal aging process. They may facilitate a healthy pregnancy and help prevent birth defects. Mothers who ate peanuts during pregnancy gave birth to children with lower rates of asthma and allergies. Flavored peanuts do not have the same health benefits as unflavored peanuts. Peanuts are frequently added to granola, mixed nuts, trail mixes, and oriental recipes such as peanut chicken. "Natural" peanut butter without added sugars or added oils is a practical way to add peanuts into your diet. A little peanut butter can be spread on apples, bananas, or celery. However, some people have a serious allergic reaction to peanuts.

Pecans: (Approximately 19.6 calories per pecan half, or 193 calories per 28 grams or 1 ounce.) They are the second highest source of monounsaturated fats compared to other nuts. They contain a lot of antioxidants. They are one of the richest sources of polyphenols in the world. Pecans may enhance bladder health, bone health, brain health, digestion, eye health, hair health, heart health, the immune system, kidney health, skin health, and weight loss. They may help minimize inflammation and menstrual discomfort. They may help lower blood pressure and cholesterol. They may reduce the risk of cancer (breast, colon, lung, prostrate), diabetes, gallstones, hair loss, and heart disease. They may help stabilize blood sugar levels. They may help slow down the normal aging process. Pecans are extremely popular in pecan pie, candies, and other desserts. They are frequently added to chicken salad, sweet potato casserole, and to some beef recipes.

Pill Nuts: (201 calories per 28 grams or 1 ounce.) They have the highest amount of fat of all nuts. They also have a significant amount of magnesium.

Pine Nuts: (188 calories per 28 grams or 1 ounce.) Some people may experience "pine mouth" after eating pine nuts. "Pine mouth" is a bitter metallic aftertaste that can remain in the mouth for up to two weeks. Pine nuts are a good source of vitamins B3 (niacin), E, K, manganese, and zinc. They may be eaten raw or added to granola, trail mix, or salads.

Pistachios: (Approximately 3.1 calories per nut, or 157 calories per 28 grams or 1 ounce.) Pistachios are high in fiber, protein, vitamins B1 (thiamine) and B6, and they have the most vitamin A and potassium of any nut. They may enhance blood health, brain health, digestion, erectile function, eye health, heart health, the immune system, metabolism, lean muscle mass, nerve health, skin health, and weight loss. They may help minimize inflammation. They may help lower blood pressure, cholesterol, and triglycerides. They may reduce the risk of cancer, diabetes, heart disease, and macular degeneration. They may help stabilize blood sugar levels. Pistachios are usually available in the shell. However, removing the pistachios from their shell is not easy. It requires less effort to buy pistachios without their shells. Pistachios sometimes contain mold that exceeds the legal "safe" limit. Therefore purchase pistachios from a reliable source. A little salt can enhance the flavor of pistachios.

Walnuts: They have the lowest omega-6 to omega-3 fatty acid ratio of all nuts which is good. They contain a lot of antioxidants. They may enhance bone health, brain health, cardiovascular health, digestion, male fertility, heart health, the immune system, liver health, metabolism, skin health, sleep, and weight loss. They may help minimize inflammation and stress. They may help lower blood pressure and cholesterol. They may reduce the risk of cancer (breast, cervical, colon, prostate), cardiovascular diseases, diabetes, and heart disease. They may slow down the normal aging process. They may help reduce birth defects. Walnuts are frequently added to brownies and to other desserts. Walnuts are removed from their shells in pieces and they are sold as pieces (or chopped). The two types of walnuts are black and English:

1. **Walnuts, Black:** (173 calories per 28 grams or 1 ounce.)
2. **Walnuts, English:** (183 calories per 28 grams or 1 ounce.)

Seeds

Seeds contain the nutrients required to grow into a plant of the same type. Therefore seeds can be very nutritious. Seeds contain fiber, protein, vitamins, minerals, antioxidants, and high amounts of vitamins B1 (thiamine) and B3 (niacin). They may help reduce blood sugar levels, blood pressure, and cholesterol.

Chia Seeds: (150 calories per 30 grams, or 100 calories per tablespoon.) They are one of the most nutrient dense foods available. They contain a significant amount of fiber, vitamin A, calcium, magnesium, manganese, omega-3 fatty acids including alpha-linolenic acid (ALA), antioxidant polyphenols, and several other nutrients. They may enhance blood health, bone health, cardiovascular health, digestion, the immune system, nerve health, skin health, sleep, and weight loss. They may help minimize inflammation. They may help lower blood pressure, cholesterol, and triglycerides. They may reduce the risk of Alzheimer's disease, cardiovascular disease, diabetes, heart attack, heart disease, and stroke. They may slow down the normal aging process. They may help stabilize blood sugar levels.

Flax Seeds or Flaxseed (Lin Seed): (152 grams per 28 grams or 1 ounce, or 55 calories per tablespoon.) They contain a lot of fiber and the omega-3 alpha-linolenic acid (ALA). They contain a variety of polyphenols which act as antioxidants. The seeds may be eaten raw but they are easier to digest if ground. In addition, when they are ground the human body can more easily process the omega-3 fatty acids in the shell of the seed. They may enhance bowel movements, cardiovascular health, digestion, eye health, female fertility, hair health, heart health, the immune system, metabolism, skin health, and weight loss. They may minimize asthma and inflammation. They may lower blood pressure and cholesterol. They may reduce the risk of cancer (breast, colon, prostrate, skin), diabetes, heart attack, heart disease, and stroke. They may help stabilize blood sugar levels. They can be made into an oil. They are used in some Indian recipes.

Hemp Seeds: (155 grams per 28 grams or 1 ounce, or 43 calories per tablespoon.) Hemp seeds are one of the best sources of vegetable protein and the quality of that protein is superior compared to other sources of vegetable protein. They contain more vitamin B3 (niacin), magnesium, phosphorus, potassium, and zinc than other seeds or nuts. They have a low omega-6 to omega-3 fatty acid ratio of 3:1 which is very good. Hemp seed may help relieve eczema, skin dryness, and itchiness. They also contain all nine of the essential amino acids that the human body needs but cannot make. Hemp seeds may be eaten raw or they can be made into hemp seed oil or into hemp milk.

Pumpkin Seeds: (151 calories per 28 grams or 1 ounce, or 45 calories per tablespoon.) They are a good source of monounsaturated fats, protein, magnesium, phosphorus, zinc, amino acids, and omega-3 fatty acids. They may help lower cholesterol, reduce the risk of bladder stones, breast cancer, and heart disease. Remove the seeds from a pumpkin, wash the seeds, and allow them to dry for a few days. They may be eaten raw or roasted. Pumpkin seeds are used in some Mexican recipes. They may also be added to homemade granola.

Sesame Seeds: (160 calories per 28 grams or 1 ounce, or 52 calories per tablespoon). They are a good source of fiber, protein, vitamin B6, calcium, and zinc. Sesame seeds are one of the best sources of the lignan sesamin. When digested sesamin can convert some of the bacteria in the intestines into a sex hormone similar to estrogen. They may enhance blood health, bone health, bowel movements, digestion, hair health, heart health, male fertility, the immune system, lung health, metabolism, lean muscle mass, oral health, skin health, sleep, and thyroid health. They may minimize arthritis, asthma, depression, inflammation, and stress. They may help lower blood pressure, cholesterol, and triglycerides. They may reduce the risk of anemia, cancer (breast, colon, leukemia, lung, pancreatic, prostate), diabetes, heart attack, heart disease, and stroke. They may help stabilize blood sugar levels. Sesame seed may be added to home baked bread, cereal, or salads.

Sunflower Seeds: (164 calories per 28 grams or 1 ounce, or 51 calories per tablespoon.) Sunflower seeds need to be removed from their shells. They contain more vitamin E than any other seed or nut. They are also a good source of dietary fat, fiber, and antioxidant polyphenols. They may enhance bone health, brain health, digestion, cardiovascular health, energy, male fertility, hair health, heart health, the immune system, skin health, sleep, thyroid health, and weight loss. They may help minimize arthritis, depression, and inflammation. They may help lower blood pressure and cholesterol. They may reduce the risk of cancer (breast, colon, lung, prostate), diabetes, and heart disease. They may help stabilize blood sugar levels. They may facilitate a healthy pregnancy. Sunflower seeds may be added to home baked bread, cereal, oatmeal, salads, granola, or trail mix.

A Low-Calorie Healthy Snack of Mixed Nuts

You can create your own mixed nut combination by purchasing small quantities of each of the nuts that you prefer and then combining them into small snack size plastic zipper bags for a very healthy snack.

Sodium: One serving of salted nuts contains about 5% to 7% of the RDA of sodium, and one serving of lightly salted nuts contains about 2% to 4% of the RDA of sodium. Therefore select the nuts you enjoy eating and don't be too concerned about the amount of salt.

The following RDA percents are based on a mixed nut combination that contains 4 almonds, 4 cashews, 4 hazelnuts, 4 macadamia nuts, 2 pecan halves, 2 peanuts, and 1 Brazil nut, for a total of 21 nuts.

A Mixed Nut Snack Containing 21 Nuts			
Total Calories = 182			
Vitamin B1	15.2%	Calcium	3.2%
Vitamin B2	5.6%	Copper	46.9%
Vitamin B3	4.3%	Iron	15.2%
Vitamin B5	4.6%	Magnesium	14.8%
Vitamin B6	6.8%	Manganese	42.5%
Vitamin B9	3.7%	Phosphorus	17.0%
Vitamin C	0.5%	Potassium	36.3%
Vitamin E	17.1%	Selenium	109.5%
Vitamin K	2.4%	Zinc	9.7%

Chapter Twenty-Four

Sweets and Snacks

On page 298 in the appendix there is a table that shows the nutrition, vitamin, and mineral data for most of the sweets mentioned in this chapter.

Sweets will be reviewed first and then some healthy snacks will be discussed.

Atkins Snack Bars

They include sugar free candy, cookies, and protein bars. One or two of these treats per day can help you make the transition from a diet that contained candy and cookies to a healthy diet that does not include commercially processed candy and cookies. However, the Atkins treats contain a variety of unhealthy ingredients and they should not be part of your long-term weight-loss strategy. After your body has adjusted to the healthy foods in your new diet then you will probably lose your appetite for the Atkins treats in preference for a variety of healthy snacks such as the ones mentioned in this chapter. A table that shows the calories and the ingredients in a variety of the Atkins treats is on the next page.

Voortman Sugar Free Wafers

These wafers are available in chocolate, lemon, orange, peanut butter, and strawberry at 47 calories per wafer. Also key lime and vanilla at 43 calories per wafer. All of these cookies have the same type of wafers and it is the filling between the wafers that provide the unique flavor. If you include these wafers in your diet then be careful that you do not exceed your total daily calorie consumption limit.

Cocoa Beans and Chocolate

Cocoa beans contain three major components:

1. **Chocolate Liquor:** It is also called cocoa mass or cocoa paste. It is created by grinding the center of the bean, called the nib, into a smooth liquid.

2. **Cocoa Butter:** It is the natural fat in the cocoa bean. It melts inside the mouth at the normal temperature of the human body and this is what gives chocolate its unique mouth consistency.

3. **Cocoa Powder:** After the cocoa butter is removed, this is the part of the cocoa bean that is ground into a dry powder.

As the percentage of cocoa increases in a chocolate product, the chocolate flavor gradually becomes more intense, the amount of sugar gradually decreases, and the taste gradually becomes more bitter.

Calories and Ingredients in a Variety of the Atkins' Food Products (per Sealed Pack or Each)															
Item	Oz.	Cal.	Fat	Chol.	Sodium	Potass.	Carbs	Fiber	Sugar	S.A.	Prot.	A	Calc.	C	Iron
Protein-Rich Meal Bars															
Choc. Chip Granola	1.69	200	9g	5mg	210mg	135mg	18g	7g	1g	8g	17g	0%	10%	0%	10%
Choc. P.B. Pretzel	1.69	200	9g	0mg	270mg	135mg	18g	7g	1g	7g	16g	0%	8%	0%	8%
Cookies & Crème	1.76	200	11g	0mg	200mg	160mg	22g	9g	1g	9g	14g	20%	8%	20%	10%
P.B. Granola	1.69	220	11g	0mg	230mg	100mg	18g	6g	1g	8g	16g	0%	8%	0%	8%
Snacks															
Caramel Choc. Nut Roll	1.55	190	13g	<5mg	200mg	135mg	19g	6g	2g	10g	7g	15%	4%	15%	2%
Triple Choc. Bar	1.41	160	8g	5mg	200mg	150mg	15g	8g	1g	3g	13g	0%	0%	0%	10%
Treats															
Caramel Nut Chew Bar	1.20	130	8g	<5mg	70mg	80mg	17g	6g	1g	1g	5g	0%	2%	0%	2%
Choc. Peanut Candies	1.20	150	11g	0mg	25mg	115mg	18g	2g	1g	15g	4g	0%	2%	0%	4%
Lemon Vanilla Wafers	1.27	200	14g	0mg	55mg	90mg	8g	4g	1g	1g	11g	0%	10%	0%	2%
Milk Choc. Caramel Sq.	0.41	43	3g	<2mg	12mg	0mg	7g	2g	0.3g	5g	0.3g	0%	1%	0%	1%
Nutty Fudge Brownie	1.41	170	12g	0mg	90mg	170mg	18g	6g	0g	10g	7g	0%	2%	0%	8%
P.B. Cups	0.60	160	13g	0mg	85mg	50mg	18g	4g	0g	12g	2g	0%	0%	0%	4%
Peanut Caramel Cluster	1.20	140	10g	<5mg	180mg	110mg	13g	6g	1g	4g	7g	2%	4%	0%	2%
Pecan Caramel Clusters	0.49	60	5g	<3mg	30mg	20mg	7g	4g	0.5g	3g	0.5g	0%	1%	0%	1%
Peppermint Patties	1.31	90	6g	5mg	30mg	70mg	23g	11g	1g	10g	4g	0%	2%	0%	2%

Atkins Food Products report "Atkins Net Carbs" at a lower value than the Total Carbs shown in the above table. The above information was collected on Atkins' Food Products in January 2020.

Cocoa is used to make three basic types of chocolate:

1. **Dark Chocolate:** Depending on the company that makes the dark chocolate the cocoa percentage will vary from about 50% up to about 75% or higher.

2. **Milk Chocolate:** It contains cocoa, milk solids (or powder), sugar, lecithin, and vanilla. Normal milk chocolate may contain as little as 10% cocoa. However, to increase sales some companies have created new milk chocolate products with higher cocoa percentages from about 38% up to about 55% and this value is shown on the product label to attract customers.

3. **White Chocolate:** It contains about 40% cocoa derived from cocoa butter. White chocolate does not have any cocoa powder or chocolate liquor. In addition to cocoa butter, white chocolate usually contains milk powder, sugar, and frequently vanilla. Healthy white chocolate should be made from cocoa butter and not from imitation fats that have no chocolate taste, such as palm oil.

The nutrition summary table on page 298 in the appendix shows the nutrients, vitamins, and minerals in a variety of different types of chocolate including milk chocolate, white chocolate, and three types of dark chocolate. The vitamin levels are not significantly different for the different types of chocolate. However, there are approximately 8% more calories in dark chocolate even though dark chocolate has less sugar than milk chocolate or white chocolate. Dark chocolate contains less calcium but more iron, magnesium, and potassium than milk chocolate or white chocolate. Although copper is not shown in the nutrition summary table in the appendix, dark chocolate contains significantly more copper than milk chocolate or white chocolate.

Most diets that permit a limited amount of chocolate recommend dark chocolate with a cocoa content of at least 70%. They mention that the minerals and amino acids are higher in dark chocolate but they neglect to mention that dark chocolate contains less calcium and more fat. They also do not mention that as the cocoa level gradually increases the bitterness of the chocolate also increases. And they minimize the fact that dark chocolate contains about 8% more calories when compared to milk chocolate and white chocolate. Since dark chocolate has been recommended for so many years, and by so many intelligent people, and in so many different publications, in the year 2020 most people believe that dark chocolate is the healthiest type of chocolate.

However, if we use *common sense* to impartially evaluate all the different types of chocolate then we should begin by considering the health benefits of cocoa which is in all chocolates. Cocoa contains a significant amount of antioxidants compared to all other foods. Cocoa also contains more catechins, flavanols, and polyphenols than any fruit including blueberries. Cocoa may significantly reduce oxidized LDL cholesterol. It may also increase good HDL cholesterol. Since all chocolate contains cocoa, in one or more forms, these benefits will be present in all chocolate to a more or less degree.

Based on all the preceding information, the Common Sense Diet recommends that chocolate be avoided because it is habit forming and it contain too many calories. However chocolate is permitted in extremely modest quantities if you can control your appetite for chocolate and you do not spend most of your day thinking about when you are going to get your next piece of chocolate. The Common Sense Diet does not recommend a specific type of chocolate over other types of chocolate. If you are able to include chocolate in your diet without exceeding your total daily calorie consumption limit, and you are still able to lose weight, then you should select the type of chocolate that you enjoy eating the most.

However, if you look at the calories, vitamins, and minerals for cocoa powder in the nutrition table in the appendix then you will notice that cocoa powder contains the following when compared to chocolate:

1. **Vitamins and Minerals:** It has approximately the same amount of vitamins and minerals as any chocolate.
2. **Phosphorus and Potassium:** It has between two to three times the phosphorus and potassium of any chocolate.
3. **Fiber:** It contains more than three times the fiber of any chocolate.
4. **Calories:** It has less than half the calories of any chocolate,
5. **Sugar:** It has a trivial amount of sugar compared to any chocolate.
6. **Chocolate Flavor:** It can enhance a dessert or a beverage with a pleasant chocolate flavor if it is properly included in the recipe for the dessert or beverage.

If you decide to include some cocoa in your diet then you should look for recipes that use cocoa powder instead of chocolate.

Peanut Butter and Honey (116 Calories)

Add 1 teaspoon of honey (20 calories) to 1 tablespoon of peanut butter (96 calories) and stir until well blended. It you like they way it tastes then use it on sandwiches and on some of the following snacks.

Quick, Easy, and Extremely Healthy Snacks

Apple or Banana Slices with Peanut Butter: Fruit is extremely nutritious. Organic apples are preferred. Peanut butter may reduce the bad LDL cholesterol, and reduce triglycerides, and increase the good HDL cholesterol. However, peanut butter contains a lot of calories so it should be added to the apple or banana slices in moderation.

Blueberries: 30 fresh blueberries contain about 17 calories and they contain fiber and a reasonable amount of vitamins and minerals.

Baby or Petite Carrots with a Mayonnaise-Based Salad Dressing: Carrots are an excellent source of carotenoids, including beta-carotene which the body can convert into vitamin A. The carotenoids in carrots may reduce the risk of cancer, cataracts, and heart disease. The fat in a mayonnaise-based salad dressing will enhance the body's absorption of the carotenoids in carrots.

Celery Sticks with Peanut Butter: Spread a small amount of your favorite brand of peanut butter on the groove in a celery stick.

Corn Chips: Corn chips may be consumed in moderation. Plain corn chips, such as Doritos, Fritos, and Tostitos, are made with corn, vegetable oil, and salt. They do not contain any artificial ingredients or preservatives. However, flavored corn chips, such as Cheese Doritos or Ranch Doritos, contain a long list of artificial ingredients and preservatives. If you enjoy the flavor of plain corn chips and you can eat them without adding too many additional calories, such as cheese dip, then plain corn chips are a healthy snack. However, if you compare the number of calories in plain corn chips to flavored corn chips then you will notice that the number of calories is very similar. About 32 original Fritos contain 160 calories, about 24 bite size Tostitos contain 150 calories, about 7 full size Tostitos contain 140 calories, and about 12 full size ranch, nacho cheese, or spicy nacho flavored Doritos contain 150 calories. Therefore if you are going to enhance the flavor of plain corn chips with dips then you may be better off eating the flavor of corn chips you prefer. A very limited number of artificial ingredients and preservatives in your diet will probably not significantly impact your short-term or long-term health.

Mixed Nuts: Nuts contain a healthy balance of fat, fiber, and protein. Mixed nuts contain approximately 180 calories per ounce (28 grams). Eating nuts in moderation may enhance weight loss. The healthiest mixed nut snack is one that you create yourself based on how many calories you desire in a snack, the type of unflavored nuts that you prefer, and the nutrients in those nuts. Additional detailed information is on pages 203 and 204.

Pear Slices with either Cottage Cheese or Ricotta Cheese: Fresh organic pears are preferred. Organic pear peels are not contaminated with harmful pesticides and they do not contain any residue from artificial fertilizers. Pear peels contain polyphenol antioxidants. Cottage cheese and ricotta cheese both contain protein and calcium. When combined with the nutrients in a fresh pear, including its peel, this creates a well-balanced extremely healthy delicious snack.

Flavored Cottage Cheese (4% milk fat)

The flavor of cottage cheese can be enhanced by sprinkling a small amount of your favorite flavor of Jello gelatin on top of one serving of cottage cheese, and then stirring until the gelatin is mixed evenly throughout the cottage cheese. *Small curd cottage cheese* evenly absorbs the flavor and color of the gelatin. If you flavor one serving of cottage cheese at a time, then you can use a different flavor of gelatin to enhance the flavor of the cottage cheese each time you eat it. Since you will only be adding a trivial amount of gelatin to each serving of cottage cheese, you may purchase the normal gelatin that contains sugar, or you can purchase the sugar-free gelatin. The difference in calories will be negligible so you should purchase the type of gelatin you prefer.

Popcorn

Air Popped Popcorn: Most diets recommend air popped popcorn because it has fewer calories. But you may discover that it has a dry bland taste and this eliminates the pleasure of eating popcorn.

Microwave Popcorn: Microwave popcorn is quick and easy to prepare with no cleanup. Snack size bags contain between 100 to 210 calories per bag depending on the net weight of the bag, whether or not butter is included, and how much butter is included. Snack size bags provide an reasonable amount of fresh hot popcorn each time you eat it. The flavor of different brands of microwave popcorn are uniquely different and you should try different brands to find the taste you prefer.

Traditional Popcorn Popper: It is possible to make homemade popcorn using a traditional corn popper and a small amount of a healthy oil, such as extra virgin olive oil or hemp oil. This method takes a little longer but it does provide a little arm exercise as you rotate the stirring handle which is good. It also yields healthy fresh hot popcorn that does not contain any unhealthy artificial ingredients or preservatives. And you can pop the exact amount of popcorn you desire each time you decide to make some popcorn.

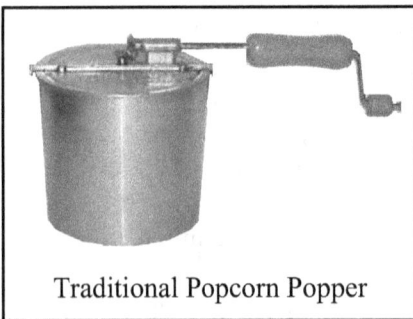

Traditional Popcorn Popper

Flavor Enhancement: A little iodized salt can be added to unsalted popcorn to enhance its flavor. Melted butter can be drizzled on hot popcorn. If you use salted butter then do not add any more salt to the popcorn. Or finely shredded Parmesan cheese can be sprinkled on hot popcorn. Butter and cheese will add calories to this snack so use butter and cheese in moderation.

Chapter Twenty-Five

Metabolism

Metabolism includes all the physical and chemical processes used by an organism to accomplish the following three functions:

1. Convert the nourishment it receives into fuel or energy.
2. Convert fuel into the exact substances that are needed by each of its various biological systems. Thousands of these metabolic activities are simultaneously happening all the time inside the human body.
3. Identify, separate, destroy, expel, or discharge unnecessary and undesirable substances from the body.

The human body metabolizes calories in the following ways:

1. **Digestion:** The simple process of digesting your food requires your body to burn calories. This is called the thermic effect of food (TEF). It has been estimated that the average adult consumes approximately 300 calories per day digesting the food they eat. But the actual amount can be more or less depending on how much food a person eats each day. In addition, some foods, such as protein rich foods, require more calories to digest. And some foods, such as fat rich foods, require fewer calories to digest. However, the difference in the total number of calories required to digest these different types of foods is usually not a significant factor in weight loss.

2. **Metabolism:** Some of the calories you eat are used in a consistent manner to maintain your involuntary normal body functions such as breathing, and the beating of your heart, and maintaining your normal body temperature. This is called your basal metabolic rate (BMR) and it represents the number of calories you burn when you are completely at rest. It has been estimated that the BMR of the average adult requires a minimum of approximately 900 calories per day (not including digestion).

3. **Physical Activity (Work or Exercise):** Most of the remaining calories you eat each day are used to supply energy so you can perform all the other activities you participate in each day.

4. **Creation of Fat and/or Muscle:** Any extra calories that are not burned in one of the above three ways are converted into fat cells or into glycogen in your muscles. Your body automatically saves the extra calories you eat each day in order to provide fuel in the event that your future daily calorie requirement is more than your future daily calorie consumption.

A person's resting metabolic rate (RMR) is the sum of their thermic effect of food (TEF) and their basal metabolic rate (BMR). An inactive person (no work or exercise) will burn a **minimum** of approximately 1,200 calories per day as a result of all their normal body functions (RMR). However, the following factors can influence the number of calories a person burns each day to maintain their normal body functions:

1. **Weight:** People who are overweight will burn more calories each day as a result of their normal body functions because it requires more energy to maintain the extra weight. This is one of the reasons why a person who is significantly overweight can lose weight more easily than a person who is just 10 or 15 pounds overweight.

2. **Height:** People who are taller will burn more calories each day as a result of their normal body functions because it requires more energy to move blood a longer distance to their toes and to their brain. This is one of the reasons why a taller person can usually lose weight a little more easily than a shorter person.

3. **Muscle to Fat Ratio:** A pound of body muscle requires more energy to maintain than a pound of body fat even when you are at rest. This is one of the reasons why a person with a reasonable amount of lean muscles will be able to lose weight (body fat) more easily than a person who has very little lean muscle on their body.

4. **Gender:** The average male weighs more than the average female. The average male is taller than the average female. The average male has a higher muscle to fat ratio than the average female. Therefore the average male burns more calories per day than the average female.

5. **Age:** After a person has reached his or her peak growth potential, then the person's muscle to fat ratio very gradually begins to decline with advancing age. On the average females reach their peak growth potential sometime around the age of 18 and males reach their peak growth potential sometime around the age of 22. After reaching their peak growth potential a person's metabolism very gradually slows down as a result of age and they burn fewer calories simply because of their gradually decreasing muscle to fat ratio. It has been estimated that a person burns about 5 *fewer* calories per day to maintain their normal body functions for each year of their age after they have reached their peak growth potential. A 40-year old person will burn about 90 *fewer* calories per day than a 22-year old person just for their normal body functions [(40 - 22) x 5 = 90]. A 70-year old person will burn about

240 *fewer* calories per day than a 22-year old person just for their normal body functions [(70 - 22) x 5 = 240]. This is one of the reasons why it is not unusual for a person to gradually gain a little weight each year as they age even though they do not change their lifestyle or their eating habits.

The Thyroid Gland

Your thyroid gland is very important to all your body's normal metabolic processes, from growing your toenails to growing your hair. An underactive thyroid (hypothyroidism) can result in weight gains even when a person is not eating too many calories per day and the person is exercising faithfully. If you are not able to lose weight then you should consider visiting your doctor to have your thyroid function evaluated.

The following symptoms may indicate an underactive thyroid:

1. **Unexplained Weight Increase:** Your weight is increasing steadily but you have not changed your diet or your daily routine.

2. **Inability to Lose Weight:** You are keeping track of your daily calorie consumption and you are exercising regularly but you can't lose any weight.

3. **Dry Skin:** Your skin has become dry and it no longer has it normal healthy appearance.

4. **Brittle Nails:** Your nails are more brittle and they have ridges.

5. **Hair Loss:** You are losing some of you hair. When you bathe you can see some of your hair in the bottom of the tub or shower, or in the towel that you dry your hair with.

6. **Pulse Rate:** Your current average pulse rate is lower than your average pulse rate in the past.

7. **Headaches:** Headaches are occurring more often than they did in the past.

8. **Coldness:** You feel cold most of the time even though you are properly dressed.

9. **Sexual Motivation:** You do not feel the same degree of sexual motivation that you did in the past. If you are a female then your menstrual cycle may have become irregular and you are cramping more than usual.

10. **Tired:** You feel fatigued most of the time.

11. **Depressed:** You feel depressed most of the time.

12. **Forgetful:** You have trouble remembering some things.

If you suspect that you may have a thyroid problem then you should consult your doctor for a physical examination that includes a thyroid test.

How to Estimate Your Daily Minimum Metabolic Rate

The human body needs a minimum number of calories per day to function properly. This minimum number of calories is the sum of the thermic effect of food (TEF) plus your basal metabolic rate (BMR) minus your age adjustment factor.

1. **RMR based on Gender:** RMR (resting metabolic rate) is the sum of TEF (digesting food) plus BMR (breathing, heart function, and maintaining normal body temperature). RMR has been estimated separately for men and women based on their weight.

   a. **Female:** Women will require approximately 9.84 calories per pound of body weight per day (or 21.70 calories per kilogram) for their normal body functions.

   b. **Male:** Men will require approximately 10.32 calories per pound of body weight per day (or 22.75 calories per kilogram) for their normal body functions.

2. **Age based on Gender:** As we age our bodies require fewer calories per day per year of age for our Resting Metabolic Rate (RMR) after we have reached the age of our peak growth potential.

   a. **Female:** The average woman will require approximately 3 fewer calories per day for her RMR after she reaches her peak growth potential sometime around the age of 18. Her muscle to fat ratio will decline slower than a man because she started with fewer lean muscles.

   b. **Male:** The average man will require approximately 5 fewer calories per day for his RMR after he reaches his peak growth potential sometime around the age of 22. His muscle to fat ratio will decline more rapidly than a women because he started with more lean muscles.

Height is not included as a variable in the above analysis for RMR for the following two reasons:

1. People with the same basic type of body but who are taller or shorter than one another will have the same approximate muscle to fat ratio because the only difference is that they are taller or shorter. Therefore their height differences will be reflected in their weights.

2. The Resting Metabolic Rate is for a person who is lying down and who is idle. When a person is lying down their height does not have a significant impact on RMR because the heart is not having to pump blood against gravity since the person is lying down. The demand on the heart for a person who is resting will be determined primarily by the person's weight and not by their height.

Based on these factors we can *estimate the minimum* number of calories we need per day based on our gender, weight, and age. The equations are:

Women:
Minimum Daily Calories = (RMR x weight) - (3 x (Age - 18))

Men:
Minimum Daily Calories = (RMR x weight) - (5 x (Age - 22))

Example One: Female 28 years old, weight 134 pounds (60.78 kg).
Minimum Daily Calories = (RMR x weight) - (5 x (Age - 18))

Based on pounds:
Minimum Daily Calories = (9.84 x 134 lb.) - (3 x (28 - 18))
Minimum Daily Calories = (1,318.6) - (30) = 1,289 (rounded)

Based on kilograms:
Minimum Daily Calories = (21.70 x 60.78 kg) - (3 x (28 - 18))
Minimum Daily Calories = (1,318.9) - (30) = 1,289 (rounded)

Example Two: Male 52 years old, weight 217 pounds (98.43 kg).
Minimum Daily Calories = (RMR x weight) - (5 x (Age - 22))

Based on pounds:
Minimum Daily Calories = (10.32 x 217 lb.) - (5 x (52 - 22))
Minimum Daily Calories = (2,239.4) - (150) = 2,089 (rounded)

Based on kilograms:
Minimum Daily Calories = (22.75 x 98.43 kg) - (5 x (52 - 22))
Minimum Daily Calories = (2,239.3) - (150) = 2,089 (rounded)

The above values are just *estimates*. The above *minimum* number of daily calories are what would be required to maintain all of a person's normal body functions while the person was sleeping, or lying down and doing nothing, or sitting down and doing nothing. However, it assumes that a person is not idle all day and the person eats and digests food each day. If a person is fasting and does not eat for 24 hours then their RMR value would be reduced by approximately 300 or fewer calories per day.

The activities a person participates in each day would add to the total number of calories the person needed each day to maintain their body weight. This will be discussed in more detail in the next chapter.

Other Methods of Calculating BMR

The Harris-Benedict equations on the next page take into account weight, height, age, and gender.

The original 1918 Harris-Benedict BMR equations are:

Women:
655 + (9.6 × weight in kg) + (1.8 × height in cm) – (4.7 × age in years)

Men:
66 + (13.7 × weight in kg) + (5 × height in cm) – (6.8 × age in years)

The revised 1984 Harris-Benedict BMR equations are:

Women:
447.593 + (9.247 × weight in kg) + (3.098 × height in cm) – (4.330 × age in years)

Men:
88.362 + (13.397 × weight in kg) + (4.799 × height in cm) – (5.677 × age in years)

In the 1990s Mifflin-St. Jeor provided equations that estimate RMR using a different method.

The 1990s Mifflin-St. Jeor RMR equations are:

Women:
(10 × weight in kg) + (6.25 × height in cm) – (5 × age in years) – 161

Men:
(10 × weight in kg) + (6.25 × height in cm) – (5 × age in years) + 5

Mifflin-St. Jeor uses the same basic equation for women and men but they allow for a constant 166 more calories per day for men than for women regardless of weight, height, or age.

All the above equations are simply estimates based on averages. Even the 1984 Harris-Benedict equations that show values to three decimal places are just estimates. Showing three decimal places creates the illusion of superior accuracy but three decimal places do not significantly improve the final results when compared to the same exact equation with the values rounded to two decimal places.

One of the problems with the Harris-Benedict 1918 and 1984 equations, and with the 1990s Mifflin-St. Jeor equations, is that the age adjustment factor includes the actual age of men and women. However, daily calorie requirements related to age do not begin to decline until after we have attained our peak growth. This usually occurs in the late teens for females and in the early twenties for males. Until we reach our peak growth our calorie requirements do not decrease each year. However, after we attain our peak growth then our resting metabolic rate (RMR) begins to decrease by approximate 0.2% per year. Therefore any age adjustment factor should not use the actual age of a person. Instead it should adjust the person's actual age by the average age at which the person stops growing because a person's RMR does not begin to decrease until that age.

Chapter Twenty-Six

Exercise and Sports

On pages 274 to 277 in the appendix there is a table that shows the approximate number of calories burned while doing a variety of the different activities, exercises, and sports mentioned in this chapter.

Regular exercise may enhance weight loss and energy levels. It may reduce fatigue and tummy fat. It may enhance blood circulation and the cardiovascular system. It may enhance brain functions, digestion, heart health, the immune system, sexual health, and skin health. It may lower bad LDL cholesterol and increase good HDL cholesterol. It may reduce blood pressure and stabilize blood sugar levels. It may increase the production of hormones that enhance the ability of muscles to absorb and utilize amino acids and this may strengthen muscles and bones and enhance joint flexibility. It may decrease feelings of anxiety, depression, and stress. It may enhance the onset of sleep, sleep duration, and sleep quality. It may reduce the risk of Alzheimer's disease, dementia, cancer (breast, colon, lung, uterine), type 2 diabetes, heart disease, osteoporosis, and stroke. It may slow down the normal aging process. It may extend life expectancy.

Exercise is a very healthy activity. However, exercise is not appropriate for everyone. In addition, some exercises may actually cause health problems for some people.

Please do not be too ambitious if you are out-of-shape and it has been a long time since you have been exercising regularly. Remember that exercise is not a short-term temporary strategy. Instead regular exercise is something you will continue doing for the rest of your life in order to maintain firm lean muscles and to also maintain your ideal weight in the long-term. Therefore it is okay to start exercising very modestly at first, such as two or three minutes per day. Then very gradually you can slowly increase the amount of time you exercise each day depending on how your body is responding to the exercises you have selected, and based on what feels comfortable to you. It may take several months or longer to reach 5 or 10 minutes of exercise per day. And it may take one or two years or longer to reach 15 or 20 minutes of exercise per day. But by starting modestly you will be able to do some exercises each day because everyone can afford to spend 2 or 3 minutes on a new activity each day. However, devoting 10 minutes, or 20 minutes, or more every day to an activity may not immediately fit into your daily schedule. But by very, very slowly increasing the time you exercise each day then you will be able to very, very slowly adjust your daily schedule for the amount of time you invest in daily exercise.

Please do not expect an immediate significant weight loss when you first begin exercising. It may take your body a few days to adjust to the exercises you do and then your weight loss will be in proportion to the amount of exercise you do in relation to the number of calories you eat.

Physical Exam

Everyone should have a compete physical exam by their doctor that includes a comprehensive blood test before they begin any type of exercise program.

A physical exam is absolutely critical for individuals who are taking any type of medication, or who have any type of chronic disease. This includes people with low blood pressure, high blood pressure, diabetes, cardiovascular problems, or breathing problems. It also includes people who are overweight or underweight, or who smoke or who have recently quit smoking, or who have any type of lung or heart problems. It includes people who have not been exercising regularly.

The Most Important
Common Sense Exercise Advice

Always be considerate of your ankles, knees, hips, and spine. Don't do any exercises that may compromise the well being of your ankles, knees, hips, or spine. Most people seriously underestimate the importance of these specific bones and joints to their continued long-term health and happiness. Anyone who is more than just a little bit overweight should avoid exercises that put continual "pounding" pressure on their ankles, knees, hips, and spine. This includes running, jogging, skipping rope, jumping jacks, and hopping on one foot.

Health Concerns

If you have high blood pressure then exercise may help lower your blood pressure and decrease the risk of cardiovascular problems, heart disease, stroke, and eye and kidney damage. If you have high blood pressure then ask your doctor to recommend specific exercises for you.

If you have low blood pressure then select exercises that are compatible with low blood pressure and that do not result in dizziness, blurred vision, or nausea. For example, avoid exercises that include bending over and rising back up quickly. If you have low blood pressure then ask your doctor to recommend specific exercises for you.

Exercise may help increase your good HDL cholesterol level. Exercise may help you lose weight.

When you exercise free radicals are created inside your body. These free radicals can be neutralized by including foods rich in antioxidants in your diet.

In general, exercise is very, very good. However, after a person exercises and burns some calories then the person may feel hungrier than usual and the person may eat more than normal. If this happens then the net impact will be a weight gain and not a weight loss.

Therefore it is usually better to select an exercise that interests you instead of one that you do simply because you want to exercise. If the exercise is one that appeals to you, or one that has a benefit to you, then there is a good chance that you will continue to do that exercise after the novelty of exercising has worn off. There is also a good chance that you will not increase your daily calorie intake more than the number of calories you burn as a result of the exercise.

Before, During, and After Exercising

Before you begin any vigorous exercise it is usually a good idea to do some stretching or some simple warm up exercises. This gives your body and your joints a chance to loosen up and to gradually adjust to the more vigorous exercise you have planned. This is very important for someone with high blood pressure.

When doing your exercises do not become too enthusiastic and exercise too rigorously. A reasonable pace is one where you can still talk to someone as you exercise.

After you have finished a vigorous exercise do not suddenly stop exercising. Slow down the pace of the exercise and continue at that slow pace for a few minutes to give your body a chance to gradually adjust back to your normal activity level. This is very important for someone with high blood pressure.

Amount of Exercise

If you don't overexert yourself then you may be able to avoid sore muscles after exercising. A good strategy would be to do your exercises for a short period of time at first. Then very gradually increase the amount of time you devote to your exercises each week. This will give your body a chance to gradually adjust to the exercises you have planned for it.

Exercise Warning Signals

If you become short of breath, or if your heart feels as if it is beating too fast or irregularly, then immediately slow down or stop. If you experience dizziness, sudden weakness, a severe headache, nose bleed, chest pain, or a sharp or sudden pain in any part of your body, then stop exercising immediately. If these symptoms do not go away quickly then immediately seek medical assistance. If these symptoms reoccur the next time you exercise then seek immediate medical assistance and also consult your regular medical doctor.

When to Exercise

There is no best time of day for everyone to exercise. A lot depends on our daily schedule and the commitments we must honor during the day to our employer and to our family.

Exercising shortly before bedtime may interfere with the benefits of a peaceful night's rest. A good night's sleep may help stabilize your blood pressure.

A good time to do our daily exercises is shortly after we wake up in the morning, and after we have relieved our bodies in the bathroom, and before we take a shower, and before we eat or drink anything. There are three reasons why this is a good time to exercise:

1. Exercising on an empty stomach puts less stress on our heart and on our digestive system.
2. It may help burn fat and tone our muscles because our stomachs are empty and therefore the energy we require to do our exercises may be provided by the fat cells on our bodies.
3. It may help lower our blood pressure immediately and this benefit may last for the entire day.
4. It may help increase our body's metabolism early in the day and this can help us burn more calories during the day even though our metabolism rate will very gradually begin to slow down when we stop exercising.

However, if exercising in the morning is not possible due to your specific schedule, then exercising at some other time is better than not exercising at all.

If possible exercise before eating. If that is not possible, then wait at least 90 minutes after you have finished eating before exercising.

Where to Exercise

If possible exercise indoors where the temperature is relatively stable, and where the air is filtered to remove pollens and pollutants.

If you wish to exercise outdoors then avoid temperature extremes such as bitter cold winter weather and sweltering hot summer weather.

It may also be prudent to not exercise outdoors if you see a lot of long white streaks that are all over the sky where aircraft have expelled something into the atmosphere.

Exercises to Avoid

Before you begin any type of exercise, ask your doctor which exercises would be appropriate for you based on your recent physical exam and your medical history.

Carefully consider your age, the flexibility of your joints, and how much you weigh. The purpose of exercising should be to enhance your health and it should not have a negative impact on your body.

If you have high blood pressure then your doctor may have advised you to not lift weights because it may aggravate your blood pressure and result in damage to your blood vessels.

If you are significantly overweight then avoid sit-ups, hopping on one foot, crunches, deep squats, and jumping. You should also probably avoid exercises that result in stress and pounding on your ankles, knees, hips, and spine. This includes running, jogging, skipping rope, and jumping jacks. After you lose a reasonable amount of your extra weight then these exercises may be considered if approved by your doctor. Walking and riding a bicycle are usually okay because they do not put the continuous "pounding" pressure on your ankles, knees, hips, and spine which may cause long-term physical disabilities.

Exercising Alone, or With a Friend, or in a Group

There is no best way to exercise for everyone. Some people are more comfortable exercising alone. And some people prefer to exercise with a friend or as part of a large group.

The choice may depend on how much time we have to exercise, and when it is convenient for us to exercise, and whether or not we can coordinate our schedule with the schedules of other people.

The important thing is that we exercise and that we don't use excuses to avoid exercising, such as our exercise partner was not available today, or our exercise class was cancelled today.

Slow and Steady Wins the Race

In Aesop's Fable "The Rabbit and the Turtle" the final words spoken by the turtle to the rabbit after the turtle won the race were: "Slow and steady wins the race." This ancient moral still has a present day application for people who desire to improve their health, lose weight, and enhance their physical appearance, strength, and stamina.

Those of us who are physically out-of-shape would benefit from slowly and gradually beginning a very simple basic exercise program that includes exercises we can do, and does not take too much time, and does not have any potential negative health side effects. For example, we should do three to five repetitions of a few simple exercises. All the different exercises combined should not consume more than two or three minutes per day. It is okay to pause and rest between each different exercise. An example would be bending over at the waist and trying to touch our toes even though our toes may be out of reach when we first begin exercising and they remain out of reach for a few months. Squatting and bending our knees and then standing back up. Extending our arms straight out from our shoulders and twirling our arms for 20 or 30 seconds. These are simple exercises that most of us can do in the privacy of our own bedroom every day and it will allow us to initiate a physical fitness program so our bodies can gradually adjust to the exercises we are doing.

It is okay to ignore the advice of some exercise professionals who say "No pain, no gain." It may be better to use *common sense* and to allow your body to adjust to new exercises gradually.

If you have sore muscles in different parts of your body after you exercise then you should not exercise those specific muscles until the soreness in those muscles is gone. However, you should still do other simple exercises that do not involve the sore muscles.

Beginning slowly with exercises that you know you could do may help you accomplish the following objectives:

1. You will not do any exercises that might be harmful to your long-term health.
2. Since you will only be exercising for two or three minutes per day when you first begin exercising then you should be able to easily find the time to do the exercises.
3. You will not be in competition with anyone because you will be doing the exercises in the privacy of your own bedroom.
4. It will not cost any money because you do not have to join a gym or buy any exercise equipment.
5. It will minimize or eliminate the pain and the sore muscles that result when you force your body to do something it is not accustomed to doing.
6. It may encourage you to start today and to continue doing exercises for the rest of your life.
7. It may help if you will remember that you are customizing a weight loss program that is designed specifically for your body and you do not have to do what the average person does, and you do not have to do what some professional trainer expects you to do.

The remainder of this chapter will discuss some information about some exercises you may wish to consider as you gradually design an exercise program that is just right for you.

Sitting versus Standing

Standing burns between 30 to 55 more calories per hour than sitting.

In the 21st century sitting is becoming more common for more people for longer periods of time. A variety of research studies have reported that sitting for long periods of time may contribute to a variety of health problems, including obesity.

If you have a desk job that requires sitting for most of the day then find a reason to get up and walk around for a few minutes every hour. For example, walk to the restroom or to the break room even if you don't need to use the restroom, or even if you don't wish to purchase something from a vending machine in the break room.

If you are at home then consider standing up for a few minutes (or longer) while you are watching television and while eating (if feasible).

Consider standing up the entire time you are using your cell phone when it is feasible.

Be creative and think of activities that you currently do while sitting that you could do just as well while you are standing up.

Household Chores

There are many benefits to doing some or all of your household chores manually. For example, your ancestors did their household chores manually and on the average your ancestors were probably healthier and stronger than the average person in the USA in the 21st century. If you decide to do some of your household chores manually then the result will be that you will live in a cleaner, healthier home and you will be healthier because you will have firmer muscles and you will be exposed to fewer germs inside your home.

1. Wash and dry your dishes by hand instead of using the automatic dishwasher. This will be easier if you purchase a dish drainer and place it beside your kitchen sink so that you can put your washed and rinsed dishes and tableware into the container until you are ready to dry everything at the same time using a dish drying towel. Put your clean dried dishes into their normal positions in your kitchen cabinets.

2. Dust your furniture once a week.

3. Manually clean your bathroom and your kitchen once a week with a good cleaner/disinfectant.

4. Sweep your wood and tile floors with a broom and use a dustpan to transfer the debris into a trashcan.

5. Mop your wood and tile floors with a good mop once per week. Squeeze the dirty water out of the mop into the toilet or into the bathroom sink and rinse the sink with hot water when you are done.

6. Vacuum your carpets with a manual push vacuum cleaner.

7. Lightly wax your wood and tile floors once every three months.

8. Shampoo your carpets once every six months.

9. If it is feasible where you live, then during the warm weather months on sunny days wash your clothes in a washing machine but hang them outdoors on a clothesline, using clothespins, to dry in the sun and in the fresh air (except when the pollen is falling, or when the sky is full of long white streaks from aircraft). Neatly fold your clothes as you remove each item from the clothesline. Your clothes will smell better and they will have fewer wrinkles because they will air dry in the sun while hanging straight down on the clothesline. And you will be exercising and losing weight. It is more difficult to find clothesline poles at hardware stores in the 21st century than it was in the 1980s. You may need to search the internet to find clothesline poles and clotheslines. If you have two solid trees that are less than 50 feet apart then you can string a clothesline between the two trees, or between one tree and a building. (Note: I do not recommend washing clothes by hand, and squeezing the water out of the clothes by hand, or squeezing the water out between two manually rotated hard rubber rollers. An automatic washing machine is a labor saving device that does a much better job of washing clothes and spinning the water out of clothes when compared to what most people can do by hand.)

10. If you have a lawn then consider mowing the grass with a push lawn mower and not a self-propelled lawn mower or a riding lawn mower. If you have hedges then consider trimming the hedges with a hand operated trimmer and not an electric trimmer.

Personal Vehicle

If you have your own car or truck then you may wish to consider the following suggestions:

1. Park far away from the entrance to your place of work and walk to the door of your building to benefit from the exercise of walking.

2. When you drive to a store park far away from the entrance into the store in order to benefit from the exercise of walking.

3. If you will be using a shopping cart then during good weather do not walk directly into the store. Instead detour to the empty cart storage corral in the parking lot and select an empty cart and push it into the store with you. You will be doing the employees of the store a good deed and you will benefit from the exercise of pushing the cart into the store.

4. While you are shopping inside a store, walk down every aisle in the store to benefit from the exercise of walking. You may walk slowly

or quickly down the different aisles depending on your interest in what is displayed on those aisles.

5. Wash your vehicle by hand instead of using a drive-through car wash. Dry the water off your vehicle using cloths or small towels.

6. Wax your vehicle by hand every two or three months during good weather in the shade. Follow the instructions on the container of car wax.

Stairs and Elevators

Always hold onto the handrail when going up or down some stairs. Or at least loosely grasp the handrail with your hand so you can quickly tighten your grasp if you trip, stumble, or begin to lose your balance. Holding onto the handrail can prevent or minimize the damage of a potentially serious accidental injury on the stairs.

If you have the option to use an elevator or to use the stairs, then you should consider using the stairs. Going up and down the stairs is an excellent exercise. However, if you are not physically able to safely use the stairs due to age, weight, or health, then use the elevator. If you are at work and using the stairs would result in sweating and its unpleasant odor, then using the elevator will enhance your work relationship with your fellow employees.

Dance Lessons

Dancing is a very good exercise. You can practice the dance steps you learn each week at home while listening to the appropriate music. If you need a partner then a pillow could be a temporary substitute, and holding a pillow at arms length can also help to strengthen your arm muscles. Depending on your age and your social environment, learning how to do the current dance steps may also improve your social life.

Sports

If you enjoy a non-violent sport, such as bowling, golf, tennis, soccer, basketball, or baseball, then this is a good way to get outdoors (except for bowling) and get some healthy exercise.

Exercise and Breathing

Breathe normally while exercising. If you must hold your breath to safely complete one repetition of an exercise then as soon as that one repetition is done you should immediately begin breathing normally again. Do not hold your breath for a long period of time while exercising unless it is necessary such as swimming under water.

Exercises that Require No Equipment

Some people can do all the following exercises. Some people cannot do any of the following exercises. However, the average person can do some of the following exercises because some people have stronger arm muscles and other people have stronger leg muscles. Please do not feel guilty if your body does not have muscles in the correct place to do some of the following exercises.

You may do as many repetitions of the following exercises as you believe appropriate but please do not overexert yourself, and do not do so many repetitions that you make your muscles sore. If you make your muscles sore then your sore muscles may discourage you from resuming your exercises after the soreness is gone.

Jumping Jacks: Stand with your feet together and your arms by your sides. Jump up and move your right foot about 9 inches to the right and move your left foot about 9 inches to the left and when you land on the floor your feet should be about 18 inches apart. Also while you are jumping raise both of your hands sideways up into the air so that your hands touch above your head as you land on both feet. Reverse the action, jump up, bring both hands down to your sides, and bring both feet together below the center of your body. This exercise is not recommend for individuals who are significantly overweight.

Leg Raises: Lie down on the floor with your back against the floor and with your legs together and in a straight line with your body with your toes pointed towards the ceiling. Place your palms flat against the floor near your hips. Keep your legs straight and lift your feet about 6 inches off the floor and hold them there for 3 seconds. Then lower your feet back down to the floor. An alternate method is to raise your feet 6 inches off the floor, and then spread your feet about 18 inches apart, and then bring your feet back together again, and finally lower your feet down to the floor.

Push-Ups: Lie face down on the floor with the palms of your hands flat against the floor below your shoulders. Position your toes against the floor about as far apart as your shoulders and curl your toes on the floor towards your head. While looking straight down at the floor exhale as you use your arms to lift your body up off the floor while keeping your back, rear end, and legs in a straight line. Inhale as your lower your body back down to the floor. As you do this exercise you will be gradually bending your elbows as you lower your body to the floor and you will be gradually straightening your arms as you raise your body up. If you are not able to do this type of push-up then it is okay to keep your knees on the floor as you use your arms to lift and lower your upper body.

Running (or Marching) in Place: Stand straight up. Keep your left foot on the floor and lift your right foot until it is about level with your left knee and then lower your right foot back down to its original starting position on the floor. Then raise and lower your left foot while your right foot remains on the floor. The height that you lift your feet and the speed at which you lift your feet should feel comfortable to you. This exercise is not the same thing as running because you are not moving forward and you are not putting the continual "pounding" pressure of all your weight on each of your knees, one at time, or on your ankles, or on your hips, or on your spinal column.

Sit-Ups: Sit-ups may injure your neck or spine if done improperly. Lie down flat on the floor with your back against the floor and your legs straight out. Place the palms of your hands against the floor beside each of your hips. Raise your upper body to an upright position as you exhale. Then lower your upper body back down to the floor as you inhale. This exercise can be made more difficult by bending your knees and placing the bottom of your feet flat on the floor instead of allowing your legs to lie straight out on the floor.

Squats (or Deep-Knee Bends): Stand straight up with your arms at your sides. Exhale as you bend your knees to lower your rear end as low as you can above your feet without losing your balance. As you are lowering your body extend your arms straight out in front of your shoulders. Inhale as you return to a standing position and allow your arms to return to your sides.

Toe Touch, Sitting: Sit upright on the floor with your legs straight and with your feet about 18 inches apart and your toes pointed towards the ceiling. Hold your arms straight out to both sides and level with your shoulders. Exhale as you bend forward and twist at the waist and reach with your right fingertips as far as you can towards your left toes. Inhale as you return to the starting position. Bend forward and twist at the waist and reach your left fingertips as far as you can towards your right toes. Return to the starting position.

Toe Touch, Standing: Stand straight up with your arms extended straight out to each side level with your shoulders. Keep your legs straight and do not bend your knees. Exhale as you bend and twist at the waist and lower the fingers of your right hand as far as you can toward the toes of your right foot (or your left foot if you want to make it more difficult) while lifting your left hand straight up into the air above you. Inhale as you return to the starting position. Then reverse the exercise and try to touch your left fingers to your left toes (or your right toes). Return to the original upright starting position. When you first attempt this exercise you may not be able to touch your toes. But if you will continue this exercise for several weeks you will notice that you very gradually become more limber and your fingertips get closer and closer to your toes. As you continue to lose weight and as your waistline gradually decreases, eventually you may be able to touch your toes and you will be delighted in what you have accomplished.

Walking: Walking may significantly benefit the heart and lungs. Walking is an excellent exercise that significantly enhances your legs, ankles, knees, hips, and the flexibility of your joints. Your legs are longer and thicker than your arms and your legs probably have more fat on them compared to your arms. Walking may help strengthen the existing lean muscles in your legs, and gradually add more lean muscles to your legs, and gradually reduce the amount of fat on your legs. Walking may also significantly reduce tummy fat. While you are walking you can listen to music or a digital book on your mobile phone. Walking outdoors is good if you live in an area with fresh clean air and the sky above you is not polluted with a lot of white residue streaks from aircraft. It is also possible to walk indoors in a grocery store or a store such as Walmart. (Note: Walking inside some large shopping malls is not as safe as it used to be.) Pushing a shopping cart around a store will increase the number of calories you burn. If you have some weight in the shopping cart then you will also be strengthening and toning your arm muscles. If you have the time consider walking down all the aisles of the store to maximize your total weight loss.

Exercises that Require a Minimum Amount of Equipment

You may do as many repetitions of the following exercises as you believe appropriate but please do not overexert yourself, and do not do so many repetitions that you make your muscles sore. If you make your muscles sore then your sore muscles may discourage you from resuming your exercises after the soreness is gone.

Ab Wheel: I first used an ab wheel in 1987 as a result of a television commercial. The exercise wheel looked like it could be an

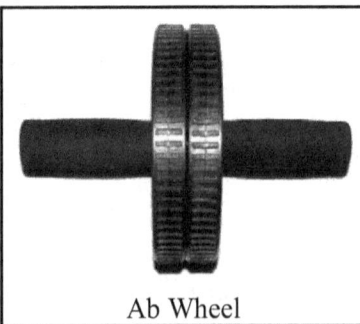

Ab Wheel

easy way to firm up my tummy. But when I actually started using it I discovered that it was not as easy at it looked. Some ab wheels have one wide center wheel and some ab wheels have two center wheels side by side. The most important issues are that the two hand grips feel comfortable when you grasp them because you will be putting your weight on them, and the wheel or wheels should rotate smoothly around the center axle. Kneel on the floor on both knees with your legs and feet together. Grasp the handles on the ab wheel palms down with both hands and position the ab wheel on the floor below your shoulders.

While looking directly at the ab wheel and while supporting your upper body weight on the handles of the ab wheel, slowly push the ab wheel forward while keeping your back straight and tighten your tummy muscles and do not allow your tummy or pelvis to sag down. Push forward to a position where you can still safely maintain your balance and not collapse onto the floor. Then pull the ab wheel back towards you and under your shoulders. Do not hold your breath. Continue to breath normally as you exercise with the ab wheel. Please do not be deceived. This is not an easy exercise for someone just starting an exercise program. The reason the ab wheel is included in this chapter is to make you aware of the difficulty of using an ab wheel and to warn you that if it is used too ambitiously it can result in serious back pain.

Chin-Ups and Pull-Ups: This exercise requires a strong stationary bar that will support your weight. The height of the bar should be at least 8 inches or more above the bottom of your chin. To do a *chip-up* grasp the bar with both hands in line with your shoulders and with the palms of your hands facing you (an underhand grip). To do a *pull-up* reverse your grasp with the palms of your hands facing away from you (an overhand grip). Bend your knees so your feet are off the floor. Exhale and use your arms to raise your chin until it is level with the bar. Inhale as you slowly lower yourself down until your arms are straight.

Hand Squeeze Balls: Purchase two firm rubber balls about the size of a baseball or a tennis ball. The balls should bounce when you drop them on a hard floor. A baseball is too firm and it will not compress when you squeeze it. A tennis ball may be used but it will compress a little more easily than a rubber ball but this may be a good choice if you do not have a strong grip. A child's toy bouncing ball will compress just a little bit when you squeeze it and this is a good type of ball to use. Grasp a ball in each hand. Squeeze each ball using firm pressure until the ball compresses just a little. Then relax the pressure.

Hand Squeeze Grips: There are two types of hand grips: some have a fixed amount of pressure (bottom of picture) and some have a pressure adjustment (top of picture). The ones that have a pressure adjustment are more expensive but they are worth it because they allow you to set the resistance at a low value when you first begin using them. Then you can increase the resistance a little bit with each passing week until you reach a comfortable resistance that is a little bit challenging but

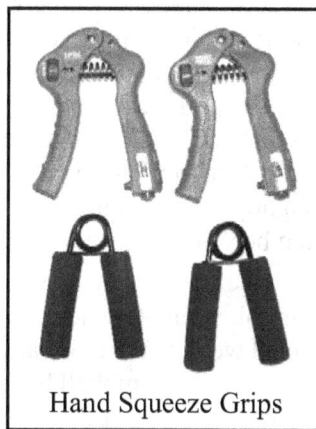

Hand Squeeze Grips

which does not cause soreness in your hand muscles. Grasp a hand grip in each hand and squeeze the grip. Then relax the pressure.

Jump Ropes: Ropes are available in two designs: some are made of traditional rope material (left rope in picture), and some are made with plastic coated metal cables (right rope in picture). Purchase a jump rope with comfortable hand grips and with an adjustable length. Adjust the length so you can comfortably jump without tripping on the rope or hitting yourself in the head with the rope. Hold one hand grip in each hand with the rope behind you. Swing the rope up over your head and back down in front towards your feet. Jump over the rope with both feet as the rope travels under your feet. Repeat. The speed of this exercise can be increased or decreased based on your rope jumping ability. There are also a variety of different way you can jump a rope to increase its exercise value and your coordination skills.

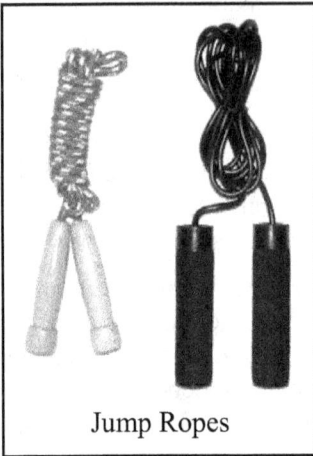

Jump Ropes

Exercises that Use Hand Dumbbells

Hand dumbbell exercises are good exercises that can help firm and enhance the muscles in your arms and chest. Hand dumbbells have a lot of advantages compared to weight training that uses a barbell. Dumbbell exercises should always be done with a dumbbell in each hand. Each arm and each side of the body does exactly the same amount of exercise and this enhances body symmetry and appearance. They are easier and safer to use when exercising alone. They provide more options and more flexibility in your workouts so you can focus on the muscles groups you wish to enhance. They allow for a greater range of motions which can enhance more muscles. They allow for more freedom of movement and they do not restrict you to a specific location. They are significantly less expensive than a set of barbell weights and a barbell weight bench. It is very easy to switch dumbbell weights depending on the exercise involved. As you gradually increase your lean muscles you can purchase two more very affordable but slightly heavier dumbbells to increase your lean muscles. Dumbbells can be stored in a very small area when not in use.

There are two types of dumbbells: (a) fixed weights, and (b) variable weights where you can add more weights to a dumbbell bar. Fixed weights are more affordable and the weights cannot get loose and rotate on the dumbbell bar.

Before you purchase a pair of dumbbells please experiment with the different weights available (2, 3, 5, 8, 10, 15, 20, 25, and 30 pounds). This can be done at most Walmarts and most physical fitness stores. Select a weight you can lift from your side towards your chest with an average amount of effort. In other words, it should not feel too easy or too challenging. Purchase a hand dumbbell of the optimal weight for each hand. Usually the weight will be the same for both dumbbells. But occasionally one arm may be

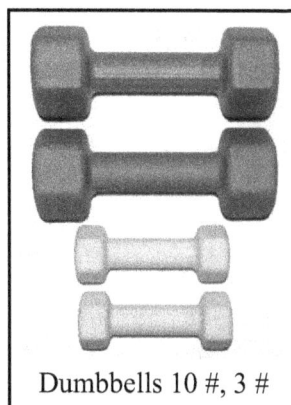

Dumbbells 10 #, 3 #

significantly weaker than the other arm and a lower weight would be appropriate for the weaker arm. After you have enhanced the strength in your weaker arm then you can increase the weight of that dumbbell.

Always use two dumbbells simultaneously, or one dumbbell for each hand. Always do dumbbell exercises with both hands at the same time. Never alternate back and forth between your hands. In other words, never do one repetition of a dumbbell exercise with one hand and then do one repetition of a dumbbell exercise with the other hand.

Dumbbell Arm Twirls: Since you will be holding the dumbbells at arms' length from your body, and you will not be raising and lowering the barbells, each dumbbell should weigh a lot less than the dumbbells you use for all your other hand dumbbell exercises. The dumbbells should only be 2 or 3 pounds each depending on how much weight you can hold at arms' length. Hold a dumbbell in each hand at arms' length straight out to the left and right with your arms level with your shoulders. Breathe normally as you move the dumbbells in a 6 inch diameter circle while holding your arms straight out to your sides. Continue rotating your arms for 10 seconds. In future weeks gradually increase the time you rotate your arms each day.

Dumbbell Bending Side Lifts: Hold a dumbbell in each hand at arms' length. Bend over at the waist in a 45 degree angle and look at the floor. Do not bend so far over that your upper body is level to the floor. Hold the dumbbells together with your arms straight down in front of you directly below your shoulders. Exhale as you raise your arms straight out to your right and to your left without bending your elbows until the dumbbells are level with your shoulders. Inhale as you lower the dumbbells back down to the starting position.

Dumbbell Curls: If you cannot do pushups or chin-ups then this is a good exercise that will help strengthen your arm muscles. Grasp a dumbbell in each hand and start with your hands straight down at your sides. Exhale as you simultaneously lift both dumbbells up towards and level with your chest. Then inhale as you lower the dumbbells back down to your sides.

Dumbbell Flies, Bent Elbows (lying on a bench or on the floor): Lie down on your back on a bench with your knees bent at the end of the bench and with your feet on the floor. Or lie on your back on the floor. Bend your knees and put your feet flat on the floor about 12 inches apart. Grasp a dumbbell in each hand and extend your arms out to the left and right in line with your shoulders but bend your elbows so each dumbbell is up in the air directly above one of your elbows. Exhale as you bring both arms straight up with the dumbbells above the center of your chest and with your arms straight without any bend in your elbows. Inhale as you lower the dumbbells back down to the starting position with your elbows bent.

Dumbbell Flies, Straight Elbows (lying on a bench or on the floor): Lie down on your back on a bench with your knees bent at the end of the bench and with your feet on the floor. Or lie down on your back on the floor and bend your knees and put your feet flat on the floor about 12 inches apart. Push your arms straight up in the air above the center of your chest and with your palms facing one another and with a dumbbell in each hand and with your elbows slightly bent so the two dumbbells are about one inch apart. This is the normal starting position. Inhale as you lower both arms out to your sides without bending your elbows and with the dumbbells in a straight line with your shoulders. Exhale as you raise the dumbbells back up to the starting position above the center of your chest with the dumbbells about one inch apart.

Dumbbell Press (lying on a bench or on the floor): Lie down on your back on a bench with your knees bent at the end of the bench and with your feet on the floor. Or lie down on your back on the floor and bend your knees and put your feet flat on the floor about 12 inches apart. Grasp a dumbbell in each hand with your elbows bent at your sides and with one dumbbell just above each shoulder. Exhale as you push the dumbbells straight up above your shoulders until your elbows are straight. Inhale as you lower the dumbbells back down to the starting position just above your shoulders.

Dumbbell Pullovers: Lie on your back on the floor. Bend your knees and put your feet flat on the floor about 12 inches apart. Grasp a dumbbell in each hand and extend your arms straight out on the floor above your head in line with your body. Exhale as your bring both arms straight up with one dumbbell above each of your shoulders. Inhale as you lower the dumbbells back down to the floor above your head.

Dumbbell Standing Overhead Front Lift: Stand straight up with a dumbbell in each hand and with your arms straight down at your sides. Exhale as you raise each dumbbell up while keeping your arms straight until each dumbbell is directly in front of you and level with your shoulders. Continue to raise the dumbbell in each hand until a dumbbell is directly above your right and left shoulder. Inhale while keeping both arms straight and lower both dumbbells forward until they are directly in front of you and then continue lowering the dumbbells to each side.

Exercises for Significantly Overweight Individuals

The following exercises are appropriate for individuals who are significantly overweight and who have not done any type of regular exercises for a long time. Select the exercises that do not cause you any discomfort or pain in any of your joints or muscles. If you begin to exercise modestly as recommended then you may be able to gradually condition your body, tone your existing muscles, and add new muscles without injuring your muscles or joints, or causing soreness in your muscles or joints. If you experience soreness then you are doing too much and you should stop exercising until your soreness is gone, and then you should do fewer repetitions when you begin doing the exercise again.

Arm Twirls: Hold your arms straight out to your sides and level with your shoulders. Twirl both of your hands in a 6 inch circle for 10 seconds. Then lower you hands to your side and relax for 10 seconds. Repeat two more times until you have done a total of 3 repetitions. The next week do 4 repetitions per day. Very gradually add more repetitions until you reach 12 repetitions per day.

Leg Lift, Sitting: Sit in a chair and raise one foot until your foot and your leg is straight out in front of you and level with the floor, but keep the other foot on the floor. Hold your foot up for 2 seconds and then lower your foot to the floor. Relax for 5 seconds and then do the other leg. The first week do 3 repetitions per day for each leg. The next week do 4 repetitions per day for each leg. Gradually continue to add repetitions until you can do a total of 12 repetitions per day for each leg. When you reach 12 repetitions per day per leg then increase the time that you hold your foot up from 2 seconds to 3 seconds. About six weeks later increase the time from 3 seconds to 4 seconds.

Knee Lift: Stand facing a wall and put both hands against the wall. Lift your right knee until your right knee is at the same height as your hips and then immediately lower your right foot back down on the floor. Then lift your left knee until your left knee is at the height of your hips and immediately lower your left foot back down to the floor. Continue doing this exercise for 30 seconds per day the first week. The next week do it for 35 seconds per day. Continue to add 5 seconds per week until you can do this exercise for a total of 3 minutes per day.

Single Leg Lift: Lie down with your back flat against the floor. Bend your left leg at the knee and put your left foot flat on the floor. Keep the right leg straight out on the floor with your toes pointed towards the ceiling. Keep your right leg straight and raise your right foot about 4 inches off the floor and hold your right foot in this position for 2 seconds. Lower your right foot back down to the floor and relax for 5 seconds. Do 3 repetitions with the right leg. Then switch and extend the left leg straight out on the floor and bend the right leg at the knee and put the right foot flat on the floor. Do 3 repetitions of lifting the left foot off the floor for 2 seconds and resting for 5 seconds. The next week do 4 repetitions per leg per day. Gradually add repetitions until you reach 12 repetitions for each leg per day. Then gradually increase the time you hold your foot up off the floor.

Sit and Stand: Select a chair with a firm seat that has a soft but firm cushion. The height of the seat should be approximately level with your knees or just a little higher. The chair seat should not be lower than your knees. Sit in the chair, lean forward with your head approximately over your knees, and then stand up at a speed that is comfortable to you. If possible, do this without using your hands to push or pull yourself up. Remain standing for about 5 seconds. Then sit down at a comfortable speed without banging your rear end on the seat cushion. Sit for 5 seconds. Then repeat the standing - sitting cycle. If you are just starting an exercise program then 3 repetitions per day is enough for the first week. The next week do 4 repetitions per day. The next week do 5 repetitions per day. Gradually continue to add repetitions until you can do a total of 12 repetitions per day.

Upper Body Twist: Stand straight up with your hands on your hips and your feet flat on the floor about 10 inches apart. Rotate your upper body to the right and hold that position for 2 seconds. Then rotate your upper body all the way to your left and hold that position for 2 seconds. Continue doing this exercise for 30 seconds per day the first week. The next week do it for 35 seconds per day. Continue to add 5 seconds per week until you can do this exercise for a total of 3 minutes per day.

Exercises that Focus on a Specific Part of the Body

All exercises can improve your health except for the exercises you have been told not to do by your physician. But some exercises only exercise the muscles in one part of the body, such as the arms or the legs. If you desire to focus on a specific muscle group then the following exercises are shown for the muscle group that they have the maximum impact on.

1. **Abdomen (Ab) Muscles:** Several different research studies have compared the impact of different types of exercises on two groups of people. All the studies reached the same conclusion. Exercises that focused on the muscles in the abdomen, such as sit-ups and the ab wheel, did enhance the strength of the muscles in the abdomen but those exercises did not result in any additional reduction in waist circumference when compared to all other types of exercise. All exercises had the same average impact on reducing waist circumference.

2. **Arm and Hand Muscles:** Hand dumbbell exercises, hand squeeze balls and grips, pull-ups and chin-ups, and push-ups.

3. **Arm Muscles and Leg Muscles:** Jumping jacks and jumping rope.

4. **Leg Muscles:** Walking, jogging, running, and squats.

Exercises for Women Who Wish to Enhance their Breasts

Women's breasts consist mostly of fat. But underneath the fat there are pectoral muscles (pecs). These muscles are primarily used to control arm movement. Therefore arm exercises that involve enhancing and strengthening these chest muscles will help firm and lift a woman's breasts. These same arm exercises will also enhance the fat and glandular tissues in the breasts which may add to the fullness of a woman's breasts.

Push-ups are a good exercise that will achieve the above objectives. In addition all the hand dumbbell exercises will also achieve the above objectives. Select a few exercises that you can do. Please do not overwork your arm and chest muscles. Only do the number of repetitions you feel comfortable doing.

Gyms

If you want to join a gym then you may do so. However, it is possible to exercise without paying a monthly gym fee.

1. **Weight Lifting:** I know that weight lifting is one of the highly recommended exercises for replacing fat with muscle. However, lifting weights may not be appropriate for you if you have high blood pressure. You can monitor your blood pressure for free at most pharmacies, including pharmacies in Walmart and many grocery stores. If you discover that you have high blood pressure then you need to visit your family doctor and consider taking the

blood pressure medicine recommended by your family doctor. Your family doctor will also probably recommend that you not lift weights because lifting weights can aggravate your high blood pressure. If you decide to lift weights then learn the correct way to lift weights to reduce the chance of injury. Consider lifting lighter weights for more repetitions to achieve the same benefits as lifting heavier weights for fewer repetitions. Breathe normally while you lift weights and do not hold your breath.

2. **Dance Aerobics:** A dance aerobics class is usually led by a trained instructor and exercises are usually done to music (but not always). An alternative to enrolling in a formal dance aerobics class would be to do simple exercises for a few minutes each day in the morning after you wake up. This would be exercises such as touching your toes, leg raises while lying down, sit-ups, pushups, and chin-ups. Select exercises that match your current health and your ability to do the exercises. Or, if you prefer, you can purchase an exercise video and do the exercises along with the exercise instructor.

Exercise Equipment

Consider purchasing either a stationary bicycle, or a treadmill, or both. The reason is because they will allow you to exercise every day regardless of the weather. They also require significantly less time each day because you do not have to get dressed for the exercise, and you do not have to travel to the area where you can ride a real bicycle or take a casual walk or jog. They are also safer because you stay inside your home and you do not expose yourself to someone who may wish to victimize you. You simply sit on the bicycle, or step onto the treadmill, and begin to exercise. Walking and bicycling have both been proven to significantly reduce tummy fat.

1. **Stationary Bicycle:** Ride the bicycle for a few minutes every day while you listen to an audio book or watch a few minutes of a movie. Use a timer to keep track of the time so you can concentrate on the audio book or movie and enjoy it while you exercise. One of the most important parts of a stationary bicycle is the seat you sit on while pedaling the bicycle. Your rear end should feel comfortable while sitting on the seat, and the inside of your legs should not rub against the front of the seat because this will result in blisters on your legs. The height of the seat should be adjustable so that when one of your legs is fully extended then you should have one of the pedals almost at its lowest position. However, the height of the seat should also be low enough so you can easily get on it without needing a stepstool. When you first begin using the bicycle please set the resistance to a low level so you do not develop pains in your

legs as a result of the exercise. After you have used the bicycle for a week or so then very gradually increase the resistance to provide a little more challenge but not to the point where it causes leg pains. If you increase the resistance slowly over time then you will continue the ride the bicycle and reap the benefits of a daily exercise that will firm up your leg muscles and help you lose weight and tummy fat. If you would also like to firm up your arm muscles, then lift and lower hand dumbbells with each hand as your ride. Finally, while you are riding your stationary bicycle you can enjoy listening to your favorite music, or to an audio book that you have downloaded onto your mobile device, or to an audio version of the Holy Bible that you downloaded onto your mobile device. A Holy Bible audio app that can be downloaded and used for free is available at the following website (www.gideons.org). The app has the Holy Bible in English, French, Spanish, and more than 1,000 other languages. The Gideons download includes a free dramatic reading of the KJV Holy Bible with sound effects and different voices. If you listen to someone read the Holy Bible while you ride your stationary bicycle then you will be able to simultaneously enhance your physical and spiritual health.

2. **Treadmill:** Walk a few minutes each day on a treadmill while you listen to an audio book or watch a few minutes of a movie. Unless you are an athlete, do not purchase a treadmill designed for a professional athlete. Instead purchase a treadmill that is designed for a person your age and who is in your physical condition. Do not purchase a treadmill until after you have actually walked on a demo model of the treadmill in a store and you have verified that it is one you could walk on for a few minutes every day without resulting in a heart attack because it is too strenuous for you to use even at its lowest settings. When you first begin set the resistance very low and then very slowly and gradually increase the resistance.

3. **Sophisticated Exercise Machine:** I once purchased a fancy piece of exercise equipment that let me do a lot of different exercises by changing the position of the components on the exercise machine. I used this machine for a few months and then I stopped because I realized that I was spending more time changing the position of the components in order to do the different exercises than I was spending doing the exercises. Because I am an Industrial Engineer I realized this was not an efficient use of my time to achieve my original objective of exercising for a few minutes each day in order to tone up my muscles. Therefore I do not recommend the purchase of a fancy piece of exercise equipment unless you are a professional athlete and you earn a living based on your physical abilities.

Fuel for Exercise

The following information may be useful to you in the long-term as you gradually enhance your exercise program to match your life style and the amount of time you have available to exercise.

The body uses carbohydrates to provide fuel for the first 20 minutes of an exercise session. However, after the first 20 minutes the body uses fat to fuel the body. Therefore exercising for a minimum of 30 minutes each time you exercise is a good habit to acquire. However, do not be in a hurry to reach the 30 minute goal. Instead you should very slowly and very gradually increase the number of minutes you exercise each month. It may take a year or longer to get to 30 minutes per day but it is possible to get there without sacrificing your health or having long periods of time with sore muscles.

Finally, exercising burns more calories if you will do a short period of intense fast exercise followed by a longer period of normal speed exercise. For example, walk really fast for 30 seconds and then walk at normal speed for between 1 to 3 minutes. Repeat this alternating fast-slow routine for the remainder of the time you devote to walking.

Number of Calories Required to Do Different Activities

In 1970 I took a college course in ergonomics that introduced me to the concept that if an activity could be simplified so it required less physical effort then a person could do the task and burn fewer calories with the result being the person would become less fatigued. The primary goal of industrial engineers in the 1970s was not to reduce the number of calories required but to reduce employee fatigue.

In 1970 I also took college courses in weight lifting, gymnastics, and golf. Because I was studying industrial engineering I became extremely interested in the number of calories that were consumed when doing a variety of different activities. In the 1970s there was a lot of basic data on the number of calories required to do different tasks.

Since 1984 I have been teaching industrial engineering courses at a major state university and one of the courses I teach on a regular basis is work measurement and ergonomics. One of the obvious things that I noticed with the passing years is that the data very gradually become more refined and more sophisticated. As an industrial engineer I also noticed that the data from different sources did not agree with one another. However, the numbers were usually within plus or minus 10% of one another, although there were some exceptions.

In the appendix the number of calories burned while doing different activities is based on a composite of all the data that has been available to me. Therefore please do not be surprised when you discover that the numerical values do not match the data from any source that has made its data available to the general public. The reason is because the number of calories consumed to do a specific task will vary from one person to the next due to the following variables: gender, weight, height, age, muscle to fat ratio, a person's average metabolic rate, and a person's inherent physical abilities that the person was born with. For example, some people are naturally gifted at music and some people are not. Some people can throw a ball and consistently hit a target, which sometimes includes a moving target, and some people cannot. Therefore the number of calories you burn doing an activity will not be the same number of calories that someone else burns doing the same exact activity. However, all people will burn approximately the same number of calories doing a specific activity within plus or minus 10% of other people who do that same activity.

With this in mind, please use the numbers in the appendix tables as a reasonable estimate of how many calories you could burn when doing one of the activities listed. Although you may burn a few more calories doing one activity in the list, when you do a different activity in the list you may burn a few less calories. But overall your calorie consumption should be reasonably close to the values provided in the appendix.

The data in the appendix can be used to compare activities to determine which activities require more calories, such as walking, and which activities require fewer calories, such as watching television. The calorie consumption numbers will help you strategically select your daily activities in order to maximize your weight loss based on the activities you do. When you are selecting optional activities please do not base your choice simply on which activity burns the most calories. Instead please select activities you are interested in and which also burn at least an average number of calories.

Calories Burned in 30 Minutes Based on Body Weight
Tables in Appendix on Pages 274 to 277

The first two activities at the top of the first table are the number of calories burned in 30 minutes to maintain all of a person's normal body functions such as breathing, heart beating, and digestion (RMR = BMR + TEF). The RMR values are shown as a separate value at the top of the table but these values are also included in the number of calories burned for each activity at an average RMR value of 0.21 calories per 30 minutes. Therefore you do **not** need to add the RMR value for your gender to the activity values shown in the table.

The calories burned while doing different activities varies based on the type of activity and the weight of the person doing the activity. In other words, a person who weighs more will burn more calories in 30 minutes doing the same exact activity as someone who weighs less.

The calories burned per 30 minutes for each activity is shown in calories per pound, calories per kilogram, and the total number of calories for a person who weighs 150 pounds or 68 kilograms.

To determine the number of calories you would burn in 30 minutes for a specific activity, multiply your body weight (in pounds or kilograms) by the number of calories burned per 30 minutes. If you weigh less than 150 pounds (68 kg) the answer should be less than the number shown in the last column. If you weigh more than 150 pounds (68 kg) the answer should be more than the number in the last column.

It is rare to do an activity for exactly 30 minutes. Fortunately the values can easily be adjusted for the length of time devoted to the activity by dividing the calories burned during 30 minutes by 30 to yield the calories burned per minute. Then multiply that value by the number of minutes actually invested in doing the activity.

The number of calories burned is only an *estimate*. The actual number of calories burned may be a little more or a little less based on:

1. **Pace or Speed:** Most of the activities are assumed to be done at an average pace. A person doing the activities slower than average will burn fewer calories and a person doing the activities faster than average will burn more calories.

2. **Environmental Conditions:** Fewer calories will be expended in a comfortable climate controlled environment when compared to a hot or cold gymnasium, or outdoors in extreme weather conditions.

3. **Muscle to Fat Ratio:** A person with more muscle will be able to perform the activities using less effort, but a person with less muscle will expend more effort doing the same exact activity.

Chapter Twenty-Seven

How to Reduce Tummy Fat and Decrease Your Waistline

Everyone who is overweight has extra tummy fat. If you are significantly overweight then you should not focus your attention on your tummy. Instead you should allow your body to remove the weight that it is programmed to lose in the most healthy manner possible.

After you have trimmed down your entire body and the only area left is the fat on your tummy, then you can focus your attention on strategies that have been proven to help reduce tummy fat and your waistline.

Tummy Fat Reduction Strategies

Refined Sugar: If you have not already eliminated refined sugar and sugary beverages from you diet then now is the time to do so. The liver can only process a limited amount of refined sugar and your body will store the extra sugar as body fat.

Fish and Shellfish: All fish and shellfish contain docosahexaenoic acid (DHA) which is an omega-3 fatty acid. DHA may help reduce tummy fat because it may deactivate the genes that add fat to the tummy, and this may prevent tummy fat cells from expanding and becoming larger. Bass, herring, mackerel, salmon, sardines, and trout contain the most DHA.

Protein: Eat foods that have high amounts of protein. At least 25% of your daily calories should be in the form of protein. Protein can reduce food cravings by up to 60%. Protein can boost your metabolism so your body burns about 90 more calories per day. Foods with significant amounts of protein include beef, eggs, fish, legumes, nuts, and shellfish.

Fiber: Soluble fiber and viscous fiber slows down the digestive process which results in a feeling of fullness for a longer period of time and a reduction in appetite. Good choices are fruits, legumes, whole oats, and vegetables.

Beans: They may help decrease cholesterol, reduce blood pressure, help control blood sugar, and reduce tummy fat. The fiber in beans is both soluble and insoluble. Both types of fiber reduce the amount of fat your body stores. Digesting the fiber and protein in beans consumes extra calories during the digesting process.

Eggs: Eggs contain choline, which is also high in beans, lentils, collard greens, seafood, and lean meats (beef, chicken, turkey). Choline may help reduce the amount of fat stored around your liver. Reducing the fat stored around your liver may help reduce your waistline from the inside of your body.

Green Tea: It contains some caffeine and it contains a significant amount of antioxidants. It may increase the burning of overall body fat by 4%, and it may increase the burning of tummy fat by up to 17%. Matcha green tea is a powdered green tea and it may have more health benefits than other types of green tea. People who regularly drink hot coffee or hot tea may find the flavor of green tea acceptable to their palate. However, people who do not regularly drink hot beverages may not enjoy the flavor of green tea. Everyone should use *common sense* and if you don't like green tea then please don't force yourself to drink it just because it might be a healthy beverage.

Coconut: Either coconut oil or unsweetened shredded coconut may help reduce your waistline if you have extra fat stored on your tummy. Coconut oil can be used instead of extra virgin olive oil in some recipes. Coconut oil may help satisfy your appetite and enhance your metabolic rate so you burn more calories while eating less food.

Glucomannan: It has no odor or taste. It is a "natural fiber" supplement that may help you more easily lose some tummy fat. It is obtained from the konjac plant which is also called "elephant yam." Since it is a soluble fiber it naturally reduces the absorption of protein and fat. It may slow down the absorption of sugar and help stabilize blood sugar levels. It is low in calories and it may help keep food inside the stomach longer which helps delay the feeling of hunger for a longer period of time. It feeds the beneficial bacteria in your intestines. It may help lower cholesterol and triglycerides and it may help relieve constipation. However it may cause bloating, soft stools, and it may interfere with some medications if the medications are taken at approximately the same time. It should be taken with water about 30 minutes before a meal.

Yogurt: It may improve your digestive processes and help reduce tummy fat.

Ab Exercises: Exercises that are focused specifically on the abdomen do **not** have a measurable impact of waist circumference.

Aerobic Exercises: Exercises such as walking, swimming, and bicycling, have resulted in major waistline reductions in a lot of different research studies.

Chapter Twenty-Eight

Weight in Relationship to Endurance, Strength, Fatigue, Flexibility, and Sex

Overweight individuals have to deal with a variety of problems that are directly related to the extra weight they are carrying on their bodies.

Endurance and Strength

Being overweight has a strong relationship to a reduction in endurance and strength.

Fatigue

If you are overweight then there is a chance that your arteries are accumulating plaque inside them. If this happens then the flow of blood to your heart is reduced and this may result in fatigue in addition to a variety of other medical problems.

If you are overweight then there is a chance that the muscles in your throat may relax while you are asleep and you will inhale less air. This will result in less oxygen in your blood and this may automatically awaken you several times during the night. When you do not get a peaceful night of rest then you may experience fatigue the next day.

Being overweight is one of the major causes of type 2 diabetes and type 2 diabetes may contribute to fatigue.

Being overweight means your body has to work harder to do all types of activities and this can contribute to fatigue. Since doing any type of work is difficult then you may compensate by trying to minimize the amount of work you do. This results in the work becoming even more difficult to do and you gradually become less and less active, and more and more fatigued.

Flexibility

Overweight individuals may move less frequently than individuals who are not overweight. In addition, a lot of excess fat at specific locations on the body may interfere with the full range of motions at nearby joints.

If a person becomes sedentary and spends a significant amount of time sitting then the person may experience tightening of the muscles and connective tissues which may reduce flexibility

Sexual Performance

Being overweight increases the risk of erectile dysfunction. In one study 31% of the men who lost a reasonable amount of weight over a two year period, and who also engaged in some type of regular exercise, reported restored erectile function at the end of two years. In the same study only 5% of the men who lost a trivial amount of weight over a two year period reported restored erectile function.

Several different studies have reported lower testosterone levels in overweight men when compared to men who were not overweight. Lower testosterone levels in men has been linked to a reduction in sexual desire. However, when the same men lost weight and participated in some form of regular exercise then their testosterone levels increased along with their sexual desire.

How to Minimize or Eliminate these Problems

1. **Food:** Foods that contain a lot of sugar but no protein or fiber will disrupt the energy balance in your body regardless of how much you weigh. Foods that contain more protein and more fiber will require more time to digest and this may help stabilize your blood sugar levels and provide more energy so you can do the tasks you desire to do. Consider adding a wider variety of meat, vegetables, fruits, and nuts to your diet, and eliminate foods with added sugar.

2. **Water:** Increase your total daily consumption of pure plain cold water. Drink some water shortly after you wake up in the morning, and during the day, and just before every meal. Always drinking cold water before you eat is an extremely healthy habit that you should adopt. However, although most people have heard this simple advice for many, many years, they have made a decision they are not going to follow this advice for one reason or another. And their body suffers for their refusal to drink lots of cold water.

3. **Caffeine:** If you enjoy beverages with caffeine, such as coffee, tea, or sodas, then consider drinking smaller quantities of those beverages at different times during the day but not in the evening before bedtime. Many sodas are now available in 7.5 ounce cans.

4. **Exercise:** Do some simple basic exercises every morning in the privacy of your bedroom. This will improve the flexibility of your joints, firm up your muscles, increase your metabolism, and enhance your energy level during the day. The effect should easily wear off before bedtime so it may be easier to go to sleep at night.

5. **Sleep:** If possible, go to bed at the same time every night, and wake up at the same time every morning, seven days per week. Having a regular sleeping schedule is as important as having a regular meal schedule.

Chapter Twenty-Nine

Weight in Relationship to
Age, Gender, Health, and Life Expectancy

On pages 272 and 273 in the Appendix there is a table that shows reasonable weight ranges for men and women based on their height and age.

Some of the information in this chapter has been mentioned previously in other chapters of this book. However, I thought it would be useful to consolidate the information into one chapter so you can more easily evaluate its impact on your health and your weight loss strategy.

Weight and Height Percentiles

In 1970 I first began studying ergonomics, anthropology, and anthropometry.

1. Ergonomics is the study of people in their normal work and social environments and it draws heavily on anthropometry, industrial engineering concepts, and psychology.

2. Anthropology is the study of mankind in relationship to:

    a. Races, culture, and national origin.

    b. Physical and mental abilities.

3. Anthropometry is the study of human physical characteristics, with emphasis of the analysis of the physical dimensions, size, shape, and characteristics of the human body. The data is usually separated into groups based on gender, race, and national origin.

Since 1984 I have been teaching classes in ergonomics and anthropometry at a major state university. During this time I have observed that the anthropometric data on people in the USA has been gradually and consistently changing due to changes in the following variables:

1. **Marriages:** More and more people are getting married to a person of a different national origin and their children inherit some of the characteristics of both parents.

2. **Food:** There has been a gradual improvement in the availability of a variety of different foods to people of every nationality.

3. **Nutrition:** There has been an improvement in the nutrition available to people of every nationality beginning at conception and continuing through the time children spend in the public school system. Some of this nutrition improvement is the result of the free social programs in many communities for pregnant women and for children of economically challenged parents.

4. **Weight:** There has been an increase in the average weight of people of every nationality due to the amount of food that has gradually become more easily acquired by almost everyone.

5. **Height:** There has been an increase in the average height of the people of some nationalities due to the availability of food and the nutrition in that food as the children were growing into adults.

6. **Strength:** There has been a decrease in the average physical strength and the physical abilities of people of every nationality due to the gradual decrease in the amount of physical exercise in public schools, lower expectations for physical performance, less physical exercise due to improved modes of transportation, and an increase in the gradual acceptance of a more sedentary lifestyle due to the increase in the use of computer technology, mobile phones, and tablets. Many people today are content to play a game or a sport on their phone or tablet instead of participating in the real thing.

The combined impact of all the above changes has resulted in the gradual systematic revision of the anthropometric data on both men and women of all age groups, of all races, and of all national origins. And I do not foresee any change in this trend in the near future. Therefore anthropometric data will continue to be gradually updated so that it continues to adequately describe the average weight, height, and other characteristics of the current population.

This is important because *common sense* should warn us that we should not compare ourselves or our family members to the averages that currently describe us in the USA. In other words, please do not become too proud or too disappointed if you or one of your family members is in a certain percentile group. It may be better to evaluate ourselves and our family members based simply on the general level of our health, our ability to avoid disease, our ability to recover from sicknesses, our mental abilities, and our physical abilities to perform a variety of physically challenging tasks.

Age and Weight

After a person has reached his or her peak growth potential, then the person's muscle to fat ratio very gradually begins to decline with advancing age. Females reach their peak growth potential sometime around the age of 18 and males reach their peak growth potential sometime around the age of 22. After reaching their peak growth potential a person's metabolism slows down as a result of age and they burn fewer calories simply because of their gradually decreasing muscle to fat ratio. After a person has attained their peak growth then their resting metabolic rate (RMR) begins to decrease by approximate 0.2% per year.

Gender and Weight

The average male weighs more than the average female. The average male is taller than the average female. The average male has a higher muscle to fat ratio than the average female. Therefore the average male burns more calories per day than the average female.

Health and Weight

Approximately two-thirds of all adults in the USA are overweight and approximately one-half of those overweight people are obese. The USA Center for Disease Control (CDC) has reported a strong relationship between obesity and all the following health issues: breathing problems (asthma and sleep apnea), chronic pain, coronary heart disease, gallbladder disease, gallstones, high blood pressure, mental illness, osteoarthritis, stroke, type 2 diabetes, unhealthy cholesterol levels, and a variety of cancers including breast, colon, gallbladder, kidney, and liver cancers. The CDC has also linked obesity to a lower quality of life and to an early death.

People who are overweight are also putting more weight on their ankles, knees, and hips, and this extra pressure will cause problems in these joints as the person gradually ages. Most people don't appreciate their ability to walk and to move about freely until after they have lost their mobility and it is too late to reverse the damage that has been done. Perhaps you will be one of the fortunate people who can minimize or avoid this problem by shedding some, most, or all of the extra weight you may be carrying on your body.

Life Expectancy and Weight

A study on 650,000 people, including both men and women, revealed that the average life expectancy of an overweight man was 3 years less than a man who was not overweight. And the average life expectancy of an overweight woman was 5 years less than a women who was not overweight. (Source: Mayo Clinic)

The same study reported that a man who has a waist in excess of 43 inches (110 centimeters) had a 50% higher risk of death than a man with a waist of 37 inches (94 centimeters) or less. A woman who has a waist in excess of 37 inches (94 centimeters) has an 80% higher risk of death than a woman with a waist of 27.5 inches (70 centimeters) or less. (Source: Mayo Clinic)

A different study on more than 600,000 people revealed that for each one pound that an overweight person loses, that person will add an average of one month to their normal life expectancy. Or stated differently, for each extra pound of weight above average that an overweight person is carrying on their body then that person will lose an average of one month off their normal life expectancy. (Source: Nature Communications)

Both of the above studies agree that any person who is overweight will be sacrificing months or years off their normal life expectancy depending on how much extra weight they are carrying on their bodies.

Hopefully it is not too late for you to take corrective action and to lose some, most, or all of your extra weight so you can live a longer life that is also more enjoyable to live.

Reasonable Weights for Adults

The weight tables on pages 272 and 273 in the Appendix are for adults with normal healthy bodies who are not overweight. The weights are shown in pounds (and kilograms) and the weights are based on gender, age, and height.

The data in the Appendix is for individuals who were considered to be physically fit and healthy from the mid-1960s through the early-1980s. As mentioned previously, men and women in the USA in the 2020s weigh more than they did 40 years ago. Therefore more recently published weight tables are based on the weights of people in the 21st century. If you prefer to compare your weight to the heavier people of the 21st century then you may do so. However, if you prefer to compare your weight to people who were healthier and more physically fit in the 1960s through the 1980s then you should use the tables in the appendix of this book.

Chapter Thirty

Weight Loss Slows Down, Stops, or Reverses.

The most significant and dramatic weight losses will occur the first week you begin dieting. Then your weight loss will very, very gradually begin to decline with the passage of time.

When you begin a new diet it is important to understand that weight loss will not happen every day for one or more of the following reasons:

1. **Food:** The different foods you eat on a specific day may contain a few more calories than what you normally eat.

2. **Water:** The amount of water your body retains will increase and decrease from one day to the next.

3. **Activities:** Unless you have a very rigid schedule, the various discretionary activities you participate in each day will consume a different number of calories. And the amount of time you invest in each of these activities may also vary which will impact the number of calories burned each day.

4. **Digestion:** Some foods take longer to digest and those foods will remain inside you longer before your body expels the residue it does not need.

In order to enhance your long-term weight loss please remember that a pound of muscle requires about three times as many calories to maintain as a pound of fat. Each pound of muscle requires about 6 calories per day to sustain it. Therefore you should gradually add activities to your daily schedule that will gradually enhance the amount of lean muscles on your body. If you begin adding activities and exercises to your weight loss plan at the beginning of the second month of your diet then you will be gradually adding lean muscles to your body. This will not only enhance your health and your appearance but it will also help your body to continue to lose weight over an extended period of time.

Your Weekly Weight Loss Slows Down

Your weight loss will gradually slow down as you continue to lose weight for the following reasons:

1. **Total Body Weight:** More calories are required to maintain a heavier body than a lighter body. As you gradually lose weight then the number of calories you need each day will also gradually begin to decrease.

2. **Food Restrictions:** If you only eat a limited number of different foods then it becomes easier for your body to more efficiently convert those foods into fuel. As your body's metabolism adjusts to the limited number of foods in your new diet then your weight loss will gradually begin to slow down. The easiest way to prevent this specific problem is to have a much wider variety of healthy foods in your diet, and do not eat exactly the same foods every day. Instead try to vary your daily diet and eat some of the foods you really enjoy one day and then eat some of the other foods you really enjoy the next day. Try to maintain some reasonable variety in your weekly diet. This will keep your metabolism more active and your metabolism will not slow down because it has adjusted to processing the same exact foods day after day after day. You will also be enhancing your health because you will be eating foods that have a wider variety of extremely healthy nutrients.

Weight Loss Plateau

As you lose weight your body will periodically reach different weight loss plateaus and your weight will stabilize at that approximate weight for one or two weeks. During this time your body is adjusting itself to your new weight and to your diet. This is normal and it should not discourage you and you should not abandon your diet. Please be patient with your body and allow your body to make all the adjustments it needs to make in order to optimize both your short-term and your long-term health. After your body has adjusted all of its normal functions to your new average weight then your body will once again begin to burn fat cells and your weight loss will resume. However, if you do not begin losing weight after a reasonable amount of time then consider implementing the strategies in the next section.

You Stop Losing Weight

If you stop losing weight and your weight does not change by more than plus or minus one pound in one month then you have reached the point where your daily calorie intake is approximately equal to the number of calories you burn each day.

If you are comfortable with your current weight then you should continue doing what you are now doing.

However if you wish to lose some more weight then you will have to burn more calories per day than you eat. There are three ways you can achieve this goal:

1. **Eat Fewer Calories Per Day:** Make a list of all the different foods you are now eating along with the number of calories in each food.

Consider replacing some of the high calorie foods with low calorie foods. Some fruits and vegetables have significantly fewer calories than other fruits and vegetables. Some meals have significantly fewer calories than other meals.

2. **Increase the Number of Calories You Burn Each Day:** Make a list of the activities that you normally do along with the amount of time you invest in each activity. Then calculate the approximate number of calories you burn doing each of those activities. If you have some flexibility in your schedule then consider replacing some of the low calorie consuming activities with some of the activities that burn more calories. However, use discretion because if you increase your daily burn rate too much then you may also increase your appetite and this may result in the consumption of more food which will offset the extra calories you are burning.

3. **Combine the Above Two Strategies:** Reduce the number of calories you eat each day by a small amount and increase the number of calories you burn each day by a small amount.

You Start Gaining Weight

If you gradually begin to gain weight then the average number of calories you are eating each day is exceeding the average number of calories you burn each day. The reasons for your weight gain are the same reasons mentioned in the previous section for not losing weight, and the same exact solutions apply to this new problem.

However, there are three other options you may wish to consider.

1. **New Low Calorie Foods:** Begin experimenting with healthy foods that you have not eaten before and which contain very, very few calories. You may discover that you like some of these new foods. If you like these new foods then you should add these new very low calorie foods into your diet in place of some of the highest calorie foods that are currently in your diet. This will help reduce your total daily calorie intake. And it may help reactivate your metabolism because your body will now have to process foods it had not been receiving before and that your body is not familiar with. And it is possible that these new foods may contain some nutrients your body wasn't getting enough of, and after you start eating these new foods then you may discover that your body is more easily satisfied with what you are now eating because these new foods contain exactly what your body needs, and your appetite decreases, and you actually eat less food each day because you are not as hungry as you used to be.

2. **Count Exactly How Many Calories You Eat Each Day:** The easiest and quickest way to do this is with a food scale that will automatically tell you exactly how many calories are in the food you put on the scale (after you enter the food code into the scale). The scale is preprogrammed to compute calories based on the weight of the food. Some scales will keep track of the total number of calories you put on the scale each day and then reset for the next day. In January of 2020 a scale that will do all of this for you is the "NutraTrack Mini Kitchen/ Calorie & Nutrition Scale." This scale has 1,998 different foods preprogrammed into its computer and it also allows you to enter 999 additional unique food codes into its computer. It has the names of the 160 most common foods printed on the top of the scale along with the code number of each food. The digital display shows the weight of the food and the calories, salt, protein, fat, carbohydrates, cholesterol, and fiber in the amount of food placed on the scale. The scale will show weights in grams or in 0.1 ounces. The scale uses 3 AAA batteries.

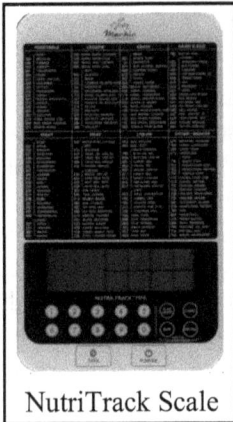

NutriTrack Scale

3. **Reread this Book:** As a last resort you may wish to consider rereading this entire book beginning on page one. You may discover a suggestion that you overlooked or a suggestion that you originally decided not to pursue. Unless you have a good reason to continue to avoid that suggestion then you might wish to give it a try because it may help you to stop gaining weight. And it may help you to once begin losing some weight just like you did when you first began the Common Sense Diet.

Weight Maintenance

After you reach your desired weight goal then one of the best things you can do to not regain the weight you lost is to continue to exercise regularly. Long-term weight maintenance is discussed in detail in the next chapter.

Chapter Thirty-One

Weight Loss Goal and Weight Maintenance

When you started your new diet you established a weight loss goal that was reasonable but attainable. Hopefully you did not set your goal at your weight when you were 18 years old, or 21 years old, or any specific age. Instead it would have been more reasonable to have set a goal based on your current age, your general health, and your daily mandatory activities (such as a job).

If you have achieved that goal then you deserve to be congratulated. And it is now time to focus on weight maintenance instead of weight loss.

However, if you have made significant progress towards your goal but you still have just a few more pounds that you would like to lose but you have been stuck at your current weight for two months or more, then may I suggest that you accept your current weight as your new normal weight, and that you focus your efforts on maintaining that weight for the rest of your life.

Frequently when a person doesn't reach their original weight loss goal then the person becomes discouraged. It is also normal to decide that it is just not worth the effort and to simply give up and surrender. Then the person starts eating foods they shouldn't eat and they gradually gain back all the weight they lost.

You can avoid this weight gain problem if you will visualize your original total weight loss goal as a moving target. For a long time you have been moving towards your total weight loss goal and you have been making good progress. But now it is time for your original total weight loss goal to move towards you and to match whatever your weight now is. This will give you a sense of completion and you can take pride in what you have accomplished. This will also add closure to your weight loss efforts and you can now begin to focus on weight maintenance instead of weight loss.

Weight Maintenance

All of the following suggestions may help you maintain your current weight and keep the weight you lost off your body for the rest of your life.

1. **Transition:** Make a very slow and gradual transition from your weight loss stage into your weight maintenance stage. Give your body a chance to gradually adjust to the changes you have planned

for it now that you are at your desired weight. Don't make too many changes too quickly. Very gradually change the things you do and monitor their impact on your weight. If your weight remains stable then you can experiment with the next change you have planned. But if your weight begins to increase, then the last change you made isn't working and you need to stop doing it.

2. **Exercise:** One of the best things you can do to not regain the weight you lost is to continue to exercise regularly. Not only will exercising help you keep the weight off, but exercising will continue to firm up your existing lean muscles and keep your body flexible and strong. And if you continue to add more lean muscles to your body then those new muscles will allow you to consume more calories each day to maintain your new muscles.

3. **Play Games and Sports with your Children or Grandchildren:** Not only will you enjoy and benefit from the exercise but your family will sincerely appreciate the time you spend with them. And they will remember you with much affection if they outlive you.

4. **Calories:** The number of calories you can eat each day can now be approximately equal to the number of calories you burn each day.

5. **Foods:** Continue to eat the healthy foods you have been eating to maintain your long-term health and to maximize your life expectancy. Continue to eat protein, fiber, and healthy dietary fat. Now that you have lost weight don't start eating all the foods that you have not been eating since you began your diet. Don't add refined sugar back into your diet.

6. **Nutrition:** To keep the weight off and to enhance your health it is important to keep the nutrition of the foods you eat each day in mind. During the week try to eat a reasonable variety of healthy foods including fish, nuts, fruit, and vegetables. These foods have been consistently proven to help people avoid weight gains, improve their health, and extend their life expectancy.

7. **New Foods:** It is okay to try new foods. But consider the calories in those foods and adjust the quantity of the other foods you eat so that your daily calorie intake still approximately matches the number of calories you burn each day.

8. **Strategically Plan Your Meals:** Give careful consideration to what you will eat at each meal of the day. Do not allow your meals to be spur of the moment decisions. It is okay to revise your meal plan as the day progresses and as mealtime gradually approaches but you should have a general idea of what you intend to eat each day at the beginning of the day.

9. **Breakfast:** If you have been eating breakfast regularly while you were losing weight then there is no reason to stop eating breakfast now that you have reached your weight loss goal. However, if you have not been eating breakfast while you were losing weight then there is no reason to start eating breakfast now that you have reached your weight loss goal. If you have **not** been eating breakfast and you start eating breakfast then you may begin to gain weight and this would not be desirable after you have reached your weight loss goal.

10. **Eat Slowly and Chew Each Bite Thoroughly:** Don't abandon this healthy eating habit that helped you lose weight. This same healthy eating habit can help you keep the weight you lost off your body.

11. **Weekends and Holidays:** Do not seriously overindulge in food on weekends or on holidays. It is okay to *slightly* increase your total calorie intake on special occasions but don't make a habit of doing it every weekend.

12. **Food Storage:** Continue to put food in food cabinets or in the refrigerator or freezer. Do not leave food on top of counters or tables where it can easily be seen. Food that is always visible encourages snacking, and snacking will increase your daily consumption of calories.

13. **Water:** Continue to drink a lot of plain pure cold water every day. Do not reduce your daily consumption of water just because you are now at your desired weight. (Note: Drinking a lot of plain pure cold water is the most widely known and believed good dieting advice, but it is also the least followed dieting advice. If you want to keep the weight you lost off your body then drinking a lot of cold water every day will help you achieve this goal.)

14. **Weigh Yourself:** Continue to weigh yourself every day. This daily feedback can help you to not eat something you know you really shouldn't eat because it may tip the scale the next day.

15. **Sleep:** Continue to get a good night's rest. The lack of sleep can easily trigger aggressive eating and an increase in weight. If you have difficulty sleeping then please remember that eating six or fewer fresh, frozen, or canned tart cherries in the evening will not add too many calories to the total number of daily calories that you consume and the melatonin in the cherries may help you sleep better. (Note: Avoid maraschino cherries because they contain added ingredients that may be harmful to your health.)

16. **Education:** Continue to read a variety of new information about weight loss and healthy foods. You may discover something interesting that you would like to try, or you may read some really positive information about a food you normally do not eat. This will allow you to continue to add new activities and new foods into your life.

17. **My Father's Advice:** While my father, Jason Lester Atkins, was alive he frequently told his children, "If it doesn't get past your lips, then it won't show up on your hips."

Chapter Thirty-Two
We Are What We Eat

I attended public schools during the 1950s and 1960s in a variety of different middle class neighborhoods in a variety of different towns in the USA. Some of my classmates did not miss a single day of school during an entire school year. Those students were usually recognized at the end of the year with a small paper certificate that had the words "Perfect Attendance Record" and the student's name. When I was in the fifth grade I received one of those awards.

I was a normal child and I occasionally got sick and I would miss one or two days of school each year. However, none of the schools I attended were ever closed because of some sickness that was sweeping through the public schools and making almost everyone sick.

My children attended public schools in the 1980s and 1990s. My children were healthy most of the time but they did occasionally miss two or three days of school per year due to some type of illness. I do not remember any of the schools being closed due to a sickness that was sweeping through the public schools and making almost everyone sick.

My grandchildren began attending public schools in the 2000s and I still have grandchildren in public schools and in private schools in the 2020s. During the decade of the 2010s it seemed like many of the public schools and private schools in my area were closed for one week or more every year due to some type of illness that was making most of the students and the teachers sick.

There are a variety of official reasons for the spread of these different illnesses and for our reduced immunity and our susceptibility to a variety of different bacteria and viruses.

However, it may be possible that the foods we have been eating in the USA for a very long time are now gradually taking their toll on our health and our immune systems. If this is true, then the good news is that we still have a chance to reverse this trend. All we need to do is to start feeding our family really nutritious healthy foods and our bodies will gradually begin to heal themselves. And our immune systems will once again become strong enough to resist the bacteria and viruses that may sweep through our geographical area.

The primary goal of the information presented in this book was to provide the knowledge you need so you can improve your long-term health and the health of your entire family. As you gradually implement the suggestions in this book then the health of your family members should gradually improve, and their natural immune systems should gradually be strengthened so that they will not succumb to every bacteria and virus they are exposed to.

Specific Health Problems and
Foods that May Minimize that Problem

The following health benefits may be enhanced by consuming the following vitamins, minerals, foods, and beverages in *moderation*. Recommended Daily Dietary Allowances (RDA) for vitamins and minerals is shown on pages 278 to 282. Excessive consumption of any vitamin, mineral, food, or beverage may have a negative health impact.

If you or your family members have a history of one or more specific medical problems, or if you wish to reduce the risk of a specific medical problem, then you may wish to consider adding some of the foods that are recommended for that specific medical condition into you diet, if you enjoy eating those foods. The maximum potential health benefit could be achieved by including a variety of foods in your diet instead of just a limited number of foods because each food has its own unique chemistry and impact on the body.

Please remember that food will **not** solve a medical problem. Your doctor can recommend medications, treatments, or an exercise program that may be of significant benefit to resolving your medical problem. However, making the right food choices may also enhance your health and help minimize your medical problem.

1. **Decrease Blood Pressure:** Fiber. **Vitamins:** B3, B5, D. **Minerals:** calcium, magnesium, potassium. **Vegetables:** beans, beets, cabbage, carrots, cauliflower, garlic, kale, lentils, mushrooms, okra, squash, sweet potatoes, Swiss chard. **Fruits:** bananas, blueberries, cantaloupes, grapefruits, grapes, honeydew melons, kiwi, lemons, olives, oranges, peaches, raspberries, strawberries, watermelons. **Grains:** oats, wheat. **Nuts:** almonds, cashews, peanuts, pecans, pistachios, walnuts. **Seeds:** chia seeds, flax seeds, sesame seeds, sunflower seeds. **Dairy:** eggs, milk, Greek yogurt. **Meat:** chicken. **Fish and Shellfish:** all. **Beverages:** beer (in moderation). **Supplements:** wheat germ oil.

2. **Decrease Cholesterol:** Fiber. **Vitamins:** B3, C. **Minerals:** calcium, chromium. **Vegetables:** beans, broccoli, cabbage, carrots, eggplant, fruits, garlic, green peas, kale, lentils, lettuce, mushrooms, okra. **Fruit:** blackberries, blueberries, cherries, grapefruits, grapes, lemons, limes, olives, oranges, peaches, plums, watermelons. **Grains:** barley, corn, popcorn, oats, wheat. **Nuts:** almonds, Brazil nuts, cashews, hazelnuts, macadamia nuts, peanuts, pecans, pistachios, walnuts. **Seeds:** chia seeds, flax seeds, pumpkin seeds, sesame seeds, sunflower seeds. **Meat:** chicken, turkey. **Fish and Shellfish:** all. **Beverages:** beer (in moderation), wine (in moderation). **Sweets:** cocoa. **Supplements:** glucomannan, wheat germ oil. **Condiments:** ketchup, mustard.

3. **Decrease Triglycerides: Mineral:** chromium. **Vegetables:** Brussels sprouts, okra. **Fruits:** peaches, plums. **Grain:** wheat. **Nuts:** Brazil nuts, cashews, hazelnuts, macadamia nuts, peanuts, pistachios. **Seeds:** chia seeds, sesame seeds. **Dairy:** eggs. **Fish:** bass, halibut, herring, mackerel, salmon, sardines, trout, tuna. **Supplements:** glucomannan.
4. **Enhance Bladder Health: Vitamin** A. **Vegetables:** broccoli, sweet potatoes. **Fruits:** pears. **Nuts:** pecans. **Seeds:** pumpkin seeds.
5. **Enhance Blood Health: Vitamins:** B2, B3, B6, B7, B12, D, K. **Minerals:** calcium, copper, fluoride, iron, magnesium, sodium. **Vegetables:** beets, broccoli, cabbage, cauliflower, celery, squash, Swiss chard. **Fruits:** apples, apricots, lemons, limes. **Nuts:** Brazil nuts, cashews, hazelnuts, pistachios, walnuts. **Seeds:** chia seeds, sesame seeds. **Dairy:** Greek yogurt. **Meats:** beef, turkey. **Fish and Shellfish:** all. **Supplements:** wheat germ oil.
   a. **Enhance Blood Circulation: Vitamins:** B1, B6, E, K. **Vegetables:** lentils, mushrooms, squash. **Fruits:** limes, olives, pears, plums. **Supplements:** wheat germ oil.
   b. **Stabilize Blood Sugar Levels:** Fiber. **Vitamins:** B7, D. **Minerals:** chromium, magnesium, manganese. **Amino Acid:** leucine. **Vegetables:** beans, Brussels sprouts, carrots, celery, cucumbers, green peas, kale, lentils, okra, potatoes, sweet potatoes, Swiss chard. **Fruits:** bananas, blackberries, blueberries, grapes, honeydew melons, kiwi, limes, peaches. **Grains:** oats, wheat. **Nuts:** almonds, hazelnuts, macadamia nuts, pecans, pistachios. **Seeds:** chia seeds, flax seeds, sesame seeds, sunflower seeds. **Fish:** mackerel, perch, sardines. **Supplement:** glucomannan, wheat germ oil.
6. **Enhance Bone Heath: Vitamins:** A, D. **Minerals:** calcium, copper, magnesium, manganese, okra, phosphorus. **Vegetables:** beans, cucumbers, green peas, tomatoes, turnips. **Fruits:** blackberries, blueberries, cantaloupes, grapes, honeydew melons, olives, peaches, pears, plums, strawberries. **Grains:** corn, popcorn, wheat. **Nuts:** almonds, cashews, macadamia nuts, pecans. **Seeds:** chia seeds, sesame seeds, sunflower seeds. **Dairy:** eggs, milk, Greek yogurt. **Meats:** beef, chicken, lamb, pork, turkey. **Fish and Shellfish:** all. **Beverages:** beer (in moderation), wine (in moderation). **Condiments:** ketchup, mustard.
7. **Enhance Bowel Movements and Minimize Constipation:** Fiber. **Mineral:** phosphorus. **Vegetables:** beets, broccoli, Brussels sprouts, cucumbers, lentils, okra, green peas. **Fruits:** kiwi, oranges, pears, plums, strawberries. **Grains:** corn, popcorn, oats, wheat. **Nuts:** almonds, Brazil nuts, hazelnuts. **Seeds:** chia seeds, flax

seeds, sesame seeds. **Fish:** cod, mackerel. **Supplements:** wheat germ oil.

8. **Enhance Brain Health and Functions: Vitamins:** B1, B2, B3, B6, E. **Minerals:** choline, manganese, **Amino Acids:** asparagine, glycine. **Vegetables:** beets, broccoli, cabbage, carrots, cauliflower, celery, lettuce, mushrooms, okra, squash, sweet bell peppers, sweet potatoes, Swiss chard. **Fruits:** apricots, blackberries, blueberries, cantaloupes, grapes, olives, oranges, peaches, plums, raspberries, strawberries. **Grains:** corn, popcorn, wheat. **Nuts:** almonds, hazelnuts, macadamia nuts, peanuts, pecans, pistachios, walnuts. **Seeds:** sunflower seeds. **Dairy:** eggs. **Meats:** beef, chicken, pork. **Fish and Shellfish:** all. **Beverages:** beer and wine (in moderation). **Supplements:** wheat germ oil. **Condiment:** peanut butter.

9. **Enhance Cardiovascular Health:** Fiber. **Vegetable:** squash. **Fruit:** grapefruits. **Grains:** corn, popcorn, oats. **Nuts:** almonds, cashews, hazelnuts, macadamia nuts, walnuts. **Seeds:** chia seeds, flax seeds, sunflower seeds. **Dairy:** cheese, eggs. **Meat:** chicken, turkey. **Fish and Shellfish:** all.

10. **Enhance Detoxification and Expel Toxins and Free Radicals from the Body: Vitamin** A. **Vegetables:** carrots, kale, lettuce, okra, sweet potatoes, spinach, squash. **Fruits:** avocados, cantaloupes. **Dairy:** butter, cheese, heavy whipping cream.

11. **Enhance Digestion: Vitamins:** B1, B3, B9. **Minerals:** chloride, manganese, phosphorus. **Amino Acids:** histidine, threonine. **Vegetables:** asparagus, beets, broccoli, Brussels sprouts, cabbage, carrots, green peas, hot peppers, lentils, mushrooms, okra, potatoes, squash, sweet bell peppers, sweet potatoes, Swiss chard, tomatoes, turnips. **Fruits:** apples, apricots, bananas, blackberries, cantaloupes, grapefruits, honeydew melons, kiwi, lemons, limes, olives, oranges, peaches, pears, pineapples, raspberries, strawberries, watermelons. **Grains:** corn, popcorn, oats, wheat. **Nuts:** almonds, Brazil nuts, macadamia nuts, pecans, pistachios, walnuts. **Seeds:** chia seeds, flax seeds, sesame seeds, sunflower seeds. **Dairy:** Greek yogurt. **Meat:** chicken. **Fish:** cod, halibut, perch, salmon, snapper. **Beverages:** wine (in moderation). **Supplements:** wheat germ oil.

12. **Enhance Energy, Endurance, and Stamina: Vegetable:** beets. **Grains:** corn, popcorn, wheat. **Nuts:** almonds, hazelnuts. **Seeds:** sunflower seeds. **Meats:** beef, chicken, lamb, pork, turkey. **Fish and Shellfish:** all. **Supplements:** wheat germ oil.

13. **Enhance Eye Health: Vitamins:** A, B3, B6, B12, C. **Vegetables:** beans, broccoli, cabbage, carrots, cauliflower, celery, garlic, green peas, kale, okra, squash, sweet bell peppers, sweet potatoes, tomatoes. **Fruits:** apples, apricots, blackberries, cantaloupes,

grapes, honeydew melons, kiwi, lemons, limes, olives, oranges, peaches, pears, pineapples, plums, raspberries, strawberries, watermelons. **Grains:** corn, popcorn, wheat. **Nuts:** cashews, macadamia nuts, pecans, pistachios. **Seeds:** flax seeds. **Dairy:** butter, eggs. **Meat:** chicken. **Fish:** bass, cod, herring, mackerel, salmon, sardines, snapper, tuna. **Shellfish:** crab, lobster, shrimp. **Beverages:** beer (in moderation). **Condiment:** ketchup.

 a. **Reduce Risk of Cataracts: Fruit:** apples. **Grain:** wheat. **Nuts:** cashews, macadamia nuts. **Dairy:** butter, eggs. **Fish:** bass. **Shellfish:** crab.

 b. **Reduce Risk of Macular Degeneration: Vitamin A. Grain:** wheat. **Nuts:** cashews, pistachios. **Dairy:** eggs. **Fish:** bass, cod, mackerel, sardines, tuna. **Shellfish:** crab, lobster, shrimp. .

14. **Enhance Gall Bladder Function and Reduce Risk of Gallstones:** Fiber. **Fruit:** lemons. **Grain:** wheat. **Nuts:** cashews, peanuts, pecans. **Condiment:** peanut butter.

15. **Enhance Hair Health: Vitamins:** A, B1, B2, B3, B5, B7, B12. **Mineral:** sulfur. **Amino Acids:** cysteine, methionine. **Vegetables:** carrots, Swiss chard, tomatoes. **Fruits:** apples, cantaloupes, lemons, limes, oranges, pears, plums, strawberries, watermelons. **Grain:** wheat. **Nuts:** almonds, Brazil nuts, hazelnuts, macadamia nuts, peanuts, pecans. **Seeds:** chia seed, flax seeds, sesame seeds, sunflower seeds. **Meat:** turkey. **Fish:** cod, halibut, mackerel, tilapia, trout. **Shellfish:** scallops, shrimp. **Supplements:** wheat germ oil. **Condiment:** mustard.

16. **Enhance Heart Health and Function: Vitamins B1 B3, B12. Minerals:** calcium, magnesium, potassium. **Amino Acid:** arginine. **Vegetables:** cabbage, celery, turnips. **Fruits:** apricots, bananas, blackberries, blueberries, cherries, grapefruits, kiwi, limes, olives, oranges, peaches, pears, plums, strawberries, watermelons. **Grains:** corn, popcorn, oats. **Nuts:** Brazil nuts, cashews, hazelnuts, macadamia nuts, peanuts, pecans, pistachios, walnuts. **Seeds:** flax seeds, sesame seeds, sunflower seeds. **Meats:** chicken, pork. **Fish and Shellfish:** all. **Sweets:** cocoa. **Supplements:** wheat germ oil.

17. **Enhance Immune System: Vitamins:** A, B2, B5,B6, C, D, E. **Minerals:** copper, iron, manganese, selenium, zinc. **Amino Acids:** arginine, histidine, isoleucine, lysine, serine, threonine. **Vegetables:** asparagus, broccoli, cabbage, carrots, cauliflower, celery, garlic, green peas, mushrooms, okra, squash, sweet bell peppers, sweet potatoes, turnips. **Fruits:** apricots, blackberries, blueberries, cantaloupes, grapefruits, grapes, honeydew melons, kiwi, lemons, limes, olives, oranges, peaches, pears, pineapples, plums, raspberries, strawberries, watermelons. **Grains:** corn, popcorn,

oats, wheat. **Nuts:** almonds, Brazil nuts, cashews, hazelnuts, macadamia nuts, peanuts, pecans, pistachios, walnuts. **Seeds:** chia seeds, flax seeds, sesame seeds, sunflower seeds. **Dairy:** butter, Greek yogurt. **Meat:** beef, chicken, lamb, turkey. **Fish and Shellfish:** all. **Beverages:** beer (in moderation), wine (in moderation). **Supplements:** wheat germ oil.

18. **Enhance Joint Flexibility: Mineral:** magnesium. **Amino Acid:** proline. **Vegetables:** beans, celery, cucumbers, okra. **Nuts:** peanuts. **Fish:** salmon, sardines.

19. **Enhance Kidney Health and Reduce the Risk of Kidney Stones: Vitamins:** B12, C, K. **Minerals:** calcium, potassium. **Vegetables:** carrots, okra. **Fruits:** bananas, cantaloupes, grapefruits, kiwi, limes, oranges, watermelons. **Grains:** corn, popcorn. **Nuts:** macadamia nuts, pecans. **Fish:** snapper, trout, tuna. **Shellfish:** scallops. **Beverages:** beer (in moderation).

20. **Enhance Life Expectancy and Slow Down the Normal Aging Process:** Fiber. **Mineral:** selenium. **Vegetables:** carrots, broccoli, garlic, lentils. **Fruits:** apples, blueberries, grapes, peaches, strawberries. **Nuts:** almonds, Brazil nuts, hazelnuts, peanuts, pecans, walnuts. **Seeds:** chia seeds. **Dairy:** cheese, milk. **Meat:** beef. **Fish and Shellfish:** all. **Beverages:** beer (in moderation), wine (in moderation). **Supplements:** wheat germ oil.

21. **Enhance Liver Health and Functions: Vitamins:** B12, choline. **Minerals:** chloride, phosphorus. **Vegetables:** carrots, cauliflower, okra. **Fruits:** apples, apricots, lemons. **Nuts:** cashews, walnuts. **Fish:** halibut, trout. **Beverages:** wine (in moderation).

22. **Enhance Lung Health:** Fiber. **Fruits:** apples, cantaloupes, kiwi, lemons. **Nuts:** almonds. **Seeds:** sesame seeds. **Fish:** herring.

23. **Enhance Metabolism: Vitamins:** B1, B2, B5, B7, choline. **Minerals:** chromium, copper, magnesium, manganese, molybdenum, phosphorus, potassium, sodium, sulfur. **Amino Acids:** alanine, glutamine, leucine, lysine, proline, threonine. **Vegetables:** hot peppers, okra, turnips. **Fruits:** lemons, plums. **Grains:** oats, wheat. **Nuts:** almonds, hazelnuts, macadamia nuts, pistachios, walnuts. **Seeds:** flax seeds, sesame seeds. **Dairy:** butter. **Meats:** beef, chicken, lamb, pork, turkey. **Fish and Shellfish:** all. **Supplements:** wheat germ oil.

24. **Enhance Muscle Health and Lean Muscle Mass: Vitamins:** B1, choline. **Minerals:** chromium, iodine, iron, magnesium, potassium, sodium. **Amino Acids:** isoleucine, leucine, serine, valine. **Vegetables:** beans, lentils, okra, Swiss chard. **Fruit:** apricots. **Grain:** wheat. **Nuts:** almonds, Brazil nuts, cashews, macadamia nuts, peanuts, pistachios. **Seeds:** sesame seeds. **Dairy:** cheese, eggs,

milk, Greek yogurt. **Meats:** beef, chicken, lamb, pork, turkey. **Fish and Shellfish:** all. **Supplements:** wheat germ oil.

25. **Enhance Nail Health: Vitamins:** B7, B12. **Mineral:** sulfur. **Amino Acids:** cysteine, methionine. **Vegetables:** carrots, Swiss chard. **Meats:** chicken, turkey. **Fish:** halibut, tilapia, trout. **Shellfish:** shrimp.

26. **Enhance Nerve Health and Functions: Vitamins:** B1, B2, B3, B6, B9, K, choline. **Minerals:** calcium, chloride, iodine, magnesium, manganese, potassium, sodium. **Amino Acids:** asparagine, glutamate, histidine. **Vegetables:** okra, Swiss chard. **Fruit:** peaches, plums. **Grains:** corn, popcorn. **Nuts:** Brazil nuts, cashews, hazelnuts, macadamia nuts, peanuts, pistachios. **Seeds:** chia seeds. **Meat:** beef. **Fish and Shellfish:** all. **Supplements:** wheat germ oil.

27. **Enhance Oral Health**: **Vegetables:** broccoli, carrots. **Fruits:** apples, blackberries, cantaloupes, lemons, oranges, pineapples, watermelons. **Grain:** wheat. **Nuts:** almonds, cashews, macadamia nuts. **Seeds:** sesame seeds. **Dairy:** butter, Greek yogurt. **Meats:** chicken, turkey. **Fish:** catfish, mackerel, sardines, snapper, tilapia, trout. **Shellfish:** shrimp.

28 **Enhance Sexual Health and Functions:**
Male and Female:
   a. **Enhance Sexual Functions: Mineral:** phosphorus. **Amino Acid:** histidine. **Fish:** halibut, perch.
   b. **Reduce Risk of Sterility: Vitamin** E. **Supplements:** wheat germ oil.
Male:
   a. **Enhance Male Fertility: Minerals:** iodine, manganese. **Nuts:** Brazil nuts, cashews, walnuts. **Seeds:** sesame seeds, sunflower seeds. **Condiment:** ketchup.
   b. **Enhance Testosterone Production:** Cholesterol. **Minerals:** manganese, zinc. **Vegetable:** asparagus. **Fruit:** oranges. **Nuts:** Brazil nuts, cashews. **Meat:** turkey.
   c. **Minimize Erectile Dysfunction: Nuts:** Brazil nuts, pistachios.
Female:
   a. **Enhance Female Fertility: Minerals:** iodine, manganese. **Seeds:** flax seeds. **Dairy:** butter.
   b. **Enhance Estrogen Production:** Cholesterol. **Mineral:** manganese, **Vegetable:** asparagus. **Fruit:** oranges. **Seeds:** sesame seeds.
   c. **Facilitate a Normal Pregnancy: Vitamins:** B6, B9, B12, choline. **Mineral:** zinc. **Vegetables:** beans, broccoli, lentils,

lettuce, okra. **Fruits:** blueberries, cantaloupes, honeydew melons, kiwi, peaches, plums, strawberries. **Grains:** corn, popcorn, wheat. **Nuts:** peanuts. **Seeds:** sunflower seeds. **Dairy:** butter. **Fish:** catfish. **Shellfish:** crab. **Supplements:** wheat germ oil.

    d. **Reduce Risk of Birth Defects: Vitamins:** B9, B12, choline. **Mineral:** iodine. **Vegetables:** beans, broccoli, lentils, lettuce, okra. **Fruits:** blueberries, cantaloupes, kiwi, peaches, plums, strawberries. **Grains:** corn, popcorn, wheat. **Nuts:** hazelnuts, peanuts, walnuts. **Dairy:** butter. **Fish:** catfish. **Supplements:** wheat germ oil.

    e. **Minimize Menstrual Discomfort: Nuts:** pecans. **Shellfish:** shrimp.

    f. **Minimize Yeast Infections: Vegetable:** garlic. **Fruit:** grapes. **Dairy:** Greek yogurt.

29. **Enhance Skin Health: Vitamins:** A, B1, B2, B3, B5, B7, B9, B12, C. **Minerals:** copper, iron, potassium, sulfur. **Amino Acids:** cysteine, methionine, proline, threonine. **Vegetables:** broccoli, carrots, cauliflower, green peas, okra, sweet bell peppers, Swiss chard, tomatoes, turnips. **Fruits:** apples, apricots, avocados, blackberries, blueberries, cantaloupes, honeydew melons, kiwi, lemons, limes, oranges, peaches, pineapples, plums, raspberries, strawberries, watermelons. **Grains:** corn, popcorn, wheat. **Nuts:** almonds, Brazil nuts, cashews, hazelnuts, macadamia nuts, peanuts, pecans, pistachios, walnuts. **Seeds:** chia seeds, flax seeds, hemp seeds, sesame seeds, sunflower seeds. **Meats:** beef, chicken, lamb, pork, turkey. **Fish & Shellfish:** all. **Supplements:** wheat germ oil.

30. **Enhance Sleep and Minimize Insomnia: Vitamin** B6. **Mineral:** calcium. **Amino Acids:** histidine, tryptophan. **Vegetables:** lettuce, mushrooms. **Fruits:** cherries, kiwi. **Nuts:** Brazil nuts, walnuts. **Seeds:** chia seeds, sesame seeds. **Meats:** beef, turkey.

31. **Enhance Thyroid Function: Minerals:** iodine, selenium. **Amino Acid:** tyrosine. **Nuts:** Brazil nuts. **Seeds:** sesame seeds, sunflower seeds. **Dairy:** butter, Greek yogurt. **Meats:** pork, turkey. **Fish:** mackerel, salmon, tilapia. **Shellfish:** crab, lobster, shrimp.

32. **Enhance Urination and Diuretics: Amino Acid:** asparagine. **Seasoning:** black pepper. **Vegetable**: okra. **Beverages:** caffeine.

33. **Enhance Weight Loss:** Fiber. **Vitamin** D. **Mineral:** chromium. **Amino Acids:** isoleucine, leucine, serine, valine. **Vegetables:** hot peppers, lentils, okra, potatoes. **Fruits:** apples, cherries, grapefruits. **Grains:** corn, popcorn, oats, wheat. **Nuts:** almonds, Brazil nuts, cashews, hazelnuts, macadamia nuts, peanuts, pecans, pistachios, walnuts. **Seeds:** chia seeds, flax seeds, sunflower seeds. **Dairy:**

butter, cottage cheese, eggs. **Meats:** beef, chicken, lamb, pork, turkey. **Fish and Shellfish:** all. **Supplements:** glucomannan, wheat germ oil.

34. **Minimize (Treat) Acne: Vitamin** A. **Fruit:** lemons. **Grain:** wheat. **Nuts:** Brazil nuts. **Beverages:** wine (in moderation).

35. **Minimize Allergies (Sinus and Seasonal): Vegetable:** hot peppers. **Fruits:** olives, peaches.

36. **Minimize (Treat) Anemia (iron deficiency): Vitamins:** B2, B6, B9, B12. **Mineral:** iron, molybdenum. **Vegetables:** asparagus, beans, kale, lentils, spinach, squash. **Fruits:** limes, olives. **Grains:** corn, popcorn, oats, wheat. **Nuts:** almonds, cashews, hazelnuts, macadamia nuts, pine nuts. **Seeds:** all. **Meats:** beef, chicken, turkey. **Fish:** mackerel, sardines. **Beverages:** beer (in moderation).

37. **Minimize Arthritis, Gout, and Rheumatism Discomfort: Vegetables:** celery, hot peppers. **Fruits:** cherries, pears, strawberries. **Fish:** tuna. **Shellfish:** crab, lobster. (Also see "a" and "b" below.)

    a. **Minimize Arthritis Discomfort: Vitamins:** B5, D. **Fruits:** avocados, cantaloupes, pineapples, oranges. **Nuts:** macadamia nuts, peanuts. **Dairy:** milk. **Seeds:** sesame seeds, sunflower seeds. **Fish:** cod, mackerel, herring, halibut, mackerel, salmon, sardines, snapper. **Condiment:** mayonnaise.

    b. **Minimize Gout Discomfort: Vitamin** B9. **Fish:** cod.

38. **Minimize Asthma: Vegetables:** garlic, okra, squash. **Fruits:** apples, cantaloupes, kiwi, lemons, limes, oranges. **Grains:** oats, wheat. **Seeds:** flax seeds, sesame seeds. **Fish:** bass, cod, herring, mackerel, salmon, sardines, trout.

39. **Minimize Depression: Vitamins:** B6, D. **Amino Acids:** threonine, tryptophan. **Vegetables:** asparagus, beans, celery, mushrooms, okra. **Grain:** wheat. **Nuts:** Brazil nuts, hazelnuts, peanuts. **Seeds:** sesame seeds, sunflower seeds. **Meats:** beef, turkey. **Fish:** bass, herring, mackerel, salmon, sardines, trout, tuna. **Beverages:** wine (in moderation).

40. **Minimize Fatigue: Mineral:** iron. **Amino Acids:** arginine, isoleucine, valine. **Vegetables:** garlic, okra. **Dairy:** eggs. **Meats:** beef, pork. **Fish:** halibut, perch, sardines. **Shellfish:** scallops.

41. **Minimize Headache Pain: Vegetable:** hot peppers.
    a. **Migraines: Vitamin** B3. **Mineral:** magnesium. **Vegetable:** okra. **Nuts:** cashews. **Fish:** cod. **Condiment:** Peanut butter.

42. **Minimize Inflammation: Vitamin** C. **Vegetables:** beets, broccoli, Brussels sprouts, cabbage, cauliflower, celery, green peas, hot peppers, lettuce, mushrooms, okra, squash, sweet bell peppers, sweet potatoes, tomatoes, turnips. **Fruits:** apricots, blueberries,

cantaloupes, cherries, grapes, kiwi, limes, olives, oranges, pears, pineapples, watermelons. **Grains:** oats, wheat. **Nuts:** almonds, Brazil nuts, hazelnuts, macadamia nuts, peanuts, pecans, pistachios, walnuts. **Seeds:** chia seeds, flax seeds, sesame seeds, sunflower seeds. **Dairy:** butter. **Meat:** beef. **Fish:** bass, cod, herring, mackerel, salmon, sardines, trout, tuna. **Shellfish:** crab, lobster, scallops, shrimp. **Beverages:** wine (in moderation). **Supplements:** wheat germ oil. **Condiment:** mayonnaise.

43. **Minimize Muscle Soreness: Fruits:** blueberries, cherries, pineapples, watermelons.

44. **Minimize Stress: Vitamins:** B5, B6, C. **Minerals:** iron, magnesium. **Nuts:** walnuts. **Seeds:** sesame seeds. **Dairy:** milk. **Meats:** chicken, turkey. **Fish:** halibut. **Supplements:** wheat germ oil.

45. **Minimize or Reduce Tummy Fat:** docosahexaenoic acid (DHA). **Vegetable:** beans. **Supplements:** glucomannan, green tea.

46. **Reduce Risk of Alzheimer's Disease: Vitamins:** B1, E. **Vegetables:** garlic, okra. **Grains:** corn, popcorn. **Nuts:** almonds, macadamia nuts, peanuts. **Seeds:** chia seeds. **Meat:** chicken. **Fish:** cod, halibut, salmon. **Shellfish:** crab, lobster.

47. **Reduce Risk of Cancer:**

   a. **General: Vitamin** D. **Minerals:** chromium, selenium. **Vegetables:** broccoli, kale, lentils. **Fruit:** grapes. **Nuts:** pistachios. **Dairy:** butter, milk. **Meat:** turkey. **Fish:** salmon, snapper, tilapia. **Supplements:** wheat germ oil.

   b. **Breast: Vitamins:** B6, B9, C, choline. **Vegetables:** broccoli, carrots, cauliflower, okra, sweet potatoes, Swiss chard, tomatoes, turnips. **Fruits:** apples, cantaloupes, limes, olives, oranges, peaches, pears, pineapples, plums. **Grains:** oats, wheat. **Nuts:** hazelnuts, macadamia nuts, peanuts, pecans, walnuts. **Seeds:** flax seeds, pumpkin seeds, sesame seeds, sunflower seeds. **Dairy:** butter, eggs. **Meat:** lamb. **Fish:** mackerel, trout, tuna. **Shellfish:** lobster. **Beverages:** wine (in moderation). **Condiments:** ketchup, peanut butter.

   c. **Cervical: Vitamin** A. **Vegetable:** carrots. **Nuts:** macadamia nuts, walnuts.

   d. **Colon:** Fiber. **Vitamins:** B6, B9. **Mineral:** calcium. **Vegetables:** beans, broccoli, carrots, cauliflower, green peas, okra, potatoes, sweet potatoes, Swiss chard, tomatoes, turnips. **Fruits:** apples, cantaloupes, kiwi, lemons, limes, olives, oranges, peaches, pineapples. **Grains:** corn, popcorn, oats, wheat. **Nuts:** almonds, cashews, hazelnuts, peanuts, pecans, walnuts. **Seeds:** flax seeds, sesame seeds, sunflower seeds.

Dairy: butter. **Meats:** chicken, lamb. **Fish:** halibut, mackerel, sardines, trout, tuna. **Shellfish:** lobster, scallops. **Beverages:** wine (in moderation). **Condiment:** peanut butter.

e. **Esophageal: Vegetable:** carrots. **Fruit:** strawberries. **Nuts:** Brazil nuts. **Fish:** Lobster.

f. **Intestinal: Vegetable:** beans. **Fruits:** kiwi, plums.

g. **Kidney: Vegetable:** broccoli. **Fruit:** limes. **Fish:** halibut, tuna.

h. **Liver: Fruits:** lemons, plums. **Nuts:** hazelnuts. **Dairy:** butter. **Meat:** lamb.

i. **Lung: Vitamin** A. **Vegetables:** carrots, cauliflower, squash, Swiss chard, tomatoes, turnips. **Fruits:** cantaloupes, limes, oranges, peaches, pears, plums. **Grains:** corn, popcorn. **Nuts:** macadamia nuts, pecans. **Seeds:** sesame seeds, sunflower seeds. **Shellfish:** lobster.

j. **Mouth, Oral: Vitamin** C. **Vegetable:** carrots,

k. **Ovarian: Vegetable:** tomatoes. **Fruit:** pears. **Grain:** oats. **Shellfish:** lobster.

l. **Pancreatic: Vegetable:** hot peppers. **Fruits:** cantaloupes, lemons, limes. **Seeds:** sesame seeds.

m. **Prostate: Vitamin** A. **Mineral:** zinc. **Vegetables:** broccoli, carrots, cauliflower, hot peppers, Swiss chard, tomatoes, turnips. **Fruits:** apples, cantaloupes, limes. **Nuts:** Brazil nuts, cashews, macadamia nuts, peanuts, pecans, walnuts. **Seeds:** flax seeds, sesame seeds, sunflower seeds. **Dairy:** butter. **Meat:** lamb. **Fish:** mackerel, sardines, trout. **Shellfish:** lobster, shrimp. **Beverages:** wine (in moderation). **Condiments:** ketchup, peanut butter.

n. **Skin: Vegetable:** hot peppers. **Fruits:** apples, lemons, oranges, pineapples. **Nuts:** peanuts. **Seeds:** flax seeds.

o. **Stomach: Vitamin** C. **Vegetables:** broccoli, cauliflower, green peas, sweet potatoes, tomatoes. **Fruits:** kiwi, lemons, limes, olives, oranges, pears. **Nuts:** macadamia nuts, peanuts. **Dairy:** butter. **Meat:** lamb.

p. **Testicular: Nuts:** cashews.

48. **Reduce Risk of Dementia: Vitamins:** B1, choline. **Vegetables:** cauliflower, garlic. **Fruit:** apples. **Nuts:** peanuts. **Fish and Shellfish:** all. **Supplements:** wheat germ oil.

49. **Reduce Risk of Diabetes: Vitamins:** B3, C, D, **Mineral:** chromium. **Vegetables:** beans, Brussels sprouts, carrots, cauliflower, lentils, okra. **Fruits:** cantaloupes, cherries, grapefruits, grapes, honeydew melons, olives, pears, raspberries, strawberries. **Grains:** corn, popcorn, oats, wheat. **Nuts:** almonds, cashews,

hazelnuts, macadamia nuts, peanuts, pecans, pistachios, walnuts. **Seeds:** chia seeds, flax seeds, sesame seeds, sunflower seeds. **Dairy:** butter, cheese, milk. **Fish:** bass, cod, mackerel, salmon, snapper. **Shellfish:** lobster, scallops, shrimp. **Beverages:** beer (in moderation), caffeine, wine (in moderation). **Supplements:** wheat germ oil. **Condiment:** peanut butter.

50. **Reduce Risk of Hair Loss: Nuts:** peanuts, pecans. **Meat:** beef. **Shellfish:** shrimp.

51. **Reduce Risk of Heart Attack: Mineral:** chromium. **Vegetables:** beans, cabbage, squash, Swiss chard, tomatoes. **Fruits:** blueberries, plums. **Grains:** oats, wheat. **Nuts:** macadamia nuts. **Seeds:** chia seeds, flax seeds, sesame seeds. **Dairy:** butter, eggs. **Fish and Shellfish:** all. **Beverages:** beer (in moderation). **Condiment:** mayonnaise.

52. **Reduce Risk of Heart Disease:** Fiber. **Vitamins:** B1, B6, B9, C, D, E, choline. **Minerals:** magnesium, phosphorus, selenium. **Vegetables:** beans, beets, broccoli, cabbage, carrots, cauliflower, garlic, lentils, green peas, kale, lentils, okra, tomatoes: **Fruits:** blackberries, blueberries, cantaloupes, cherries, grapes, limes, olives, pears, raspberries. **Grain:** wheat. **Nuts:** almonds, Brazil nuts, cashews, hazelnuts, macadamia nuts, peanuts, pecans, pistachios, walnuts. **Seeds:** chia seeds, flax seeds, pumpkin seeds, sesame seeds, sunflower seeds. **Dairy:** eggs. **Meats:** beef, chicken, **Fish and Shellfish:** all. **Beverages:** beer (in moderation), wine (in moderation). **Supplements:** wheat germ oil. **Condiment:** ketchup.

53. **Reduce Risk of Hemorrhoids:** Fiber. **Vegetable:** beets. **Fruit:** apples. **Grains:** corn, popcorn.

54. **Reduce Risk of Osteoporosis: Vegetable:** okra. **Fruit:** olives. **Nuts:** cashews. **Dairy:** milk. **Fish:** halibut, sardines, snapper. **Shellfish:** crab, lobster.

55. **Reduce Risk of Stomach Ulcers: Vegetables:** kale, hot peppers, okra.

56. **Reduce Risk of Stroke: Vitamins:** B12, choline. **Mineral:** chromium. **Vegetables:** beans, carrots, cauliflower, squash, Swiss chard, tomatoes. **Fruits:** apples, bananas, grapes, limes, pears, plums, strawberries. **Grains:** oats, wheat. **Nuts:** cashews, macadamia nuts, peanuts. **Seeds:** chia seeds, flax seeds, sesame seeds. **Dairy:** butter, eggs. **Meat:** chicken. **Fish:** halibut, salmon, snapper, tuna. **Shellfish:** crab, scallops, shrimp. **Beverages:** beer (in moderation), wine (in moderation). **Condiment:** mayonnaise.

57. **Reduce Risk of Urinary Track Infections: Vegetable:** asparagus. **Fruits:** blueberries, limes.

Chapter Thirty-Three

Conclusion

As I mentioned at the beginning of chapter four, most of us in the USA who are overweight are truthfully not responsible for the extra pounds we are carrying on our bodies. Instead we are the innocent victims of a variety of different food processing companies, restaurants, and food advertisements. If you have read all the chapters prior to this chapter then you may now agree with me. And you may have already begun to change your diet so you can lose weight and improve your long-term health. The good news is that your body will work with you to help you achieve your goals.

The human body is truly amazing. It automatically knows exactly what it should do in order to keep itself alive. When it gets sick it will try to heal itself. When it gets wounded it will try to heal its wounds. When it is fed too much food it will store the extra food it doesn't need as fat so that its fat reserves can be used to provide energy if we don't eat enough food each day.

When we eat unhealthy stuff our bodies will still process that food. Even if the food contains nasty stuff that will gradually kill us, our bodies will do the very best they can do to eliminate that stuff from our systems. The problem begins when we keep putting more and more of that bad stuff into our bodies at a rate that exceeds the speed at which our bodies can get rid of it. If we do not take corrective action then that bad stuff will continue to accumulate inside our bodies. And eventually the bad stuff will overwhelm one of our organs, or one of our bodies' systems, and we will die.

But there is hope. Our bodies are so amazing that our bodies can heal themselves and gradually get rid of all the bad stuff that has built up inside our bodies if we will just stop putting more of that bad stuff into our bodies.

Our bodies can gradually repair many of our self-inflicted health problems if we will simply start eating healthy food, such as organic foods and whole grain bread that contains all of its original bran and germ instead of just a portion of its bran and only a trivial amount of its germ (or none of its germ). The reason is because our cells are in a continual state of replenishment that includes the creation of new cells and the elimination of old cells. For example, our skin cells are regenerated every 39 days. And our liver cells are regenerated every 400 days. Some intestinal cells are replaced every 5 days but some intestinal cells are gradually replaced over a period of 16 years. Some heart cells are gradually replaced over a period 6 years. Therefore your body can gradually rebuild itself into a significantly more healthy body if you will just supply your body with the healthy foods it needs.

If you have read the previous chapters in this book then hopefully you now know how to become a significantly healthier person while you simultaneously lose weight. But it is still up to you to create a list of healthy foods that you really desire to eat so that you can achieve your two goals of losing weight and improving your long-term health.

Appendix

Tables for
Normal Weights Based on Gender, Age, and Height,
Calories Burned When Doing Common Activities,
Recommended Daily Dietary Allowances (RDA),
USDA Nutrition Information on Specific Foods,
and Average Calories in Specific Foods

The United States Department of Agriculture (USDA) does not report starch, betaine, choline, copper, and manganese on the foods they evaluate with the same consistency that they report other vitamins and minerals. Therefore starch, betaine, choline, copper, and manganese are not shown on some of the nutrition tables in this appendix due to the absence of that data on the USDA site.

It should also be mentioned that the USDA updates the information in the tables on their website as they collect more data on the foods that they monitor. Therefore the values for the nutrients in a specific food will be revised based on their most recent analysis of that food. The values for some nutrients may be more, or less, or about the same as the values the USDA previously published for those nutrients in a specific food. The reported values are impacted by the number of days between planting and harvest, the fertility of the soil, the average weather conditions, and the number of days between harvest and actual testing.

Normal Weights based on Gender, Age, and Height
Height shown in Feet (Ft.) and Centimeters (cm)
Weight shown in Pounds (lbs.) and Kilograms (kg)
(Data from the mid-1960s to early 1980s)

The weight tables on the next page are for adults with normal healthy bodies who are not underweight or overweight. The weights are based on gender, age, and height.

The weight data is for individuals who were considered to be physically fit and healthy from the mid-1960s through the early-1980s. The Common Sense Diet recommends that a person in the 21st century use the weight benchmarks from the 1960s to the 1980s to set a reasonable weight goal to work towards.

In the 2020s men and women in the USA weigh more on the average they did 40 years ago for all the reasons mentioned in Chapter Twenty-Nine. Therefore more recently published weight tables based on more recently collected data will reflect this increase in the acceptable weight ranges for men and women. If you wish you may consult these more recently published weight tables to set a weight goal for yourself.

The choice is yours.

Normal Weights: Gender, Age, Height (mid-1960s to early 1980s)

Height Ft. In.	Women lb. Age 21-40	Women lb. Age 41-60	Height Ft. In.	Men lb. Age 21-40	Men lb. Age 41-60
4'10"	107 to 119	119 to 132	4'10"	- -	- -
4'11"	109 to 121	121 to 134	4'11"	- -	- -
5'0"	111 to 123	123 to 137	5'0"	- -	- -
5'1"	113 to 126	126 to 141	5'1"	125 to 135	138 to 149
5'2"	116 to 130	129 to 145	5'2"	128 to 139	141 to 153
5'3"	120 to 134	133 to 149	5'3"	131 to 143	144 to 157
5'4"	123 to 137	137 to 152	5'4"	134 to 146	147 to 161
5'5"	126 to 140	140 to 156	5'5"	137 to 149	151 to 164
5'6"	130 to 144	144 to 160	5'6"	140 to 153	154 to 168
5'7"	133 to 147	148 to 164	5'7"	143 to 156	157 to 172
5'8"	137 to 151	152 to 168	5'8"	146 to 160	161 to 176
5'9"	140 to 154	155 to 171	5'9"	149 to 164	164 to 180
5'10"	143 to 157	159 to 174	5'10"	153 to 168	168 to 185
5'11"	147 to 161	163 to 178	5'11"	156 to 172	172 to 189
6'0"	150 to 164	167 to 182	6'0"	160 to 176	176 to 194
6'1"	154 to 168	171 to 186	6'1"	163 to 180	180 to 199
6'2"	158 to 172	175 to 191	6'2"	167 to 184	184 to 202
6'3"	- -	- -	6'3"	170 to 188	187 to 207
6'4"	- -	- -	6'4"	174 to 193	191 to 212

Height cm	Women kg Age 21-40	Women kg Age 41-60	Height cm	Men kg Age 21-40	Men kg Age 41-60
147 cm	48.5 to 54.0	54.0 to 59.9	147 cm	- -	- -
150 cm	49.4 to 54.9	54.9 to 60.8	150 cm	- -	- -
152 cm	50.3 to 55.8	55.8 to 62.1	152 cm	- -	- -
155 cm	51.3 to 57.2	54.9 to 64.0	155 cm	56.7 to 61.2	62.6 to 67.6
157 cm	52.6 to 59.0	58.5 to 65.8	157 cm	58.1 to 63.1	64.0 to 69.4
160 cm	54.4 to 60.8	60.3 to 67.6	160 cm	59.4 to 64.0	65.3 to 71.2
163 cm	55.8 to 62.1	62.1 to 68.9	163 cm	60.8 to 66.2	66.7 to 73.0
165 cm	57.2 to 63.5	63.5 to 70.8	165 cm	62.1 to 67.6	68.5 to 74.4
168 cm	59.0 to 65.3	65.3 to 72.6	168 cm	63.4 to 69.4	69.9 to 76.2
170 cm	60.3 to 66.7	67.1 to 74.4	170 cm	64.9 to 70.8	71.2 to 78.0
173 cm	62.1 to 68.5	68.9 to 76.2	173 cm	66.2 to 72.6	73.0 to 79.8
175 cm	63.5 to 69.9	70.3 to 77.6	175 cm	67.6 to 74.4	74.4 to 81.6
178 cm	64.9 to 71.2	72.1 to 78.9	178 cm	69.4 to 76.2	76.2 to 83.9
180 cm	66.7 to 73.0	73.9 to 80.7	180 cm	70.8 to 78.0	78.0 to 85.7
183 cm	68.0 to 74.4	75.8 to 82.6	183 cm	72.6 to 79.8	79.8 to 88.0
185 cm	69.9 to 76.2	77.6 to 84.4	185 cm	73.9 to 81.6	81.6 to 90.3
188 cm	71.6 to 78.0	79.4 to 86.6	188 cm	75.8 to 83.5	83.5 to 91.6
191 cm	- -	- -	191 cm	77.1 to 85.3	84.8 to 93.9
193 cm	- -	- -	193 cm	78.9 to 87.5	86.6 to 96.2

Calories Burned in 30 Minutes Based on Body Weight

The first two activities at the top of the first table are the number of calories burned in 30 minutes to maintain all of a person's normal body functions such as breathing, heart beating, and digestion (RMR = BMR + TEF). The RMR values are shown as a separate value at the top of the table but these values are also included in the number of calories burned for each activity at an average RMR value of 0.21 calories per 30 minutes. Therefore you do **not** need to add the RMR value for your gender to the activity values shown in the table.

The calories burned while doing different activities varies based on the type of activity and the weight of the person doing the activity. In other words, a person who weighs more will burn more calories in 30 minutes doing the same exact activity as someone who weighs less.

The calories burned per 30 minutes for each activity is shown in calories per pound, calories per kilogram, and the total number of calories for a person who weighs 150 pounds or 68 kilograms.

To determine the number of calories you would burn in 30 minutes for a specific activity, multiply your body weight (in pounds or kilograms) by the number of calories burned per 30 minutes. If you weigh less than 150 pounds (68 kg) the answer should be less than the number shown in the last column. If you weigh more than 150 pounds (68 kg) the answer should be more than the number in the last column.

It is rare to do an activity for exactly 30 minutes. Fortunately the values can easily be adjusted for the length of time devoted to the activity by dividing the calories burned during 30 minutes by 30 to yield the calories burned per minute. Then multiply that value by the number of minutes actually invested doing the activity.

The number of calories burned is only an *estimate*. The actual number of calories burned may be a little more or a little less based on:

1. **Pace or Speed:** Most of the activities are assumed to be done at an average pace. A person doing the activities slower than average will burn fewer calories and a person doing the activities faster than average will burn more calories.
2. **Environmental Conditions:** Fewer calories will be expended in a comfortable climate controlled environment when compared to a hot or cold gymnasium, or outdoors in extreme weather conditions.
3. **Muscle to Fat Ratio:** A person with more muscle will be able to perform the activities using less effort, but a person with less muscle will expend more effort doing the same exact activity.

Calories Burned in 30 Minutes Based on Body Weight (Page 1 of 3)			
Resting Metabolic Rate	**Calories per 30 min. per lb.**	**Calories per 30 min. per kg**	**Calories per 30 min. 150 lb. - 68 kg**
Female normal body functions	0.205	0.452	30.75
Male normal body functions	0.215	0.474	32.25
Routine Activities			
Carrying Infant in Arms	0.78	1.720	117
Computer, Typing, Data Entry	0.33	0.728	49.5
Driving Vehicle	0.39	0.860	58.5
Eating, Sitting	0.30	0.662	45
Eating, Standing	0.42	0.926	63
Job, Sitting at Desk	0.39	0.860	58.5
Job, Standing at Machine	0.55	1.213	82.5
Job, Avg. Physical Labor	0.73	1.610	109.5
Pushing Baby Stroller	0.55	1.213	82.5
Pushing Shopping Cart	0.67	1.478	100.5
Sitting, Idle	0.21	0.463	31.5
Sitting, Reading	0.28	0.617	42
Sitting, Watching TV	0.21	0.463	31.5
Sleeping, Lying Down	0.21	0.463	31.5
Stairs, Climbing	1.12	2.470	168
Stairs, Descending	0.64	1.412	96
Stairs, Going Up & Down	0.88	1.941	132
Standing, Idle, Waiting	0.34	0.750	51
Games, Hobbies, Sports			
Archery, Target Practice	0.80	1.764	120
Badminton	1.03	2.272	154.5
Baseball, Casual	1.16	2.559	174
Basketball, Casual	1.51	3.331	226.5
Bicycling, 12 mph	1.58	3.485	237
Billiards, Casual	0.57	1.257	85.5
Bowling	0.69	1.522	103.5
Card Games, Sitting	0.30	0.662	45
Catch, Baseball, Football	0.55	1.213	82.5
Cricket (Batting, Bowling)	1.12	2.470	168
Dancing, Slow	0.67	1.478	100.5
Dancing, Fast	1.21	2.669	181.5
Fencing	1.38	3.044	207
Fishing, Sitting	0.55	1.213	82.5
Fishing, Standing	0.78	1.720	117
Football, Flag, Touch	1.86	4.103	279
Frisbee, Casual	0.68	1.500	102

Games, Hobbies, Sports	Calories per 30 min. per lb.	Calories per 30 min. per kg	Calories per 30 min. 150 lb. - 68 kg
Golf, Driving Range	0.67	1.478	100.5
Golf, Miniature	0.67	1.478	100.5
Golf, Ride Cart	0.78	1.720	117
Golf, Walk, Carry Clubs	1.10	2.426	165
Hiking, Carry Backpack	1.46	3.220	219
Handball	2.77	6.110	415.5
Hockey, Field and Ice	1.86	4.103	279
Horseback Riding	0.98	2.161	147
Horseshoe Pitching	0.67	1.478	100.5
Hunting	1.16	2.559	174
Ice Skating, Slow	1.26	2.779	189
Ice Skating, Average	1.61	3.551	241.5
Ice Skating, Fast	2.06	4.544	309
Kickball	1.58	3.485	237
Lacrosse	1.84	4.058	276
Martial Arts Practice	2.32	5.117	348
Ping Pong, Table Tennis	0.91	2.007	136.5
Racketball, Casual	1.62	3.573	243
Roller Skating	1.61	3.551	241.5
Rugby	2.30	5.073	345
Skateboarding	1.14	2.515	171
Soccer, Casual	1.62	3.573	243
Softball, Casual	1.16	2.559	174
Squash	2.76	6.088	414
Snow Skiing, Downhill	1.38	3.044	207
Snow Skiing, Cross Country	1.86	4.103	279
Swimming, Laps	1.58	3.485	237
Swimming, Casual	1.39	3.066	208.5
Tennis, Casual	1.62	3.573	243
Volleyball, Casual	1.20	2.647	180
Water Skiing	1.32	2.912	198
Music, Playing Instruments			
Cello, Flute, Guitar, Horn	0.44	0.970	66
Drums	0.89	1.963	133.5
Piano, Trumpet, Violin	0.55	1.213	82.5
Housework			
Cooking	0.57	1.257	85.5
Dusting	0.55	1.213	82.5

Calories Burned in 30 Minutes Based on Body Weight (Page 3 of 3)			
Housework	**Calories per 30 min. per lb.**	**Calories per 30 min. per kg**	**Calories per 30 min. 150 lb. - 68 kg**
Housework, Easy	0.55	1.213	82.5
Housework, Average	0.78	1.720	117
Housework, Difficult	0.94	2.073	141
Laundry, Folding, Hanging	0.42	0.926	63
Washing Dishes by Hand	0.50	1.102	75
Outdoor Work			
Digging with Spade	1.10	2.246	165
Gardening	0.95	2.095	142.5
Mowing, Push Mower	1.30	2.867	195
Mowing, Riding Mower	0.55	1.213	82.5
Raking Leaves	0.96	2.117	144
Shoveling Snow by Hand	1.39	3.066	208.5
Washing Car	0.88	1.941	132
Exercise			
Aerobics, Easy	1.12	2.470	168
Aerobics, Average	1.46	3.220	219
Aerobics, Difficult	1.62	3.573	243
Calisthenics, Easy	0.78	1.720	117
Calisthenics, Average	0.92	2.029	138
Calisthenics, Difficult	1.84	4.058	276
Gymnastics	0.94	2.073	141
Jumping Rope, Slow	1.84	4.058	276
Jumping Rope, Average	2.23	4.919	334.5
Jumping Rope, Fast	2.76	6.088	414
Running, 5 mph	1.85	4.081	277.5
Stair Step Platform, On & Off	0.88	1.941	132
Stationary Bike, Slow	1.26	2.779	189
Stationary Bike, Average	1.62	3.573	243
Stationary Bike, Fast	2.44	5.382	366
Stationary Rowing, Slow	0.80	1.764	120
Stationary Rowing, Average	1.64	3.617	246
Stationary Rowing, Fast	1.97	4.345	295.5
Walking, 2 mph slow	0.56	1.235	84
Walking, 3 mph normal	0.75	1.654	112.5
Walking, 4 mph brisk	1.13	2.492	169.5
Stretching Exercises	0.57	1.257	85.5
Weight Lifting, Light	0.67	1.478	100.5
Weight Lifting, Average	0.70	1.544	105
Weight Lifting, Heavy	1.39	3.066	208.5

Recommended Daily Dietary Allowances (RDA) and Adequate Intakes (AI)

The National Center for Biotechnology Information (NCBI) was the source of the data on the next four tables. The data is current at the beginning of the year 2020. However, the NCBI is continuously collecting and analyzing new data and this may result in future revisions of some RDAs and AIs. These future updates would only change the numbers in the next four tables and those updates would have no impact on the data in the other tables in this appendix.

The next four tables show either the Recommended Daily Allowance (RDA) or the Adequate Intakes (AI) for each nutrient. When enough statistical data was available then the RDA was calculated for a nutrient. If there was not enough statistical data to support a recommendation then Adequate Intakes were estimated based on the data that was available.

The information in the next four tables can be used to determine the actual nutritional value of the different foods that are shown in the tables at the end of this appendix based on your gender and age.

The unit of measure that was used by the NCBI for Potassium and for Sodium were both changed from g/d to mg/d to match the unit of measure that is used by the USDA. The unit of measure for Copper was also changed from µg to mg. This allows for the information in all the tables in this Appendix to be compared on a one-to-one basis without having to make any adjustments to the numbers due to differences in the units of measure.

(RDA) Recommended Daily Dietary Allowances and (AI) Adequate Intakes for MALES							
Nutrients		Age in Years					
		9-13	14-18	19-30	31-50	51-70	>70
Vitamins:							
A (Retinol)	(µg/d)	600	900	900	900	900	900
B1 (Thiamine)	(mg/d)	0.9	1.2	1.2	1.2	1.2	1.2
B2 (Riboflavin)	(mg/d)	0.9	1.3	1.3	1.3	1.3	1.3
B3 (Niacin)	(mg/d)	12	16	16	16	16	16
B5 (Pantothenic Acid)	(mg/d)	4	5	5	5	5	5
B6 (Pyridoxamine)	(mg/d)	1.0	1.3	1.3	1.3	1.7	1.7
B7 (Biotin)	(µg/d)	20	25	30	30	30	30
B9 (Folate)	(µg/d)	300	400	400	400	400	400
B12 (Cobalamin)	(µg/d)	1.8	2.4	2.4	2.4	2.4	2.4
C (Ascorbic Acid)	(mg/d)	45	75	90	90	90	90
D (Sunshine Vitamin)	(µg/d)	15	15	15	15	15	20
E (Alpha-Tocopherol)	(mg/d)	11	15	15	15	15	15
K (Phylloquinone)	(µg/d)	60	75	120	120	120	120
Unclassified:							
Choline	(mg/d)	375	550	550	550	550	550
Minerals:							
Calcium (Ca)	(mg/d)	1300	1300	1000	1000	1000	1200
Chloride (Cl)	(g/d)	2.3	2.3	2.3	2.3	2.0	1.8
Chromium (Cr)	(µg/d)	25	35	35	35	30	30
Copper (Cu)	(mg/d)	0.70	0.89	0.90	0.90	0.90	0.90
Fluoride (F)	(mg/d)	2	3	4	4	4	4
Iodine (I)	(µg/d)	120	150	150	150	150	150
Iron (Fe)	(mg/d)	8	11	8	8	8	8
Magnesium (Mg)	(mg/d)	240	410	400	420	420	420
Manganese (Mn)	(mg/d)	1.9	2.2	2.3	2.3	2.3	2.3
Molybdenum (Mo)	(µg/d)	34	43	45	45	45	45
Phosphorus (P)	(mg/d)	1250	1250	700	700	700	700
Potassium (K)	(mg/d)	4500	4700	4700	4700	4700	4700
Selenium (Se)	(µg/d)	40	55	55	55	55	55
Sodium (Na)	(mg/d)	1500	1500	1500	1500	1300	1200
Zinc (Zn)	(mg/d)	8	11	11	11	11	11

Recommended Daily Dietary Allowances (RDAs) except as follows: Adequate Intakes (AIs) for Vitamin B5 (Pantothenic Acid), Vitamin B7 (Biotin), Vitamin K (Phylloquinone), Choline, Chloride, Chromium, Fluoride, Manganese, Potassium, and Sodium.

Source: National Center for Biotechnology Information (NCBI).

(RDA) Recommended Daily Dietary Allowances and (AI) Adequate Intakes for FEMALES							
		Age in Years					
Nutrients		9-13	14-18	19-30	31-50	51-70	>70
Vitamins:							
A (Retinol)	(µg/d)	600	700	700	700	700	700
B1 (Thiamine)	(mg/d)	0.9	1.0	1.1	1.1	1.1	1.1
B2 (Riboflavin)	(mg/d)	0.9	1.0	1.1	1.1	1.1	1.1
B3 (Niacin)	(mg/d)	12	14	14	14	14	14
B5 (Pantothenic Acid)	(mg/d)	4	5	5	5	5	5
B6 (Pyridoxamine)	(mg/d)	1.0	1.2	1.3	1.3	1.5	1.5
B7 (Biotin)	(µg/d)	20	25	30	30	30	30
B9 (Folate)	(µg/d)	300	400	400	400	400	400
B12 (Cobalamin)	(µg/d)	1.8	2.4	2.4	2.4	2.4	2.4
C (Ascorbic Acid)	(mg/d)	45	65	75	75	75	75
D (Sunshine Vitamin)	(µg/d)	15	15	15	15	15	20
E (Alpha-Tocopherol)	(mg/d)	11	15	15	15	15	115
K (Phylloquinone)	(µg/d)	60	75	90	90	90	90
Unclassified:							
Choline	(mg/d)	375	400	425	425	425	425
Minerals:							
Calcium (Ca)	(mg/d)	1300	1300	1000	1000	1200	1200
Chloride (Cl)	(g/d)	2.3	2.3	2.3	2.3	2.0	1.8
Chromium (Cr)	(µg/d)	21	24	25	25	20	20
Copper (Cu)	(mg/d)	0.70	0.89	0.90	0.90	0.90	0.90
Fluoride (F)	(mg/d)	2	3	3	3	3	3
Iodine (I)	(µg/d)	120	150	150	150	150	150
Iron (Fe)	(mg/d)	8	15	18	18	8	8
Magnesium (Mg)	(mg/d)	240	360	310	320	320	320
Manganese (Mn)	(mg/d)	1.6	1.6	1.8	1.8	1.8	1.8
Molybdenum (Mo)	(µg/d)	34	43	45	45	45	45
Phosphorus (P)	(mg/d)	1250	1250	700	700	700	700
Potassium (K)	(mg/d)	4500	4700	4700	4700	4700	4700
Selenium (Se)	(µg/d)	40	55	55	55	55	55
Sodium (Na)	(mg/d)	1500	1500	1500	1500	1300	1200
Zinc (Zn)	(mg/d)	8	9	8	8	8	8

Recommended Daily Dietary Allowances (RDAs) except as follows: Adequate Intakes (AIs) for Vitamin B5 (Pantothenic Acid), Vitamin B7 (Biotin), Vitamin K (Phylloquinone), Choline, Chloride, Chromium, Fluoride, Manganese, Potassium, and Sodium.

Source: National Center for Biotechnology Information (NCBI).

(RDA) Recommended Daily Dietary Allowances and (AI) Adequate Intakes for PREGNANCY and LACTATION

Nutrients		Pregnancy Age in Years			Lactation Age in Years		
		14-18	19-30	31-50	14-18	19-30	31-50
Vitamins:							
A (Retinol)	(µg/d)	750	770	770	1200	1300	1300
B1 (Thiamine)	(mg/d)	1.4	1.4	1.4	1.4	1.4	1.4
B2 (Riboflavin)	(mg/d)	1.4	1.4	1.4	1.6	1.6	1.6
B3 (Niacin)	(mg/d)	18	18	18	17	17	17
B5 (Pantothenic Acid)	(mg/d)	6	6	6	7	7	7
B6 (Pyridoxamine)	(mg/d)	1.9	1.9	1.9	2.0	2.0	2.0
B7 (Biotin)	(µg/d)	30	30	30	35	35	35
B9 (Folate)	(µg/d)	600	600	600	500	500	500
B12 (Cobalamin)	(µg/d)	2.6	2.6	2.6	2.8	2.8	2.8
C (Ascorbic Acid)	(mg/d)	80	85	85	115	120	120
D (Sunshine Vitamin)	(µg/d)	15	15	15	15	15	15
E (Alpha-Tocopherol)	(mg/d)	15	15	15	19	19	19
K (Phylloquinone)	(µg/d)	75	90	90	75	90	90
Unclassified:							
Choline	(mg/d)	450	450	450	550	550	550
Minerals:							
Calcium (Ca)	(mg/d)	1300	1000	1000	1300	1000	1000
Chloride (Cl)	(g/d)	2.3	2.3	2.3	2.3	2.3	2.3
Chromium (Cr)	(µg/d)	29	30	30	44	45	45
Copper (Cu)	(mg/d)	1.00	1.00	1.00	1.30	1.30	1.30
Fluoride (F)	(mg/d)	3	3	3	3	3	3
Iodine (I)	(µg/d)	220	220	220	290	290	290
Iron (Fe)	(mg/d)	27	27	27	10	9	9
Magnesium (Mg)	(mg/d)	400	350	360	360	310	320
Manganese (Mn)	(mg/d)	2.0	2.0	2.0	2.6	2.6	2.6
Molybdenum (Mo)	(µg/d)	50	50	50	50	50	50
Phosphorus (P)	(mg/d)	1250	700	700	1250	700	700
Potassium (K)	(mg/d)	4700	4700	4700	5100	5100	5100
Selenium (Se)	(µg/d)	60	60	60	70	70	70
Sodium (Na)	(mg/d)	1500	1500	1500	1500	1500	1500
Zinc (Zn)	(mg/d)	12	11	11	13	12	12

Recommended Daily Dietary Allowances (RDAs) except as follows: Adequate Intakes (AIs) for Vitamin B5 (Pantothenic Acid), Vitamin B7 (Biotin), Vitamin K (Phylloquinone), Choline, Chloride, Chromium, Fluoride, Manganese, Potassium, and Sodium.

Source: National Center for Biotechnology Information (NCBI).

(RDA) Recommended Daily Dietary Allowances and (AI) Adequate Intakes for INFANTS and CHILDREN					
		Infants Age in Months		Children Age in Years	
Nutrients		0-6	6-12	1-3	4-8
Vitamins:					
A (Retinol)	(µg/d)	400	500	300	400
B1 (Thiamine)	(mg/d)	0.2	0.3	0.5	0.6
B2 (Riboflavin)	(mg/d)	0.3	0.4	0.5	0.6
B3 (Niacin)	(mg/d)	2	4	6	8
B5 (Pantothenic Acid)	(mg/d)	1.7	1.8	2	3
B6 (Pyridoxamine)	(mg/d)	0.1	0.3	0.5	0.6
B7 (Biotin)	(µg/d)	5	6	8	12
B9 (Folate)	(µg/d)	65	80	150	200
B12 (Cobalamin)	(µg/d)	0.4	0.5	0.9	1.2
C (Ascorbic Acid)	(mg/d)	40	50	15	25
D (Sunshine Vitamin)	(µg/d)	10	10	15	15
E (Alpha-Tocopherol)	(mg/d)	4	5	6	7
K (Phylloquinone)	(µg/d)	2.0	2.5	30	55
Unclassified:					
Choline	(mg/d)	125	150	200	250
Minerals:					
Calcium (Ca)	(mg/d)	200	260	700	1000
Chloride (Cl)	(g/d)	0.18	0.57	1.5	1.9
Chromium (Cr)	(µg/d)	0.2	5.5	11	15
Copper (Cu)	(mg/d)	0.20	0.22	0.34	0.44
Fluoride (F)	(mg/d)	0.01	0.5	0.7	1
Iodine (I)	(µg/d)	110	130	90	90
Iron (Fe)	(mg/d)	0.27	11	7	10
Magnesium (Mg)	(mg/d)	30	75	80	130
Manganese (Mn)	(mg/d)	0.003	0.6	1.2	1.5
Molybdenum (Mo)	(µg/d)	2	3	17	22
Phosphorus (P)	(mg/d)	100	275	460	500
Potassium (K)	(mg/d)	400	700	3000	3800
Selenium (Se)	(µg/d)	15	20	20	30
Sodium (Na)	(g/d)	120	370	1000	1200
Zinc (Zn)	(mg/d)	2	3	3	5

Infants: AIs except RDAs for Iron 6-12 months, Zinc 6-12 months.
Children: RDAs except AIs for Vitamin B5 (Pantothenic Acid), Vitamin B7 (Biotin), Vitamin K (Phylloquinone), Choline, Chloride, Chromium, Fluoride, Manganese, Potassium, and Sodium.

Source: National Center for Biotechnology Information (NCBI).

Food Nutrition Tables

All the nutritional data in the following tables was calculated by the United States Department of Agriculture (USDA). The nutrition values are based on a serving that weighs 100 grams. This allows for different foods to be compared based on their nutritional values regardless of the density of the foods, or how light or heavy the foods may be.

This is not the way that nutritional data is listed on the nutrition labels on food containers. The top of each nutrition label defines how much food is in one serving and then all the nutrition data is based on that serving size. There may only be one serving of food in the entire container, or there may be several servings of food in one container.

Most nutrition labels also include the percent of each nutritional value based on the Recommended Daily Allowance (RDA) for an adult instead of the actual amount of each vitamin or mineral, such as mg.

Nutritional data is almost always presented with one food on one page. In contrast, the tables in this appendix show the nutritional data for a variety of foods in the same basic food category on one page. This makes it easy to quickly compare the nutritional values for a lot of different foods in the same food category. For example, your doctor may tell you that you need more vitamin E in your diet. If you really enjoy fruit then you could look at the vitamin E column in the fruit table and you would discover that apricots, avocados, blackberries, kiwi, olives, peaches, and raspberries contain the most vitamin E of the 24 different fruits listed. Then you could add some or all of these fruits into the unique Common Sense Diet that you create for yourself depending on which of these fruits you like best.

The tables will also allow you to verify the claims that may be made for specific foods. You can find the specific food in the appropriate table and then compare all of its nutritional values, including vitamins and minerals, to the other foods in that same table. This will help you to decide if the claims are valid or if the claims are exaggerated. In other words, you will no longer have to accept information based on faith. You will now be able to easily and quickly verify, modify, or refute the food claims that come to your attention.

Finally the nutrition tables will help you to select a variety of foods from each of the tables that you enjoy eating and that are low in calories so you can create your own unique Common Sense Diet. You will also be able to verify that the combination of all the different types of foods that you select include a reasonable amount of fat, fiber, and protein on a weekly basis.

| Meat, Seafood | Cal | Fat | | | | Other | | | Vitamins | | | | | | | | | | Ch | Minerals | | | | | | | | |
Per 100 g Serving	kcal	Tot g	Sa g	Po g	Mo g	Cho mg	Sod mg	Pro g	A μg	B1 mg	B2 mg	B3 mg	B5 mg	B6 mg	B9 μg	B12 μg	D μg	E mg	mg	Ca mg	Co mg	Ir mg	Mg mg	Mn mg	Ph mg	Po mg	Se μg	Zn mg
Meat																												
Beef	198	13	5.3	.53	4.8	62	68	19.4	0	.05	.15	4.8	.58	.36	6	2.0	-	.35	67	12	.06	2.0	19	.01	175	289	14	4.6
Chicken	215	15	4.3	3.2	6.2	75	70	18.6	41	.06	.12	6.8	.91	.35	6	.31	.2	.30	60	11	.05	.90	20	.02	147	189	14	1.3
Ham/Pork	245	19	6.5	2.0	8.4	73	47	17.4	0	.74	.20	4.6	.69	.40	7	.63	.5	-	-	5	.07	.85	20	.02	199	315	29	1.9
Turkey	115	1.9	.46	.41	.48	67	118	22.6	9	.05	.19	8.1	.84	.65	7	1.2	.2	.09	60	11	.08	.86	27	.01	190	235	23	1.8
Fish																												
Bass	97	2.3	.51	.78	.66	80	69	17.7	27	.10	.03	2.1	.75	.30	9	3.8	-	-	-	15	.03	.84	40	.02	198	256	37	.40
Catfish	95	2.8	.72	.87	.84	58	43	16.4	15	.21	.07	1.9	.77	.12	10	2.2	13	-	-	14	.03	.30	23	.03	209	358	13	.51
Cod	82	.67	.13	.23	.09	43	54	17.8	12	.08	.07	2.1	.15	.25	7	.91	.9	.64	65	16	.03	.38	32	.02	203	413	33	.45
Halibut	91	1.3	.29	.29	.47	49	68	18.6	20	.05	.03	6.5	.34	.55	12	1.1	4.7	.61	62	7	.02	.16	23	.01	236	435	46	.36
Herring	158	9.0	2.0	2.1	3.7	60	90	18.0	28	.09	.23	3.2	.65	.30	10	14	4.2	1.1	65	57	.92	1.1	32	.04	236	327	37	.99
Mackerel	205	14	3.3	3.4	5.5	70	90	18.6	50	.18	.31	9.1	.86	.40	1	8.7	16	1.5	65	12	.07	1.6	76	.02	217	314	44	.63
Perch	79	1.5	.27	.30	.48	52	287	15.3	12	.04	.05	1.0	.27	.07	9	1.5	1.2	.76	65	28	.02	.22	23	.01	248	187	29	.29
Salmon	131	4.7	.81	1.1	1.4	51	78	22.3	49	.13	.21	8.5	1.1	.73	6	4.7	14	.83	95	9	.06	.43	30	.01	257	367	30	.46
Sardines *	208	11	1.5	5.1	3.9	142	307	24.6	32	.08	.23	5.2	.64	.17	10	8.9	4.8	2.0	75	382	.19	2.9	39	.11	490	397	53	1.3
Snapper	100	1.3	.29	.25	.46	37	64	20.5	32	.05	≈0	.28	.75	.40	5	3	10	.96	65	32	.03	.18	32	.01	198	417	38	.36
Tilapia	96	1.7	.59	.36	.50	50	52	20.1	0	.04	.06	3.9	.49	.16	24	1.6	3.1	.04	43	10	.08	.56	27	.04	170	302	42	.33
Trout	619	6.6	1.1	1.5	3.3	58	52	20.8	17	.35	.33	4.5	1.9	.20	13	7.8	3.9	.02	65	43	.19	1.5	22	.85	245	361	13	.66
Tuna	103	1.0	.33	.32	.19	47	37	22.0	16	.03	.10	15	.42	.85	9	1.9	-	-	-	29	.09	1.3	34	.02	222	407	37	.82
Shellfish																												
Crab	87	1.1	.22	.39	.19	78	293	18.1	2	.08	.04	2.7	.35	.15	44	9	-	-	-	89	.67	.74	34	.15	229	329	37	3.5
Lobster	77	.75	.18	.30	.22	127	423	16.5	1	.02	.01	1.6	1.4	.10	10	1.3	0	.87	70	84	1.3	.26	38	.06	161	200	64	3.5
Scallops	69	.49	.13	.13	.05	24	392	12.1	1	.01	.02	.70	.22	.07	16	1.4	0	0	65	6	.02	.38	22	.02	334	205	13	.91
Shrimp	71	1.0	.26	.30	.18	126	566	13.6	54	.02	.02	1.8	.31	.16	19	1.1	.10	1.3	81	54	.18	.21	34	.03	244	113	30	.97

Raw Meat, Seafood except *   Source of Data: United States Department of Agriculture   Meat does not have Carbs, Fiber, or Sugar

United States Department of Agriculture (USDA) Nutrition, Vitamins, and Minerals for Beef, Chicken, Ham/Pork, Turkey, Fish, Shellfish

Abbreviations Used at the Top of the Table on the Previous Page

g = gram   1 mg = .001 gram   1 μg = .000001 gram

Cal = Calories

Tot = Total Fat

Sa = Saturated Fat

Po = Polyunsaturated Fat

Mo = Monounsaturated Fat

Cho = Cholesterol

Sod = Sodium (Na)

Pro = Protein

Unclassified:

Ch = Choline

Vitamins:

A = Retinal, Retinol

B1 = Thiamine

B2 = Riboflavin

B3 = Niacin

B5 = Pantothenic Acid

B6 = Pridoxine, Pyridoxine, Pyridoxamine

B9 = Folic Acid, Folate, Folacin

B12 = Cobalamin, Cyanocobalamin

D = The "Sunshine Vitamin"

E = Alpha-Tocopherol

Minerals:

Ca = Calcium (Ca)

Co = Copper (Cu)

Ir = Iron (Fe)

Mg = Magnesium (Mg)

Mn = Manganese (Mn)

Ph = Phosphorus (P)

Po = Potassium (K)

Se = Selenium (Se)

Zn = Zinc (Zn)

- = Information not reported by United States Dept. of Agriculture.

≈ 0 = Approximately Zero or a Very Trivial Amount.

Beef = Grass Fed, Ground Beef.

Chicken = Includes Meat and Skin.

Cod, Halibut, Mackerel, Perch = Wild Caught Atlantic.

Salmon = Wild Caught Alaskan.

* = Sardines, Atlantic, Canned in Oil.

Tuna = Skipjack (the type used in canned chunk light tuna).

All data for 100 gram servings. 100 grams = 3.527 ounces in **weight.**
3.527 ounces in weight is **not** the same as approximately 1/2 cup.
The imperial system uses ounces for both weight and volume.
The metric system uses grams for weight and liters for volume.

A 100 gram serving of meat is the same as 3.527 ounces in **weight.**
Divide the values in the table on the previous page by 3.527 and then
multiply by the weight of the meat (in ounces) to yield the nutrition in
that piece of meat.

Vegetables Per 100 g Serving	Cal kcal	Fat Tot g	Sa g	Po g	Mo g	Carbs Car g	Fib g	Sug g	Other Sod mg	Pro g	Vitamins A µg	B1 mg	B2 mg	B3 mg	B5 mg	B6 mg	B9 µg	C mg	E mg	K µg	Minerals Ca mg	Ir mg	Mg mg	Mn mg	Ph mg	Po mg	Se µg	Zn mg
Asparagus	20	.12	.04	.05	0	3.88	2.1	1.9	2	2.2	38	.14	.14	.98	.27	.09	52	5.6	1.1	41.6	24	2.1	14	.16	52	202	2.3	.54
Bean Pinto	347	1.2	.24	.41	.23	62.6	15.5	2.1	12	21.4	0	.71	.21	1.2	.79	.47	525	6.3	.21	5.6	113	5.1	176	1.1	411	1393	28	2.3
Beets	43	.17	.03	.06	.03	9.56	2.8	6.8	78	1.61	2	.03	.04	.33	.16	.07	109	4.9	.04	.20	16	.80	23	.33	40	325	.7	.35
Broccoli	34	.37	.11	.11	.03	6.64	2.6	1.7	33	2.82	31	.07	.12	.64	.57	.18	63	89	.78	102	47	.73	21	.21	66	316	2.5	.41
Brussels S.	43	.30	.06	.16	.02	8.95	3.8	2.2	25	3.38	38	.14	.09	.75	.31	.22	61	85	.88	177	42	1.4	23	.34	69	289	1.6	.42
Cabbage	25	.10	.03	.02	.02	5.8	2.5	3.2	18	1.28	5	.06	.04	.23	.21	.12	43	37	.15	76	40	.47	12	.16	26	170	.3	.18
Carrots	41	.24	.03	.10	.01	9.58	2.8	4.7	69	.93	835	.07	.06	.98	.27	.14	19	5.9	.66	13.2	33	.30	12	.14	35	320	.1	.24
Cauliflower	25	.28	.13	.03	.03	4.97	2	1.9	30	1.92	0	.05	.06	.51	.67	.18	57	48	.08	15.5	22	.42	15	.16	44	299	.6	.27
Celery	14	.17	.04	.08	.03	2.97	1.6	1.3	80	.69	22	.02	.06	.32	.25	.07	36	3.1	.27	29.3	40	.20	11	.10	24	260	.4	.13
Green Peas	81	.40	.07	.19	.04	14.5	5.7	5.7	5	5.42	38	.27	.13	2.1	.10	.17	65	40	.13	24.8	25	1.5	33	.41	108	244	1.8	1.2
Kale	35	1.5	.18	.67	.10	53	4.42	4.1	1	2.92	241	.11	.35	1.2	.37	.15	62	93	.66	390	254	1.6	33	.92	55	348	.9	.39
Lentils	352	1.1	.15	.53	.19	63.4	10.7	2.0	6	24.6	2	.87	.21	2.6	2.1	.54	479	4.5	.49	5	35	6.5	47	1.4	281	677	.1	3.3
Lettuce	15	.15	.02	.08	.01	2.87	1.3	.78	28	1.36	370	.07	.08	.38	.13	.09	38	9.2	.22	126	36	.86	13	.25	29	194	.6	.18
Mushrooms	31	.19	.03	.09	.03	6.97	2.7	2.1	1	1.94	0	.15	.24	.59	.27	.06	21	0	.01	0	1	.30	10	.06	74	204	2.2	.75
Okra	33	.19	.03	.03	.02	7.45	3.2	1.5	7	1.93	716	.20	.06	1.0	.25	.22	60	23	.27	31.3	82	.62	57	.79	61	299	.7	.58
Onions	40	.10	.04	.02	.01	9.34	1.7	4.2	4	1.1	0	.05	.03	.12	.12	.12	19	7.4	.02	.40	23	.21	10	.13	29	146	.5	.17
Pep., Bell G	20	.17	.06	.06	.01	4.64	1.7	2.4	3	.86	18	.06	.03	.48	.10	.22	10	80	.37	7.4	10	.34	10	.12	20	175	0	.13
Pep., Hot	40	.20	.02	.11	.01	9.46	1.5	5.1	7	2	59	.09	.09	.95	.06	.28	23	243.69	.01	14.3	18	1.2	25	.24	46	340	.5	.30
Pot., Red	70	.14	.04	.06	0	15.9	1.7	1.3	18	1.89	0	.81	.03	1.2	.28	.17	18	8.6	.01	2.9	10	.73	22	.14	61	455	.5	.33
Pot., White	69	.10	.03	.04	0	15.7	2.4	1.2	16	1.68	8	.07	.03	1.1	.28	.20	18	9.1	.01	1.6	9	.52	21	.15	62	407	.3	.29
Pot., Sweet	107	2.5	.53	1.2	.78	19.7	3.1	6.2	371	1.92	948	.10	.10	1.4	-	.42	6	19	1.5	6.2	37	.66	26	-	52	453	.2	.30
Radishes	16	.10	.03	.05	.02	3.4	1.6	1.9	39	.68	0	.01	.04	.25	.17	.07	25	15	0	1.3	25	.34	10	.07	20	233	.6	.28
Spinach	23	.39	.06	.17	.01	3.63	2.2	.42	79	2.86	469	.08	.19	.72	.07	.20	194	28	2.0	483	99	2.7	79	.90	49	558	1	.53
Squash	45	.10	.02	.04	.01	11.7	2	2.2	4	1	532	.10	.02	1.2	.40	.15	27	21	1.4	1.1	48	.70	34	.20	33	352	.5	.15

All Raw Vegetables   Source of Data: United States Department of Agriculture   Vegetables have no Cholesterol.

The Common Sense Diet

United States Department of Agriculture (USDA) Nutrition, Vitamins, and Minerals for Vegetables

Abbreviations Used at the Top of the Table on the Previous Page

g = gram   1 mg = .001 gram   1 μg = .000001 gram

Cal = Calories

Tot = Total Fat

Sa = Saturated Fat

Po = Polyunsaturated Fat

Mo = Monounsaturated Fat

Sod = Sodium (Na)

Car = Carbohydrates

Fib = Fiber

Sug = Sugars

Pro = Protein

Vitamins:

A = Retinal, Retinol

B1 = Thiamine

B2 = Riboflavin

B3 = Niacin

B5 = Pantothenic Acid

B6 = Pridoxine, Pyridoxine, Pyridoxamine

B9 = Folic Acid, Folate, Folacin

C = Ascorbic Acid

E = Alpha-Tocopherol

K = Phylloquinone

Minerals:

Ca = Calcium (Ca)

Ir = Iron (Fe)

Mg = Magnesium (Mg)

Mn = Manganese (Mn)

Ph = Phosphorus (P)

Po = Potassium (K)

Se = Selenium (Se)

Zn = Zinc (Zn)

- = Information Not Reported by United States Dept. of Agriculture.
Cucumber nutritional values include the cucumber peel.
Tomatoes are technically a fruit and they are on the next page.

All data for 100 gram servings. 100 grams = 3.527 ounces in **weight.**
3.527 ounces in weight is **not** the same as approximately 1/2 cup.
The imperial system uses ounces for both weight and volume.
The metric system uses grams for weight and liters for volume.

Fruit (Per 100 g Serving)	Cal kcal	Fat				Carbs			Other		Vitamins										Minerals							
		Tot g	Sa g	Po g	Mo g	Car g	Fib g	Sug g	Sod mg	Pro g	A µg	B1 mg	B2 mg	B3 mg	B5 mg	B6 mg	B9 µg	C mg	E mg	K µg	Ca mg	Ir mg	Mg mg	Mn mg	Ph mg	Po mg	Se µg	Zn mg
Apple	52	.17	.03	.05	.01	13.8	2.4	10	1	.26	3	.02	.03	.09	.06	.04	3	4.6	.18	2.2	6	.12	5	.04	11	107	0	.04
Apricot	48	.39	.03	.08	.17	11.1	2.0	9.2	1	1.4	96	.03	.04	.60	.24	.05	9	10	.89	3.3	13	.39	10	.08	23	259	.1	.20
Avocado	160	15	2.1	9.8	1.8	8.53	6.7	.66	7	2	146	.07	.13	1.7	1.4	.26	81	10	2.1	21	12	.55	29	.14	52	485	.4	-
Banana	89	.33	.11	.07	.03	22.8	2.6	12	1	1.09	3	.03	.07	.67	.33	.37	20	8.7	.1	.5	5	.26	27	.27	22	358	1	.15
Blackberry	43	.49	.01	.28	.05	9.61	5.3	4.9	1	1.39	11	.02	.03	.65	.28	.03	25	21	1.2	19.8	29	.62	20	.65	22	162	.4	.53
Blueberry	57	.33	.03	.15	.05	14.5	2.4	10	1	.74	3	.04	.04	.42	.12	.05	6	9.7	.57	19.3	6	.28	6	.34	12	77	.1	.16
Cantaloupe	34	.19	.05	.08	0	8.16	.9	7.9	16	.84	169	.04	.02	.73	.11	.07	21	37	.05	2.5	9	.21	12	.04	15	267	.4	.18
Cherries	63	.20	.04	.05	.05	16.0	2.1	13	0	1.06	3	.03	.03	.15	.20	.05	4	7	.07	2.1	13	.36	11	.07	21	222	0	.07
Grapefruit	33	.10	.01	.02	.01	8.41	1.1	7.3	0	.69	2	.04	.02	.27	.28	.04	10	33	.13	0	12	.06	9	.01	8	148	1.4	.07
Grapes	67	.35	.11	.10	.01	17.1	.9	16	2	.63	5	.09	.06	.30	.02	.11	4	4	.19	14.6	14	.29	5	.72	10	191	.1	.04
Honeydew	36	.14	.04	.06	0	9.09	.8	8.1	18	.54	3	.04	.01	.42	.16	.09	19	18	.02	2.9	6	.17	10	.03	11	228	.7	.09
Kiwi	61	.52	.03	.29	.05	14.7	3.0	9.0	3	1.1	4	.03	.03	.34	-	.06	25	93	1.5	40	34	.31	17	-	34	312	.2	.14
Lemon	29	.30	.04	.09	.01	9.32	2.8	2.5	2	1.1	1	.04	.02	.10	.19	.08	11	53	.15	0	26	.60	8	.03	16	138	.4	.06
Lime	30	.20	.02	.06	.02	10.5	2.8	1.7	2	.70	2	.03	.02	.20	.22	.04	8	29	.22	.6	33	.60	6	.01	18	102	.4	.11
Olives *	116	11	2.3	.63	7.7	6.04	1.6	0	735	.84	17	0	0	.04	.02	.01	0	.9	1.7	1.4	88	6.3	4	.02	3	8	.9	.22
Orange	46	.21	.03	.04	.04	11.5	2.4	9.1	0	.70	11	.10	.04	.40	.25	.05	17	45	.18	0	43	.09	10	.02	12	169	.5	.08
Peach	39	.21	.02	.09	.07	9.54	1.5	8.4	0	.91	16	.02	.03	.81	.15	.03	4	6.6	.73	2.6	6	.25	9	.06	20	190	.1	.17
Pear	57	.14	.02	.09	.08	15.2	3.1	9.8	1	.36	1	.01	.03	.16	.05	.03	7	4.3	.12	4.4	9	.18	7	.05	12	116	.1	.10
Pineapple	50	.12	.01	.04	.01	13.1	1.4	9.9	1	.54	3	.08	.03	.50	.21	.11	18	48	.02	.7	13	.29	12	.93	8	109	.1	.12
Plum	46	.28	.02	.04	.13	11.4	1.4	9.9	0	.70	17	.03	.03	.42	.14	.03	5	9.5	.26	6.4	6	.17	7	.05	16	157	0	.10
Raspberry	52	.65	.02	.38	.06	11.9	6.5	4.4	1	1.2	2	.03	.04	.60	-	.06	21	26	.87	7.8	25	.69	22	-	29	151	.2	.42
Strawberry	32	.30	.02	.16	.04	7.68	2.0	4.9	1	.67	1	.02	.02	.39	.13	.05	24	59	.29	2.2	16	.41	13	.39	24	153	.4	.14
Tomatoes	18	.20	.03	.08	.03	3.89	1.2	2.6	5	.88	42	.04	.02	.59	.09	.08	15	14	.54	7.9	10	.27	11	.11	24	237	0	.17
Watermelon	30	.15	.02	.05	.04	7.55	.40	6.2	1	.61	28	.03	.02	.18	.22	.05	3	8.1	.05	.10	7	.24	10	.04	11	112	.4	.01

All Raw Fruit Except *   Source of Data: United States Department of Agriculture   Fruit has no Cholesterol

United States Department of Agriculture (USDA) Nutrition, Vitamins, and Minerals for Fruits

Abbreviations Used at the Top of the Table on the Previous Page

g = gram   1 mg = .001 gram   1 μg = .000001 gram

Cal = Calories

Tot = Total Fat

Sa = Saturated Fat

Po = Polyunsaturated Fat

Mo = Monounsaturated Fat

Sod = Sodium (Na)

Car = Carbohydrates

Fib = Fiber

Sug = Sugars

Pro = Protein

Vitamins:

A = Retinal, Retinol

B1 = Thiamine

B2 = Riboflavin

B3 = Niacin

B5 = Pantothenic Acid

B6 = Pridoxine, Pyridoxine, Pyridoxamine

B9 = Folic Acid, Folate, Folacin

C = Ascorbic Acid

E = Alpha-Tocopherol

K = Phylloquinone

Minerals:

Ca = Calcium (Ca)

Ir = Iron (Fe)

Mg = Magnesium (Mg)

Mn = Manganese (Mn)

Ph = Phosphorus (P)

Po = Potassium (K)

Se = Selenium (Se)

Zn = Zinc (Zn)

- = Information not reported by United States Dept. of Agriculture.

* Olives = Canned, Ripe, Small - Extra Large.

Apple, Raw with Skin and Flesh.

All data for 100 gram servings. 100 grams = 3.527 ounces in **weight.**
3.527 ounces in weight is **not** the same as approximately 1/2 cup.
The imperial system uses ounces for both weight and volume.
The metric system uses grams for weight and liters for volume.

Grain	Cal	Fat				Carbs			Other		Vitamins								Ch	Minerals								
Per 100 g Serving	kcal	Tot g	Sa g	Po g	Mo g	Car g	Fib g	Sug g	Sod mg	Pro g	B1 mg	B2 mg	B3 mg	B5 mg	B6 mg	B9 µg	E mg	K µg	mg	Ca mg	Co mg	Ir mg	Mg mg	Mn mg	Ph mg	Po mg	Se µg	Zn mg
Corn																												
Dent White	365	4.7	.67	2.2	1.3	74	-	-	35	9.42	.39	.20	3.6	.42	.62	-	-	-	-	7	.31	2.7	127	.49	210	287	16	2.2
Dent Yellow	365	4.7	.67	2.2	1.3	74	7.3	.64	35	9.42	.39	.20	3.6	.42	.62	19	.49	.3	-	7	.31	2.7	127	.49	210	287	16	2.2
Cornmeal	362	3.6	.51	1.6	.95	77	7.3	.64	35	8.12	.39	.20	3.6	.43	.30	25	.42	.3	22	6	.19	3.5	127	.50	241	287	16	1.8
Oats																												
Oats Raw	379	6.5	1.1	2.3	2.0	68	10	.99	6	13.2	.46	.16	1.1	-	.60	32	.42	2	40	52	.39	4.3	138	-	410	362	29	3.6
Oatmeal	367	6.3	1.1	2.3	2.0	67	9.8	1.0	4	16.0	.73	.14	.78	-	.12	32	.47	-	-	52	-	4.2	148	-	474	350	-	3.1
Oat Flour	404	9.1	1.6	3.3	2.9	66	6.5	.80	19	14.7	.69	.13	1.5	.20	.13	32	.70	3.2	30	55	.44	4.0	144	4.0	452	371	34	3.2
Rice																												
Brown Cook	122	.96	.26	.36	.37	25	1.6	.24	202	2.73	.18	.07	2.5	-	.12	9	.17	.2	9.2	3	.11	.56	39	-	102	86	5.8	.71
Jasm. Basm.	129	.28	.08	.08	.09	28	.40	.05	245	2.67	.16	.01	1.5	-	.09	58	.04	0	2.1	10	.07	1.2	12	-	43	35	7.5	.49
White Cook	96	.19	.04	.07	.07	21	1.0	.05	227	2.01	.02	.01	.29	-	.03	1	.04	0	2.1	2	.05	.14	5	-	8	10	5.6	.41
Wild Cook	101	.34	.05	.21	.05	21	1.8	.73	3	3.99	.05	.09	1.3	.15	.14	26	.24	.5	10	3	.12	.60	32	.28	82	101	.80	1.3
Rice Flour	363	2.8	.56	1.0	1.0	76	4.6	.66	8	7.2	.44	.08	6.3	1.6	.74	16	.60	-	-	11	.23	2.0	112	4.0	337	289	-	2.5
Wheat																												
Hard Red S	329	1.9	.31	.77	.30	68	12	.41	2	15.4	.50	.11	5.7	.94	.34	43	1.0	1.9	31	25	.41	3.6	124	4.1	332	340	71	2.8
Hard Red W	327	1.5	.27	.63	.20	71	12	.41	2	12.6	.38	.12	5.5	.95	.30	38	1.0	1.9	31	29	.43	3.2	126	4.0	288	363	71	2.7
Soft Red W	331	1.6	.29	.66	.18	74	13	.41	2	10.4	.39	.10	4.8	.85	.27	41	1.0	-	-	27	.45	3.2	126	4.4	493	397	-	2.6
Hard White	342	1.7	.28	.75	.20	76	12	.41	2	11.3	.39	.11	4.4	.96	.37	38	1.0	1.9	-	32	.36	4.6	93	3.8	355	432	-	3.3
Soft White	340	2.0	.37	.84	.23	75	13	.41	2	10.7	.41	.11	4.8	.85	.38	41	1.0	1.9	-	34	.43	5.4	90	3.4	402	435	-	3.5
Sprouted	198	1.3	.21	.56	.15	43	1.1	-	16	7.49	.23	.16	3.1	.95	.27	38	-	-	-	28	-	2.1	82	-	200	169	16	-
Wheat Flour	392	2.0	.43	1.2	.28	74	13	1.0	3	9.61	.30	.19	5.4	1.0	.19	28	.53	1.9	31	33	.48	3.7	117	3.4	323	394	13	3.0
Buckwheat	343	3.4	.74	1.0	1.0	72	10	-	1	13.3	.10	.43	7.0	1.2	.21	30	-	-	-	18	1.1	2.2	231	1.3	347	460	8.3	2.4
Rye Grain	338	1.6	.20	.78	.21	76	15	1.0	2	10.3	.32	.25	4.3	1.5	.29	38	.85	5.9	30	24	.37	2.6	110	2.6	332	510	14	2.7

Source of Data: United States Department of Agriculture   Grain has no Cholesterol or A, B12, C, D.

United States Department of Agriculture (USDA) Nutrition, Vitamins, and Minerals for Grain: Corn, Oats, Rice, and Wheat

Abbreviations Used at the Top of the Table on the Previous Page

g = gram   1 mg = .001 gram   1 μg = .000001 gram

Cal = Calories
Tot = Total Fat
Sa = Saturated Fat
Po = Polyunsaturated Fat
Mo = Monounsaturated Fat

Car = Carbohydrates
Fib = Fiber
Sug = Sugars
Sod = Sodium (Na)
Pro = Protein

Vitamins:
B1 = Thiamine
B2 = Riboflavin
B3 = Niacin
B5 = Pantothenic Acid
B6 = Pridoxine, Pyridoxine, Pyridoxamine
B9 = Folic Acid, Folate, Folacin
E = Alpha-Tocopherol
K = Phylloquinone
Unclassified:
Ch = Choline

Minerals:
Ca = Calcium (Ca)
Co = Copper (Cu)
Ir = Iron (Fe)
Mg = Magnesium (Mg)
Mn = Manganese (Mn)
Ph = Phosphorus (P)
Po = Potassium (K)
Se = Selenium (Se)
Zn = Zinc (Zn)

- = Information not reported by United States Dept. of Agriculture.

Corn = Dent White Field Corn, Dent Yellow Field Corn.
Cornmeal = Includes White and Yellow Cornmeal.
Rice = All rice were cooked but the Rice Flour was not cooked.
Oatmeal = Organic "Quaker" Instant Oatmeal.
Sprouted Wheat = Contains 2.6 mg of vitamin C.

Abbreviations:
Jasm. Basm. = Jasmine and Basmati Rice Cooked.
Hard Red Spring, Hard Red Winter, Soft Red Winter.
Flour Soft Wheat Whole Grain.

All data for 100 gram servings. 100 grams = 3.527 ounces in **weight.**
3.527 ounces in weight is **not** the same as approximately 1/2 cup.
The imperial system uses ounces for both weight and volume.
The metric system uses grams for weight and liters for volume.

| Nuts and Seeds | Cal | Fat | | | | Carbs | | | Other | | Vitamins | | | | | | | | | | Minerals | | | | | | | |
Per 100 g Serving	kcal	Tot g	Sa g	Po g	Mo g	Car g	Fib g	Sug g	Sod mg	Pro g	A µg	B1 mg	B2 mg	B3 mg	B5 mg	B6 mg	B9 µg	C mg	E mg	K µg	Ca mg	Ir mg	Mg mg	Mn mg	Ph mg	Po mg	Se µg	Zn mg
Nuts																												
Acorns	509	31	4.1	6.1	20	53.7	-	-	0	8.1	0	.15	.15	2.4	.94	.70	115	0	-	-	54	1.0	82	1.4	103	709	-	.69
Almonds	579	50	3.8	12	32	21.6	13	4.4	1	21	0	.21	1.1	3.6	.47	.14	44	0	26	0	269	3.7	270	2.2	481	733	4.1	3.1
Brazil Nuts	659	67	16	24	24	11.7	7.5	2.3	3	14	0	.62	.04	.30	.18	.10	22	.7	5.7	0	160	2.4	376	1.2	725	659	1917	4.1
Cashews	553	44	7.8	7.8	24	30.2	3.3	5.9	12	18	0	.42	.06	1.1	.86	.42	25	.5	.9	34	37	6.7	292	1.7	593	660	20	5.8
Chestnuts	224	1.1	.16	.29	.58	49.1	-	-	3	4.2	10	.16	.18	.80	.56	.41	68	36	-	-	18	1.4	84	1.6	96	447	-	.87
Coconut	354	33	30	1.4	.37	15.2	9	6.2	20	3.3	0	.07	.02	.54	.30	.05	26	3.3	.24	.2	14	2.4	32	1.5	113	356	10	1.1
Hazelnuts	628	61	4.4	7.9	45	16.7	9.7	4.3	0	15	1	.64	.11	1.8	.92	.56	113	6.3	15	14	114	4.7	163	6.2	290	680	2.4	2.5
Hickory N.	657	64	7.0	22	33	18.3	6.4	-	1	13	7	.87	.13	.91	1.7	.19	40	2	-	-	61	2.1	173	4.6	336	436	8.1	4.3
Macadamia	718	76	12	1.5	59	13.8	8.6	4.6	5	7.9	0	1.2	.16	2.5	.76	.28	11	1.2	.54	-	85	3.7	130	4.1	188	368	3.6	1.3
Mixed Nuts	594	51	6.5	11	31	25.4	9	4.8	345	17	0	.20	.20	4.7	1.2	.30	50	.4	11	13	70	3.7	225	1.9	435	693	7.5	3.8
Peanuts	567	49	6.3	16	24	16.1	8.5	4.7	18	26	0	.64	.14	12	1.8	.35	240	0	8.3	0	92	4.6	168	1.9	376	705	7.2	3.3
Pecans	691	72	6.2	22	41	13.9	9.6	4.0	0	9.2	3	.66	.13	1.2	.86	.21	22	1.1	1.4	3.5	70	2.5	121	4.5	277	410	3.8	4.5
Pili Nuts	719	80	31	7.6	37	4.0	-	-	3	11	2	.91	.09	.52	.48	.12	60	.6	-	-	145	3.5	302	2.3	575	507	-	3.0
Pine Nuts	673	68	4.9	34	19	13.1	3.7	3.6	2	14	1	.36	.23	4.4	.31	.09	34	.8	9.3	54	16	5.5	251	8.8	575	597	.7	6.5
Pistachios	560	45	5.9	14	23	27.2	11	7.7	1	20	26	.87	.16	1.3	.52	1.7	51	5.6	2.9	-	105	3.9	121	1.2	490	1025	7	2.2
Walnut Blk.	619	59	3.5	36	15	9.58	6.8	1.1	2	24	2	.06	.13	.47	1.7	.58	31	1.7	2.1	2.7	61	3.1	201	3.9	513	523	17	3.4
Walnut Eng.	654	65	6.1	47	9	13.7	6.7	2.6	2	15	1	.34	.15	1.1	.57	.54	98	1.3	.7	2.7	98	2.9	158	3.4	346	441	4.9	3.1
Seeds																												
Chia Seed	486	31	3.3	24	2.3	42.1	34	-	16	17	54	.62	.17	8.8	-	-	49	1.6	.5	-	631	7.7	335	2.7	860	407	55	4.6
Flax Seed	534	42	3.7	29	7.5	28.9	27	1.6	30	18	0	1.7	.16	3.1	.99	.47	87	.6	.31	4.3	255	5.7	392	2.5	642	813	25	4.3
Hemp Seed	553	49	4.6	38	5.4	8.67	4	1.5	5	32	1	1.3	.29	9.2	-	.60	110	.5	.8	-	70	8.0	700	7.6	1650	1200	-	9.9
Sesame S.	573	50	7.0	19	22	23.5	12	.30	11	18	0	.79	.25	4.5	.05	.79	97	0	.25	0	975	15	351	2.5	629	468	34	7.8
Sunflower S	584	51	4.5	23	19	20.0	8.6	2.6	9	21	3	1.5	.36	8.3	1.1	1.3	227	1.4	35	0	78	5.3	325	2.0	660	645	53	5.0

All Raw Nuts and Seeds   Source of Data: United States Department of Agriculture   Nuts & Seeds have no Cholesterol, B12, or D

United States Department of Agriculture (USDA) Nutrition, Vitamins, and Minerals for Nuts and Seeds

Abbreviations Used at the Top of the Table on the Previous Page

g = gram   1 mg = .001 gram   1 μg = .000001 gram

Cal = Calories

Tot = Total Fat

Sa = Saturated Fat

Po = Polyunsaturated Fat

Mo = Monounsaturated Fat

Car = Carbohydrates

Fib = Fiber

Sug = Sugars

Sod = Sodium (Na)

Pro = Protein

Vitamins:

A = Retinal, Retinol

B1 = Thiamine

B2 = Riboflavin

B3 = Niacin

B5 = Pantothenic Acid

B6 = Pridoxine, Pyridoxine, Pyridoxamine

B9 = Folic Acid, Folate, Folacin

C = Ascorbic Acid

E = Alpha-Tocopherol

K = Phylloquinone

Minerals:

Ca = Calcium (Ca)

Ir = Iron (Fe)

Mg = Magnesium (Mg)

Mn = Manganese (Mn)

Ph = Phosphorus (P)

Po = Potassium (K)

Se = Selenium (Se)

Zn = Zinc (Zn)

- = Information Not Reported by United States Dept. of Agriculture.

Mixed Nuts, Dry Roasted, Salted, with Peanuts.

Hazelnuts are also called Filberts.

Note: Technically coconuts and peanuts are not pure nuts even though they have the word nut in their name. A coconut is a drupe which is a type of fruit but a coconut can be loosely defined as a nut. A peanut is a legume which is a type of vegetable that has a seed inside a pod. However, since most people consider coconuts and peanuts to be nuts they are included in this chapter in order to make it easy for people to find nutrition information about them.

All data for 100 gram servings. 100 grams = 3.527 ounces in **weight.**
3.527 ounces in weight is **not** the same as approximately 1/2 cup.
The imperial system uses ounces for both weight and volume.
The metric system uses grams for weight and liters for volume.

Per 100 g Serving	Cal kcal	Tot g	Sa g	Po g	Mo g	Car g	Sug g	Cho mg	Sod mg	Pro g	A µg	B1 mg	B2 mg	B3 mg	B6 mg	B9 µg	B12 µg	D µg	E mg	K µg	Ch mg	Ca mg	Ir mg	Mg mg	Ph mg	Po mg	Se µg	Zn mg
Milk Whole	61	3.3	1.9	.20	.81	4.8	5.1	10	43	3.15	46	.05	.17	.09	.04	5	.45	1.3	.07	.3	14	113	.03	10	84	132	3.7	.37
Milk 2%	50	2.0	1.3	.07	.56	4.8	5.1	8	47	3.30	55	.04	.19	.09	.04	5	.53	.2	.03	.2	16	120	.02	11	92	140	2.5	.48
Milk 1%	42	.97	.63	.04	.28	5.0	5.2	5	44	3.37	58	.02	.19	.09	.04	5	.47	1.2	.01	.1	18	125	.03	11	95	150	3.3	.42
Milk ≤0.5%	34	.08	.06	≈0.02	.02	5.0	5.1	2	42	3.37	61	.05	.18	.09	.04	5	.50	1.2	.01	0	16	122	.03	11	101	156	3.1	.42
Buttermilk	62	3.3	1.9	.20	.83	4.9	4.9	11	105	3.21	47	.05	.17	.09	.04	5	.46	1.3	.07	.3	15	115	.03	10	85	135	3.7	.38
Half & Half	131	12	7.0	.55	3.3	4.3	4.1	35	61	3.13	97	.03	.19	.11	.05	3	.19	0	.25	1.3	19	107	.05	10	95	132	3.2	.39
Cream L.	195	19	10	.79	4.5	3.7	3.7	59	72	2.96	120	.02	.19	.09	.04	2	.14	1.1	.12	1.7	37	91	.32	9	92	136	4.6	.32
Cream H.W.	340	36	23	1.6	9.1	2.8	2.9	113	27	2.84	411	.02	.19	.06	.04	4	.16	1.6	.92	3.2	17	66	.01	7	58	95	3.0	.24
Butter																												
Salted	717	81	51	3.0	21	.06	.06	215	643	0.85	684	.01	.03	.04	.01	3	.17	0	2.3	7	19	24	.02	2	24	24	1.0	.09
Unsalted	717	81	50	3.0	23	.06	.06	215	11	0.85	684	.01	.03	.04	≈0	3	.17	0	2.3	7	19	24	.02	2	24	24	1.0	.09
Cheese																												
American	312	23	13	1.0	6.2	8.8	6.2	78	1309	17.1	270	.04	.43	.17	.12	18	1.5	6.5	.84	3.1	17	1360	.89	33	799	283	16	2.1
Cheddar	410	34	19	1.4	8.4	2.1	.27	99	644	24.3	263	.03	.43	.04	.08	27	.88	1.0	.78	2.4	17	711	.16	27	460	76	28	3.7
Colby	394	32	20	.95	9.3	2.6	.52	95	604	23.8	264	.02	.38	.09	.08	18	.83	.6	.28	2.7	15	685	.76	26	457	127	15	3.1
Cream	350	34	20	1.5	8.9	5.5	3.8	101	314	6.15	308	.02	.23	.09	.06	9	.22	0	.86	2.1	27	97	.11	9	107	132	8.6	.50
Cottage	98	4.3	1.7	.12	.78	3.4	2.7	17	364	11.1	37	.03	.16	.10	.05	12	.43	.1	.08	0	18	83	.07	8	159	104	9.7	.40
Mexican	384	32	16	.86	7.9	.13	0	95	607	23.5	174	.02	.32	.11	.06	13	1.2	.5	.25	2.5	16	659	.59	25	438	85	15	3.0
Monterey	373	30	19	.90	8.7	.68	.50	89	600	24.5	198	.02	.39	.09	.08	18	.83	.6	.26	2.5	15	746	.72	27	444	81	15	3.0
Muenster	368	30	19	.66	8.7	1.1	1.1	96	628	23.4	298	.01	.32	.10	.06	12	1.5	.6	.26	2.5	15	717	.41	27	468	134	15	2.8
Provolone	351	27	17	.77	7.4	2.1	.56	69	727	25.6	236	.02	.32	.16	.07	10	1.5	.5	.23	2.2	15	756	.52	28	496	138	15	3.2
Swiss	393	31	18	1.3	8.0	1.4	0	93	187	27.0	288	.01	.30	.06	.07	10	3.1	0	.60	1.4	14	890	.13	33	574	72	30	4.4
Yogurt	61	3.3	2.1	.09	.89	4.7	4.7	13	46	3.47	27	.03	.14	.08	.03	7	.37	.1	.06	.2	15	121	.05	12	95	155	2.2	.59
Egg Whole	143	9.5	3.1	1.9	3.7	.72	.37	373	142	12.6	160	.04	.46	.08	.17	47	.89	2	1.1	.3	294	56	1.8	12	198	138	31	1.3

Source of Data: United States Department of Agriculture

Dairy has no Fiber

United States Department of Agriculture (USDA) Nutrition, Vitamins, and Minerals for Dairy: Milk, Butter, Cheese, Yogurt, Eggs

Abbreviations Used at the Top of the Table on the Previous Page

g = gram   1 mg = .001 gram   1 µg = .000001 gram

Cal = Calories
Tot = Total Fat
Sa = Saturated Fat
Po = Polyunsaturated Fat
Mo = Monounsaturated Fat

Cho = Cholesterol
Sod = Sodium (Na)
Pro = Protein
Unclassified:
Ch = Choline

Vitamins:
A = Retinal, Retinol
B1 = Thiamine
B2 = Riboflavin
B3 = Niacin
B5 = Pantothenic Acid
B6 = Pridoxine, Pyridoxine, Pyridoxamine
B9 = Folic Acid, Folate, Folacin
B12 = Cobalamin, Cyanocobalamin
D = The "Sunshine Vitamin"
E = Alpha-Tocopherol
K = Phylloquinone

Minerals:
Ca = Calcium (Ca)
Ir = Iron (Fe)
Mg = Magnesium (Mg)
Ph = Phosphorus (P)
Po = Potassium (K)
Se = Selenium (Se)
Zn = Zinc (Zn)

- = Information not reported by United States Dept. of Agriculture.
≈ 0 = Approximately Zero or a Very Trivial Amount.
Butter and Cheese have no Vitamin C.
Milk and Cream have no or very little Vitamin C.
Yogurt = Plain using Whole Milk.

All data for 100 gram servings. 100 grams = 3.527 ounces in **weight.**
3.527 ounces in weight is **not** the same as approximately 1/2 cup.
The imperial system uses ounces for both weight and volume.
The metric system uses grams for weight and liters for volume.

Miscellaneous	Cal	Fat				Carbs			Other			Vitamins										Minerals						
Per 100 g Serving	Cal	Tot	Sa	Po	Mo	Car	Fib	Sug	Cho	Sod	Pro	A	B1	B2	B3	B5	B6	B9	C	E	K	Ca	Ir	Mg	Ph	Po	Se	Zn
	kcal	g	g	g	g	g	g	g	mg	mg	g	µg	mg	mg	mg	mg	mg	µg	mg	mg	µg	mg	mg	mg	mg	mg	µg	mg
Salt, Table	0	0	0	0	0	0	0	0	0	**38758**	0	0	0	0	0	0	0	0	0	0	0	24	.33	1	0	8	.1	.1
Black Pep.	251	3.3	1.4	1.0	0.7	64	25	.64	0	20	10.4	27	.11	.18	1.1	1.4	.29	17	0	1.0	164	443	9.7	171	158	**1329**	4.9	1.2
Garlic Raw	149	.50	.09	.25	.01	33	2.1	1	0	17	6.36	0	.20	.11	.70	.60	1.2	3	31	.08	1.7	181	1.7	25	153	401	14	1.2
Dressings																												
Caesar	542	58	8.8	33	14	3.3	.50	2.8	39	**1209**	2.17	9	.01	.01	.04	-	.03	2	.3	4.7	105	48	1.1	2	19	29	1.6	.11
Italian	240	21	2.9	11	5.6	12	0	11	0	993	.41	2	.02	0	.13	0	.06	0	.4	2.2	56	13	.26	5	15	84	2	.07
Oil & Vin.	449	50	9.1	24	15	2.5	0	2.5	0	1	0	0	0	0	0	0	0	0	0	4.6	99	0	0	0	0	8	1.6	0
Ranch	430	45	7.0	26	9.2	5.9	0	4.7	26	901	1.32	15	.02	.09	.05	.27	.03	4	0	2.2	134	28	.3	5	186	64	3.5	.17
Thousand I.	379	35	5.1	18	7.9	15	.8	15	26	962	1.09	14	1.4	.06	.42	0	0	0	0	4	69	17	1.2	8	27	107	1.5	.26
Oils, Etc.																												
Canola	884	100	7.4	28	63	0	0	0	0	0	0	0	0	0	0	0	0	0	0	17.5	71	0	0	0	0	0	0	0
Coconut	892	99	82	1.7	6.3	0	0	0	0	0	0	0	0	0	0	0	0	0	0	.11	.6	1	.05	0	0	0	0	.02
Corn	900	100	13	55	28	0	0	0	0	0	0	0	0	0	0	0	0	0	0	14.3	1.9	0	0	0	0	0	0	0
Olive	884	100	14	11	73	0	0	0	0	2	0	0	0	0	0	0	0	0	0	14.4	60	1	.56	0	0	1	0	0
Peanut	884	100	17	32	46	0	0	0	0	0	0	0	0	0	0	0	0	0	0	15.7	.7	0	.03	0	0	0	0	.01
Vegetable	886	100	14	41	42	0	0	0	0	0	0	0	0	0	0	0	0	0	0	11.7	118	0	.16	0	0	0	0	0
Lard	902	100	39	11	45	0	0	0	95	0	0	0	0	0	0	0	0	0	0	.6	0	0	0	0	0	0	0	.11
Vinegar Cid	21	0	0	0	0	.93	0	.4	0	5	.3	0	0	0	0	0	0	0	0	0	0	7	.2	5	8	73	.1	.04
Other																												
Honey	304	0	0	0	0	82	.20	82	0	4	.3	0	0	.04	.12	.07	.02	2	.5	0	0	6	.42	2	4	52	.8	.22
Ketchup	101	.1	.01	.04	.02	27	.3	21	0	907	1.04	26	.01	.17	1.4	.05	.16	9	4.1	1.5	3	15	.35	13	26	281	.7	.17
Mayonnaise	680	75	12	45	17	.57	0	.57	42	635	.96	16	.01	.02	0	-	.01	5	0	3.3	163	8	.21	1	21	20	2.3	.15
Mustard Yel	60	3.3	.21	.77	2.2	5.8	4	.93	0	**1104**	3.74	5	.18	.07	.57	.25	.07	7	.3	.36	1.4	63	1.6	48	108	152	34	.64
Peanut But.	598	51	10	13	26	22	5	10	0	17	22.2	0	.15	.19	13	1.1	.44	87	0	9.1	.3	49	1.7	168	335	558	4.1	2.5

Source of Data: United States Department of Agriculture

United States Department of Agriculture (USDA) Nutrition, Vitamins, and Minerals for Seasonings, Salad Dressings, Oils, and Condiments

Abbreviations Used at the Top of the Table on the Previous Page

g = gram   1 mg = .001 gram   1 μg = .000001 gram

Cal = Calories
Tot = Total Fat
Sa = Saturated Fat
Po = Polyunsaturated Fat
Mo = Monounsaturated Fat

Car = Carbohydrates
Fib = Fiber
Sug = Sugars
Cho = Cholesterol
Sod = Sodium (Na)
Pro = Protein

Vitamins:
A = Retinal, Retinol
B1 = Thiamine
B2 = Riboflavin
B3 = Niacin
B5 = Pantothenic Acid
B6 = Pridoxine, Pyridoxine, Pyridoxamine
B9 = Folic Acid, Folate, Folacin
C = Ascorbic Acid
E = Alpha-Tocopherol
K = Phylloquinone

Minerals:
Ca = Calcium (Ca)
Ir = Iron (Fe)
Mg = Magnesium (Mg)
Ph = Phosphorus (P)
Po = Potassium (K)
Se = Selenium (Se)
Zn = Zinc (Zn)

- = Information Not Reported by United States Dept. of Agriculture.
Abbreviations: Oil & Vinegar, Thousand Island, Vinegar Cider, Mustard Yellow, Peanut Butter Smooth.
In the year 2020 most national brands of mustard have no calories.

All data for 100 gram servings. 100 grams = 3.527 ounces in **weight.**
3.527 ounces in weight is **not** the same as approximately 1/2 cup.
The imperial system uses ounces for both weight and volume.
The metric system uses grams for weight and liters for volume.

Per 100 g Serving	Cal kcal	Fat				Carbs			Other			Vitamins										Minerals						
		Tot g	Sa g	Po g	Mo g	Car g	Fib g	Sug g	Cho mg	Sod mg	Pro g	A µg	B1 mg	B2 mg	B3 mg	B5 mg	B6 mg	B9 µg	B12 µg	E mg	K µg	Ca mg	Ir mg	Mg mg	Ph mg	Po mg	Se µg	Zn mg
Cocoa Pow.	228	14	8.1	.44	4.6	58	37	1.8	0	21	19.6	0	.08	.24	2.2	.25	.12	32	0	.10	2.5	128	14	499	734	**1524**	14	6.8
Chocolate																												
Baking Un.	642	52	32	1.6	16	28	17	.91	2	24	14.3	0	.15	.10	1.4	.17	.03	28	0	.40	9.7	101	17	327	400	830	8.1	9.6
Milk Choc.	535	30	19	1.4	7.2	59	3.4	52	23	79	7.65	59	.11	.30	.39	-	.04	12	.75	.51	5.7	189	2.4	63	208	372	4.5	2.3
Semi-Sweet	480	30	18	1.0	10	64	5.9	55	0	11	4.2	0	.06	.09	.43	-	.04	13	0	.26	5.6	32	3.1	115	132	365	4.2	1.6
Spec. Dark	556	32	-	.44	5.1	60	7	48	5	6	5.54	-	0	.01	0	0	0	0	-	-	-	30	2.1	31	51	502	.30	.01
White Choc.	539	32	19	1.0	9.1	59	.2	59	21	90	5.87	9	.06	.28	.75	-	.06	7	.56	.96	9.1	199	.24	12	176	286	4.5	.74
Dark Choc.																												
45%–59%	546	31	19	1.1	9.5	61	7	48	8	24	4.88	2	.03	.05	.73	.30	.04	-	.23	.54	8.1	56	8.0	146	206	559	3	2.0
60%–69%	579	38	22	1.2	12	54	8	37	6	10	6.12	3	.03	.05	.84	.30	.03	-	.18	.59	7.2	62	6.3	176	260	567	8.4	2.7
70%–85%	598	43	24	1.3	13	46	11	24	3	20	7.79	2	.03	.08	1.1	.42	.04	-	.28	.59	7.3	73	12	228	308	715	6.8	3.3
Cookies																												
Choc. Chip	492	25	8.1	8.4	6.3	65	2	33	0	311	5.1	0	.29	.30	2.7	-	.06	72	.03	2.0	34	21	5.6	41	109	171	3.9	.72
Oatmeal	447	18	3.6	5.6	7.7	66	-	-	36	598	6.8	160	.26	.17	1.3	.36	.05	33	.09	-	-	105	2.7	43	167	182	17	.93
Peanut But.	475	24	4.4	7.2	11	59	-	-	31	518	9	137	.22	.21	3.5	.35	.08	55	.09	-	-	39	2.2	39	116	231	15	.82
Ice Cream																												
Chocolate	251	17	10	.66	4.8	20	.9	17	60	57	4.72	201	.03	.17	.18	.34	.03	5	.18	.46	1.5	142	1.0	32	115	238	2.1	.64
Strawberry	192	8.4	5.2	-	-	28	.9	-	29	60	3.2	96	.05	.26	.17	.72	.05	12	.30	-	-	120	.21	14	100	188	1.9	.34
Vanilla	249	16	10	4.5	.68	22	0	21	92	61	3.5	182	.04	.17	.08	.46	.05	8	.39	.51	1.3	117	.34	11	105	157	3.5	.47
Syrup																												
Chocolate	269	0	0	0	0	67	0	60	0	150	0	0	.01	.03	.17	.02	.01	3	0	.01	.02	0	0	40	58	122	1.5	.55
Corn	283	0.2	0	0	0	77	0	77	0	62	0	0	.06	0	0	-	0	0	0	0	0	13	0	1	0	1	0.7	.44
Maple	260	.06	.01	.02	.01	67	0	60	0	12	0.04	0	.07	1.3	.08	.04	≈0	0	0	0	0	102	.02	21	2	212	0.6	1.5
Pancake	234	0	0	0	0	61	0	21	0	82	0	0	.02	.01	0	≈0	0	0	0	0	0	3	.03	2	9	15	0	.08

Source of Data: United States Department of Agriculture

United States Department of Agriculture (USDA) Nutrition, Vitamins, and Minerals for Cocoa Powder, Chocolate, Cookies, Ice Cream, Syrup

Abbreviations Used at the Top of the Table on the Previous Page

g = gram   1 mg = .001 gram   1 μg = .000001 gram

Cal = Calories
Tot = Total Fat
Sa = Saturated Fat
Po = Polyunsaturated Fat
Mo = Monounsaturated Fat

Car = Carbohydrates
Fib = Fiber
Sug = Sugars
Cho = Cholesterol
Sod = Sodium (Na)
Pro = Protein

Vitamins:
A = Retinal, Retinol
B1 = Thiamine
B2 = Riboflavin
B3 = Niacin
B5 = Pantothenic Acid
B6 = Pridoxine, Pyridoxine, Pyridoxamine
B9 = Folic Acid, Folate, Folacin
C = Ascorbic Acid
E = Alpha-Tocopherol
K = Phylloquinone

Minerals:
Ca = Calcium (Ca)
Ir = Iron (Fe)
Mg = Magnesium (Mg)
Ph = Phosphorus (P)
Po = Potassium (K)
Se = Selenium (Se)
Zn = Zinc (Zn)

- = Information Not Reported by United States Dept. of Agriculture.
≈ 0 = Approximately Zero or a Very Trivial Amount.

Abbreviations: Cocoa Dry Powder Unsweetened, Baking Chocolate . Unsweetened Squares, Milk Chocolate Plain Candy, Semi-Sweet Chocolate Morsels, Special Dark Chocolate Bar, White Chocolate, Dark Chocolate % Cocao Solids, Chocolate Ice Cream Rich, Vanilla Ice Cream Rich, Chocolate Syrup Nestle, Corn Syrup Light or Dark, 100% Maple Syrup, Pancake Syrup Blends.

All data for 100 gram servings. 100 grams = 3.527 ounces in **weight.** 3.527 ounces in weight is **not** the same as approximately 1/2 cup. The imperial system uses ounces for both weight and volume. The metric system uses grams for weight and liters for volume.

Average Calories in
Vegetables, Fruits, Nuts, Dairy, Meat, and Grain

The average number of calories in many common food items are shown in the tables on this page and on the next page.

The symbol "=" means exactly equal to. The symbol "≈" means approximately equal to. The symbol "≈" is used it the tables because the number of calories is only an average. A specific food item, such as an apple, may be a little smaller or a little bigger than an average apple and the apple you eat may contain a few more or a few less calories than average. A cup of cantaloupe may contain slightly larger or smaller pieces than average and the number of calories may be a little more or less than average. However, the average calories for each food can be used to estimate the total number of calories you eat each day.

Vegetables	Fruits
Asparagus ≈ 6 calories per spear	Apple ≈ 85 calories each
Beans ≈ 210 calories per cup	Apricot ≈ 18 calories each
Beets ≈ 67 calories per cup	Avocado ≈ 29 cal. / tablespoon
Broccoli ≈ 30 calories per cup	Banana ≈ 100 calories each
Brussels Sprouts ≈ 12 cal. each	Blackberry ≈ 1 calorie each
Cabbage ≈ 23 calories per cup	Blueberry ≈ 0.8 calories each
Carrot, Baby ≈ 4.5 calories each	Cantaloupe ≈ 52 calories / cup
Carrot, Petite ≈ 2.7 calories each	Cherry ≈ 4 calories each
Cauliflower ≈ 25 cal. per cup	Grape ≈ 2 calories each
Celery ≈ 10 calories per stalk	Grapefruit ≈ 84 calories each
Corn ≈ 200 calories per cup	Honeydew ≈ 58 calories / cup
Cucumbers ≈ 13 calories per cup	Kiwi ≈ 46 calories each
Green Peas ≈ 130 cal. per cup	Lemon ≈ 19 calories each
Kale ≈ 28 calories per cup	Lime ≈ 19 calories each
Lentils ≈ 230 calories per cup	Olive ≈ 4.6 calories each
Lettuce ≈ 8 calories per cup	Orange, Clementine: 32 cal. each
Mushroom ≈ 26 calories per cup	Orange, Navel ≈ 65 calories each
Onion ≈ 70 calories per cup	Peach ≈ 40 calories each
Pepper, Bell ≈ 32 cal. per cup	Pear ≈ 85 calories each
Pepper, Hot ≈ 60 cal. per cup	Pineapple ≈ 80 calories / cup
Potato, Baked ≈ 220 cal. each	Plum ≈ 32 calories each
Potatoes ≈ 107 calories per cup	Raspberry ≈ 1 calorie each
Potato, Sweet ≈ 147 cal. per cup	Tangerine ≈ 52 calories each
Radish ≈ 2.6 calories each	Strawberry ≈ 6.0 calories each
Spinach ≈ 8 calories per cup	Tomato, Cherry ≈ 3.5 cal. each
Squash ≈ 50 calories per cup	Tomato, Roma ≈ 22 cal. each
Turnip ≈ 36 calories per cup	Watermelon ≈ 49 calories / cup

Nuts

Almond ≈ 6.3 calories each
Brazil Nut ≈ 18.9 calories each
Cashew ≈ 8.5 calories each
Chestnut ≈ 24 calories each
Coconut ≈ 55 calories/Tbsp.
Hazelnut ≈ 7.1 calories each
Macadamia ≈ 7.2 calories each
Peanut ≈ 5.0 calories each
Pecan Half ≈ 19.6 calories each
Pill Nut ≈ 13.5 calories each
Pine Nut ≈ 0.51 calories each
Pistachio ≈ 3.1 calories each
Walnut, Black ≈ 76.9 cal./Tbsp.
Walnut, English ≈ 59.3 cal./Tbsp.

Seeds

Chia Seeds ≈ 100 cal./tablespoon
Flax Seeds ≈ 55 cal./tablespoon
Hemp Seeds ≈ 43 cal./tablespoon
Pumpkin Seeds ≈ 45 cal./Tbsp.
Sesame Seeds ≈ 52 cal./Tbsp.
Sunflower Seeds ≈ 51 cal./Tbsp.

Dairy

Milk, Whole ≈ 150 cal. per cup
Milk, 2% ≈ 125 cal. per cup
Milk, 1% ≈ 103 cal. per cup
Milk, Skim ≈ 85 cal. per cup
Half & Half ≈ 20 cal. per Tbsp.
Heavy W. Cream ≈ 50 cal./Tbsp.
Butter ≈ 100 calories per Tbsp.
Cheese (avg.) ≈ 105 cal. / ounce
Cheese Cottage ≈ 220 cal. / cup
Yogurt ≈ 17 calories per ounce
Egg ≈ 72 calories each

Meat (3.5 ounce serving)

Beef ≈ 198 calories per serving
Chicken ≈ 215 cal. per serving
Turkey ≈ 115 cal. per serving
Pork ≈ 245 calories per serving
Fish (average) ≈ 112 cal./serving
Shellfish (average) ≈ 76 cal./ser.

Breakfast Pork

Bacon ≈ 45 calories per slice
Sausage ≈ 215 cal. per 2 ounces

Grain (dry, uncooked)

Corn, dried ≈ 193 cal. per cup
Grits ≈ 560 calories per cup
Oatmeal ≈ 300 calories per cup
Wheat Berries ≈ 162 cal. per cup

Pasta (dry, uncooked)

Macaroni ≈ 100 cal. / 1 ounce
Spaghetti ≈ 100 cal. / 1 ounce

Corn Chips

Fritos ≈ 160 cal. / 32 chips
Doritos ≈ 150 cal. / 12 chips
Tostitos Bite Size ≈ 150 c./24 ch.
Tostitos Big ≈ 140 cal. / 7 chips

Wheat Crackers / Pretzels

Cheez-Its ≈ 150 cal. / 27 crackers
Ritz ≈ 160 cal. / 10 crackers
Pretzel Sticks ≈ 110 c. / 53 sticks

Other

Brown Gravy ≈ 5 calories / Tbsp.
Cocktail Sauce ≈ 15 cal. / Tbsp.
Honey ≈ 60 calories / Tbsp.
Jelly ≈ 50 calories / Tbsp.
Ketchup with sugar ≈ 20 cal. / T.
Ketchup no sugar ≈ 10 cal./Tbsp.
Maple Syrup, 100% ≈ 53 cal./T.
Marinara Sauce ≈ 9 cal. / Tbsp.
Mayonnaise ≈ 95 cal. / Tbsp.
Molasses ≈ 60 calories / Tbsp.
Mustard, Dijon ≈ 15 cal. / Tbsp.
Mustard, Yellow ≈ 0 cal. / Tbsp.
Pancake Syrup ≈ 53 cal. / Tbsp.
Peanut Butter ≈ 96 cal. / Tbsp.
Pizza Sauce ≈ 7.5 cal. / Tbsp.
Salad Dressing (mayo) ≈ 65 c./T.
Salad Dressing (oil) ≈ 80 cal./T.
Spaghetti Sauce ≈ 9 cal. / Tbsp.

Average Nutrition in One Large Egg (Grade A) (50g)

Nutrition	One Normal Large Egg	One Organic Large Egg
Calories	72	60
Fat	5 g	4 g
Saturated Fat	1.56 g	1 g
Monounsaturated Fat	1.9 g	2 g
Polyunsaturated Fat	1 g	1 g
Omega-3 Fatty Acids	49 mg	125 mg
Omega-6 Fatty Acids	700 mcg	700 mcg
Trans Fat	0 g	0 g
Cholesterol	196 mg	170 mg
Sodium	70 mg	65 mg
Total Carbohydrates	0.44 mg	0 g
Dietary Fiber	0 mg	0 g
Sugars	0.15 mg	0 g
Protein	6 g	6 g
Vitamin A (Retinol)	80 mg	80 mg
Vitamin B2 (Riboflavin)	0.23 mg	0.3 mg
Vitamin B5 (Pantothenic Acid)	0.8 mg	1 mg
Vitamin B7 (Biotin)	11 mg	11 mcg
Vitamin B12 (Cyanocobalamin)	0.45 mcg	1 mcg
Vitamin D	1 mcg	6 mcg
Vitamin E (Tocopherol)	0.5 mg	5 mg
Calcium	28 mg	28 mg
Choline	147 mcg	147 mcg
Folate	25 mcg	45 mcg
Iodine	28 mcg	60 mcg
Iron	0.9 mg	0.9 mg
Lutein	145 mcg	200 mcg
Molybdenum	8 mcg	8 mcg
Potassium	69 mg	69 mg
Selenium	15 mcg	22 mcg
Zinc	0.7 mg	0.7 mg
ALA	18 mg	60 mg
EPA	2 mg	2 mg
DHA	29 mg	63 mg

Organic = Egg-Land's Best Organic, Cage Free, Farm Fresh, Large Brown Eggs from Vegetarian Fed Hens.

Index

About the Author
Robert Wayne Atkins, P.E. (Grandpappy)
Born in 1949. Accepted Jesus Christ as Savior in April of 1976.
B.S. Degree in Industrial Engineering & Operations Research, Virginia Polytechnic Institute and State University, June 1972.
Master of Business Administration, Georgia State University, 1985.
Licensed Professional Engineer (P.E.), Florida 1980, Georgia 1982.
Professor of Industrial Engineering and Industrial Engineering Technology, Southern Polytechnic College of Engineering and Engineering Technology, Kennesaw State University, 1984-2021.
Member of The Gideons International continuously since 1979.
Ordained Deacon in Christian Church, Ocala, Florida, 1980.
Author of Nine Computer Software Games including **"The Lost Crown of Queen Anne,"** 1988-1991.
Contributing Author to **"Maynard's Industrial Engineering Handbook,"** Fifth Edition, pg. 5.10, 2001.
Contributing Author to **"Maynard's Industrial & Systems Engineering Handbook,"** Sixth Edition, pg. 102, 2023.
Listed in **"Who's Who in America,"** 64th Edition, 2010.
Listed in **"Who's Who in the World,"** 29th Edition, 2012.
Recipient of **"Who's Who"** Lifetime Achievement Award, 2019.

Other Books by this Same Author:
1. Handbook of Industrial, Systems, and Quality Engineering (English).
2. Manual de Ingeniería Industrial, de Sistemas y de Calidad (Spanish).
3. Introduction to Engineering Management.
4. Engineering Statistics and Applications.
5. Engineering Economy and Financial Analysis.
6. Introduction to Quality Engineering.
7. Introduction to Industrial and Systems Engineering.
8. Instructor's Manual: Introduction to Industrial & Systems Engineering.
9. Work Measurement and Ergonomics.
10. Instructor's Manual: Work Measurement and Ergonomics.
11. Facilities Design and Plant Layout.
12. Instructor's Manual: Facilities Design and Plant Layout.
13. Practical Small-Scale Electrical Energy Systems.
14. Practical Strategies for Long-Term Survival.
15. The Practical Prepper's Survival Handbook.
16. Self-Defense Weapons: Traditional and Modern.
17. How to Maximize Your Eating Pleasure and Your Life Expectancy.
18. The Food Book.
19. Grandpappy's Gourmet Cookbook.
20. Grandpappy's Recipes for Hard Times.
21. Grandpappy's Campfire Survival Cookbook (English).
22. Recetas del Abuelo para la Supervivencia al Acampar (Spanish).
23. Grandpappy's Survival Manual for Hard Times, Third Edition.
24. The Most Important Survival Skills of the 1800s.
25. How to Tan Animal Hides and How to Make High Quality Buckskin Clothing.
26. How to Live Comfortably for Several Years in a Hostile Wilderness Environment.
27. Some Difficult Questions Answered Using the Holy Bible.
28. Religion and Christianity in the Twenty-First Century.
29. Grandpappy's Christian Poems.
30. The New Heaven and the New Earth (English).
31. El Cielo Nuevo y La Tierra Nueva (Spanish).
32. Grandpappy's Stories for Children of All Ages.
33. Ancient Board Games and Solitaire Games from Around the World.
34. The Four Pillars of Prosperity: Government, Business, Religion, and Banks.

www.ingramcontent.com/pod-product-compliance
Lightning Source LLC
Chambersburg PA
CBHW060836280326
41934CB00007B/808